INSIDE THE MIXED MARRIAGE

Accounts of Changing Attitudes, Patterns, and Perceptions of Cross-Cultural and Interracial Marriages

Edited by

Walton R. Johnson
The State University of New Jersey–Rutgers
New Brunswick, New Jersey

and

D. Michael Warren
Iowa State University
Ames, Iowa

UNIVERSITY
PRESS OF
AMERICA

Lanham • New York • London

Copyright © 1994 by
University Press of America®, Inc.
4720 Boston Way
Lanham, Maryland 20706

3 Henrietta Street
London WC2E 8LU England

Library of Congress Cataloging-in-Publication Data

Inside the mixed marriage : accounts of changing attitudes, patterns,
and perceptions of cross-cultural and interracial marriages / edited by
Walton R. Johnson and D. Michael Warren.
p.   cm.
Includes bibliographical references.
1. Intermarriage.   I. Johnson, Walton R.   II. Warren, Dennis M.
HQ1031.I567   1993   306.84'6—dc20   93–2203 CIP

ISBN 0–8191–9205–8 (cloth : alk. paper)
ISBN 0–8191–9206–6 (pbk. : alk. paper)

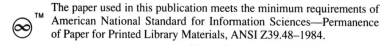

The paper used in this publication meets the minimum requirements of
American National Standard for Information Sciences—Permanence
of Paper for Printed Library Materials, ANSI Z39.48–1984.

Table of Contents

Acknowledgements   v

Introduction   1
Walton R. Johnson and D. Michael Warren

Part I: Defining and Exploring the Mixed Relationship

1. Cross-Cultural Definitions of Persons of Mixed Racial Heritage   17
Robert E.T. Roberts

2. Black-White Inter-marriage in the United States   25
Robert E.T. Roberts

3. Cross-Cultural Marriage as a Literary Motif in Africa and Caribbean Literature   81
Charlotte H. Bruner

4. Literary Images of Intercultural Relationships between Westeners and Middle Easteners   95
Christy Brown

Part II: Adjusting to Racial and Cultural Pluralism

5. Racial Pluralism, Racism and Exile from America   117
Bolaji and Jeanne Bamijoko

6. Up from the Fifties   127
Donald R. and Blanche O. Hill

7. The Impact of the Peace Corps on America   141
Patricia and Kevin Lowther

8. Interracial or Cross-Cultural?   147
Carlie and Gary Tartakov

9. The Other Side of the Coin   155
Richard W. and Myoung Chung Wilson

Part III: Becoming a Minority through the Study Abroad Experience

10. Alive and Well in Lovely Lagos   163
Tolani and Judy Asuni

11. Crossing Religious Lines in America   173
Christy Brown and Ayoub Farahyar

12. Differences Can be Strengths   193
Judith and Walton R. Johnson

13. The Cameroon-Iowa Connection   203
    Ajaga and Katherine Langhurst Nji

14. The Lure of Great Britain   211
    Pamela and John Rooks

15. Beyond the Homelands: A Euro-Asian Marriage in Africa   219
    Leendert Jan and Mady Slikkerveer-Oek Kiat Lien

Part IV: Immersion in a New Culture: Living and Working Abroad

16. The Ghanaian-Namibian Connection in Zambia   227
    Leslie and Elizabeth Bruce-Lyle

17. The British-Barbadian Connection in America   235
    Hugh and Maris Corbin

18. Linking Trinidad, East India and EuroAmerica   245
    Pearl Ramcharan-Crowley and Daniel J. Crowley

19. Crossing Racial and Cultural Boundaries in Europe   257
    Aaron Davenport and Noa Davenport-Zanolli

20. The British-Pakistani Connection in Nigeria   265
    Shahina Ghazanfar and Yusuf Martin

21. Learning to Live and Love in Different Worlds   273
    Mary Salawuh Warren and Dennis Michael Warren

Acknowledgements

We would like to acknowledge the editorial suggestions provided by several anonymous reviewers, and the preparation of the camera ready copy by Dr. B. Rajasekaran.

INTRODUCTION

Walton R. Johnson and D. Michael Warren

"...A long time ago I decided that if I did marry, it would have to be exciting, and I think that I got my wish..."

Taboo! Most societies shroud "mixed" marriages in veils of mystery, fascination and disapproval. The very idea of such unions can elicit feelings of deep, very personal opposition in people who have never even seen such a marriage. Societal reaction is often so strong that families are torn apart, loved ones lost forever, and immeasurable hurt is inflicted on decent and gentle people. Recounting some of these experiences, people from these marriages tell us,

"...my father said our marriage would kill his father; my brother said it would kill my father; my father said he would disown me...";
"...my parents decided that they never wanted to see me again...";
"...my parents lost friends when I married into another group...";
"...to this day part of my husband's family has no communication with him...The older brother has expressed fears throughout the years that we would 'pop up' at his home and embarrass his in-laws."

Despite the intense feelings, mixed marriages are increasing throughout the world. Most countries are struggling to cope with the implications of culturally diverse and ethnically heterogeneous populations. Marriage, a most basic social institution, finds itself inextricably caught in the struggle. Though the nuptials are between two individuals, mixed marriages are the object of attention in every society because of their symbolic meaning. Marriage is more than a relationship between individuals. It is a relationship between groups--a relationship signifying equality between those groups.

Families are the groups most directly involved. But, indirectly, status groups--in the forms of social classes, ethnic groups, religious groups, and cultural groups--are always involved as well. Every social structure disadvantages some of its members, while promoting the interests of others. Through myths, values, norms and broad worldviews, the social order, skewed as it is, is portrayed as a "natural" order. The disadvantaged are consistently categorized as a distinct social group--a caste, an ethnic group, a minority. These designations function to clearly distinguish those who are to be advantaged from those who are to be disadvantaged.

In other words, social groups are not equal in terms of their access to the society's rewards. Yet, marriage is perhaps the most "equal" of all social relationships. For those who enjoy preferential treatment, the symbol of social equality inherent in someone else's marriage can be threatening. The advantaged always seek legitimization of their privileged status; so among other things, they prohibit mixed marriages because of the social symbolism involved.

Some mixed unions are both cross-cultural and interracial, and some were established before laws prohibiting such marriages were nullified. Furthermore, many couples say they are living happy, stimulating lives.

"...The mixture of our backgrounds has turned out to be a strength rather than a weakness...";
"...our relationship has been a beautiful, worthwhile journey and we have never regretted it...";
"...we feel our interracial marriage has been of nothing but benefit to us..."

Such are the contrasts when dealing with mixed marriages. Broader society disapproves, but mixed couples continue to appear. Even in South Africa, interracial couples stand up to right wing "hit squads," family excommunication, and police intervention, not to mention extraordinary social pressure (Anon. 1988a).

"Racial" intermarriage is the most despised mixed marriage in most dominated societies. Other societies have different obsessions, however. In Nigeria, religious intermarriage is a major problem. One reason religion is a key factor is that Islam, the country's dominant religion, accepts polygamous marriages. Most Nigerian women object to the presence of other wives or concubines. Lagos newspapers tell of scorned wives who pour boiling water on their husband's mistresses or who, out of revenge, set fire to all of his valuables (Anon. 1988b). Furthermore, in Nigeria, religious differences are often seen to coincide with ethnic differences. The society as a whole reacts to the tension by questioning the efficacy of "mixed" marriages.

There has not been much written about mixed marriages. The small literature which does exist usually uses quantitative and statistical data to describe national patterns. Typically, it frowns on these marriages and says very little about the people in the marriages or about their relationships. As a case in point, American textbooks on marriage make the following types of unappealing comments about mixed marriages:

* "Opposites attract" in some aspects of personality. However, in terms of groups, the general rule is "like marries like."
* Mixed couples...find their internal difficulties magnified by the counter pulls of their separate "tribal" involvements.
* Contrasting backgrounds create potential problems.
* A mixed marriage is a "house divided against itself."
* The negative effect on children increases the greater the barriers to intermarriage.
* Alienation from in-laws is a natural corollary of mixed marriages.
* Mixed marriages not only have more difficulties but fewer "patterned intergenerational family activities."
* Mixed marriages...are risky. But high-risk games have high payoffs - for those who win (Blood).

Most of the relationships which are now defined as 'mixed' have emerged during the last 150 years. Western colonial and neocolonial domination have drawn rather sharp lines between certain groups.[1] For instance, the enslavement of

Africans and the widespread servitude of non-western people has reduced virtually all persons of color to inferior status. Even the fiction makes this clear. Though people in Africa are black, an admirable character like Tarzan has to be white so as not to upset our images of proper group relationships. Paul Scotts, in The Raj Quartet, stated the situation accurately:

> Daphne's British suitor, was the type of lower middle class administrator whose sense of racial superiority derived from the fact that he had more social status in India than he ever would have had in England simply because all British were considered superior to all Indians by virtue of their skin color (Brown 1993: 99).

Viewed in this light, we can understand that powerful interests outside the mixed marriage are always affected by the mere existence of the marriage. Negative attitudes toward mixed marriages then must be understood as part of the more general forces of social control. Mixed marriages undermine social hierarchies as Brown observed in A Passage to India:

> "The British social snobbery even towards the most educated and wealthy Indians...indicates the difficulty of maintaining even a friendship, not to mention a marriage, when one people is subordinated to another (Brown 1993: 99).

Alan Paton's Too Late the Phalarope portrays a society which is even harsher on those whose behavior undermines the boundaries between the dominators and the dominated:

> It opens with several instances of legal action against contact between races, contact even with slight social or sexual implication. A young white Afrikaner asks a black girl for her name, and narrowly avoids punitive judgement because the magistrate only scolds him in secret. A farmer named Smith is sentenced to death because he and his white wife killed his black servant for fear that his sexual relationship with a black woman would come to light. The novel's main protagonist, Afrikaner police lieutenant, Jakob van Vlaanderen, rugby idol, "Lion of the North," church deacon, model family man, is brought down because he confessed to committing an offense under the Immorality Act (Bruner 1993: 85).

As Europe extended its control over the rest of the world, it propagated a culture which justified the resulting superior/inferior relationships on the basis of "civilization." There were, of course, great paradoxes - not the least of which had to do with sexual behavior.

> The Victorians condemned [various sexual] practices, which made them feel superior to these other cultures; on the other hand, they were titillated by them (Brown 1993: 99).

Indeed, some have criticized European sexual behavior while outside of Europe because of:

The inherent exploitiveness of such relationships in which the politically and economically more powerful Westerner feels superior and is essentially using the Third World male or female (Brown 1993: 100).

While by far the most prevalent cause, European hegemony is not the only cause of social differentiation which affects people's feelings about matrimony. An illustration is Ghanaian playwright Ama Ata Aidoo's story of an African student in the United States who plans to marry a black American, only to find that the grandmother at home "...is scandalized that [he] could marry a descendant of former slaves" (Bruner 1993: 82). Similarly, in No Longer At Ease, Chinua Achebe depicts an African community's opposition to a marriage between a "promising been-to" and "an osu, member of a despised class" (Bruner 1993: 82).

The commonality of this behavior is that social equality implicit in the mixed marriage violates socially sanctioned patterns of privilege and superiority. In fact, it is this characteristic which causes a society to label it "mixed" - mixed between two groups which are in different positions in the pecking order. The further apart the groups are in their access to social rewards, the greater the sense of "mixture."

We can now understand why people become so personally involved in this marriage question. It is not just an amorphous "society" which takes offense. Rather, the objectors often convey the sense that they are somehow directly and individually affronted by mixed couples, and that, therefore, they have a right to object to these marriages. Strangely, they are correct. The affront is direct and personal because the mixed marriage makes a public statement, saying "You are not special or superior and your privilege is not justified."

It is noteworthy that only the marriage relationship implies complete equality. Hence of all intergroup liaisons, it is the most prohibited. Miscegenation and concubinage, so long as it does not involve dominant group women, is frowned upon, but it does not evoke nearly the same hostility as intermarriage. Richard Burton's remark, "...while thousands of Europeans have cohabited for years with and have had families by native women, they are never loved by them," illustrates that only marriage could have compromised the dominant/subordinate relations between the British and the Indians (Brown 1993: 97).

Emphasizing the power of marriage, society usually looks the other way when it comes to concubinage and miscegenation. The only exception is when these interactions involve notables. With Thomas Jefferson, for instance, historians have rushed to protect his name by vehemently disputing allegations that he had a long term affair with his slave, Sally Hemings, and that he fathered several children by her. Being so central to America's culture and mythology - which frequently wants to eschew relations with blacks - Jefferson cannot be seen as having this kind of intimate relationship. But, except for idols, miscegenation and concubinage continue to be tolerated because they do not have the same meaning as marriage.

Complicating the study of mixed marriages is the fact that "mixed" is culturally defined. Whether "like marries like" depends on which characteristics are regarded as significant. Take, for instance, the case of a marriage between a black American and a white American, same nationality and culture, from the same neighborhood, same economic background, same university, same religion, same norms and values, and same profession. In the United States, such a marriage is regarded as "mixed," not because there are important attributes of the individuals which are different, but because American society uses "race" as a measure of social differentiation. "Race" determines one's access to rewards, one's place in the pecking order. It is group privileges which are at stake and America frequently uses "race" to distinguish status groups. Hence, this couple is "mixed."

These definitions differ from society to society. Sometimes it's religion which counts; sometimes it's class; sometimes it is "race;" sometimes geographic location. Take the highly emotive concept of "race." Biologically speaking, there are no such categories as "races." "Race" is entirely a social construct. It is not surprising, then, that different societies have constructed different "races." In the United States, there is a two-tier racial categorization system. Anybody with known black ancestry, no matter how small, is considered black and is distinguished socially from "whites."[2] As a result, there are Americans with light skins, light hair, and blue eyes who are defined as "black." Ludicrously, they may even "pass" as white, but they are "really" black.

By contrast, most other multiethnic societies have created separate social categories for people with different combinations of ancestors. Mulattoes, mestizos, creoles, coloreds, Euroasians, Euroafricans, are among these categories. In Brazil, there may be as many as forty such "racial" categories.

To protect the system of differential rewards, the more useful a social category is as a means of discrimination, the greater the barriers to marriages with that category. For example, those American communities with the largest number of blacks rely most heavily on "race" as a criterion of social status and as a measure of legitimate access to wealth and power. The strongest prohibitions on mixed marriages exist in these communities, because they blur these important social lines. One finds, on the other hand, that in states like Vermont, the taboo on interracial marriages is significantly less. Two of the couples contributing to this volume were well received in small towns in Vermont, where, "...race was certainly not an issue." The population of blacks is so small in Vermont that "race" is not sufficient as a differentiating criterion. For this reason, marriage across "racial" lines does not disrupt the established social hierarchy and is not strongly opposed.[3]

In those situations where certain "groupings" have meaning for the allocation of social rewards, "mixed" marriage is a major issue. Because "race" is an important instrument of social differentiation in the United States, apart from ethnically homogeneous places like Vermont, white Americans generally raise great objection to marriages between whites and blacks. In Ireland, where one's life chances are linked to religion, "Mixed marriages...stand for marriage between Protestant and Catholic and are fraught with immense difficulties...an interracial marriage between a black African and a white Irish girl was much more easily acceptable...if they were both Catholic." In Korea, people "...do not use the term "interracial" or "mixed" marriage...the term is "international"...race tends not to be an overriding or primary issue."

In North Africa,

> ...family, clan and village ties are particularly strong. Ethnic diversity is not featured...nearly as much as are schisms in religious or even sectarian dogmas. Dichotomies between Muslim-Christian, Suni-Shiite, Western dominance-Persian control are strong, and even nationalistic patriotism may give way to the fervor of all-encompassing Muslim religious state.

Similarly, today Iranians may encircle Armenian Catholics, but seek to exterminate followers of their own "race" who follow Bahai (Bruner 1993: 87).

The point is we are all taught to categorize people into socially defined groups which tell us about their relations with other socially defined groups, including where they stand in the "pecking order." This instruction occurs during socialization, much of which is through the literature about our culture.

Take Shakespeare, for example:

> In Othello, Shakespeare drew upon Renaissance stereotypes of dark skin as ugly and North Africans as excessively jealous, yet Othello is presented as noble because he is a Christian and serves the Venetian state. Still, it seems incredible to all...that Desdemona should fall in love with the black-skinned Othello unless she has been bewitched(Brown, 1993: 97).

Similarly,

> In Antony and Cleopatra, Shakespeare drew upon Plutarch, whose view of the Orient conformed to the then current view of the East as sexually unrestrained and opulently wealthy and decadent, as feminine in its emotionalism as opposed to the masculine discipline and order of Rome. Mark Antony's tragedy is that he turns his back on his duty to his country and to his Roman wife Octavia to indulge himself in the pleasure offered by the Eastern queen so 'infinite in her variety' (Brown, 1993 97).

Furthermore, modern films as well as modern literature continue to implant unfavorable and unrealistic images of "other" groups.

It should be evident then that mixed marriages have at least two crucial dimensions - the interpersonal dimension and the intergroup dimension. So far, we have dwelled on the intergroup dimension because it is this aspect of mixed marriages which accounts for the great public interest. We should further realize though that most of the "groups" are constructs of a particular culture. They are conceptual fabrications which have been made into social realities.

This explains why the most fierce taboos and the greatest sanctions, including lynching and imprisonment, often befall people who marry across these group lines. The fear is that the fact of fabrication will be revealed, that the artificiality of group boundaries will become evident and the system of preferential access to wealth and power will crumble. The sweeping prohibitions on mixed marriages, therefore, have little to do with the married individuals. They have everything to do with protecting the interests of the socially advantaged.

Because they too normally act in support of the status quo, scholars have given inadequate attention to mixed marriages. The most widely-known context for understanding these marriages has to do with assimilation, socio-cultural change and social integration. Mixed marriage, it is argued, is seen as a manifestation of broader social processes. When group cohesion breaks down, intermarriage occurs. The mixed marriage is the ultimate indication that social distance does not exist.

Without a doubt, there is some validity in these analyses. They fail, however, in not conceptualizing the larger picture. If these scholars could step out of their peculiar cultural indoctrinations, they would appreciate the absurdity of concepts like homogamy and heterogamy. Not only are the categories of "likeness" defined by the broader society, but they are done so on bases which have nothing to do with the individuals' personal attributes. What then is homogamy, "like marrying like?" A couple can be very much alike, but a culture can impose the differences it wants to see. Does that then make it a marriage between people who are not alike?

Furthermore, when marriage is consensual, the very fact of consent demonstrates substantial "likeness" and shows the absence of meaningful differences. The larger picture, which scholars too often chose to ignore, is that the processes of conceptualizing "groups," stimulating social distance, instilling ideas like "homogamy," and defining certain marriages as "mixed," are important instruments of social control and social domination. Many of the "scholarly" analyses perform the same function. In actual fact, most mixed marriages are no more "mixed" than other marriages.

In any event, scholars have little impact on popular sentiments. The general public is so concerned about mixed marriages that many ideas flourish outside the academy. At one point, "crossbreeding" was seriously regarded as a "disharmonious combination of genes," which would lead to biological or social deficiencies. Other myths have associated mixed marriage with mental retardation among the children and high divorce among parents. Evidence to support these stereotypes has not been found, but the negative images of mixed marriages nevertheless persist.

It is paradoxical, in one sense, that most western societies have such great anxiety about mixed marriages, since such marriage should be expected in multicultural, multiracial, egalitarian democracies. Indeed, social values should encourage these marriages since they are one measure of the society's progress toward fulfilling its ideals. That strong interdictions on such marriages remain in these societies underscores the fact that sophisticated techniques of social control and social superiority are in operation.

While society is solely concerned with mixed marriages as they relate to intergroup relations, the marriages themselves are between individuals. This is the interpersonal dimension, which quite obviously for the partners is by far the most important aspect of the marriage. "Race" seldom seems to matter in the interpersonal dimension, though religious and cultural differences, which can coincide with "racial" differences, often matter quite considerably. As an example, marriages between Africans and West Indians or Afro-Americans often encounter cultural problems. Living in West Africa, the foreign blacks can be frustrated by "...expectations of polygamy, sharing of concerns with members of the extended family and the resultant loss of privacy, conflicts in belief systems, etc" (Bruner, 1993: 82). "Further complications occur often because of the traditional African idea of the status of women, or the husband's own alienation from his culture if he is a been-to, and also the system of obligations to the extended family put upon the couple by traditional society" (Bruner, 1993: 82).

By contrast, on the interpersonal dimension, marriages between people with a similar culture, even if there is a "racial" difference, seem to encounter fewer serious stresses. Although the interpersonal dimension of mixed marriages is generally ignored, a few academics have theorized about it. Bound by their own ethnocentrism, however, these theories usually promote the notion that mixed couples are "deviant." The theme is on the anti-normative character of this behavior rather than its healthy, natural nature. The message is that mixed marriages are "wrong." It is seldom that they are portrayed as desirable or even acceptable.

Also, dominant group scholars find it difficult to wrest themselves from the "intergroup" frame of reference, despite the fact that they seek to explain interpersonal behavior. The basic problem is that dominant cultures want to deny that there can be a warm, rich interpersonal dimension to a mixed marriage. They want to maintain boundaries, and usually the scholars oblige. For these reasons, the most popular analysis of the interpersonal dimension of mixed marriages actually demeans the marriages by impuning purely mercenary motives to the partners. This analysis is called exchange theory. It holds that

> minority men are able to exchange nonracial status (e.g. occupation or education) for the racial status of white women. This option is assumed not to be open to minority women because men are not as interested in the occupation or education of potential spouses as are women...within the framework of exchange theory: the status of the minority group member becomes higher through marriage to a white spouse, and the status of the majority group member improves through marriage to someone with higher status on dimensions other than race (Sandfur and McKinnell 1986: 351).

Absurdly, this analysis sees marital decisions as decisions taken solely on the basis of relative status and group stratification. What about the normal motivations of love, common interests, sharing, similar values, and desire for companionship? Obviously, the main concern of the exchange theorists is still social control and social dominance. Healthy, successful, gratifying mixed marriages remain culturally forbidden, so the interpersonal rewards of these unions are deliberately ignored. Sadly, because their privilege seems to be at stake, dominant groups only focus on the "mixed;" they refuse to see the "marriage."

The inadequacy of most interpretations of mixed marriage is apparent when we listen to the mixed couples' own views:

> "...As long as one maintains interest in the personality and the changing personality of the other partner and in his/her interests and concerns, whether or not the marriage is mixed or non-mixed is not relevant..."
>
> "...In spite of our obvious differences...[we] share some basic values that hold our marriage together...the basic consensus on how to live mediates our differences and external problems."
>
> "...My experiences have taught me that the problems of mixed marriages were always, without exception, the problems of the wider society, and not the problems of that particular couple."
>
> "...We were attracted to each other not only physically, but also for personal characteristics. Qualities such as caring, loving, understanding, comprehensiveness, dedication, and desire to reach forward, were very important aspects that minimized our cultural, economic and education differences."
>
> "...one of the advantages of a cross-cultural marriage is that the broadening of each other's mind is enhanced by this very fact... another... is the beauty and intelligence of the children."

Inside the Mixed Marriage is about the personal experiences of people in mixed marriages. The book emerged from our own awareness of the increase in mixed marriages and our desire to inform ourselves and others about this experience. Here the marital partners consider the changing sets of advantages and constraints mixed marriages have imposed on them and their children. And, in addition to discussing the impact of society on our marriages, we speculate on the impact our marriages have had on the attitudes of others.

These narratives do not attempt to construct a theoretical analysis of mixed marriages. Although a disproportionate number of the contributors are scholars, our point of departure was our own marriages, seen from the inside. These are personal accounts. Their purpose is to breathe life into the statistics on mixed marriages, to try to put a human face on sterile terms like homogamy, social integration, assimilation, cultural 'barriers', and the like. All but one of the contributors are currently in a mixed marriage. Having chosen to be in a mixed marriage, and having chosen to write about it, we are in a sense advocates. Ours are the voices which are not normally heard. And while we acknowledge some of the peculiar stresses which can plague mixed marriages, we clearly do not subscribe to the broader society's myths and fears about such unions.

The contributors are not a representative sample of mixed marriages. The invitees were chosen from the personal networks of the editors. It is not at all coincidental that a high percentage of the partners are anthropologists. Cross-cultural relations is what many of our professional lives have been all about. Moreover, only a small number of invitees actually contributed chapters. Over 50 couples were invited to participate. About 35 indicated a desire to be involved, but, in the end, there were 17 submissions.

Herein lies an important insight into the nature of this volume. First of all, only couples who were still married were invited to participate. There was no attempt to assess those mixed marriages which had dissolved. Secondly, and most importantly, the process of writing showed just how personal and delicate many of these issues are. This is of course a characteristic of all marriages, not just mixed ones. Public discussion of the expectations, frustrations, bitternesses, and differences which are inevitably intertwined with the joys and successes, is a difficulty for all marriages. Most wedded couples find ways of closeting the 'excess baggage' in their relationships. In our cases, this 'baggage' usually had nothing to do with the 'mixed' character of the relationship. It was the personal 'baggage' which accompanies all marital relationships. The idea of dusting off and thoroughly inspecting this 'baggage' for purposes of public consumption is frightening and sometimes dangerous. Many couples, perhaps wisely, withdrew.

The couples who have contributed chapters, therefore, are representative of relatively stable mixed marriages. They have, of course, been subjected to the general stresses of matrimony and the pressures which impose themselves on mixed marriages. Nevertheless, they have had the personal or situational circumstances which have given stability to the union.

It is interesting to observe the demographic characteristics of the contributors, because their profiles, in many ways, tell us a great deal about the phenomenon of mixed marriages. The couples included here are non-traditional in a number of ways. It is not simply that they are in a mixed marriage. Many of the individuals entered marriage when they were older. This is to be expected in the cases of people who were previously married. Nonetheless, in addition to the question of wisdom coming with age and experience, the older person is probably less susceptible to social pressures and conventions. Add to that the fact that the individuals are professionals, often functioning in a 'liberal' university environment, it is easier to see how they might decide to transgress social custom.

Almost half of the partners here were previously married. In most cases the previous marriage would have been defined as 'homogamous'. Is it that these individuals were searching for someone totally different from their previous spouse? Was it excitement they were looking for? Or is it that they were wiser, having realized which attributes really contribute to a successful marriage and which ones do not?

In every case, except one, at least one of the partners had a terminal degree in his/her field. In the one exception, both partners had college degrees, one had a Master's degree, and both were practicing professionals. In other words, the authors here come from the most educated, professional segment of the population. These data confirm the current thinking that mixed marriages tend to occur between individuals of higher than average education. Interestingly, this was not always the case, but, at the moment, education seems to be related to greater tolerance of other groups and to the perception of less social distance between the individual and other groups.

For several of the couples writing here, there were no children from the mixed marriage. While this, too, can be a function of various factors, the absence of children is significant. A mixed marriage without children is subject to much less social sanction. One couple put it this way, "One of our weapons before parenthood in fighting racism and the possible repercussions...had been our ability to be selectively quiet about our marriage. Parenthood put a stop to that."

Society's taboos are not fully transgressed if there are no children because there is no permanent blurring of the boundaries between groups. Children obliterate the boundaries. Their very existence challenges the system. Children underscore the arbitrary, substancelessness of socially contrived 'groups'. We are told, for instance, "...our children are 'white' in Nigeria and 'black' in America..." Because they highlight absurd situations in this manner, mixed children constitute a perpetual demand for the dominant group to justify its distinctions. The extreme discomfort caused by this demand undoubtedly explains why society frequently strikes out most viciously at 'mixed' children, the most innocent of all parties.

Perhaps the most noteworthy characteristic of the couples here is their international links. Major international experience is common to every couple. It is easy to suggest therefore that the cultural ethnocentrism, which restricts most people's marital choices, had already been significantly loosened by the time these individuals contemplated marriage. Their norms and values had already been modified before the marriage. They had already experienced the excitement of cross-cultural interaction. In many cases, this loosening of cultural ethnocentrism occurred precisely during the 'marriage years' - that is, the middle '20s.

For many, the international links continue. There are hints that living 'overseas' has allowed some marriages to cope with the social pressures at home. Two of the couples here still live 'overseas':

"...expatriate communities [are] ... completely accepting of interracial families."

"...the challenge of living in a developing country has been helpful to our marriage."
"To avoid this conflict [of cultures] and in order to establish a balance between us, we decided that moving to a third country would be a wise thing to do."

Furthermore, many of the longer term marriages were contracted during the 1960's and early 1970's when the American civil rights movement and the war in Vietnam were promoting new, non-racial, culturally plural norms. No doubt many thought these were the values of the future and wanted to put them in practice in their own lives.

The point is that most of these marriages were embarked upon within a quite well defined normative framework. The literature which subtlely rebukes them as ethically deviant is, in reality, simply revealing how bankrupt a dominant culture actually can become in its attempt to remain dominant. That literature is simply incorrect as regards the absence of strong, socially approved values in individuals who marry across 'group' lines.

The instructions to the contributors were few. Both spouses were expected to participate in the preparation of the chapter. This was not always easily done, given different perceptions and individual preoccupations. Couples were asked to discuss the personal factors which led them as individuals to enter mixed marriages. They were asked to discuss the factors which have contributed to the stability of their marriage. Finally, they were asked to assess the relationship of their marriage to the broader society, especially how their marriage has influenced others.

The results were fascinating. The personal accounts reveal that, despite the social taboos, mixed marriages can offer exciting, fulfilling relationships. People in these marriages often lead very rewarding lives.

"...Tasting the richness of varied cultures in this country has been my way before and since my marriage..."
"...when I converted to Islam I didn't only discover a different religion, I joined a whole culture, a whole way of life..."
"...we have never experienced the feeling that our marriage is singularly unusual, and certainly not despicable..."
"...We are both individualists, taking pleasure in being different..."
"...It is hard for us to think of any real disadvantages we experienced because our marriage is interracial..."
"...We cherish our different backgrounds and do not try to deny it in any way..."
"...we have not encountered adversity because of our mixed marriage, in fact quite the contrary..."

Indeed, time after time, couples stressed that the important aspects of their marriage had to do with elements other than its 'mixed' character. The externally imposed categories of 'ethnicity' or 'culture', in the end, had very little to do with the nature of their relationship. The problem differences were usually not the differences outsiders saw, but were the differences which exist between any two human beings trying to live together.

"...the interracial aspect of our marriage has turned out to seem less important and less interesting than the cross cultural aspects..."
"...I believe the success or failure of my marriage has had less to do with race than class and perceptions of sex roles..."
"...cultural differences may be less important than differences between individuals..."
"...Most conflicts were naturally of the trivial domestic sort, in which it is difficult to distinguish cultural from personal differences..."
"...I do not think that our mixed marriage differs very much from those which are not mixed..."

It is evident from the narratives in this compendium that mixed marriages have no special access to marital bliss. As one contributor put it, "Any discussion of the mixed marriage is invariably a discussion of marriage itself." Relationships within all marriages are at times difficult and trying. But not always more so because they are 'mixed'. Happiness, loving and sharing are equally attributes of marriage. No less so because they are 'mixed'.

It is the view from inside the mixed marriage which makes these narratives significant. They provide sharp contrasts to those who understand mixed marriages solely in the context of intergroup relations, social control, and social dominance. They hit directly at popular myths and fears. These narratives illustrate the artificiality of social constructs like ethnicity, race and culture. By calling attention to the relationships between the individuals, Inside the Mixed Marriage is a testimony to the marvelous scope and variety of the human experience.

Notes

[1]   Mixed marriages involving people from other parts of the world, for example, cannot be understood outside the context of western hegemony over that part of the world.

[2]   A most recent variation has been the introduction of Hispanics, many of whom have black and white ancestry. But even here, the United States distinguishes between Hispanic black and Hispanic white.

[3]   Similarly, as Native Americans shrink as a percentage of the United States population, and thereby become less threatening, intermarriage with them has become more acceptable.

References

Anon.
  1988 "Love will Triumph," Sowetan, 28 January.

Anon.
  1988 "Reporting Matters of the Heart in Nigeria," The New York Times, January.

Blood, Robert O.
  1978 <u>Marriage</u> . 3rd edition. The Free Press, New York.

Brown, Christy
  1993 "Literary Images of Intercultural Relationships between Westerners and
      Middle Easterners," in <u>Inside the Mixed Marriage: Accounts of Changing
      Attitudes, Patterns, and Perceptions of Cross-Cultural and Interracial
      Marriages</u>, Walton Johnson and D. Michael Warren (eds.), Lanham,
      Maryland: University Press of America.

Bruner, Charlotte H.
  1993 "Cross-Cultural Marriage as a Literary Motif in Africa and Caribbean
      Literature," in <u>Inside the Mixed Marriage: Accounts of Changing Attitudes,
      Patterns, and Perceptions of Cross-Cultural and Interracial Marriages</u>,
      Walton Johnson and D. Michael Warren (eds.), Lanham, Maryland:
      University Press of America.

Roberts, Robert
  1993 "Black-Inter-marriage in the United States," in <u>Inside the Mixed Marriage:
      Accounts of Changing Attitudes, Patterns, and Perceptions of Cross-
      Cultural and Interracial Marriages</u>, Walton Johnson and D. Michael Warren
      (eds.), Lanham, Maryland: University Press of America.

Sandfur, G. and Trudy McKinnell
  1986 "American Indian Intermarriage," <u>Social Science Research</u>, vol. 15, p. 351.

PART I :

DEFINING AND EXPLORING THE MIXED RELATIONSHIP

CHAPTER 1

CROSS-CULTURAL DEFINITIONS OF PERSONS OF MIXED RACIAL HERITAGE

Robert E.T. Roberts

During the past five centuries, millions of Europeans, Asians, and Africans have crossed the oceans and settled in distant lands, creating numerous biracial and multiracial societies. Such societies, with a history of conquest, colonization, slavery, and exploitation have long remained stratified on a racial and ethnic basis, with Europeans forming the upper stratum and non-Europeans occupying lower rungs in the status hierarchy. Individuals of mixed racial background may constitute a named, self-conscious social group, recognized as such by members and non-members alike; they may be defined as belonging to the status group of either parent, or they may be of ambiguous status without assigned racial group affiliation.

Biracial Groups of Asia and South Africa

In South and Southeast Asia and South Africa, early racial mixing between European men and indigenous or slave women has produced intermediate named and recognized social groups. Hybrid groups such as Anglo-Indians and Goans of India, Burghers of Sri Lanka, Eurasians of Malaysia and Indonesia, and the Cape Coloured of South Africa have long constituted endogamous units with strong group identity. They are socially and culturally distinct from the indigenous population, and have few or no family or kinship ties with either parental group. They are predominantly Christian, European in orientation, culture and language, and intermediate in status between the two ancestral races from which they derive. They have been proud of their European ancestry and cultural background, and since independence was attained by their Asian homelands, many Eurasians have emigrated to Britain, Europe, North America, and Australia rather than cast their lot with culturally distinct and now politically dominant Asians (Stonequist 1937: 10-53; Dover 1937; Gist, Dworkin 1972: 57, 78, 92-100).

During the past half century, African, Asian, and other non-European students and workers in European countries, and American military and civilian personnel in Asia have produced a new generation of racial hybrids who have not been absorbed into established mixed racial groups. Children of marriages between Indian men and European women do not become Anglo-Indians (Cottrell 1979). Children of non-marital unions of alien soldiers and Asian women may be rejected by both parental societies and find no place in a subsociety of mixed racial background. Thousands of such children in Japan, Korea, and Vietnam, although socialized and enculturated in the norms of their countries of birth, face rejection on the basis of race and illegitimate birth in nations which lack established Eurasian communities (Hurh 1972: 10-22).

There have been situations in which numerous offspring of marriages and other unions between Europeans and non-Europeans have gained entry into the dominant white group. In the early years of the Cape Colony, a large percentage of mixed offspring of European fathers and mainly Asian mothers of slave background married white men, and their descendants form a considerable element in the dominant white Afrikaner population of South Africa today.

In his research on race relations in the Cape, Frederickson found evidence that one-fifth of German immigrants between 1652 and 1806 married women who had been born slaves and that about 24 percent of marriages recorded between 1688 and 1807 of white immigrants who appear to be ancestors of Afrikaner families founded before 1867 involved one spouse, usually female, of some known degree of non-white ancestry (Frederickson 1981: 108-119).

During most of the period of Dutch rule of the East Indies, migration from the Netherlands was predominantly male, and Dutch settlers frequently married or lived with Indonesian women. The children of marital unions, and those who were adopted or formally legitimized by their fathers were legally designated as European and had the same legal and political rights as persons of unmixed Dutch ancestry. Following Indonesian independence in 1949, a majority chose to retain Dutch citizenship and settle in the Netherlands where it appears likely that many will be fully assimilated into Dutch society (Wittermans 1972: 79-102; van Amersfoort 1982: 81-100).

Status of Persons of Mixed Race in Latin America and the West Indies

In the Western hemisphere, especially in Latin America, centuries of race mixture have produced a largely hybrid population. In Mexico and much of Central America, a majority of the population are mestizos of Spanish-Amerindian descent. The mestizo element also predominates in large areas of South America, while Eurafricans constitute a large percentage of the population of Brazil, Cuba, Puerto Rico, and the Dominican Republic.[1]

Costa Rica, Chile, Uruguay, and Argentina have largely absorbed into the dominant white population those Amerindians and blacks who did not succumb to warfare and disease during the colonial and early republican periods (Beals 1969: 242; Thompson 1973: 74-86).

In Guatemala and Mexico, the African slave population has been virtually absorbed into the mestizo or Ladino group which is predominantly of mixed Spanish and Indian composition. In most of Central America and much of South America unmixed Europeans have declined to a small numerical minority, and the culturally European dominant social group includes both unmixed whites and persons of mixed racial ancestry. The definition of Indian identity is cultural rather than biological, and many Ladinos resemble Indians phenotypically, while differing in language, dress, and lifestyle. In Guatemala, the former distinctions between Spaniard, mestizo, mulatto, zambo, and Negro have given way to use of the term "Ladino" to designate any person, regardless of physical type, who is non-Indian, thus including whites, mulattoes, mestizos, and Europeanized Indians (Tax 1942; Roberts 1948: 136; Aguirre Beltran 1970).

In the tropical areas of Latin America and the West Indies, the population is predominantly of European and African descent, including varying degrees of mixture. The racially mixed segment of the population exceeds that of unmixed blacks in most of South America, Cuba, Puerto Rico, and the Dominican Republic, but does not constitute a separate social unit. Rather, we find a continuum of color and other racial characteristics, with no sharp dividing line, and with highest evaluation given to Caucasian traits. Classification is based on physical appearance combined with cultural attainment so that a wealthy lawyer or doctor with some Negroid features might be classed as white, while an unskilled and unlettered slum-dweller might be classed as black despite the presence of some Caucasoid physical characteristics.

In Colombia, with a population estimated to be 25 percent white, 42 percent mestizo, 8 percent Negro, 20 percent mulatto, and 5 percent Indian, we are informed that:

> Humans and genes being what they are, racial features cut across the Colombian classification. The classification is based not on biology but on behavior. Thus an Indian ceases to be an Indian when he gives up Indian ways, when he adopts a Spanish surname, speaks the Spanish language, wears European clothes, and does the things that White Colombians do. The case of the Negro is not as clear cut, because the behavioral classification does not completely override his dark skin. If a person of obvious Negro ancestry does not work in a sugarcane field, does not have the reputation of being lazy and carefree, and whose education permits him to have an office job, he will likely be moreno (brown). Moreno becomes solely a descriptive term, which denotes the color of the skin, and its racial connotation falls away (Richardson 1970: 15).

In the port city of Cartagena, Colombia 120 adults, 30 each of upper, middle, working, and lower class levels, were shown 22 photographs of men and women representing a spectrum of racial types and patterns of dress and were asked to indicate the "race" of the individuals in the photographs. While the terms negro and blanco were most frequently used to describe the polar extremes of color and feature, the number of terms used for each picture varied from 9 to 25, with an average of 16.5 terms per picture. Racially mixed individuals were frequently described by racially neutral or ambiguous terms. The researchers state that the third most commonly used term, moreno, derived from Moor, has been used to describe Spanish white brunettes, a wide variety of miscegenated individuals, and as a euphemism for negro.

. . . Despite an ideological preference for white, a significant number of persons who are not white are fully integrated and accepted by whites on an equal status basis: they are socially defined as "white" (Solaúm and Vélez 1985: 143-149).

Racial definitions vary from place to place, as indicated by Julian Pitt-Rivers:

> In Barranquilla, Colombia, color is qualified by other social factors, and the term Negro confined to the slum-dwellers of the city. In the modern housing developments where no one is to be seen who would not qualify as a Negro in the United States, one may be told: "Only white people live here." The definition of Negro varies from place to place and, of course, from class to class. A man may be defined as Negro in one place, but

simply as <u>moreno</u>, <u>trigueño</u>, <u>canela</u>, or even white in another. A man who would be considered Negro in the United States might, by travelling to Mexico, become <u>moreno</u> or <u>prieto</u>, then <u>canelo</u> or <u>trigueño</u> in Panama, and end up in Barranquilla white (Pitt-Rivers 1968: 270).

In Brazil, one finds ambiguity in racial or color terminology with as many as forty racial terms used in a single community. There are no fixed lines of demarcation between positions on the color continuum. Phenotypically Caucasian Brazilians need not conceal African ancestry or relatives, for individuals who appear to be white are accepted as white as are many with visible Negroid characteristics who possess wealth and professional status. In the absence of a color caste line or descent rule, siblings of differing complexion may be identified by color terms which differ from those of either parent and each other. One brother or sister may be classed as white, while others who display visible evidence of African ancestry may be described by one or more of the numerous terms for persons of mixed racial appearance (Harris 1964: 57-59; Harris 1970; Pierson 1972: 244-247, 261-262; Van den Berghe 1978: 71; Wagley 1971: 123-124; Degler 1971: 101-112).

In Cuba, Puerto Rico, and the Dominican Republic, unmixed blacks are a small minority, with Cuba and Puerto Rico recording a white majority, and the Dominican Republic having a mulatto majority. There is no sharp color line and racial classification is based on physical appearance rather than descent. As in Brazil, children of intermarriages of whites and mulattoes may be either white or colored according to their physical appearance (Boas 1932: 71-73; Hoetink 1967: 167-170; Mathews 1974: 315-317; Rogler 1946; Steward 1956).

Almost all of the non-Hispanic West Indian islands have large black majorities and few unmixed whites. Historically the upper class was white and near-white, the middle class was predominantly mulatto, and the lower class of peasants and laborers was for the most part black. A white elite drew a color line in marriage and intimate social relationships, and many persons who would be classed as white in Puerto Rico or the Dominican Republic would be colored in Jamaica or Barbados. The colored segment of the population does not constitute a unified social group, but is divided by shade of color as well as socio-economic and cultural differences (Braithwaite 1953; Henriques 1953; Lowenthal 1972; Smith 1965).

The Two-Category Racial Descent System of the United States

Almost alone among societies composed mainly of people of European and African descent and mixtures thereof, the United States of America evolved a two-category status system based on a rigid descent rule which excluded anyone with known African ancestry from white identity, and recognized no intermediate "colored" or mixed racial status. In some areas of Louisiana, the Gulf Coast, and South Carolina "free people of color" once occupied an intermediate status resembling that of colored West Indians and held themselves aloof from unmixed African American. The refusal of whites to exempt even the lightest of mulattoes from legal and social discrimination eventually forced the colored Creoles of Louisiana and other light mulattoes to cast their lot with black Americans and often to become enthusiastic supporters and leaders of African American causes

(Williamson 1980: 62, 73-75, 108-109; Frederickson 1981: 129-131; Mills 1977; Woods 1972; Dominquez 1986: 133-148, 172-174).

The most conspicuous exception to classification as black of persons of the slightest degree of Negro ancestry in the United States is that of many Latin Americans of mixed racial descent who occupy an ambiguous status. In addition to persons of Latin American and other foreign birth, some individuals and groups of known or suspected part-African ancestry resist classification as or association with blacks and seek recognition as white, American Indian, or another non-African American identity.

Little known to outsiders are more than 200 variously mixed communities or groups, originating mainly in obscure seventeenth and eighteenth century blending of European adventurers and settlers with remnants of American Indian tribes, and often also with escaped slaves. Most live or have lived in poverty in isolated rural areas in the Eastern United States, from Louisiana to New England. Though suspected of having some black ancestry, they have persistently rejected African American identity and have had some success in gaining recognition as American Indian or white. Most such groups have remained apart from both whites and blacks and their communities constitute isolated endogamous pockets of ambiguous racial status (Berry 1963; Berry 1972: 191-212; Frazier 1951: 164-189; Beale 1972).

Notes:

1. In the Americas, native Americans are commonly referred to as Indians and I shall use this term and Amerindian interchangeably. Mestizo refers to white-Amerindian mixtures; mulatto or colored to mixture of white and Negro; and Negro or black to unmixed or nearly unmixed African ancestry, except in the United States where Negro, black, colored, and Afro-American or African American are all terms used to designate anyone having any degree of known black African ancestry.

References:

Aguirre Beltran, Gonzalo
1970 "The Integration of the Negro into the National Society of Mexico," in Magnus Morner, ed., Race and Class in Latin America. New York: Columbia University Press, 11-27.

Beale, Calvin L.
1972 "An Overview of the Phenomenon of Mixed Racial Isolates in the United States," American Anthropologist, Vol. 74, No. 3: 704-710.

Beals, Ralph L.
1969 "Indian-mestizo-white Relations in Spanish America," in Melvin M. Tumin, ed., Comparative Perspectives on Race Relations. Boston: Little, Brown, 239-257.

Berry, Brewton
1963 Almost White. New York: Macmillan.

Berry, Brewton
  1972 "America's Mestizos," in N.P. Gist and A.G. Dworkin, eds., The Blending
       of Races. New York: Interscience, 191-212.

Boas, Franz
  1932 Anthropology and Modern Life, revised ed. New York: Macmillan.

Braithwaite, Lloyd
  1953 "Social Stratification in Trinidad: a Preliminary Analysis," Social and
       Economic Studies, Vol. 2, No. 2/3: 5-175.

Cottrell, Ann Baker
  1979 "Today's Asian-Western Couples are not Anglo-Indians," Phylon, Vol. 40:
       351-361.

Degler, Carl N.
  1971 Neither Black nor White: Slavery and Race Relations in Brazil and the
       United States. New York: Macmillan.

Dominquez, Virginia R.
  1986 White by Definition: Social Classification in Creole Louisiana. New
       Brunswick, N.J.: Rutgers University Press.

Dover, Cedric
  1937 Half-Caste. London: Martin Secker and Warburg.

Frazier, E. Franklin
  1951 The Negro Family in the United States. New York: Dryden.

Frederickson, George M.
  1981 White Supremacy: a Comparative Study in American and South African
       History. Oxford: Oxford University Press.

Gist, Noel P. and Anthony Gary Dworkin, eds.
  1972 The Blending of Races: Marginality and Identity in World Perspective.
       New York: Wiley-Interscience.

Harris, Marvin
  1964 Patterns of Race in the Americas. New York: Norton.

Harris, Marvin
  1970 "Referential Ambiguity in the Calculus of Brazilian Racial Identity,"
       Southwestern Journal of Anthropology, Vol. 26, No. 1: 1-14.

Henriquez, Fernando
  1953 Family and Colour in Jamaica. London: Eyre and Spottiswodde.

Hoetink, H.
1967 The Two Variants in Caribbean Race Relations. London: Oxford
University Press.

Hurh, Won Moo
1972 "Marginal Children of War: an Exploratory Study of American-Korean
Children," International Journal of Sociology of the Family, Vol. 2, No. 1:
10-20.

Lowenthal, David.
1972 West Indian Societies. New York: Oxford University Press.

Mathews, Thomas G.
1974 "The Question of Color in Puerto Rico," in Robert Brent Toplin, ed.,
Slavery and Race Relations in Latin America. Westport, CT.: Greenwood
Press.

Mills, Gary B.
1977 The Forgotten People: Cane River's Creoles of Color. Baton Rouge and
London: Louisiana State University Press.

Pierson, Donald
1972 "Brazilians of Mixed Racial Descent," in N.P. Gist and A.G. Dworkin,
eds., The Blending of Races. New York: Wiley-Interscience, 237-
263.

Pitt-Rivers, Julian
1968 "Race, Color, and Class in Central America and the Andes," in John Hope
Franklin, ed., Color and Race. Boston: Beacon Press, 264-281.

Richardson, Miles
1970 San Pedro, Colombia: Small Town in a Developing Society. New York:
Holt, Rinehart and Winston.

Roberts, Robert E.T..
1948 "A Comparison of Ethnic Relations in Two Guatemalan Communities,"
Acta Americana, Vol. 6, No. 3/4: 135-151.

Rogler, Charles
1946 "The Morality of Race Mixing in Puerto Rico," Social Forces, Vol. 25, No.
1: 77-81.

Smith, M.G.
1965 The Plural Society in the British West Indies. Berkeley: University of
California Press.

Solaún, Mauricio and Eduardo Vélez
1985 "Racial Terminology and Discriminatory Integration in Latin America,"
Research in Race and Ethnic Relations, Vol. 4: 139-159.

Steward, Julian H. ed.
  1956 The People of Puerto Rico. Urbana: University of Illinois Press.

Stonequist, Everett V.
  1937 The Marginal Man. New York: Charles Scribner's Sons.

Tax, Sol
  1942 "Ethnic Relations in Guatemala," America Indigena, Vol. 2, No.4: 43-48.

Thompson, Era Bell
  1973 "Argentina: Land of the Vanishing Blacks," Ebony, October: 74-86.

Van den Berghe, Pierre L.
  1978 Race and Racism: a Comparative Perspective, 2nd Edition. New York:
       John Wiley and Sons.

Van Amersfoort, Hans
  1982 Immigration and the Formation of Minority Groups: the Dutch Experience
       1945-1975. New York: Cambridge University Press.

Wagley, Charles.
  1971 An Introduction to Brazil, Revised Edition. New York: Columbia
       University Press.

Williamson, Joel
  1980 New People: Miscegenation and Mulattoes in the United States. New York:
       Free Press.

Wittermans, Elizabeth P.
  1972 "The Eurasians of Indonesia," in N.P. Gist and A.G. Dworkin, eds., The
       Blending of Races. New York: Wiley-Interscience, 79-102.

Woods, Sister Frances Jerome
  1972 Marginality and Identity. Baton Rouge: Louisiana State University Press.

CHAPTER 2

BLACK-WHITE INTERMARRIAGE IN THE UNITED STATES
Robert E.T. Roberts

The Colonial Period: 1619-1776

When in 1619 twenty Africans shipped on a Dutch man-of-war were sold to British colonists at Jamestown, Virginia, they were treated much the same as the numerous British and Irish indentured servants who were held in bondage for a fixed number of years. It required a generation or two for lifelong chattel slavery and the utter debasement of the Negro, whether slave or free, to crystallize. In the 1660's, Maryland and Virginia made legal distinctions between white and black servants, recognizing lifelong bondage for blacks even if they had been baptized as Christians.[1]

There was little social distance during the 17th century between white servants and black servants and slaves who shared similar tasks and living conditions and had friendly social relationships, including sexual intercourse and marriage. Antagonism between poor whites and blacks was a later development.

Sexual relations between whites and blacks appear to have been more distasteful to most free white colonists than ordinary fornication (which was considered sinful and punished by whipping or fine). As early as 1630, in Jamestown, it was ordered that "Hugh Davis be soundly whipped before an assemblage of Negroes and others for abusing himself to the dishonor of God and the shame of Christians by defiling his body in lying with a Negro, which fault he is to acknowledge next Sabbath day" (Johnston 1970: 166).

Early anti-miscegenation laws of Maryland and Virginia appear to have been enacted in order to protect the interests of the master class which would have lost valuable property if mulatto children of white mothers assumed the status of the mother. As early as 1661, Maryland legislated that "whatsoever free-born woman shall intermarry with any slave, shall serve the master of such slave during the life of her husband; all issues of such free-born women, so married, shall be slaves as their fathers were" (Woodson 1918: 339-340).

Planters sometimes took advantage of this law and encouraged their white female servants to marry black slaves in order to extend the period of indenture of the servant, as well as to gain additional slaves in the event that children were born of the union. When, in 1681, Lord Baltimore returned to Maryland with a white domestic servant, Irish Nell, who married a slave the same year, he used his influence to have the law repealed in August, 1681 (Catterall 1932: IV, 2).

In 1691, Virginia legislated against interracial marriages, decreeing that:

> ...for the prevention of that abominable mixture and spurious issue which may hereafter increase in this dominion...Be it enacted...that for the time to come, whatsoever English or white man or woman being free shall intermarry with a Negro, mulatto, or Indian man or woman, bound or free

shall within three months thereafter be banished and removed from the dominion forever... (Johnston 1970: 172-173).

Following the example of Maryland and Virginia, marriage between whites and blacks was made punishable by law in Massachusetts in 1705, North Carolina in 1715, Delaware in 1721, Pennsylvania in 1725, and Georgia in 1750. Such legislation typically fined those who performed interracial marriage ceremonies as well as the participants, and extended the terms of indenture of white women servants who were found guilty, without necessarily voiding such marriages.

There is little information apart from reports of cases brought to trial and a few letters, diaries, and travelers' accounts, of the frequency and circumstances of marriages between whites and blacks during the colonial period. Legal and social pressure gradually reduced the once frequent intermarriage of white servant women with slaves and other Afro-Americans.

Public opinion in the Northern colonies soon came to be much opposed to unions between whites and blacks both in and out of marriage. An early account tells of a white woman who married a Negro in New England in 1681, lived with him for years and reared mulatto children, and was completely ostracized by her family and the community.

A number of judicial cases in which mulattoes petitioned for freedom on the basis of descent from a white woman document marriages of blacks with white servant women during the colonial era. In the following Maryland case, the petitioner gained his freedom:

> Shorter v. Rozier. . . October 1794. The petitioner claimed his freedom as being lineally descended in the female line from Elizabeth Shorter, a free white woman. He offered in evidence the following papers, dated June 15, 1702: These are to certify, that in the year 1681, or near about that time, I Nicholas Geulick, priest . . . did join together in the holy estate of matrimony, according to the then law, a negro man named Little Robin, to a white woman, whose name was Elizabeth Shorter, which couple all that time were both servants unto Mr. William Roswell, deceased . . . Emma Roswell . . . declareth upon her oath, that she . . . was present at the marriage of the said negro man and white woman, the said white woman had three mulatto girl children, named Mary, Jane, and Martha (Catterall 1932: IV, 52).

The noted self-taught late 18th century black mathematician, astronomer, publisher of an almanac, and surveyor of the streets of the District of Columbia, Benjamin Banneker, was the grandson of

> ...Molly Welsh, a native of England, who came to Maryland--, with a ship load of emigrants, and, to defray the expense of the voyage was sold to a master with whom she served an apprenticeship of seven years. After her term of service had expired, she bought a small farm--, and purchased as laborers, two Negro slaves, from a ship which lay in Chesapeake Bay. One of them . . . she liberated from slavery and afterwards married . . . They had four children (Johnston 1970: 189).

Unlike the widespread New World practice of assigning to persons of mixed Caucasian and Negro ancestry a status intermediate between white and black, no special status was accorded persons of mixed ancestry in most areas of the United States. Early in the colonial period there was established a two-category status system with the so-called "one-drop" descent rule by which any amount of known Negro ancestry excluded a person from the dominant white group. Even remote African ancestry was seen as degrading, and many slaves who were physically indistinguishable from Europeans were held in bondage.

Until well into the 19th century, however, along the Gulf Coast from Louisiana to Florida, where under previous French or Spanish rule mulattoes had been accorded intermediate status (and in South Carolina as well), there were localities in which was found a prosperous slave-holding mulatto elite, a few of whom married whites. An interesting case of acceptance by the white establishment of some industrious free people of color is that of the family of Gideon Gibson, the carpenter son of a free mulatto man from Virginia who accompanied by a white wife and several other mulatto men with white wives, won acceptance from the Governor and a legislative investigating committee to settle on the South Carolina frontier in 1731.

Governor Johnson reported to the South Carolina Commons House of Assembly that investigation indicated that Gideon Gibson had a good reputation in Virginia where he had paid taxes for two tracts of land and had seven slaves, and added:

> ...That he is a Carpenter by Trade and is come hither for the support of his Family ... The account he has given of himself is so Satisfactory that he is no Vagabond that I have in Consideration of his Wifes being a white woman and several White women Capable of working and being Serviceable in the Country permitted him to Settle in this Country upon entering into Recognizance for his good behaviour which I have taken accordingly (Jordan 1969: 172).

During the next half century the Gibson family flourished and gained acceptance as white. One of Gideon Gibson's daughters married an English planter, and after his accidental death married one of the richest men in the area. Several sons gained wealth and married into prominent southern families (Williamson 1980: 30-31).

From Independence to Final Emancipation: 1776-1865

Between 1776 and the mid-nineteenth century, the United States expanded from thirteen colonies along the Atlantic seaboard to the Pacific Ocean, and while slavery ceased to exist in the North by about 1840, it continued to thrive in the South where the institution was defended with increased vigor. Despite sectional differences over the existence and spread of slavery, there was almost universal agreement among white Americans of all regions that white supremacy must be forever maintained, and that the white race must be protected from infusion of Negro genes in order to prevent biological and cultural deterioration. In the Supreme Court's Dred Scott decision of 1857, Chief Justice Taney declared that:

. . . [Negroes] are not included, and were not intended to be included, under the word 'citizen' in the Constitution and therefore can claim none of the rights and privileges which that instrument provides for and secures to citizens of the United States. . . .

. . . They had, for more than a century before, been regarded as beings of an inferior order and altogether unfit to associate with the white race, either in social or political relations; and so far inferior that they had no rights which the white man was bound to respect (Miller 1967: 72).

There was almost universal agreement that white Americans would never permit full equality to blacks, nor social mixing which might lead to amalgamation of the races. And they feared that emancipation would lead to an intolerable amount of intermarriage. Thomas Jefferson, Abraham Lincoln, and many opponents of slavery viewed colonization of freedmen in Africa, the West Indies, Central or South America, or elsewhere beyond the boundaries of the United States as the only means of preventing racial conflict and amalgamation.

During the long period of slavery in the South, the taboo against intermarriage and sexual relations involving black men and white women increased in strength, while interracial sex relations became normal experiences for a large percentage of white men, and ranged from casual encounters devoid of sentiment to more or less permanent unions with black and mulatto mistresses and concubines.

In mid-nineteenth century New Orleans, white men hired slave girls by the month, and wealthy men purchased slave women as concubines. Others met and courted beautiful and well-educated quadroons, and under a system known as plaçage, they secured the approval of the girl's parents and agreed to purchase a house for the mistress or concubine and to provide for any children resulting from the relationship. Some of these arrangements led to long-term and permanent unions similar to marriage.

It appears that while it was not unusual for white men to keep Negro mistresses, and even live in open concubinage with favorite slaves, there were few legal marriages of white men to women of known African ancestry in the South before 1865. In addition to the colonies which prohibited such marriages prior to independence, all of the remaining Southern states and fourteen Northern and Western states passed laws prohibiting marriages between white persons and blacks or mulattoes between 1798 and 1865.

Legislation prohibited marriage between whites and blacks, restricted the right to the franchise, jury duty, office holding, the right to carry arms, etc. to white persons, and required a definition of the proportion of African ancestry which would exclude a person of mixed descent from white legal status. Long before the end of the colonial period, many persons of mixed racial descent were indistinguishable in appearance from Caucasians. There has been no consistency in defining who would be excluded from marriage to a white person, with some states placing the barrier at one-fourth or one-eighth, and others excluding anyone with any amount of African or Negro "blood." Massachusetts accepted as sufficiently white to marry a Caucasian a person descended from one black and three white grandparents. Although such a marriage did not violate the law, the participants could not expect acceptance by white society unless the non-white partner concealed his or her black ancestry.

Marriages of white women, especially of servants and others of low status, to black men continued to occur in the South, but with decreasing frequency, during the decades prior to the Civil War. An examination of the 1830 Census returns for Nansemond County, Virginia revealed nine free Negro heads of family with white wives. In 1849, a free mulatto was declared by a North Carolina court not to be a mulatto within the meaning of the law, and to be entitled to exercise all of the rights accorded white citizens after evidence was presented that:

> . . . the said Joseph was a reddish copper colored man, with curly red hair and blue eyes; that the said Joseph's wife was a white woman, and that they had a son, named William; that the said William also married a white woman, and had issue by her a son, named Whitmel; and that the said Whitmel married a white woman, and that they are the parents of the defendant (Johnston 1970: 196).

Occasionally, the relationship between a white man and his black mistress or concubine was accompanied by such strong affection and devotion that the man was willing to defy convention and marry his beloved. Some such couples traveled abroad or to Canada or Mexico, or to a state or territory where interracial marriage was not illegal. A number of southern white men freed and married slave mistresses in Ohio and Pennsylvania. John W. Blassingame reports concerning intermarriages in defiance of the law in antebellum New Orleans:

> . . . The white cashier of a New Orleans bank, for example, married a Negro woman by transferring some of her blood to himself and claiming to be a Negro. Priests were regularly bribed to perform religious marriages, and a few white men moved to Cuba or France and married their concubines. On occasion, black men also married white women during the antebellum period. Public reaction to such unions was ambivalent; a man who was known to be a mulatto man could, if he were wealthy, marry a white woman with no furor developing.
> . . . A number of white women claimed they were Negroes and married the black men they loved (1973: 19-20).

There is little information concerning marriages between whites and blacks in the North prior to the 1850's, but it appears that apart from white men who came from the South to marry black concubines, most interracial marriages were between black men and white women. Samuel Dexter, a Boston merchant and member of the Massachusetts legislature, stated in a letter to a friend in 1795: "Intermarriages between whites and blacks are rare, oftener between black men and white women than on the contrary" (Greene 1942: 201-202).

Although New York has never legislated against interracial marriages, marriages of whites to blacks appear not to have been numerous and to have met with strong opposition from whites. An English traveler reported in the 1850's that he found in Buffalo, New York:

> . . . a woman of English birth, well-informed, good-looking, married to a negro, seemingly owing to his fortune. Tho the man was not an undesirable citizen, the wife was despised by the wives of white citizens

and both were shunned. White etiquette would not let him attend her at their theater box; they never ventured out together. If one did go out, it was usually after dark. On one occasion the man was mobbed and nearly lost his life (Calhoun 1945: II, 30).

William G. Allen, a light mulatto professor of rhetoric and belles-lettres at Central College in McGrawville, New York, married one of his white pupils, the daughter of an abolitionist minister. After escaping from a mob at Phillipsville, New York, the couple settled in England from where Allen wrote in 1853:

> . . . Whatever a man be in his own person, . . . and though, in personal appearance, he should be as fair as the fairest Anglo-Saxon, yet, if he have but one drop of the African flowing in his veins, no white young lady can ally herself to him in matrimony, without bringing upon her the anathemas of the community, with scarce an exception, and rendering herself an almost total outcast, not only from the society in which she formerly moved, but from society in general (Allen 1853: 12-13).

Writers who described the notorious Five Points slum area of Manhattan in the 1850's noted that it was not uncommon for black men to have white wives. G.G. Foster wrote of this neighborhood of blacks and Irish and other whites living in poverty in 1850:

> The Negroes form a large and rather controlling portion of the population of Five Points. . . . They associate at least on equal terms with the men and women of the parish, and many of them are regarded as desirable companions and lovers by the girls. They most of them have either white wives or mistresses, sometimes both; and their influence in the community is commanding (Foster 1850: 56).

Carter G. Woodson states that interracial marriage was common in Pennsylvania after repeal of the anti-intermarriage act in 1790, but that there was a reaction against such marriages in the first decade of the nineteenth century, followed by a campaign against marriages of blacks to whites in 1820 (Woodson 1918: 348-349).

Thomas Branagan writing from Philadelphia in 1805 noted that familiarity between black male and white female servants in homes of the wealthy often led to sexual intimacy and intermarriage. He remarked:

> It is a stubborn fact that there are more bound and hired white girls in rich men's houses, deluded by black men than anywhere else. . . . There are perhaps hundreds of white women thus fascinated by black men in this city; and there are thousands of black children by them at present (Johnston 1970: 187; Woodson 1918: 348).

During the generation before the Civil War, Massachusetts was a center of abolitionist activity and agitation for Negro rights. During this period abolitionist pressure and legal action removed racial segregation in the schools and many public places, and the black man gained the right to vote, hold public office, sit as a juror, and testify in court. The 1705 law prohibiting interracial marriage, too, came under attack and was repealed in 1843.

Frederick L. Hoffman found in checking annual reports of the city registrar that there were fifty marriages of Negroes to whites in Boston during the five years, 1855 to 1859, and forty-five such marriages for the years, 1862-1866. This represents a high rate of intermarriage for Boston's blacks who numbered but 2,160 in 1855 and 2,348 in 1865. It is probable that the great majority of these marriages were of black men and white women, for when the sex and race combination of marriage partners was first published for Boston, for the years 1900 to 1904, there were 133 black grooms and only 10 black brides who married whites (Hoffman 1896: 198-201; Stone 1908: 62).

From Emancipation to the Second World War: 1865-1939

Between 1867 and 1874, during the period of Reconstruction which followed the Confederate defeat, the anti-intermarriage laws of Maryland, Alabama, South Carolina, Mississippi, Florida, Louisiana, and Arkansas were repealed, declared void, or omitted, and it is probable that such statutes were not rigidly enforced in other southern states (Mangum 1940: 241-242; Reuter 1931: 82-96).

There is strong indication that as a result of the absence of a legal barrier hundreds, perhaps even thousands, of marriages took place between white men and black women, many of whom had been living together in informal unions, and that a lesser number of black men married white women in the South during the quarter-century following emancipation. Although such marriages were strongly opposed by the vast majority of white southerners, the assumption or hope that the old social order had been permanently overthrown emboldened some individuals to defy public opinion and marry across the color line.

Newspaper accounts and other sources describe scores of marriages between whites and blacks in the former Confederate States, mainly for the period from 1865 to 1880. A.A. Taylor noted more than two dozen marriages of whites to blacks in Virginia, which were reported in the Richmond Enquirer, between 1865 and 1870, and stated that such unions continued to take place throughout the state after the end of Military Reconstruction, with the parties sometimes going out of the state to marry (Taylor 1926: 299-303). Taylor also noted several references in local newspapers to marriages of white men to black women in Tennessee, stating:

> In 1866, the Nashville Republican Banner reported several instances of miscegenation. On June 30th, that journal published an account of a bi-racial marriage said to have occurred in the Negro First Baptist Church of Nashville. "Thompson--a white man--walked up to the front of the pulpit accompanied by a coal black negro woman, and producing his marriage license, the twain were made one flesh and blood in due form by the officiating minister of the church. . ." (Taylor 1941: 228-229).

The South Carolina legislature repealed the prohibition of marriages between whites and blacks in 1868, and soon the local press mentioned the occurrence of several such marriages. Taylor cites cases of intermarriage reported in South Carolina newspapers and traveler's accounts, and observes:

Yet, Edward King did not believe in 1871 that there were in the state a half dozen married couples with the wife white and husband black or colored. But there were three or four instances in every county of colored women married to white men. So strong was the sentiment among the whites against such unions that . . . It condemned them to bitter hatred and irrevocable social ostracism among their own race. They generally had no recourse but to associate with the colored people and become Negroes in all but color (Taylor 1924: 10-11).

During the 1870's, the number of interracial marriages had greatly increased in South Carolina and, in 1879, a member of the state legislature, in support of legislation that would again prohibit intermarriage, stated that in his township in York County "there were at least twenty-five or thirty white women living with colored men as husbands, most of them having come from North Carolina which already had a law against interracial marriage" (Tindall 1966: 296).

In 1866, G. Thornton, a prominent and wealthy white politician, married a black woman in North Carolina. He found his social life among African-Americans and was buried from a Black church (Rogers 1942: II, 231).

The Mississippi anti-intermarriage law was repealed in 1870 by a bill introduced by Senator Albert T. Morgan whose marriage on August 3, 1870 to Carrie Highgate, a mulatto school teacher who had come from New York, was perhaps the most publicized intermarriage in the post-bellum South. Morgan came to the South as a colonel in a Michigan regiment of the Union Army and remained in Mississippi, where he became an affluent planter in Yazoo and served in turn as a member of the state constitutional convention, a state senator, and sheriff of Yazoo county. Morgan describes his association with his bride to be in a book of memoirs of post-bellum Mississippi:

The first time I saw Carrie I lost my head, banged if I didn't. It happened in this way: I was in Jackson on some business or other connected with the election. General Copeland invited me to visit the school with him; he said he had something to show me better for the eyes than fine gold; ay, than many pearls. . . .
. . . The lady in question is one of the most brilliant and accomplished I ever met, a splendid woman, no mistake about that . . . That's all there is to it, and when I saw that my visits to her father's house were being misconstrued by the public, I got Carry to accompany me to the House of Representatives one day during a recess of the Senate, and caused announcement to be made of our intended marriage (Morgan 1884: 346-347, 352).

Marriages of white men to black women were of frequent occurrence in Louisiana after the anti-intermarriage law was omitted in 1870. An Englishman who visited the Louisiana State Senate in 1871 wrote that the body "was being addressed by an honourable white Senator of an intellectual cast of head and face, who appears to have gained more notoriety than all the rest by marrying a black woman" (Somers 1871: 226).

The Census of 1880 listed 176 white men with Negro wives, and 29 Negro men with white wives in New Orleans. As the average age of these white husbands was 50.14 years and of the wives, 38.61 years, it would appear that many of these men had married women who had for many years been their concubines. Fifty-five percent of the white husbands were foreign born and only 15 percent of the 176 were unskilled laborers. The leading occupations were laborers, clerks, cigarmakers, sailors, carpenters, merchants, and brokers. Of the 29 white women married to black men in New Orleans, ten were foreign-born, while three of the husbands were foreign born. The average age of the black husbands was 40 years and of their white wives, 35 years. Seven of these men were laborers, and other occupations included cigarmaker, broker, drayman, minister, and gardener (Blassingame 1973: 206-207).

While most whites and the press expressed strong opposition to marriages between blacks and whites in New Orleans, the strongest hostility was directed against the black male-white female combination. Blassingame states:

> The burdens on the partners in mixed marriages were great; they were almost crushing in the case of black men and white women. White employers shunned the black men in such unions. For instance, S.S. Ashley wrote in 1871 of one New Orleans Negro man, who had been born in Scotland and had married a white woman there: "He can get no employment here. The fact that his wife is white is unfavorable. I do not think that in any family or hotel when the fact is known they could obtain, or retain employment." While white male partners of interracial marriages were socially ostracized, their complexion guaranteed them employment, and sometimes their wealth and social standing led to a degree of acceptance for their Negro wives. . . (Blassingame 1973: 207-208).

Geographically, the District of Columbia lies in the South, and like the states of Maryland and Virginia, from which it was detached, maintained slavery and appeared to have had little or no interracial marriage before the end of the Civil War. Thomas P. Monahan examined marriage records for selected years beginning with 1874, and found that until 1910 there was an average of only three marriages per year between Caucasians and Negroes, representing less than 0.5 percent of all marriages. There was an increase in the number of marriages between whites and blacks in 1915, 1920, and 1925, but only one such marriage in 1930 and in 1940, as indicated in Table 1 (Monahan 1977:222).

Except for 1874-1875, 1890, and 1915, less than one in 200 marriages with a Negro partner was interracial in the years to 1940. Until 1940, 64.4 percent of marriages between whites and blacks were of white men to black women, as revealed in Table 2 (Monahan 1977: 223, 227).

The brief period of Reconstruction which permitted some interracial marriages to take place in the South was followed by the restoration of absolute white supremacy, the disfranchisement of blacks, an exclusion of African-Americans from association with whites in other than inferior roles, a hardening of anti-Negro attitudes, the legal segregation in public and institutional settings, and a reintroduction of legislation which made interracial marriage a criminal offense.

The southern states which had repealed, omitted, or not enforced their anti-intermarriage laws during the Reconstruction era all reenacted or again enforced legislation prohibiting marriage of whites to persons of Negro descent, beginning with Alabama in 1877 with Louisiana completing the process in 1894. Whereas prior to the Civil War, persons of less than one-fourth or one-eighth Negro descent were permitted to marry whites in several states, the restriction came increasingly to exclude anyone with one-sixteenth or even any trace of Negro "blood." In Virginia, the prohibition applied to persons who had one-fourth or more African ancestry until 1910 when the statute was changed to read one-sixteenth or more. In 1930, the law was again revised to prohibit anyone with any Negro ancestry from marrying a Caucasian. The penalties for violation of the law ranged from a fine of not less than one hundred dollars or up to thirty days in jail in Delaware to much heavier fines and imprisonment of up to ten years in Maryland, North Carolina, Florida, and Mississippi (Mangum 1940: 236-248; Wirth and Goldhamer 1944: 360-361).

Table 1. Interracial marriage in the District of Columbia for selected years

Year	Total	Mixed Marriages			Percent (total) Mixed
		Negro with White	Negro with Other Race	All Other Mixed	
1874-75*	6	6	---	---	.58
1890	2	2	---	---	.16
1897	1	1	---	---	.04
1900	3	3	---	---	.09
1905	4	3	---	1	.10
1910	5	3	---	2	.13
1915	18	13	1	4	.43
1920	14	10	--	4	.20
1925	12	7	2	3	.21
1930	11	1	4	6	.21
1940	29	1	2	26+	.38
1956	92	23	9	61+	1.13

Source: 1874-75, Health Department Register; all other years, a search of the Supreme Court register and documents by the author. Monahan, 1967: 222.
*August 8, 1874 to December 31, 1875.
+ The great majority of these are other race males with white females. In 1940, Filipino males with white females, 21 cases; and white males with Filipino females, 5 cases.

Between 1866 and 1920, six northern and western states and territories repealed or omitted their statutes prohibiting interracial marriage, while seven western states and territories introduced such legislation. By 1920, thirty states prohibited marriages between whites and Negroes, and this number remained constant until 1948. All of the southern and border states, Indiana, and states West of the Mississippi River, with the exception of Minnesota, Washington, Iowa, Kansas and New Mexico, and the territories of Alaska and Hawaii, had legal prohibitions. Fifteen states also included various Asian ethnic groups (Japanese, Chinese, Mongolians, Hindus, and Malayans) as ineligible to marry Caucasians; five banned marriages between whites and American Indians, and three between blacks and American Indians (Mangum 1940: 252-254; Wirth and Goldhamer

1944: 360-362). Only New Hampshire, Vermont, Connecticut, New York, New Jersey, Wisconsin, Minnesota, Alaska, and Hawaii have never prohibited interracial marriage.

Table 2. Race of groom and race of bride in marriages between Whites and Blacks in the District of Columbia for selected years

Year	White Groom Negro Bride	Negro Groom White Bride	Total
1874-75	1	5	6
1879-89	14	9	23
1915	11	2	13
1920	8	2	10
1930-39	13	8	21
Totals	47	26	73

The taboo on sexual relations between black men and white women remained powerful in most areas of the South throughout the first half of the twentieth century. It was widely believed that the only possible sex relationship of this type was rape, for it was thought to be unimaginable for a white woman to willingly endure the embrace of a Negro. Black men were extremely wary of even innocent contact with white women for severe punishment, even death, might result from glancing at, touching, or neglecting to observe the required deference toward a woman of the dominant race.

Research by social scientists in communities in Mississippi in the 1930's revealed that despite increased pressure from white society against cohabitation of white men and black women, casual relationships with prostitutes, servants, or girls picked up on the streets were common. Many or most white youths began their sexual experience with black girls, and many had no sexual intimacy with white women before they married. Black men were powerless to protect their wives, sisters, or daughters from the sexual demands of white men. There was little opportunity for black women to find employment other than in domestic service, where the probability of receiving sexual proposals from white men in the household was an occupational hazard. If he were discrete and decently concealed the relationship, a white man could indulge in interracial sexual relationships without seriously losing status in the white community. Too open or notorious association with a black mistress was no longer acceptable, and those who actually lived with black women and their biracial children were more or less ostracized by their own relatives and white society (Davis, Gardner and Gardner 1941; Dollard 1937; Powdermaker 1939).

It had become increasingly rare in the South for white men to reside in the same household as their black mistresses, and resultant mulatto children nearly always lived in fatherless homes, although they often received financial support. In the Mississippi town referred to as "Old City" there were, however, several lasting relationships in which the couples were united by bonds of respect and affection. A black woman in such a relationship remarked:

I love Jim's daddy [her son's white father], 'n Jim's daddy loves me.
Nothing else matters. We were boy and girl sweethearts 'n we're
sweethearts today. So the rest of the world can go by. . . . I feel I'm living
a great deal more decently with a union based on love than some who are
married before the law. And I don't feel that I've heaped any disgrace on
Jim. He's got a dad and a good one who is doing everything possible to be
a good dad to him. And we live here in our little shack, happily, and
according to my standards, decently (Davis, Gardner and Gardner 1941:
33-34).

There were probably very few marriages of visibly Negroid persons to
whites in the South during the first half of the twentieth century. An unknown
number of fair Negroes passed as white and married whites, while some whites
claimed to possess a fraction of African ancestry and passed as Negro in order to
marry blacks. In a series of articles published in eleven consecutive issues of the
Richmond Times-Dispatch in February, 1926, John Powell of the Virginia Bureau
of Vital Statistics reported on numerous cases in which near-white persons of
partial African descent had married whites, often having themselves been legally
white at the time of marriage. In one case in which children of a mixed family were
denied admission to a white high school in Dinwiddie County, Virginia:

. . . The records were examined and it was found that the grandfather of
these children had been less than one-fourth Negro, and as he was legally
white under the statute at that time, had married a white woman. The
children were, therefore, less than one-sixteenth Negro, and at that time,
although the law had been again amended, they were legally white and had
every right to attend the white school (Rogers 1942: 279).

Early in this century the New Orleans Picayune reported on white men in
Louisiana who claimed to be colored in order to avoid conviction under the anti-
intermarriage act, stating:

. . . All around Lee Station the white farmers and fishermen and other
classes have intermarried with colored people and reared large families
regardless of the law against such. A number of arrests have been made,
but it has been impossible to convict one for the reason that the white parties
all went on the stand and swore they were colored. Just what the
prosecuting attorney can do remains to be seen (Rogers 1942: 325).

A few white men and black women continued to leave the South to marry
and take up residence in the North, as did a very few black men and white women.
It was possible in some areas of the border states for black and white couples of
either combination of gender and race to live together after marrying in the North.
Newspaper publicity was given in 1932 to a court battle over the estate of a wealthy
Georgian who had died the previous year and left his fortune to his Negro wife, the
daughter of a family servant. The deceased octogenarian had studied at Yale and
practiced law as a young man. He inherited a fortune in real estate in Georgia, and
built an expensive home in Atlanta's most fashionable section for his black

mistress. Their forty-year relationship continued in Atlanta until 1927 when the couple moved to Chicago and married (Afro-American: December 3, 1932).

In the course of research on interracial marriage in the late 1930's the present writer encountered several white husbands with African-American wives who had moved to Chicago from the South to marry and take up residence. (Roberts 1940).

During the quarter century following the Civil War, there was some improvement in the status of blacks in the North where, as in the South, they were granted political and legal rights by the 14th and 15th amendments to the Constitution. After the Civil Rights Act of 1875 was overturned by the Supreme Court in 1883, most of the northern states enacted similar legislation prohibiting racial discrimination in places which served the public. While several western states legislated against interracial marriage, Ohio, Rhode Island, Maine, and Michigan repealed their restrictive laws between 1877 and 1883, leaving Indiana as the only northern state East of the Mississippi River to retain such legislation.

The gains experienced by Negroes in the North did not extend to the area of social relationships. To most northern whites, blacks remained a despised group, believed to be inherently inferior, and they were severely limited in economic opportunity and excluded from the social life of the dominant race. There was no relaxation of the severe taboo against marriage between blacks and whites.

Prior to 1940, there was very little published information on the social characteristics or experiences of the participants in interracial marriages in the United States. It was widely held that blacks and whites who intermarried represented the worst elements of both races, were of bad character if not criminal, or that the white partners were recent immigrants unaware of the social penalties they would face. In the absence of careful research, Frederick L. Hoffman's comments on 37 cases of cohabitation or intermarriage of Negroes and whites which he had obtained chiefly from newspaper reports of vice and crime--including among the participants twelve white prostitutes, two women murdered by black husbands, and three white men who were criminals or suspected of being such-- were cited by scholars decades later. In discussing interracial marriage in a chapter on the "Nature of Race Intermixture in the United States," Edward B. Reuter, a leading authority on the subject, summarized these same 37 cases and quoted Hoffman's biased conclusion, prefacing his remarks with the statement that "Hoffman made a careful study of 37 such mixed unions" (Hoffman: 1896: IX, 204-206; Reuter 1918: 136-137).

In his pioneer fifteen-month study during 1896 and 1897 of the condition of Philadelphia's Negroes, W.E.B. DuBois made a house-to-house canvass of the 9,000 blacks of the city's seventh ward, and gathered information on 33 interracial families living in the ward. There were four white husbands who were employed as street car driver-laborer, motorman on electric cars, tobacconist, and painter. Nineteen of the 27 black husbands were born in the South. Of the 27, there were 9 waiters, 3 porters, 2 each of barber, steward, cook, and restaurant keeper, and 1 each of helper and engineer, stationary engineer, laborer, stevedore, caterer, messenger, and bootblack. Fifteen of the white wives were born in foreign countries (six in Ireland, three in England, two each in Scotland and Germany, and one each in Canada and Hungary), eight in the North, and three in the South. The 33 interracial families represented 1.35 percent of the 2441 families in the ward. DuBois concludes:

It is often said that only the worst Negroes and lowest whites intermarry. This is certainly untrue in Philadelphia; to be sure among the lowest classes there is a large number of temporary unions and much cohabitation. . . On the other hand it is an error certainly in this ward to regard marriages of this sort as confined principally to the lower classes; on the contrary they take place most frequently in the laboring classes, and especially among servants where there is the most contact between the races. . .

. . .It is certainly a strain on affections to have to endure not simply the social ostracism of the whites but of the blacks also. Undoubtedly, this latter acts as a more practical deterrent than the first. For, while a Negro expects to be ostracized by the whites, and his white wife agrees to it by her marriage vow, neither of them are quite prepared for the cold reception they invariably meet with among the Negroes. Nevertheless, one must candidly acknowledge that there are respectable people who are thus married and are apparently contented and as happy as the average of mankind (DuBois 1899: 358-367).

In a doctoral dissertation Richard R. Wright, Jr. stated:

Although the law against inter-marriage in Pennsylvania was repealed more than a century ago, there has been but little marriage between blacks and whites. According to the records of the city of Philadelphia, there were during the years 1901, 1902, 1903, 1904 only 31 marriages of this kind. In 1900 there were six cases of inter-marriage out of 633 marriages. Three Negro men, aged 26, 35, and 49, respectively, married three white women, aged 26, 23, and 38, respectively; and three white men aged 26, 29, and 34 years, respectively, married three Negro women, aged 28, 33 years, and of unknown age, respectively. There were more intermarriages when there were fewer Negroes than there are to-day. . . .

. . . The so-called mixed marriages are not approved by either the white or Negro group. Negro women especially object. When, however, such marriages are consummated in spite of Negro public opinion, the couple is almost always ostracized by the Negroes. Perhaps there is no more pathetic injustice inflicted by Negroes than the cruel scorn and contempt which they show toward those who have chosen to marry "outside the race." In church, or society, there is very little opportunity for such persons and though no law prevents, there are very few persons who dare disregard this public opinion (Wright 1912: 174-175).

Between 1906 and 1908, an eminent journalist, Ray Stannard Baker, examined living conditions of African-Americans in the South and the North, and reported on his investigation of interracial marriages in several northern cities. He stated, in summary:

I have made a careful investigation of the facts in several northern cities, and I have been surprised to discover how little intermarriage there really is. . . . At Boston and in other northern towns, I made inquiries in regard to the actual specific instances of intermarriage.

There are two classes of cases, first, what may be called the intellectuals; highly educated mulattoes who marry educated white women. I have the history of a number of such intermarriages, but there is not space here to relate the really interesting life stories which have grown out of them. One of the best-known Negro professors in the country has a white wife. I saw the home where they live under almost ideal surroundings. . . .
But such cases as these are rare. In the great majority of intermarriages the white women belong to the lower walks of life. They are German, Irish, or other foreign women, respectable, but ignorant. As far as I can see from investigating a number of such cases, the home life is as happy as that of other people in the same stratum of life. But the white woman who marries a Negro is speedily declassed: she is ostracized by the white people, and while she finds a certain place among the Negroes, she is not even readily accepted as a Negro. In short, she is cut off from both races. . . . (Baker 1964: 171-173).

Data on the number of marriages which took place between whites and blacks have been published for limited time periods between 1855 and 1939 for Rhode Island, Connecticut, Michigan, Boston, Philadelphia, New York State, exclusive of New York City, and two boroughs of New York City. F.L. Hoffman collected much of the nineteenth century data from marriage records made available by officials. He found that from 1883 to 1893 there were 51 marriages of Negro men to white women and 7 of white men to Negro women in Rhode Island, while there were 65 marriages of whites to blacks in Connecticut from 1883 to 1894. These marriages represented less than one in 1200 of all marriages in Rhode Island and approximately one in 2,000 of all marriages in Connecticut for those years (Hoffman 1896: 198-200).

In Michigan, although illegal until 1883, there was one intermarriage for every 6,220 persons married during the years 1874 to 1883 and one to every 7,931 persons married from 1884 to 1893. Hoffman presents the following table enumerating interracial marriages in Michigan from 1874 to 1893, by color of grooms and brides:

Table 3. Intermarriages of Whites and Negroes in Michigan, 1874-1893

Year	White males married to		White females married to		Total
	Black Females	Mulatto Females	Black Males	Mulatto Males	
1874-78	2	5	8	7	22
1879-83	1	2	8	12	23
1884-88	1	4	21	14	40
1889-93	2	1	10	13	26
1874-93	6	12	47	46	111

Source: Hoffman 1896: 198

Here we may note that more than five times as many white women as men married interracially and that they selected supposedly unmixed black partners as frequently as those of mixed ancestry, while the white men who married Negroes selected mulatto brides twice as frequently as those described as black.

The longest and most nearly continuous series of years for which interracial marriage data have been published is for Boston, Massachusetts, for periods between 1855 and 1938, summarized in Table 4, below:

Table 4. Negro-White intermarriages, Boston, Mass., 1855-1938

Year	Number of Intermarriages				Percentage intermarried by race			
	Groom Negro	Groom White	Total	Average per annum	Negro grooms	Negro brides	White grooms	White brides
1855-59			50	10.0				
1862-66			45	9.0				
1867-71			88	17.6				
1873-77			172	34.4				
1878-82			121	24.2				
1883-87			124	24.8				
1890			24	24.0				
1900-04	133	10	143	28.6	12.8	1.1		
1900-07	203	19	222	27.7				
1914-18	68	21	89	17.8	4.0	1.2	.04	.13
1919-23	42	5	47	9.4	2.7	.3	.01	.08
1924-28	41	12	53	10.6	2.8	.8	.03	.09
1929-33	36	4	40	8.0	3.2	.4	.01	.09
1934-38	40	7	47	9.4	3.1	.6	.02	.10
1914-38	227	49	276	11.0	3.2	.7	.02	.10

Source: Hoffman 1896:200; Stephenson 1910:98; Stone 1908:62; and Wirth, Goldhamer 1944:277.

In comparison with other localities for which we have comparable figures, the percentage of Negroes who married Caucasians in Boston was extraordinarily high during the half century before the first World War.

When, from 1900 to 1904, 12.8 percent of Negro grooms and 1.1 percent of Negro brides married Caucasians, there had already been a decline in marriages between blacks and whites from a peak of 34.4 per year during 1873 to 1877 to 28.6 per year. As the black population of Boston had more than doubled during the last quarter of the 19th century, it would appear that more than 20 percent of black grooms married white brides in Boston during the 1870's. The marked decline in intermarriages, particularly of black men and white women, may have resulted from a weakening of pro-Negro sentiment, which had been strong when Boston was a center of abolitionist agitation, coupled with an influx of poorly educated blacks from the South. The low percentage of blacks in Boston's population, which increased slowly from 2.1 percent of the total population in 1900 to 2.2 percent in 1920 and 2.6 percent in 1930, meant that although 390 of every 10,000 Negroes who married during 1914-1938 married Caucasians, only 13 of every 10,000 whites who married during the same period married blacks (Wirth and Goldhamer 1944: 278-281).

In analyzing the Boston intermarriage data, Wirth and Goldhamer found that there was a slightly higher proportion of foreign born men and of native-born women among the white grooms and brides, in comparison with white men and women of comparable age in the general population. Twenty-two (44.8 percent) of the 49 white grooms who married blacks were foreign born, while 40.5 percent of the white male population aged 20 to 54 were of foreign birth. Of the 227 white brides who married black men, 68 (30 percent) were of foreign birth as compared with 34.2 percent foreign born of the white female population aged 15 to 49. Of the 22 foreign-born white grooms, 8 were born in Italy, 3 in Greece, 2 in Central or South America, 2 in Portugal and 7 in other countries. Twenty-four of the 68 foreign-born white brides were born in Canada, 16 in Ireland, 8 in Great Britain, 3 in Portugal and 17 in other countries (Wirth and Goldhamer 1944: 285-289).

It was found that the average age at marriage of the interracially married grooms and brides was well above that of men and women who married endogamously. This may have been related to the fact that many had been previously married. Of the 222 marriages of black men to white women in Boston from 1914 to 1938, 11.5 percent of the grooms had been previously divorced and 16.7 percent were widowers, while 11.9 percent of their brides had been divorced and 21.6 percent were widows. Of the 49 marriages of white men to black women, none of the white grooms had been previously divorced and 18.4 percent were widowers, while 12.2 percent of their brides had been divorced and 24.5 were widows (Wirth and Goldhamer 1944: 296-298).

In Table 5, below, is presented the occupational status of the grooms and brides who married interracially in Boston during the period 1914-1938:

Table 5. Parties to Negro-White marriages in Boston, 1914-1938, by Sex, Color and Occupation

Occupation	Grooms				Brides			
	Negro		White		Negro		White	
	No.	%	No.	%	No.	%	No.	%
Professions	19	8.4	3	6.1	1	2.6	14	8.7
Managers and officials	7	3.1	2	4.1				
Clerks	13	5.7	4	8.2	1	2.6	24	14.9
Skilled workers	42	18.6	8	16.3			1	0.6
Semiskilled workers	52	23.0	12	24.5	7	17.9	20	12.3
Unskilled workers	93	41.2	20	40.8	30	76.9	103	63.6
Gainfully employed	226	100	49	100	39	100	162	100
Not gainfully employed	1				10		65	
Total	227		49		49		227	

Source: Wirth and Goldhamer 1944: 290.

There is very little difference in the occupational distributions of the black and white grooms, with both groups heavily represented in the unskilled and semiskilled workers categories. Comparison with the occupational distributions of all white and black gainful workers in Boston, as reported by the 1930 census, reveals that the black grooms in interracial marriages occupied higher occupational positions than other black males. While 8.4 percent of the black grooms were professionals and 41.2 percent were unskilled workers, only 3.8 percent of other black males were professionals while 60.4 percent were unskilled workers. On the other hand, the racially intermarried white grooms were inferior in occupation to other white males, with 40.8 percent of their number classed as unskilled workers in contrast to 19 percent of all white gainful workers being so classified by the 1930 census. The white grooms were underrepresented in the categories of proprietors, managers and officials, clerks, and skilled workers, which occupational groups accounted for only 28.6 percent of the white grooms, but 53.5 percent of Boston's gainfully employed white males. The white brides who married black men occupied higher occupational positions than the racially intermarried black brides, but occupied lower positions than gainfully employed white females. They were underrepresented in clerical positions (14.9 percent vs. 40.4 percent) and overrepresented in the unskilled workers category (63.6 percent vs. 15.7 percent). Twenty-eight, or 72 percent, of the black brides who were employed were in the "servant classes," and half of these were engaged in housework which would have afforded them close contact with whites (Wirth and Goldhamer 1944: 289-296).

In his study of intermarriage, primarily of nationality groups, in New York City, based on records of 101,854 marriage licenses for the boroughs of Manhattan and Bronx for the years 1908-1912, Joseph Drachsler includes information on marriages of African-Americans with whites, shown in Table 6, below:

Table 6. Interracial marriage of U.S. Blacks in New York City (Boroughs of Manhattan and Bronx), 1908-1912

Total marriages	101,854
Man U.S. Black-woman Black (U.S. and foreign)	2,260
Man U.S. Black-woman White	41
Woman U.S. Black-Man Black (U.S. and foreign)	2,472
Woman U.S. Black-man White	11
Percent of U.S. Blacks married to White persons	1.08
Percent of U.S. Black grooms to White brides	1.74
Percent of U.S. Black brides to White grooms	0.44

Source: Julius Drachsler, Intermarriage in New York City: a Statistical Study of the Amalgamation of European Peoples, Columbia University Studies in History, Economics, and Public Law, Vol. XVIV, no. 2 (New York, 1921), 49-50.

Drachsler's study was primarily concerned with rates of interethnic marriage of European immigrants and their children, but included a brief section on "Miscegenation Among Negroes." He designated as "United States (colored)" African-Americans whose parents had been born in the United States, and classified separately 323 first and second generation "West Indian colored." The intermarriage rate of black Americans to whites in New York City of 1.08 percent of total black marriages during the five years, 1908-1912, is far lower than early twentieth century rates for Boston. The 41 interracial marriages of white women represent only 4 in 10,000 marriages of all white brides, while the 11 marriages of white men to black women constitute but one in 10,000 of all marriages of white men in the boroughs of Manhattan and Bronx during the five-year period (Drachsler 1921: 49-51).

Statistics listing the number of marriages by race, including intermarriages of blacks and whites, were published annually for New York State, exclusive of New York City, by the New York State Department of Health from 1916 to 1964, and some further analysis of unpublished data has been made by sociologists. Some of the published data are summarized in Table 7, below:

Table 7. Negro-White intermarriage, New York State, exclusive of New York City, 1916-1947

Year	Number of Intermarriages				Percentage intermarried by race			
	Groom Negro	Groom White	Total	Average per annum	Negro grooms	Negro brides	White grooms	White brides
1916-18	15	10	25	8.3	1.3	.9		
1919-21			55	18.3				
1922-24	88	32	120	40.0	3.5	1.3		
1925-27	76	20	96	32.0	2.6	0.7	.01	.06
1928-30	81	24	105	35.0	3.0	0.7	.03	.08
1931-33			74	24.7	2.5			
1934-36			63	21.0	2.0	0.6		
Totals								
1916-37	424	145	569	25.9				
1925-32	195	53	248	31.0	2.4	.7	.01	.05
1938-47	157	46	203	20.3	1.4	.4	.01	.03

Source: New York State Department of Health, Annual Reports; Wirth and Goldhamer 1944:278; Monahan 1971a:98.

As Negroes constituted less than two percent of the population of Upstate New York for most years before 1940, very few whites married blacks, with approximately one in 10,000 white men and fewer than one in 1,000 white women doing so. There was a slight decline over the years in the percentage of white and black brides and grooms who married interracially from 1922 to the 1940's. Of 145 white grooms who married black women in New York State, exclusive of New York City, from 1916 to 1937, 49, or 33.8 percent, were foreign born, while of 424 white brides who intermarried during the same period only 38, or 9.9 percent were of foreign birth. Eleven of the foreign-born grooms were born in Italy, 4 in Canada, 3 in Germany, 2 in Austria, 3 in Hungary, and 26 in other countries. Of the foreign-born white brides, 13 were born in Canada, 6 in Germany, 6 in Great Britain, 3 in Austria, 2 in Poland, 2 in Italy, and 6 in other countries (Wirth and Goldhamer 1944: 286-289; Monahan 1971a: 94-105).

There appears to be little published information on marriages between blacks and whites in states West of the Mississippi River for the 19th and early 20th centuries. Frederick Hoffman summarized and quoted excerpts from an unpublished study conducted about 1910 by a graduate student at the University of Minnesota of Negro-White intermarriage in St. Paul and Minneapolis, including excerpts from eight case studies of marriages between white women and black men. Hoffman states:

> The conclusions of this investigation are summed up in the statement that "the white women who have married blacks are of the weaker class, either mentally, morally or physically; while conversely the negro men represent the better class in most respects, at least physically and mentally. It is felt that the women who have so married have married into a much better economic condition of life than they would have had they married among their own race or kind. Most of the women are of foreign birth or parentage, and though they all professed a prejudice in the beginning it certainly could not have been as deeply ingrained in them as among those in which it was inborn or of native stock." Most of the women were working girls who married porters or waiters. The fine physique, the politeness, the sentiment and evident appreciation with regard to his white wife, would seem to have been the winning virtues.

Hoffman quotes from the report concerning Case 5, the marriage seven years previously in St. Paul of a foreign-born (probably Danish) woman who worked as a scrub girl or chambermaid to a waiter. The wife was reported to be neat and clean and their house was neatly kept:

> Mr. and Mrs. R. have no children. Asked if she were not somewhat ostracized because of her marriage with the negro, she said yes, by the whites, but not so much by the negroes, although she said that she seldom neighbored with her negro neighbors. She said that it was not necessary for her to be on specially good or friendly terms with either race, for the families of the twin cities in which the husbands were black and the wives were white had a club of their own, the purpose of which was to overcome social inconveniences which their marital relations might have brought upon them. This club is known as the 'Manassas Club,' [actually, Manasseh] and has about 200 members in the twin cities, its only rule being that the negro seeking admission have a white wife. Each city formerly had an organization but recently the prime mover of the St. Paul organization had died and the club has somewhat disbanded. However, they keep in touch with the Minneapolis organization and from time to time join with them in their dances and card parties (Hoffman 1923: 175-188).

The period between the first and second world wars was one during which marriages between blacks and whites, especially those of black men and white women, declined as a percentage of Negro marriages and aroused strong feelings of hostility from most whites. It was suggested that interracial marriage was not made illegal in some of the northern and western states because strong public disapproval reduced their number to such an extent that legislation was not thought to be necessary. Reuter wrote in 1931 that the Secretary of State of a northern state which had no legal prohibition of such marriages had stated his belief that most judges refuse to issue licenses to marry to interracial couples, and quotes an example from an Associated Press Dispatch of February 11, 1930 from Spokane, Washington:

> Antonio Biggs, Negro, and Miss Cecil Robinson, attractive white girl, were denied a marriage license Monday at the office of the Spokane County auditor.
> Although there is no law in Washington forbidding such a marriage, Acting County Auditor Frank Glover said the County Auditor "has the right to ascertain whether the mentality of applicants for marriage licenses is sound, and I can but question the sanity of a white woman who will marry a Negro" (Reuter 1931: 102).

As the statistics presented in most studies of interracial marriage do not reveal the social setting which prevailed during the half century before 1940, I shall attempt to summarize the problems which confronted interracial couples during that period, and give excerpts from interviews conducted during 1937-1939 when the writer was conducting dissertation research on "Negro-White Intermarriage in Chicago" (Roberts 1940). This was a period, especially in the 1920's and 1930's, when such marriages were viewed very unfavorably by the general public, and subjected to severe opprobrium and negative sanctions. The Great Migration of poorly educated, largely rural blacks from the lower South doubled Chicago's Negro population during 1915-1920, resulting in increased racial segregation in housing, schools, parks, playgrounds, and places of public accommodation. The public tended to assume that whites who married blacks were of the lowest class. They were subjected to social ostracism by parents, relatives, and former associates. They and their children were subjected to the discrimination faced by blacks with added difficulty in securing housing and employment.

In the writer's Chicago study of interracial marriages it was found that of those who married before 1940, 41 percent of the white husbands, 46 percent of their black wives, 37 percent of black husbands and 33 percent of the white wives had been previously married, with consequent late age at marriage. A majority of the black spouses were born in the South, while 44 percent of the white husbands and 27 percent of the white wives were of foreign birth. As was the case in other northern cities, more than three-quarters of the couples were of black husbands and white wives. The most common situation in which these interracial couples first met was through occupational relationships. Especially frequent before 1910 were situations in which black men and white women lived at the workplace, as domestic servants in homes of the wealthy or as waiters and pantry girls or maids in hotels, where they were in daily contact, and were confined to the premises for long hours with little opportunity to meet others.

Despite the ostracism and social sanctions which they faced, a majority of those interviewed indicated that they were happily married, although a considerable number of the white wives expressed the view that the social penalties to which they were subjected because of their marriage were a heavy price to pay. Most of the participants sought to give the impression that love and appreciation for the fine qualities of those they married had caused them to disregard societal attitudes and marry someone of another race. A middle-aged widow said of her reason for marrying her black husband:

> "You might ask why did we marry. Love! You can't stay the hand of love.
> "I never regretted the step I made when I married my husband. I am proud to say that John Whitney was my husband. I have been engaged to four men. They were wealthy men, but I stopped because love was not there. I could have married a doctor. A nurse always has a chance. My association with my husband was always wonderful and romantic."[2]

Another white wife remarked:

> "I had loved my husband so furiously that I don't think I will ever love again. I'm the type of person who gives all he's got at once. I don't regret my love because it made me better able to understand life. . .
> "I really thought my husband was a god. I didn't think there was anything else in the world. This may sound silly. I gave up everything easily for him."

It was generally felt by interracially married persons that the strongest opposition to intermarriage came from black women and white men. Several made comments such as the following:

> "I find that the general public isn't ready for it and doesn't accept it. Colored are very strong against it and whites are too. Especially the colored women oppose mixed marriage."
> "The majority of people put us all in the same class--rotten. There are two classes of people who can't take it, who can't stand mixed marriages. They are colored women and white men."

The courtship and marriage of many, if not most, of the white partners in pre-World War II unions was of a surreptitious nature. Knowing that marriage to a Negro would probably cause embarrassment and loss of status, as well as disbelief and shock, to parents and close relatives, as well as rejection of themselves, spouse, and children, most white partners found it very difficult to inform parents and other family members of their marriage until the knot had been tied. One of the white wives stated:

> "I have only one parent, my father, but I don't know if he's living or not because I severed all connections with my people when I married because I didn't want to interfere. . . . I wouldn't want anybody else to suffer for anything I did."

Another white wife who hadn't communicated with her parents or relatives since she left home thirty years previously, although she and they resided in Chicago, remarked:

"I didn't want them to know. I had so many relatives and brothers and sisters and everybody I thought it would be better to stay by myself. There were too many of them. I used to cry for years and years about home."
"They don't know anything about it today. They never knew much about colored. There were so many people concerned. I'd much rather they didn't know where I am than know the truth."

Often white parents and family members maintained varying degrees of contact with a partner in an interracial marriage, but kept the marriage secret from more distant relatives and friends. A 64-year old white husband, married for 40 years, said of relationships with six brothers and sisters who resided in a neighboring state:

"We communicate once in a great while, when there is a death or something. We used to come together often, but drifted apart. It was because of the mixture. None of them approve of it of my brothers and sisters."
". . . They don't want the children to know it. They don't never mention my name among the children"
"The first generation, they all know it. The uncles and aunts know. But since then, they've put the soft pedal on it. The children and them, none know. They know nothing about it. I've got hundreds of relatives I wouldn't know if I saw them on the street. I don't even know some of my sisters' names after they got married. No one approves, you know that."

There were several cases in which parents of the white spouse, usually when elderly and dependent, made their home with the interracial couple. Complete acceptance of their child's intermarriage by white parents most often occurred when the parents were foreign-born and free of the usual American abhorrence of racial intermarriage. In one such case in the 1890's the black husband met his French Canadian wife at the home of her uncle where he was a roomer. Her mother consented to the marriage before the couple were engaged, and after they married she lived with them until her death, more than two decades later. One of the wife's sisters also lived with the interracial family, and the older children learned to speak French before they learned English.

After marriage, the white partners frequently faced a greater degree of social isolation and ostracism than they had expected, and several white wives spoke of the difficulties they had encountered. One such wife stated:

"I think that an interracial has a hard life to live. They are shunned everywhere they go by white and colored both. They're just like a discarded race. I know because I've lived with the colored longer than with the white. I've been married 25 years and I was 22 when I married. The best part of my life has been spent with colored."
". . . . The colored don't want you and the whites won't have you at all. . . . I wouldn't advise no white woman to marry a colored man because of the hardships they have to go through. I'm not going to lie about it because it is true."
Another of the white wives interviewed in the late 1930's remarked:

"When you marry out of your race you live a double life. . . . Everywhere you go you have to be afraid someone you know will see you. . . . I feel like an innocent criminal, like some person arrested for something he has never done, and doesn't want anybody to find out."

A woman who emigrated from Sweden at the age of 17, at the turn of the century, and two years later married a bell-hop who was employed at the hotel where she worked in the fruit pantry, and by whom she had ten children, spoke of the difficulties of marriage across the color line:

"There are too many obstacles to face. . . . They make it too hard for you. I didn't know when I came here. I think if I was born and raised in this country it would have been different. I was a greenhorn, but many were born in Chicago and did it too."
"Now I have to live my life. I have lovely kids. If it wasn't for my kids I wouldn't have stayed together all this time. It isn't so hard for a woman who is intermarried but doesn't have children. She doesn't have to go out with her husband. If you have children you have to take along, it is not so pleasant. You have to take a lot of insults."

A number of the persons interviewed stated that they had experienced difficulty in finding housing, even in black neighborhoods, because of the feeling against intermarriage. One of the white wives stated:

"You don't know how hard it is for an interracial couple to rent a place. Usually they just say that the place is already rented. One renting agency comes right out and says that it won't rent to mixed couples. We were refused by colored landlords because we were a mixed couple."

One of the major threats to the security of interracial couples a half century ago was that of loss of employment if it was discovered that the husband or wife of a white employee was black. White wives were in agreement that this was a very serious threat and several stated that they had lost a number of jobs when the fact that they were interracially married was discovered. One of the white wives who had been a waitress for many years commented:

"I had a fine job downtown which I had had eleven years. Then I had to have an operation and I didn't know what to tell them because I couldn't give my address. I couldn't let them know that I lived out here. I said I was out of town. I thought that was the best thing to say. When I didn't come to work, they tried to locate me. After all those years we had worked together the girls wanted to visit me when I was sick. I couldn't let them come to the hospital because they might have seen my husband there. I had given the address of an old woman and they called her. She forgot what I told her to say when somebody asked for me and I lost my job."
"It is a terrible problem with work. It is hard for a white woman married to a colored man to hold a job. I've said intermarriage is all right if your husband can support you so you don't have to work."

A black railroad employee and his white wife both stated, when interviewed in 1937, that they found it necessary to lead a dual life because both would lose their jobs if their employers discovered that they were interracially married. Each had been employed in their current positions during the sixteen years of their marriage. The wife was secretary of the president of a large company where it was thought that she was unmarried. She remarked:

> . . . . No white women can hold a job if it is known that her husband is colored. You would lose your position immediately if it were known. The world isn't ready to accept interracial marriage yet.

The husband often posed as her chauffeur with the wife sitting in the rear seat of their car when he drove her to or from her place of work. The wife commented:

> One day my husband called to drive me home from work. Just as he was about to start the car I saw my boss. I told my husband to stop and asked my boss if he was going to the ----- station as we were going that way too. They know that I have a car at work. Mr. Lane was at the wheel and I was in the back seat. I introduced Mr. Lane to my boss but didn't say who he was. We took my boss to the station, but he never thought that we were married.
> The only trouble I have is if I would become ill and have to go to a hospital. My husband wouldn't be able to come to see me. He couldn't see me then unless I didn't have my job.

The husband (Mr. Lane) stated:

> I am a railroad employee. I am an office car employee. That's the car the officials of the road are on. If they found out that my wife is white, I would lose my job.

Mrs. Lane then remarked:

> I was with him from May to August when he was sick. I couldn't let it be known that I was his wife. I was supposed to be in Michigan. I had to write letters and send them to the office where I worked from Michigan. I had to be careful that nobody from the office saw me while I was supposed to be away. I had to step about the house because people from his [railroad] line came to visit him. I had a colored woman here and went into the kitchen when visitors came.
> We have to be careful because we're buying our home and can't afford to lose our jobs. If we had enough money to be independent, we wouldn't care who knew we were married.

Because Mrs. Lane felt the need to conceal her address in a black neighborhood from people at her place of work, the Lanes had an unlisted telephone number, and Mrs. Lane had given her brother's telephone number as hers. Asked how she received calls from her office, she replied:

That is all taken care of. [They think] I live with my brother. If anyone from the office calls me my brother says that I have stepped to the drug store but will call back. Then he calls me and I call the person who wanted me.

Mrs. Lane commented:

Of course I live a dual life. Anyway I am happy. I have to forget all about my other self when I am at the office so as not to give myself away by accident. I'm the oldest employee at our place.
I go out with them [the girls from the office] all the time. They don't come here because they think I am rooming. Of course I am older than the others at the office. Occasionally I entertain the workers on the Northside at the home of a white friend. . . . They let me use their house to entertain the group from the office. I try to entertain them in fine style once a year.
We have to be very careful in going out. We have a car and can go anywhere. We go together but can't recognize each other. The only thing that bothers me is that I can't introduce him as my husband.
. . . As soon as we leave Chicago we feel free and go together as we want to. We go in our car and have travelled in the North and the East.

From the Outbreak of World War II to the Peak of the Civil Rights Movement: 1939-1966

On the eve of World War II, blacks were segregated by law in the South and denied service in most other areas in hotels, restaurants, and other places of public accommodation, were largely excluded by a rigid color line from employment in other than unskilled or service occupations, were negatively stereotyped in the press, and portrayed as menials or buffoons or in secondary singing and dancing roles in motion pictures. Residential racial segregation was at its height, buttressed by restrictive covenants and other discriminatory real estate practices. There was little opportunity for whites and blacks of opposite sex to meet under circumstances conducive to friendship or marriage. In thirty states, marriage of whites to blacks was illegal, and elsewhere societal attitudes and sanctions made any increase in such marriages appear to be unlikely.

Then in the quarter century prior to 1967, there was greater improvement in the status of African-Americans than at any time since the 1870's. Slowly in the 1940's and with increased momentum in the 1950's and 1960's changes occurred in the attitudes of many whites and in national policy which served to reduce racial discrimination and segregation and make possible some increase in interracial association and marriage outside the South.

Biological theories of innate racial superiority of Caucasians and of the harmful effects of racial mixture were rejected by most scholars and molders of opinion and increasingly by the public. Racial stereotyping increasingly was felt to be in bad taste and blacks were portrayed in less demeaning manner than in the past by the media. Blacks were gradually given more dignified roles on the stage and screen and seldom caricatured.

At the end of World War II the position of the United States as leader of the free world was in sharp conflict with existing patterns of racial inequality, discrimination and segregation. The appearance of non-white representatives of newly independent Asian and African nations in their embassies and the United Nations countered old notions of the inferior "place" of persons of color. The protests of Asian and African diplomats when denied service by restaurants, hotels, and other places of public accommodation were a source of embarrassment for United States government officials, and a source of unfavorable publicity around the world, which spurred government efforts to end such discrimination.

With improved living standards, educational attainment, and increased visibility of a growing middle class, the image of black Americans was enhanced. Increasingly religious, humanitarian, and civic agencies promoted the cause of racial harmony and understanding. In the 1940's and 1950's hundreds of cities, counties, and states initiated community self surveys and appointed human relations commissions to address problems of racial discrimination and conflict. By 1963, twenty-one states and more than 40 cities had passed fair employment practices laws. Churches began to move against racial injustice, and some church bodies expressed the view that an interracial church should be their goal. Labor unions, particularly the C.I.O., began to include blacks in their membership in large numbers.

From 1875 to 1940 the federal government and courts made almost no attempt to overturn legally mandated racial segregation nor the discrimination which was so widely practiced. Then a number of challenges to the old order were made by executive decree, beginning with President Roosevelt's establishment of a Fair Employment Practice Committee (FEPC) in 1941 to end racial discrimination in defense industries. In 1947, President Truman's Committee on Civil Rights condemned racial discrimination and recommended strong legislative action to protect minority rights. In the early 1950's, racial segregation in the armed forces was brought to an end.

The United States Supreme Court began to require some measure of equality in the enforcement of racial segregation where required by law under the separate but equal doctrine and then, in the 1940's and 1950's, ruled against racial segregation in transportation and public education. Congress finally passed a series of Civil Rights Acts between 1957 and 1968 which voided all of the state and local laws which had required racial segregation in places of public accommodation and guaranteed equal legal and voting rights. By 1968, the entire body of racially discriminatory legislation which had supported the doctrine of white supremacy in the South had been eliminated (Bardolph 1970: 394-535). In addition, affirmative action legislation increased educational and employment opportunities for blacks.

With the changes brought about by legislation, judicial decisions and the civil rights movement, including acceptance of customers in places of public accommodation on a non-racial basis and the entry of large numbers of blacks in types of employment from which they had been previously barred or seldom found, there has been a great increase in situations in which persons of opposite race and sex meet in daily work activities as a result of which friendships might be formed. It should not be surprising that the great increase in contacts between whites and blacks of similar educational and occupational levels would lead to an increase in intermarriage where permitted by law and that the changed social climate would permit gradual voiding of state laws prohibiting racial intermarriage.

Four western states introduced legislation prohibiting racial intermarriage during the first two decades of the twentieth century, and no state repealed such laws between 1883 and 1948. Then, in 1947, the Catholic Interracial Council of Los Angeles announced that it sought a test case to challenge California's law prohibiting interracial marriages on the ground that the law deprived a white Catholic and one of any other race of their right to receive the sacrament of marriage. Such a case, that of a black male and white female Roman Catholic, was brought before the California Supreme Court (Perez v. Lippold) which found the provision of state law which read, "All marriages of white persons with Negroes, Mongolians, members of the Malay race or mulattoes are illegal and void . . .," to be a violation of the guarantee of equal protection of the laws (LeBerthon 1947: 52-56; Sickles 1972: 98).

Following the California decision in 1948, all twelve of the remaining northern and western states which had such legislation repealed their anti-intermarriage laws during the next 17 years: Oregon in 1951, Montana in 1953, North Dakota in 1955, Colorado and South Dakota in 1957, Idaho and Nevada in 1959, Arizona in 1962, Utah and Nebraska in 1963, and Indiana and Wyoming in 1965 (Weinberger 1966: 157).

A number of social scientists have published marriage record data for several widely separated cities, counties, and states for a series of years between 1940 and 1967. Table 8, below, gives the number of marriages between white and black grooms and brides by year for Los Angeles County, California for eleven years, beginning with November, 1948 when the state anti-intermarriage law was found to be unconstitutional.

Table 8. Negro-White intermarriages, Los Angeles County, Calif., 1948-1959

Year	Groom Negro Bride White	Groom White Bride Negro	Total
1948	6	0	6
1949	43	10	53
1950	30	16	46
1951	50	12	62
1952	45	13	58
1953	53	25	78
1954	61	30	91
1955	84	23	107
1956	77	27	104
1957	95	34	129
1958	111	35	146
1959	145	42	187
Totals 1948-59	800	267	1067

Source: Burma 1963: 163.

Monahan has presented data on interracial marriages in Iowa for the years 1940 to 1967 during which period there were 567,719 recorded marriages of which

7,988 included at least one black partner. Table 9, below, which groups the Iowa data into five consecutive time periods, is based on marriages of black men and women to non-Negroes, a predominantly but not exclusively white category.

Table 9. Percent of Negro marriages in Iowa which are mixed, 1940-1967

Years	Male	Female	Total
1940-42	3.08	0.81	3.84
1944-49	5.37	2.76	7.84
1950-55	6.14	1.75	7.69
1956-61	9.69	2.00	11.32
1962-67	13.88	3.73	16.67

Source: Monahan 1970a; 468.

Table 10. Negro-White intermarriages as percentages of marriages of grooms and brides by race, selected states, 1947-1967 (excluding New York City*)

Year	Kansas Negro spouse	New York* Negro groom	New York* bride	Michigan Negro groom	Michigan bride	Michigan White groom	Michigan White bride	Hawaii Negro groom	Hawaii Negro bride	Hawaii White groom	Hawaii White bride
1947	1.2	1.5	0.4								
1948	1.0	1.5	0.6								
1949	1.0	1.4	0.5								
1950	0.6	1.1	0.3								
1951	0.5	1.6	0.5								
1952	1.5	1.7	0.8								
1953	1.0	1.5	0.9	1.09	0.40	0.04	0.10				
1954	0.9	2.2	1.2	1.10	0.46	0.04	0.09				
1955	2.7	1.4	0.9	1.12	0.48	0.05	0.11				
1956	1.6	1.6	1.2	1.32	0.46	0.04	0.13	9.09	0	0	0.31
1957	1.7	1.2	1.1	1.37	0.14	0.01	0.14	13.33	0	0	0.47
1958	2.4	1.4	0.7	1.37	0.05	0.05	0.13	4.08	5.00	0.06	0.16
1959	2.6	1.8	0.7	1.62	0.40	0.04	0.16	9.80	8.33	0.11	0.36
1960	2.5	2.3	1.3	1.39	0.63	0.06	0.14	14.71	12.50	0.16	0.34
1961	3.7	2.8	0.7	1.76	0.48	0.05	0.18	16.00	8.00	0.11	0.52
1962	3.3	2.8	1.3	1.90	0.49	0.05	0.19	17.78	4.17	0.05	0.19
1963	4.0	3.3	1.2	2.34	0.77	0.07	0.23	14.81	9.38	0.14	0.43
1964	8.6	3.9	1.8					20.31	8.57	0.13	0.68
1965	6.9										
1966	6.7										
1967	5.8										
Totals											
1953-63				1.53	0.48	0.05	0.15				
1956-64								13.53	6.82	0.09	0.43

Source: Monahan 1971a: 110; Monahan 1971b: 98; Heer 1966: 264-265.

Monahan and Heer have published data showing the percentage of black grooms and brides who have married whites and, for some states, of white brides and grooms who have married blacks for selected years over several widely scattered states as indicated in Table 10.

Marriage data for the state of California for the years 1955 and 1957-1959 indicate that 3.56 percent of Negro grooms and 1 percent of Negro brides married whites, while 0.07 percent of white grooms and 0.27 percent of white brides married blacks (Heer 1966: 264, 265).

The available data from northern and western states indicate that the decline in frequency of marriages between whites and blacks between the two world wars lessened or bottomed during the 1940's and that their number at least doubled or tripled from the mid-1950's to the mid-1960's.

Table 11, below, presents data provided by several scholars which show the frequency of marriages between blacks and whites by race and sex of bride and groom for widely scattered cities and states and varying time periods. We may note that in all places for which we have information, marriages between black men and white women occur more frequently than those between white men and black women. This was most marked for marriages entered into before 1940.

Table 11. Black-White marriages by sex and race of grooms and brides

Years	Area	Number of Black-White marriages	Marriages of Black males-White females		Marriages of White males-Black females	
			Number	Percent of all Black-White marriages	Number	Percent of all Black-White marriages
1874-93	Michigan 111		93	83.8	18	16.2
1883-93	Rhode Island 58		51	87.9	7	12.1
1908-12	New York City (x) 52		41	78.8	11	21.2
1900-07	Boston 222		203	91.4	19	8.6
1914-38	Boston 276		227	82.3	49	17.7
1916-37	New York St. (y) 569		424	74.5	145	25.5
1922-47	Philadelphia* 41		24	58.5	17	41.5
1948-59	Los Angeles 1067		800	75	267	25.0
1955-59	California 1173		921	78.5	252	21.5
1931-65	Washington DC 818		523	64	295	36
1947-69	Kansas			85		15
1953-63	Michigan 1132		864	76.3	268	23.7
1956-64	Hawaii 74		59	79.7	15	20.3
1962-67	Iowa**			79		21
1960-62	Philadelphia 245		124	50.6	121	49.4
1960-62	Philadelphia***197		120	60.9	77	39.1

Sources: Wirth, Goldhamer 1944:282; Monahan 1970a, 1970b, 1971b; Lynn 1967: 429; Golden 1953; Heer 1966: 264-65.

Key: * 5 year intervals, including 1922, 1927, 1937, 1942, and 1947
      ** All non-Black included with White; *** Excluding Puerto Ricans and Mexicans
      x-Manhattan and Bronx; y-Excluding New York City

The extreme subordination, oppression and segregation of Negroes persisted with little change in the South, with the exception of the District of Columbia and the border states until the 1960's. Few imagined in 1954 when the Supreme Court ordered desegregation of the public schools that in little more than a decade a second reconstruction would be forced upon the South with civil rights legislation and judicial decisions removing all legally imposed racial segregation of public schools, means of transportation, restaurants, hotels, libraries, parks, theaters, and other places of public accommodation, and prohibiting restrictions on legal and political rights. The white South responded to this assault on the system of white supremacy with massive resistance. The strongest opposition centered upon what were perceived as threats to white dominance through enforcement of voting rights and weakening of the barriers to social equality and racial intermarriage.

The author of a major work on the legal status of black Americans declared in 1940:

> . . . . the present temper of the southern white man would not tolerate a policy permitting mixed marriages. Any attempt to change the law would be stirring up the racial prejudice of the white man to such fever heat that it would act as a boomerang against the Negroes. The white man in the South has made up his mind that he wants no intermarriage with the Negro, and nothing is going to change this attitude as yet, if ever. In fact, the state of Mississippi has enacted a criminal statute punishing anyone for publishing, printing, or circulating any literature in favor of or urging interracial marriage or social equality (Mangum 1940: 237).

The laws prohibiting racial intermarriage remained in force in all of the southern states until 1967. Black veterans of World War II who attempted to return to homes in the South with European brides were forced to leave or face imprisonment. The atmosphere of racial hatred and resistance of southern whites to court imposed desegregation and to proponents of civil rights would have made racial intermarriage almost unthinkable in most areas of the South during the 1950's and most of the 1960's. It was possible for a few interracial couples who married in the North to live together in some of the border states where resistance to court imposed desegregation was accepted with little resistance, but from 1894 to 1967 the District of Colombia was the only southern jurisdiction without anti-intermarriage laws.

In the 1940's there were very few marriages of whites to blacks in Washington, D.C., only 1 out of 10,954 in 1941, and a total of only 26 of the 97,599 marriage licenses issued during the eight years, 1940-1947, were to white-black mixed couples of which seven grooms were white and nineteen were black. During this same period, 209 Filipino men and 48 Chinese men married white women. Sister M. Annella Lynn indicates the marked increase in interracial marriages, particularly of whites with blacks and Asians, in the District of Columbia from 1931 to 1965 in table 12, below:

Table 12. Number of interracial marriages in Washington, D.C. (Number distributed by race and five year period)

	1931-35	36-40	41-45	46-50	51-55	56-60	61-65	Total
Black-White	15	8	17	26	82	177	493	818
Filipino-White	27	67	142	120	109	146	243	854
Chinese-White	3	7	32	56	67	59	74	298
Japanese-White	3	4	11	20	32	46	71	187
Indian-White	12	3	20	14	17	41	61	168
Others-White	1	3	5	15	26	55	105	210
Filipino-Black	4	7	8	6	10	4	5	44
Indian-Black	3	4	3	4	11	10	19	54
Chinese-Black		2	4	6	6	10	4	32
Japanese-Black	2				3		1	6
Others-Black				1		4	7	12
Totals	70	105	242	268	363	552	1081	2683

Source: Annella (Lynn) 1967: 430.

The 1960 United States Census for the first time presented data on marital status which included counts of interracial couples for the United States and for four regions, but not for separate states. The totals include consensual unions as well as couples who were legally married. Contrary to all available state and city marriage statistics, which show without exception the preponderance of black grooms and white brides in black-white marriages, the 1960 Census reported a total of 25,913 white husbands with black wives and 25,496 black husbands with white wives. Even more surprising was the indication that 39.7 percent of all white and black interracial couples in the United States resided in the South, including 11,808 white husbands with black wives and 8,624 black husbands with white wives (U.S. Bureau of the Census 1960: 160-161).[3]

Prior to the 1940's, a majority of black and white grooms and brides who intermarried were servants and unskilled or semiskilled workers, although a few black professionals, writers, and entertainers married whites. In a book published in 1949, Maurice R. Davie lists 65 "outstanding American Negro artists in literature, in the theater, and on the concert stage," of whom no less than eight of fifty men and four of fifteen women had married Caucasians (Davie 1949: 378-380). Since 1950 there has been a marked increase in the educational and occupational level of those who intermarry. Many middle-class interracial couples met in colleges and universities after blacks entered in large numbers in the late 1940's and 1950's, in civil rights organizations, and as members of social service organizations and government agencies engaged in social welfare and anti-poverty programs.

A high percentage of African-Americans who spent extended periods in Europe, in countries where blacks were few in number, married whites. During and after the second World War, several hundred thousand black American military personnel were stationed in Europe and many married British, French, German,

Italian, and other European women. African-American students, artists, writers, and entertainers often spend years in Europe and many marry Europeans. Foreign students at American universities frequently establish intercultural and interracial friendships which lead to marriage.

Information gathered from Census and marriage record sources from the 1950's and 1960's indicates that whites and blacks who intermarry are more likely than those who marry persons of their own race to have been previously married and to have a higher age at marriage. They tend to be homogamous as to educational level, and blacks who marry whites have on average a higher level of education than those who marry blacks (Bernard 1966: 274-276; Burma 1952: 587-589; Burma 1963: 161-165; Carter and Glick 1970: 127-129; Monahan 1970b: 294-297; Pavela 1964: 209; Roberts 1978: 197-201).

The Post-Civil Rights Period: 1967 to the Present

Although by 1967 the civil rights movement lost momentum as many white activists turned their attention to other causes and many blacks, influenced by black pride and black nationalism, rejected close association with whites, the trends of the previous two decades which saw reduction of racial discrimination and segregation, removal of racially restrictive legislation, favorable portrayal of blacks by the media, and entry of blacks into occupations and professions from which they had been excluded or restricted continued and spread to the South. Overt bigotry has diminished and public officials and others have been forced to resign after making anti-black remarks. Men seeking elective or appointive political office often hasten to resign from private clubs which exclude racial minorities.

The public has become accustomed to seeing African-Americans on their television screens as well-dressed, affluent, and intelligent political figures, concert artists, news reporters, interviewers, panelists, and experts, as well as entertainers. Whites increasingly have contact with black teachers and professors and fellow employees. With the removal of racial restrictions, the white public has become accustomed to seeing blacks frequenting hotels, restaurants, and places of entertainment and public accommodation as well as in the workplace.

During the past twenty years numerous newspaper and magazine articles have reported intermarriages between blacks and whites, with participants telling of their experiences. There have been scores of radio and television talk shows and news broadcasts featuring transracial adoption and interracial marriage, usually with sympathetic treatment and supportive audience reaction. Such presentations serve to counteract previous opinion that whites and blacks who intermarried were of the lowest social level.

Opinion surveys indicate a lessening of opposition to interracial association and intermarriage. Four Gallop Poll surveys taken between 1968 and 1983 show the following trends in attitudes of the American public toward interracial marriage:

Table 13. U.S. attitudes toward marriage between whites and nonwhites

year	Approve	Disapprove	No opinion
1968	20%	72%	8%
1972	29%	60%	11%
1978	36%	54%	10%
1983	43%	50%	7%

Source: Gallop Poll, as reported in Philadelphia Inquirer, July 2, 1983: D-1

The 1983 survey showed that nonwhites were more likely than whites to express approval of interracial marriage, with 71% expressing approval as contrasted with 38% of whites expressing approval.

There has been a reduction of the negative sanctions which had long kept interracial dating and marriage to a minimum. Prior to the changed climate of the 1950's many interracial couples, especially those of black husbands and white wives, felt uncertainty and apprehension when they left the security of home and familiar environment. There was the threat of hostile reaction from outraged whites, including harassment by policemen and verbal and physical attack.

Since the mid-1960's, white public opinion has become less violently opposed to marriages between blacks and whites, almost indifferent if the participants are strangers, while many blacks, influenced by black power, black nationalism, and black awareness rhetoric have voiced strong opposition to intermarriage, particularly to marriages of black men in leadership positions to white women.

A prominent African-American professor with a fair Caucasian wife expressed fear of physical attack by white youths in the 1940's and early 1950's and remarked in 1969:

> I thought that within the last five years the subjective experience of sanction against interracial marriages has been felt more strongly from the Negro than from the white side. Up until the last two or three years, as far as I'm concerned, I was more sensitive and apprehensive about the response of white people in the United States to being intermarried. This often involved the apprehension about physical attack. . . . For years I didn't even bother to walk around the streets with my wife, because of bad experiences I had had in the past. I have seen a significant change in temper of the general public. In the first place, I think that on the streets by and large people just take interracial couples for granted as a part of the scenery, except in certain ethnic neighborhoods after dark. But in the [Chicago] loop and in Hyde Park there isn't the stopping to stare and the gawking. You may get a look of curiosity, but not much else.
>
> . . . .
>
> Since Malcolm X became a hero with the popularity of his autobiography and his very strong feeling against association between black males and white women, with the general rise of black power and black consciousness, I know my feeling--subjectively--I find myself slipping into a feeling of guilt. You feel occasionally when you're talking to somebody you have to apologize about why you married white, and one doesn't feel that you have to do this to white people. I get into dilemmas--things I am

invited to and asked not to bring my wife, and then one has something approaching an ethical problem and a moral problem.
. . . . One final point on this is that you can get to the point where your credibility as a person to be trusted wanes. I am frequently referred to by black student groups, including the one at [my] university as "the nigger who talks black and sleeps white." This has made for strained relations with me and the Black Students Association here.
The most extreme case I ever had of this is the very attractive young lady in a certain black students group at an eastern university who invited me to dinner when I was on the campus making a speech. She was dressed in Ghanaian cloth with nothing under it, and was obviously interested in trying herself out on whether she could seduce the author of ------ ------. I saw what the name of the game was very early, but it's interesting what the line was--"You have written books and have been helpful to the black people. This is a period that needs active leaders. You should be playing that role, but you have a handicap. I hear you have a white wife. If you had any devotion to your race, you would divorce that woman immediately and face your responsibility as a leader."

In an interview in the early 1970's, a white wife reported that her husband's parents who previously had accepted her and their biracial grandchildren rejected them as a result of their involvement in the black awareness movement, stating:

I'm told that I can't bring my children home to see their white grandmother. This hurts--not for me but my children. Not only are they not accepted by the white grandparents, they are not accepted anymore by the black grandparents. The Negro grandparents don't want to be bothered with them anymore because they are now too involved in the black movement. Black people are rejecting us now as much as whites. We have nobody but ourselves. . . . (Porterfield 1978: 122-123).

The opposition of black nationalist spokespersons and of many African-American women to intermarriage with whites did not offset the trend established in the 1950's of marked increase in such marriages which was facilitated by the reduction of legal and customary restrictions and the great increase in social contacts between black and white men and women of equivalent educational and occupational background. By 1967, marriages between whites and blacks were increasing in the North and West, and by the beginning of the year, only the seventeen southern and border states still made marriages between whites and blacks a legal offense. Then in March, 1967, Maryland repealed its anti-intermarriage law. Finally, on June 12, 1967, following the elimination of all other forms of legally imposed racial segregation and discrimination, the United States Supreme Court in a unanimous decision (Loving v. Virginia) declared that the Virginia statute prohibiting racial intermarriage was unconstitutional, constituting a violation of the equal protection clause of the 14th amendment. In delivering the opinion of the Court, Chief Justice Warren declared:

. . . [T]wo members of this Court have already stated that they "cannot conceive of a valid legislative purpose . . . which makes the color of a person's skin the test of whether his conduct is a criminal offense." . . .
There is patently no legitimate overriding purpose independent of invidious racial discrimination which justifies this classification. The fact that Virginia prohibits only interracial marriages involving white persons demonstrates that the racial classifications must stand on their own justification, as measures designed to maintain White Supremacy. . . .
Marriage is one of the "basic civil rights of man," fundamental to our very existence and survival. . . . To deny this fundamental freedom on so unsupportable a basis as the racial classifications embodied in these statutes, classifications so directly subversive of the principle of equality at the heart of the Fourteenth Amendment, is surely to deprive all the State's citizens of liberty without due process of law. . . . Under our Constitution the freedom to marry, or not marry, a person of another race resides with the individual and cannot be infringed by the State (Bell 1973: 282-283).

The Supreme Court decision was not followed in the South by massive resistance or violence such as accompanied the school desegregation and voting rights acts, but several states were slow in voiding their anti-intermarriage laws. A county judge in Miami refused to issue a marriage license to a black man and white woman, but in January, 1968 the Florida Supreme Court ordered that the license be issued. In several other states federal and state courts directed defiant clerks and registrars to issue licenses to interracial couples. As late as December, 1970 a federal judge ordered Alabama officials to stop enforcing the state anti-intermarriage statutes after the Army sought an order for issuance of a marriage license which had been denied a white soldier stationed at Fort McClellan and his black fiancée (Sickels 1972: 112-115).

There appear to have been no marriages between whites and blacks in post-Reconstruction Mississippi until the summer of 1970. Then a white supremacist organization obtained a temporary injunction from a Mississippi Circuit judge preventing the issuance of a marriage license to a white law clerk from Boston and his black fiancée, a student from rural Mississippi who was attending Jackson State College. The 24-year old groom was a conscientious objector who had come to Mississippi from law school to work for the NAACP Legal Defense and Educational Fund as alternate service approved by his draft board. After the federal district court ordered the issuance of a marriage license the couple were married, with wide publicity and television coverage, by a white Presbyterian minister in a black Baptist church before some two hundred guests. The minister, like the bride and groom, had been active in the civil rights movement (Sickles 1972: 114-115).

There was no rush to intermarry in most of the southern states. The North Carolina State Board of Health reported 15 marriages of blacks to whites in 1967. Seventeen such marriages were recorded in Virginia during the last half of 1967, of which 13 of the husbands were black, and in 1968 there were 32 black-white marriages with 21 uniting black men and white women (N.Y. Times, July 28, 1968: Sickles 1972: 129).

Thomas P. Monahan checked the files of marriages for the District of Columbia, Maryland and Virginia for the late 1960's and early 1970's and found progressive increases in marriages between whites and blacks. In the District of

Columbia where the population has become predominantly black and marriages of blacks exceed those of whites, the rate of intermarriage of blacks showed little change while the percentage of whites who married blacks increased from 3.58 percent in 1965 to 6.06 percent in 1973.

Table 14. Percentage of Racial Mixture in Marriages in the District of Columbia, 1965-1973.

Year	Total Number of marriages	Marriages White with Black			Marriages of Whites: with % mixed White with		Marriages of Blacks: with % mixed, Black
		Number	% mixed	Total	Black	Total	with White
1965	9,182	172	1.87	4,811	3.58	4,437	3.88
1966	9,416	201	2.13	4,704	4.27	4,811	4.18
1967	7,506	143	1.91	3,780	3.78	3,779	3.78
1968	7,839	166	2.12	3,575	4.64	4,319	3.84
1969	7,745	174	2.25	3,416	5.09	4,394	3.96
1970	7,209	160	2.22	3,086	5.18	4,151	3.86
1973	5,656	140	2.48	2,310	6.06	3,394	4.12

Source: Original compilation from Court file of marriage records; Monahan 1977: 225.

In Maryland for the three year period of June 1, 1967 to June 30, 1970 marriages of blacks to whites doubled, from .31 percent to .65 percent of all marriages, from .37 to .79 percent of marriages of whites, and from 1.83 to 3.66 percent of marriages of blacks. In Virginia there was a pronounced and steady increase in marriages between whites and blacks, with the proportion of such marriages measured as a percentage of all marriages of blacks rising from .41 percent during the last half of 1967, to .66, .94, 1.28, 1.77, 2.31, 3.79, and 4.10 percent in successive years from 1968 to 1974 (Monahan 1977: 230-237).

Tables 15 and 16, below, present United States Census data for 1970 and 1980 which show the number of intact marital and consensual unions of whites, blacks, Native Americans (American Indian, Eskimo and Aleut), Japanese, Chinese, Filipinos, and "other races." It can be noted that although increasing, marriages between whites and blacks are proportionately far less common than those of Asians and American Indians with whites. In 1980 almost half of Native American husbands and wives were living with white spouses and Asians intermarried proportionately many times more frequently than did blacks, with those who intermarried most often selecting white spouses and rarely blacks. While the proportion of white husbands living with black wives increased slightly, the percentage of black husbands with white wives doubled during the decade.

Tables 17 and 18 indicate the geographic distribution of intermarried white and black couples as reported by the United States Censuses for 1970 and 1980. Higher proportions of white husbands with black wives resided in the Northeast and West than in the South and North Central regions and a much higher percentage of intermarried black husbands and white wives resided in the West than in the other regions. The total number of interracial couples did not vary much by region, but because of the heavy concentration of blacks in the South the percentage of blacks and whites who were interracially married was far lower in the South than in the other geographic regions.

Table 15. Racially endogamous and interracial marriages, United States, 1970*

Race of husband	% of Total	Spouse of same race	White	Negro	Amer. Indian	Japanese	Chinese	Filipino	other race
White	91.4	99.6	99.6	.1	.1	.1			.1
Negro	7.6	98.5	1.2	98.5	.1	.1			.1
Am.Indian	.3	64.2	33.4	1.3	64.2	.2	.1	.2	.7
Japanese	.3	88.6	8.3	.1	.1	88.6	1.1	.5	1.3
Chinese	.2	86.5	8.3	.4	.1	2.8	86.5	.6	1.4
Filipino	.1	66.5	24.4.	1.1	.7	3.1	.8	66.5	7.4
Other race	.2	62.7	29.4	1.2	1.0	2.4	1.6	1.6	62.7
Race of wife									
White	91.3	99.7	99.7	.1	.1				.1
Negro	7.6	99.2	.7	99.2					
Am.Indian	.3	61.0	35.6	2.3	61.0	.1		.4	.6
Japanese	.4	66.8	28.0	1.1	.1	66.8	1.5	1.3	1.1
Chinese	.2	87.8	8.1	.4	.1	1.5	87.8	.6	1.4
Filipino	.1	72.8	20.9	2.0	.4	1.0	.9	72.8	2.0
Other race	.2	54.9	36.1	2.3	.9	1.8	1.4	2.6	54.9

Source: U.S. Bureau of the Census, Census of Population 1970: PC (2)-4C: 262.
* Total of 44,597,574 married couples

Table 16. Racially endogamous and interracial marriages, United States, 1980*

Race of husband	% of Total	Spouse of same race	White	Black	Amer. Indian	Japanese	Chinese	Filipino	other race
White	88.9	98.9	98.9	.1	.3	.1		.1	.4
Black	7.0	96.4	2.6	96.4	.2	.1		.1	.5
Am.Indian Eskimo, Aleut	.5	47.6	48.3	1.1	47.6	.2	.1	.2	2.5
Japanese	.4	81.4	12.1	.3	.2	81.4	2.2	.9	2.9
Chinese	.4	86.9	7.2	.3	.1	2.6	86.9	.8	2.1
Filipino	.3	77.9	14.6	.3	.5	1.4	.7	77.9	4.6
Other race	2.5	83.8	13.6	.7	.7	.4	.2	.4	83.8
Race of wife									
White	88.9	99.0	99.0	.2	.3				.4
B	7.2	98.8	.8	98.8	.1				.3
Am.Indian Eskimo, Aleut	.5	46.3	48.0	2.1	46.3	.1	.1	.3	3.3
Japanese	.3	59.4	32.7	1.9	.2	59.4	2.3	1.1	2.5
Chinese	.3	83.2	12.1	.6	.1	1.8	83.2	.6	1.7
Filipino	.3	67.5	25.0	2.5	.3	.7	.8	67.5	3.1
Other race	2.4	81.3	15.5	1.5	.5	.3	.3	.5	81.3

Source: U.S. Bureau of the Census, Census of Population 1980: PC 80-2-4C: 175.
* Total of 49,513,933 married couples

Table 17. Number and percent intermarried of Negro and White husbands and wives by geographic region, United States, 1970

Region of residence	All married couples	Number of Interracially married			Percent intermarried of all husbands and wives, by race			
		Husband Negro, wife White	Husband White, wife Negro	Total	Negro husbands	White wives	White husbands	Negro Wives
Northeast	10,647,480	12,435	8,096	20,531	1.9	.13	.08	1.3
North Central	12,563,107	10,758	4,525	15,283	1.5	.09	.04	.6
West	7,619,806	11,744	3,862	15,606	4.5	.17	.05	1.6
South	13,767,181	6,286	7,083	13,369	4.35	.05	.06	.4
Total U.S.	44,597,574	41,223	23,566	64,789	1.2	.10	.06	.7
U.S. excluding South	30,830,393	34,937	16,483	51,420	2.2	.12	.06	1.0

Source: U.S. Bureau of the Census, Census of Population 1980: PC 2-4C: 262-267.

Table 18. Number and percent intermarried of Black and White husbands and wives by geographic region, United States, 1980

Region of residence	All married couples	Number of Interracially married			Percent intermarried of all husbands and wives, by race			
		Husband Black, wife White	Husband White, wife Black	Total	Black husbands	White wives	White husbands	Black Wives
Northeast	10,429,197	22,507	8,007	30,514	3.7	.24	.08	1.4
North Central	13,111,079	23,406	5,382	28,788	3.4	.19	.04	.8
West	9,252,549	26,563	6,312	32,875	8.4	.34	.08	2.3
South	16,721,108	21,189	7,628	28,817	1.1	.15	.05	.4
Total U.S.	49,513,933	93,665	27,329	120,994	2.6	.21	.06	.8
U.S. excluding South	32,792,825	72,476	19,701	92,177	4.5	.25	.07	1.3

Source: U.S. Bureau of the Census, Census of Population 1980: PC 80-2-4C: 177-179.

Most of the interracial marriage data which were collected before 1960 were provided by the published annual marriage statistics of a few states or secured by researchers who were given access to unpublished records of marriages or marriage applications by officials of various cities and states. There was no tabulation of interracial marriages for the United States or for a majority of states. In 1963, the Vital Statistics Division of the National Center for Health Statistics began to tabulate marriages reported by those states which constituted the Marriage Registration Area of the United States, including state and national totals, by three racial categories, white, black, and other. The number of states in the Marriage Registration Area increased from 35 in 1963 to 41 in 1971 and 42 since 1979 along with the District of Columbia. The designation of race or color has been removed from marriage records of the District of Columbia and eight states during the past three decades with the result that since 1979 data on race of brides and grooms has been recorded for only 34 states. The totals compiled are of the occurrence of marriages within a given year and are based on samples of from 5 to 100 percent of the marriage records received from the registration offices of the cooperating states. From 1963 to 1985 the annual number of marriages of blacks to whites reported by these states has increased tenfold, from 1,033 to 10,661.

Thomas P. Monahan has presented data (Table 19) showing the increase in marriages between blacks and whites and blacks and other races during two four-year periods from 1963 to 1970 based on unpublished tables for 35 states which were then in the Marriage Registration Area to which he was given access by the National Center for Health Statistics.

Table 19. Proportion of Negro marriages which were of mixed race* : U.S. Registration Area
        States

		1963-1966					1967-1970			
Area**	Total	Negro White	White Negro	Negro Other	Other Negro	Total	Negro White	White Negro	Negro Other	Other Negro
Total	1.44	.95	.36	.08	.05	2.63	1.91	.55	.11	.05
12 South	.10	.05	.03	.01	.02	.82	.55	.21	.02	.04
23 North	5.06	3.38	1.26	.29	.13	7.22	5.36	1.42	.34	.10

*In showing race combinations, the husband's race is given first.
**Northern includes the District of Columbia, Alaska and Hawaii.
Source: Monahan 1976: 225.

The data presented in Table 19 give evidence of the rapid increase in marriages between white and black Americans during the 1960's. The increase was most pronounced in the South following the voiding of anti-intermarriage statutes in 1967, but was considerable in the North as well. The proportion of black-white marriages in which the bride was white increased from 72.4 to 77.6 percent between the two time periods.

Table 20 presents marriage data by race and sex for the 34 states in the Marriage Registration Area which record the race of brides and grooms each year. Marriages between whites and blacks continued to increase steadily from 1968 to 1987, from .2 to 1.0 percent of all marriages. Of intermarriages between the two major races, those of white grooms increased from .06 to .3 percent, those of white brides from .2 to .8 percent, those of black grooms from 1.6 to 6.0 percent, and those of black brides from .5 to 2.4 percent.

As eight states were not included in the Marriage Registration Area and information as to the race of grooms and brides was not reported for eight of the other states, and for the District of Columbia after 1974, the actual number of marriages and of marriages by race of groom and bride nationwide is probably fifty percent greater than the totals given in Table 20 (McDowell 1971: 54). The addition

Table 20a. Racially endogamous and interracial marriages of White and Black grooms and brides, United States Marriage Registration Area

Year	Total marriages	White grooms	White brides	Both White	Black grooms	Black brides	Both Black	Percent Black total marriages
1968	1,047,645	927,559	928,565	924,798	115,665	114,311	113,657	11.1
1970	1,071,465	948,092	949,308	944,685	114,953	112,978	112,090	10.8
1975	1,133,347	999,353	1,002,447	994,406	123,367	119,575	118,379	11.0
1980	1,192,685	1,051,816	1,053,594	1,041,475	129,393	125,006	122,325	10.5
1981	1,207,863	1,063,935	1,065,963	1,053,534	131,076	126,387	123,539	11.1
1982	1,217,745	1,072,783	1,076,070	1,062,712	129,794	125,208	122,119	10.9
1983	1,207,193	1,061,856	1,063,795	1,050,770	130,250	125,867	122,763	11.0
1984	1,213,351	1,062,890	1,065,490	1,053,088	134,207	129,915	126,400	11.4
1985	1,191,345	1,038,031	1,041,261	1,028,232	137,163	132,166	128,790	11.8
1986	1,189,120	1,031,112	1,033,451	1,018,264	142,620	136,792	133,027	12.3
1987	1,187,292	1,030,126	1,032,406	1,016,950	140,178	134,720	130,725	12.1

Table 20b. Racially endogamous and interracial marriages of White and Black grooms and brides, United States Marriage Registration Area (continued)*

Year	Numbers			Black grooms of all White with black marriages	Mixed Black-White of all marriages	Percentages			
	White groom Black bride	Black groom White bride	Total mixed			Marriages with Blacks of		Marriage with Whites of	
						White grooms	White brides	Black grooms	Black brides
1968	596	1907	2503	76.2	.2	.06	.2	1.6	.5
1970	841	2692	3533	76.2	.3	.09	.3	2.3	.7
1973	1162	4561	5723	79.7	.5	.11	.4	3.1	.8
1975	1119	4647	5766	80.6	.5	.11	.5	3.8	.9
1980	2289	6261	8550	73.2	.7	.2	.6	4.8	1.8
1981	2443	6511	8954	76.2	.7	.2	.6	5.0	1.9
1982	2476	6824	9300	73.4	.8	.2	.6	5.3	2.0
1983	2469	6572	9041	72.7	.7	.2	.6	5	2.0
1984	3115	7127	10242	69.6	.8	.3	.7	5.3	2.4
1985	2952	7709	10661	72.3	.9	.3	.7	5.6	2.2
1986	3116	8506	11622	73.2	1.0	.3	.8	6.0	2.3
1987	3239	8447	11686	72.3	1.0	.3	.8	6.0	2.4

*The numbers of marriages are for the 34 states in the Marriage Registration Area which record the race of brides and grooms
Source: Vital Statistics of the United States, 1980-1987, and unpublished tables provided by the National Center for Health Statistics, U.S. Department of Health and Human Services.

Table 21. Racially endogamous and interracial marriages of White and Black grooms and brides, selected states in United States Marriage Registration Area*

	Numbers					Percentages			Marriage to blacks of		Marriage to Whites of	
Year	Groom & bride both White	Groom & bride both Black	White groom Black bride	Black groom White bride	Total Black with White	Black of all marriages**	Black grooms of b-w marriages**	Mixed b-w of all marriages	White grooms	White brides	Black grooms	Black brides
District of Columbia												
1968	3356	4162	50	96	146	55.1	65.8	1.9	1.5	2.8	2.3	1.2
1970	2796	3858	26	126	152	57.5	82.9	2.2	.9	4.3	3.2	.7
1973	2064	3180	28	98	126	59.8	77.8	2.3	1.3	4.5	3.0	.9
South Carolina												
1975	38375	11007	38	119	157	22.3	75.8	.3	.1	.3	1.1	.3
1980	40936	11805	102	262	364	22.5	72.0	.7	.2	.6	2.2	.9
1981	41470	11679	105	307	412	22.3	74.5	.8	.3	.7	2.6	.9
1982	40652	11531	113	324	437	22.5	74.1	.8	.3	.8	2.7	1.0
1983	41186	11242	128	292	420	21.9	69.5	.8	.3	.7	2.6	1.1
1984	42192	11669	177	343	520	22.1	66.0	.9	.4	.8	2.8	1.1
1985	39975	11404	172	364	536	22.7	67.9	1.0	.4	.8	3.1	1.5
1986	40580	11898	165	357	522	23.0	68.4	1.0	.4	.9	2.9	1.4
1987	39916	11769	193	427	620	23.2	68.9	1.2	.5	1.1	3.5	1.6
Virginia												
1980	50799	7913	155	440	595	14.3	73.9	1.0	.3	.9	5.2	1.9
1981	51551	8175	175	506	681	14.6	74.3	1.1	.3	1.0	5.8	2.1
1982	51956	8401	185	482	667	14.8	72.3	1.1	.4	.9	5.3	2.1
1983	51269	8530	234	499	733	15.2	68.1	1.2	.5	1.0	5.5	2.7
1984	54065	9769	279	611	890	16.3	68.7	1.3	.5	1.1	5.8	2.8
1985	53247	10699	291	738	1029	17.8	71.7	1.5	.5	1.4	6.4	2.6
1986	52464	10783	377	781	1158	17.9	67.4	1.7	.7	1.5	6.7	3.4
1987	53068	10876	402	846	1248	18.1	67.8	1.9	.7	1.6	7.2	3.6
Delaware												
1968	3295	470	3	8	11	12.7	72.7	.3	.1	.2	1.7	.6
1970	3752	476	5	17	22	11.7	77.3	.5	.1	.5	3.4	1.0
1975	3468	435	8	15	23	11.7	65.2	.6	.2	.4	3.3	1.8
1980	3836	532	8	33	41	13.0	80.5	.9	.2	.8	5.8	1.5
1981	3939	523	10	35	45	12.7	77.8	1.0	.3	.9	6.2	1.9
1982	4158	582	15	33	48	13.1	68.7	1.0	.4	.8	5.3	2.5
1983	4748	733	16	40	71.4	14.3	71.4	1.0	.4	.8	5.1	2.1
1984	4656	677	18	45	63	13.7	71.4	1.0	.3	1.0	6.2	2.3

1985	4563	663	17	46	63	13.8	73.0	1.2	.4	1.0	6.4	2.5
1986	4510	826	29	47	76	16.5	61.8	1.4	.6	1.0	5.3	3.4
1987	4513	721	12	61	73	14.7	83.6	1.4	.3	1.3	7.7	1.6
					Florida							
1975	74999	9568	97	283	380	11.7	74.5	.5	.1	.4	2.9	1.0
1980	94225	12240	199	551	750	12.7	73.5	.7	.2	.6	4.3	1.6
1981	99013	11851	250	523	773	11.3	67.7	.7	.3	.5	4.2	2.1
1982	100901	14060	287	517	804	11.7	64.3	.7	.3	.5	3.9	2.2
1983	103212	13150	303	596	899	11.7	66.3	.8	.3	.6	4.3	2.2
1984	108258	15228	364	736	1100	13.0	66.9	.9	.3	.7	4.6	2.3
1985	105987	16298	413	791	1204	14.1	65.7	1.0	.4	.7	4.6	2.5
1986	109357	16462	475	897	1372	13.8	65.4	1.1	.4	.8	5.2	2.8
1987	116539	16115	523	1011	1534	13.0	65.9	1.1	.4	.9	5.9	3.1
					Illinois							
1980	92975	12002	286	665	951	12.2	69.9	.9	.3	.7	5.2	2.3
1981	93613	11805	326	673	999	12.1	67.4	.9	.3	.7	5.4	2.7
1982	89638	11099	318	635	953	11.8	66.6	.9	.4	.7	5.4	2.8
1983	86799	11313	316	660	976	12.4	67.6	1.0	.4	.8	5.5	2.7
1984	86564	11120	295	670	965	11.5	69.4	.9	.3	.8	5.7	2.6
1985	81831	11003	306	665	971	12.7	68.5	1.0	.4	.8	5.7	2.7
1986	79953	11684	339	692	1031	13.6	67.1	1.1	.4	.8	5.6	2.8
1987	80045	11323	347	721	1068	13.3	67.5	1.1	.4	.9	6.0	3.0
					Missouri							
1975	44481	3458	65	176	241	7.7	73.0	.5	.1	.4	4.8	1.8
1980	45529	3977	190	393	583	9.1	67.4	1.2	.4	.9	9.0	4.5
1981	46719	4382	287	411	698	9.8	58.9	1.3	.6	.9	8.5	6.1
1982	45867	4262	340	521	861	10.1	60.1	1.7	.7	1.1	10.8	7.4
1983	46259	3818	144	309	453	8.5	68.2	.9	.3	.7	7.4	3.6
1984	43697	3752	82	274	356	8.6	77.0	.7	.2	.6	6.8	2.1
1985	43424	3986	88	311	399	8.7	77.9	.8	.2	.7	7.2	2.2
1986	42747	4179	93	353	446	9.7	79.1	.9	.2	.8	7.8	2.2
1987	41815	3983	94	324	418	9.4	77.5	.9	.2	.8	7.5	2.3
					Alaska							
1968	2321	65	3	12	15	2.8	80.0	.5	.1	.5	15.2	4.4
1970	2638	78	0	12	12	2.8	100.0	.4	.0	.4	12.6	0.0
1975	3658	114	11	38	49	3.7	77.6	1.0	.3	1.0	22.9	8.7
1980	4011	132	21	51	72	4.4	70.8	1.4	.4	1.1	22.1	13.6
1981	4221	155	15	62	77	4.6	80.5	1.5	.3	1.4	25.5	8.7
1982	4871	196	22	62	84	5.2	73.8	1.4	.4	1.2	22.2	9.8
1983	4934	152	27	55	82	4.2	67.0	1.3	.5	1.0	23.5	11.0
1984	4639	199	24	65	89	5.2	73.0	1.5	.5	1.3	23.0	10.7
1985	4268	188	26	55	81	5.3	67.9	1.5	.6	1.2	20.8	12.1

Year												
1986	4178	196	20	62	82	5.1	75.6	1.5	.5	1.4	21.5	9.2
1987	4020	204	12	74	86	5.4	86.0	1.6	.3	1.7	25.7	5.6

Hawaii

Year												
1968	3734	114	12	28	40	1.9	70.0	.4	.3	.6	17.3	9.5
1970	4378	138	14	34	48	2.3	70.8	.5	.4	.7	15.0	9.1
1975	3378	82	20	50	70	2.4	71.4	.7	.6	1.1	23.6	19.2
1980	7034	196	36	114	150	3.8	76.0	1.3	.5	1.9	27.9	15.4
1981	7426	192	34	92	126	3.8	73.0	1.0	.4	1.5	22.0	14.3
1982	5700	288	32	124	156	4.6	79.5	1.2	.6	1.8	21.2	9.9
1983	6266	320	46	130	176	4.7	73.9	1.3	.8	1.7	21.4	12.3
1984	6926	232	56	148	204	3.8	72.5	1.7	.6	2.4	35.4	23.5
1985	7410	336	58	162	220	4.7	73.6	1.4	.6	1.9	24.7	14.5

Rhode Island

Year												
1968	7032	176	8	24	32	3.0	75.0	.4	.1	.3	11.8	4.3
1970	7230	160	14	24	38	2.7	63.2	.5	.2	.3	12.9	7.9
1975	6407	138	10	52	62	3.2	83.9	.9	.2	.8	26.3	6.5
1980	7034	249	12	66	78	4.5	84.6	1.0	.2	.9	20.6	4.5
1982	7426	236	31	64	95	4.4	67.4	1.2	.4	.9	20.4	11.3
1983	7584	235	27	62	89	4.2	69.7	1.1	.4	.8	20.5	10.0
1984	7546	204	24	70	94	4.0	74.5	1.2	.3	.9	24.7	10.2
1985	7539	232	22	73	95	4.3	76.8	1.2	.3	1.0	23.5	8.4
1986	7743	189	18	79	97	3.5	81.4	1.2	.2	1.0	29.2	8.7
1987	7490	280	28	68	96	4.6	70.8	1.2	.4	.9	18.8	8.9

Nebraska

Year												
1975	12589	279	4	55	59	2.6	93.2	.5	.03	.4	16.3	1.4
1980	13678	291	12	91	103	2.8	88.3	.7	.1	.7	23.5	4.0
1981	13732	334	12	65	77	3.0	84.4	.5	.1	.5	15.9	3.4
1982	13692	366	15	73	88	3.2	83.0	.6	.1	.5	16.4	3.9
1983	13107	327	14	76	90	3.1	84.4	.7	.1	.6	18.5	4.1
1984	12689	280	19	94	113	3.0	83.2	.9	.1	.7	24.6	6.3
1985	12090	314	14	86	100	3.3	86.0	.8	.1	.7	21.2	4.2
1986	11472	378	9	85	94	3.4	90.4	.8	.1	.7	20.8	2.7
1987	11111	310	21	89	110	3.6	80.9	.9	.2	.8	22.1	6.3

New Hampshire

Year												
1968	9638	64	6	26	32	1.0	81.2	.3	.1	.3	28.9	8.6
1970	9818	88	22	30	52	1.4	57.7	.5	.2	.3	25.4	20.0
1975	8602	116	11	41	52	2.0	78.8	.6	.1	.5	25.8	8.5
1980	8966	147	7	35	42	2.1	83.3	.5	.1	.4	19.0	4.5
1981	9705	107	8	51	59	1.7	86.4	.6	.1	.5	32.1	6.8
1982	10292	108	14	41	55	1.6	74.5	.5	.1	.5	27.2	11.5
1983	10618	134	20	69	89	2.1	77.5	.8	.2	.8	33.2	13.0
1984	10983	130	16	55	71	1.8	77.5	.6	.1	.5	29.4	11.0

Year	N	c2	c3	c4	c5	c6	c7	c8	c9	c10	c11	c12
1985	10873	218	19	56	75	2.61	74.7	.7	.2	.5	20.3	8.0
1986	10757	123	16	61	77	1.8	79.2	.7	.15	.6	32.8	11.5
1987	10522	76	16	67	83	1.5	80.7	.8	.15	.6	46.5	17.0
South Dakota												
1968	10012	40	0	22	22	.7	100.0	.2	.00	.2	31.4	0.0
1970	10652	32	2	36	38	.7	94.7	.3	.02	.3	50.0	5.9
1975	10495	60	5	50	55	1.1	90.9	.5	.05	.5	41.7	7.7
1980	8210	56	4	34	38	1.2	89.5	.4	.05	.7	34	6.5
1981	8114	28	4	42	46	1.0	91.3	.5	.05	.5	51.2	12.5
1982	7786	40	8	36	44	1.1	81.8	.5	.10	.5	41.9	16.7
1983	7488	44	6	24	30	1.1	80	.4	.08	.3	30	12
1984	7450	32	4	40	44	1.2	90.9	.5	.05	.6	47.6	11.1
1985	7118	42	4	48	52	1.2	92.3	.7	.05	.6	52.2	8.7
Wyoming												
1968	3752	28	1	8	9	.9	88.8	.2	.03	.2	22.2	3.4
1970	3149	23	1	4	5	.9	80.0	.2	.03	.1	14.8	4.0
1975	4660	32	2	22	24	1.2	91.7	.5	.04	.5	40.7	5.9
1980	6228	26	6	32	38	1.0	84.2	.6	.1	.5	53.3	18.7
1981	6672	26	2	28	30	.9	93.3	.4	.03	.4	50.0	7.1
1982	6552	44	2	30	32	1.1	93.7	.5	.02	.5	40.5	4.3
1983	5874	22	4	22	26	.8	84.6	.6	.08	.3	45.8	15.4
1984	5480	36	14	18	32	1.2	56.2	.4	.25	.3	32.1	28.0
1985	5120	40	4	16	20	1.2	80	.3	.07	.3	27.6	9.1
1986	4943	33	3	14	17	1.0	82.3	.3	.06	.3	28.0	8.3
1987	4446	35	7	19	26	1.3	73.1	.6	.16	.4	32.8	16.7
Montana												
1968	5998	10	0	16	16	.5	100.0	.3	.00	.3	53.3	0.0
1970	6596	12	2	10	12	.4	83.3	.2	.03	.2	35.7	14.3
1975	6962	8	0	14	14	.3	100.0	.2	.00	.2	63.6	0.0
1980	7844	15	1	23	24	.5	95.8	.3	.01	.3	56.1	6.2
1981	7707	23	0	19	19	.6	100.0	.2	.00	.2	42.2	0.0
1982	7650	16	1	26	27	.6	96.3	.3	.01	.3	56.5	5.9
1983	7550	14	4	19	23	.5	82.6	.3	.05	.3	50.0	21.1
1984	7214	13	2	21	23	.5	95.2	.5	.03	.4	56.8	13.3
1985	6705	7	3	26	29	.5	89.7	.4	.04	.3	72.2	30.0
1986	6317	8	2	20	22	.4	90.9	.3	.03	.3	69.0	20.0
1987	6071	9	5	21	26	.5	80.8	.4	.08	.3	58.3	35.7
Maine												
1968	10168	16	0	14	14	.3	100.0	.1	.0	.1	46.7	0.0
1970	10878	22	2	28	30	.5	93.3	.3	.02	.3	56.0	7.7
1975	10972	19	5	29	34	.5	85.3	.3	.05	.3	59.2	20.8
1980	11583	23	11	35	46	.6	76.1	.4	.1	.3	56.6	31.4

Inside the mixed marriage

Year											
1981	11928	28	12	50	62	.06	80.6	.5	.1	.4	64.1	30.0
1982	12111	24	8	55	63	.7	87.3	.5	.1	.5	68.7	24.2
1983	12232	26	7	49	56	.7	87.5	.4	.1	.4	64.5	20.6
1984	12264	31	6	55	61	.7	90.2	.5	.05	.4	62.5	16.2
1985	11983	33	6	53	59	.8	89.8	.5	.05	.4	60.2	15.4
1986	11596	27	8	50	58	.8	86.2	.5	.07	.4	62.5	22.9
1987	11662	21	13	58	71	.8	81.7	.6	.11	.5	73.4	38.2

Vermont

Year											
1975	4510	3	3	13	16	.4	81.2	.4	.07	.3	81.2	50.0
1980	5185	6	4	11	15	.4	73.3	.3	.08	.2	61.1	40.0
1981	5162	5	4	19	23	.5	82.6	.4	.08	.3	79.2	44.4
1982	5495	2	5	21	26	.5	80.8	.5	.09	.4	91.3	71.4
1983	5494	3	3	20	23	.5	87	.4	.05	.4	87	50.0
1984	5380	3	5	12	17	.4	70.6	.3	.09	.2	80	62.5
1985	5464	7	4	19	23	.5	82.6	.4	.07	.3	73.1	36.4
1986	5605	6	8	22	30	.6	73.3	.5	.14	.4	78.6	57.1
1987	5791	7	9	25	34	.7	73.5	.6	.15	.4	78.1	56.2

* The data presented are for all marriage records (100 percent sample size) for all years for South Carolina, Virginia, Delaware, Florida, Illinois, Missouri, Alaska, Nebraska, Wyoming, and Vermont; for a 50 percent sample for all years for the District of Columbia, Hawaii, and South Dakota and for 1968 and 1970 for Rhode Island, Maine, and New Hampshire, and for 1968, 1970, and 1975 for Montana with 100 percent sample size for the subsequent years for the latter four states.

** All marriages, less those for which race was not stated

Source: same as for Table 20.

of fifty percent to the M.R.A. totals would indicate an increase of from approximately 3755 marriages between whites and blacks in the United States in 1968 to 17,500 in 1987.

Table 21 records marriage data for the District of Columbia and 16 of the 34 states in the Marriage Registration Area which record race of grooms and brides and have a sample size of 50 percent or 100 percent for the years included. There is a fairly close relationship between the percentage of blacks and of black marriages in a state and intermarriage patterns. The states with the lowest percentages of black marriage partners have the highest percentages of black grooms and brides who intermarry, while very low percentages of white brides and grooms marry blacks. In states with high numbers of blacks and of black marriage partners the intermarriage rates of black grooms and brides are much lower. Only the District of Columbia has a black majority of total marriages and by far the highest proportion of white with black of all marriages and of white brides and grooms who marry blacks.

The five states (South Carolina, Virginia, Delaware, Florida, and Illinois) with from 11.5 to 23.2 percent black partners in all marriages have for the years 1980-1987 intermarriage rates of from .2 to .7 percent for white grooms, .6 to 1.6 percent for white brides, 2.2 to 7.7 percent for black grooms, and .9 to 3.6 percent for black brides. The five states (Alaska, Hawaii, Rhode Island, Nebraska, and New Hampshire) with from 2.1 to 5.4 percent black partners in all marriages have for the same years intermarriage rates of from .1 to .6 percent for white grooms, .4 to 1.9 percent for white brides, 15.9 to 46.5 percent for black grooms, and 2.7 to 17.0 percent for black brides. The five states with fewest blacks, with from .3 to 1.3 percent black partners in all marriages (South Dakota, Wyoming, Montana, Maine, and Vermont) have for these years intermarriage rates of from .01 to .2 for white grooms, .2 to .7 percent for white brides, 27.6 to 91.3 percent for black grooms, and 6.5 to 71.4 percent for black brides. The southern and border states, which prohibited interracial marriages until 1967, showed the greatest proportionate increase in marriages between blacks and whites from the 1970's to 1985, and by 1985 Virginia, Missouri, Florida, and Delaware had intermarriage rates comparable with those of Illinois and other northern states with high proportions of blacks. Nebraska, South Dakota, Wyoming, Montana, and other western states which prohibited interracial marriages until the 1950's and early 1960's, and with very small black populations, now have very high proportions of black grooms and brides who marry whites.

Part of the increase in interracial marriages since the 1940's may be attributed to the elimination of legal prohibitions in the 30 states in which marriages between whites and blacks were illegal and large scale migration of African-Americans to non-prohibitive northern states. In 1910, 90 percent of black Americans lived in the South. In 1940 marriages between blacks and whites were legal in but 18 states, the District of Columbia, and the territories of Hawaii and Alaska which together contained only 19 percent of the Negro population of the nation.

While marriages of black grooms to white brides are far more numerous than those of white grooms to black brides, there are regional differences as well as changes over the years. In New England during the late 19th century the first combination exceeded the second by a large margin. During and after Reconstruction, when intermarriage was permitted in the South for a brief period during the 1870's and 1880's, most interracial marriages were of white males and Negro females. This pattern prevailed in the District of Columbia before 1940, but has since reversed. Since 1967, the black male-white female combination has predominated in the South, but to a less pronounced degree than elsewhere. In recent years, the groom was black and the bride white in from about 65 to 75 percent of marriages between blacks and whites in states in which more than 8 percent of all marriages included black partners, while this combination ranged from about 80 to well above 90 percent of marriages between blacks and whites in states in which not more than 1.2 percent of marriages included a black partner.

Table 22. Black-White and Other interracially married couples, United States, 1985-1992

Year	In thousands				Percentages			
	1985	1988	1991	1992	1985	1988	1991	1992
Total married couples	51,114	52,613	53,227	53,572	100.0	100.0	100.0	100.0
Interracial married couples	792	956	994	1,161	1.55	1.82	1.87	2.17
All Black-White married couples	164	218	231	246	0.32	0.41	0.43	0.46
Husband Black, wife White	117	149	156	163	0.23	0.28	0.29	0.30
Husband White, wife Black	47	69	75	83	0.09	0.13	0.14	0.16
Other interracial married couples*	628	738	763	915	1.23	1.40	1.43	1.71
One spouse Black	29	35	43	32	0.06	0.07	0.08	0.06
Husband Black, wife Other	26	26			0.05	0.05		
Husband Other, wife Black	3	9			0.01	0.02		
One spouse White	599	703	720	883	1.17	1.34	1.35	1.65
Husband White, wife Other	362	434			0.71	0.82		
Husband Other, wife White	237	269			0.46	0.51		

Source: U.S. Bureau of the Census, <u>Population Reports: Population Characteristics--Marital Status and Living Arrangements</u> (March, 1992 and previous years)
* Other race includes American Indian, Asian, Pacific Islander, and all other than White or Black.

    The 1980 and earlier Census enumeration of marriages by race of husbands and wives can be updated from annual population reports based on national samples as shown for selected years from 1985 to 1992 in Table 22. The number of interracial Black-White and White-Other race couples has continued a steady rise, from 164,000 Black-White married couples in 1985 to 246,000 in 1992 and from 599,000 White-Other race couples in 1985 to 883,000 in 1992.

    At present, white and black partners in interracial marriages are above those who marry endogamously in level of education. A sample of marriage data from 17 states in 1980 revealed that black grooms and brides who married whites had a higher level of education than those who married blacks. While only 9 percent of black grooms who married brides of their own race had completed college, 13 percent of black grooms who married white brides held college degrees. Twenty-four percent of white grooms who married black brides had college degrees, but only 18 percent of white grooms in endogamous marriages had completed college (Wilson 1984: 45).

Table 23. Live births by race of father and race of mother, United States, 1968-1988

	Numbers			Percentages					
Year	Father White, mother Black	Father Black mother White	Total mixed, Black & White	Father Black of Biracial children	Parents both White	Parents both Black	Father White, mother Black	Father Black, mother White	Total Mixed Black-White
1968	1,786	6,972	8,758	78.7	86.0	12.0	0.05	0.21	0.27
1970	2,920	9,636	12,556	76.7	85.8	11.9	0.08	0.28	0.36
1975	2,965	13,542	16,507	82.0	85.1	11.7	0.10	0.48	0.58
1980	5,532	19,754	25,286	78.1	84.3	11.3	0.17	0.61	0.79
1985	8,047	24,271	32,318	75.1	83.6	10.9	0.24	0.74	0.98
1986	8,758	26,110	34,868	74.9	83.2	11.1	0.27	0.80	1.06
1987	9,675	28,251	37,926	74.5	82.8	11.2	0.29	0.86	1.15
1988	10,358	30,943	41,301	74.9	82.4	11.2	0.31	0.92	1.23

Source: National Center for Health Statistics (1988 and previous years)

Table 23 provides numbers and percentages by race of live births in the United States from 1968 to 1988, with reports of race of father and mother obtained from all fifty states and the District of Columiba. While there was little change in the number of children born to two white or two black parents, there was a marked and steady increase in births of children of interracial white and black parentage, from 8,758 in 1968 to 41,301 in 1988, reaching 1.23 percent of all live births in which the race of both parents was reported.

There was a slight increase in the proportion of white fathers and black mothers in the total number of children of mixed white and black parentage after 1980. Between 1968 and 1988 children born of white fathers and black mothers increased from 0.05 to 0.31 percent of all live births while children of black fathers and white mothers increased from 0.21 to 0.92 of all live births in which the race of both parents was reported.

Despite the reduction of racial barriers and of intense opposition of the public to marriages between whites and blacks during the past three decades, there remain negative attitudes which have kept the incidence of such marriages low. Most whites place blacks at the bottom of the racial and ethnic hierarchy and social distance between the races remains strong. The stigma attached to Negro genes and known ancestry is much stronger than that attached to Mongoloid or Amerindian ancestry. A person of mixed Caucasian and Amerindian descent need not conceal his non-white ancestry to avoid social rejection, but may be identified either as a white person with some American Indian ancestry or as a Native American with some Caucasian ancestry. The time when admitted African ancestry in small degree will no longer preclude acceptance as white appears to be far in the future.

During the 19th Century, American Indians were stereotyped as primitive savages and isolated on reservations. Today a majority of Native Americans in the United States live away from the reservations and nearly half of both sexes marry whites. In the early 1940's, Japanese Americans constituted a despised minority who were subjected to strong racial prejudice and discrimination and legally prohibited from marrying whites in California and several other states. Then within thirty years, with the dramatic rise in status and acceptance of Japanese-Americans, their intermarriage rate skyrocketed and now of the highly assimilated and upwardly mobile second American-born (Sansei) generation, half of brides and grooms marry Caucasians (Tinker 1982: 62-64).

Will it be possible within the foreseeable future for African-Americans to gain similar acceptance and attain intermarriage rates comparable to those of other non-white races and ethnic groups? This would require removal of the severe stigma attached to even the slightest fraction of black African ancestry. At present, fewer than one percent of white Americans marry blacks. The size of the black population would require a large percentage of whites to intermarry if black intermarriage rates were to approach those of the much smaller Native American, Japanese, and other non-white groups. As Caucasians outnumber Japanese-Americans by a ratio of 200 to one, even if all persons of Japanese descent married whites, only a fraction of one percent of white grooms and brides would become their marriage partners. In the few states in which half or more of black grooms and one-tenth of black brides marry whites there are so few blacks that fewer than one in a thousand white grooms and two to five in a thousand white brides become their marriage partners. There is no indication that more than a very small minority of whites in the states with large concentrations of blacks, mainly in highly segregated urban areas, will soon be prepared to cross the color line in marriage. But who would have predicted in the 1940's that in little more than a generation the anti-Japanese prejudice and hostility would almost have disappeared, permitting the approach to marital assimilation of Americans of Japanese descent?

Notes

[1] I shall use the terms "Negro," "black," "Afro-American," and "African-American" to refer to persons of black African descent, whether or not of part European or other ancestry, and "mulatto" to refer to offspring of Caucasian and Negro parents, or to persons of visible mixture of black and white, in accordance with historical usage. Thus, "Negro" or "black" will be employed interchangeably for the years prior to about 1970, and "black" or "African-American" for the past two decades.

[2] In this and the following excerpts from recorded interviews all names of members of interracial families are pseudonyms.

[3] Although not without fault, state marriage registration statistics would appear to give more accurate counts of legally recognized marriages than the Census totals which include a range of unions from transitory cohabitation to licensed marriages.

[4] I wish to express my thanks to Barbara Foley Wilson, a demographer, and to Sally Cuningham Clark, a statistician, at the National Center for Health Statistics, for providing tabulations and information on marriages by race of bride and groom and live births by race of mother and father for the United States and the separate states.

References

Allen, William G.
1853 The American Prejudice Against Color. London: W. and F.G. Cash.

Baker, Ray Stannard
1964 (1st edition, 1908) Following the Color Line: American Negro Citizenship in the Progressive Era. New York: Harper and Row.

Bardolph, Richard. editor
1970 The Civil Rights Record: Black Americans and the Law: 1849-1970. New York: Thomas Y. Crowell.

Bell, Derrick A., Jr.
1973 Race, Racism and American Law. Boston: Little, Brown.

Bernard, Jessie
1966 "Note on Educational Homogamy in Negro-White and White-Negro Marriages," Journal of Marriage and the Family 27:274-276.

Blassingame, John W.
1973 Black New Orleans 1860-1880. Chicago: University of Chicago.

Burma, John H.
1952 "Research Note on the Measurement of Interracial Marriage," American Journal of Sociology 57:587-589.
1963 "Interethnic Marriage in Los Angeles, 1948-1959," Social Forces 42:156-165.

Calhoun, Arthur W.
1945 (Reprint of 1918 edition) A Social History of the American Family from Colonial Times to the Present. Vol. II. New York: Barnes and Noble.

Carter, Hugh and Paul C. Glick
1970 Marriage and Divorce: a Social and Economic Study. Cambridge: Harvard University.

Catterall, Helen Tunnicliff, editor
1932 Judicial Cases Concerning American Slavery and the Negro. Washington, D.C.: Carnegie Institution of Washington.

Crester, Gary A. and Joseph J. Leon, editors
1982 "Intermarriage in the United States," Marriage and Family Review 5, No.1.

Davie, Maurice R.
1949 Negroes in American Society. New York: McGraw-Hill.

Davis, Allison, Burleigh B. Gardner and Mary R. Gardner
1941 Deep South. Chicago: University of Chicago.

Dollard, John
1937 Caste and Class in a Southern Town. New Haven: Yale University.

Drachsler, Julius
1921 Intermarriage in New York City. Columbia University Studies in History, Economics, and Public Law 94 no. 213. New York: Columbia University.

DuBois, W.E. Burghardt
1899 The Philadelphia Negro: a Social Study. Philadelphia: University of Pennsylvania.

Foster, George G.
1850 New York by Gas-Light. New York: R.M. DeWitt.

Golden, Joseph
1953 "Characteristics of the Negro-White Intermarried in Philadelphia," American Sociological Review 18:177-183.

Greene, Lorenzo Johnston
1942 "The Negro in Colonial New England 1620-1776". Columbia University Studies in History, Economics and Public Law, No. 494. New York: Columbia University.

Heer, David M.
1966 "Negro-White Marriage in the United States," Journal of Marriage and the Family 28:262-273.

Hoffman, Frederick L.
1896 Race Traits and Tendencies of the American Negro. New York: Macmillan.
1923 "The Problem of Negro-White Intermixture and Intermarriage," Eugenics in Race and State, Vol. II:175-188. [Scientific papers of the second International congress of Eugenics] Baltimore: Williams and Wilkins.

Johnston, James Hugo
1970 Race Relations in Virginia and Miscegenation in the South 1776-1860. Amherst: University of Massachusetts.

Jordan, Winthrop D.
1969 White Over Black: American Attitudes Toward the Negro 1550-1812. Baltimore: Penguin Books.

LeBerthon, Ted
1947 "Does the Constitution Uphold Mixed Marriage?" Negro Digest, 5, no. 9 (July), 52-56.

Lynn, Sister M. Annella
1953 Interracial Marriages in Washington, D.C., 1940-1947. Washington, D.C.: Catholic University of America.
1967 "Interracial Marriages in Washington, D.C.," Journal of Negro Education 36, no. 4:428-433.

Mangum, Charles S., Jr.
1940 The Legal Status of the Negro. Chapel Hill: University of North Carolina.

McDowell, Sophia F.
1971 "Black-White Intermarriage in the United States," International Journal of Sociology of the Family (special issue on intermarriage in a comparative perspective) 1 (May):49-58.

Miller, Loren
1967 The Petitioners: the Story of the Supreme Court of the United States and the Negro. Cleveland: World Publishing Co.

Monahan, Thomas P.
1970a "Are Interracial Marriages Really Less Stable," Social Forces 48:461-473.
1970b "Interracial Marriage: Data for Philadelphia and Pennsylvania," Demography 7:287-299.
1971a "Interracial Marriage in the United States: Some Data on Upstate New York," International Journal of Sociology of the Family 1:94-105.
1971b "Interracial Marriage and Divorce in Kansas and the Question of Instability in Mixed Marriages," Journal of Comparative Family Studies 2:107-120.
1976 "An Overview of Statistics on Interracial Marriage in the United States, with Data on its Extent from 1963-1970," Journal of Marriage and the Family 38:223-231.
1979 "Interracial Marriage in a Southern Area: Maryland, Virginia, and the District of Columbia," Journal of Comparative Family Studies 8: 217-252.

Morgan, A.T.
1884 Yazoo: or, On the Picket Line of Freedom in the South: a Personal Narrative. Washington, D.C.: A.T. Morgan.

Pavela, Todd H.
1964 "An Exploratory Study of Negro-White Intermarriage in Indiana," Journal of Marriage and the Family 26:209-211.

Porterfield, Ernest
1978 Black and White Mixed Marriages: an Ethnographic Study of Black-White Families. Chicago: Nelson-Hall.

Powdermaker, Hortense
   1939 After Freedom: a Cultural Study in the Deep South. New York: Viking.

Reuter, E.B.
   1918 The Mulatto in the United States. Boston: R.G. Badger.
   1931 Race Mixture: Studies in Intermarriage and Miscegenation. New York:
        McGraw-Hill.

Roberts, Robert E.T.
   1940 Negro-White Intermarriage: a Study of Social Control. Unpublished M.A.
        thesis, University of Chicago.
   1978 "Trends in Marriages between Negroes and Whites in Chicago," in Regina
        E. Holloman and Serghei Arutiunov, editors, Perspectives on Ethnicity.
        The Hague: Mouton, 173-210.

Rogers, J.A.
   1942 Sex and Race, Vol. II, The New World. New York: J.A. Rogers.

Sickels Robert J.
   1972 Race, Marriage and the Law. Albuquerque: University of New Mexico.

Somers, Robert
   1871 The Southern States Since the War, 1870-1. London and New York:
        Macmillan.

Stephenson, Gilbert Thomas
   1910 Race Distinctions in American Law. New York: Appleton.

Stone, A.H.
   1908 Studies in the American Race Problem. New York: Doubleday Page.

Taylor, Alrutheus Ambush
   1924 The Negro in South Carolina During the Reconstruction. Washington,
        D.C.: The Association for the Study of Negro Life and History.
   1926 The Negro in the Reconstruction of Virginia. Washington, D.C.: The
        Association for the Study of Negro Life and History.
   1941 The Negro in Tennessee 1865-1880. Washington, D.C.: The Associated
        Publishers, Inc.

Tindall, George Brown
   1966 South Carolina Negroes 1877-1900. Baton Rouge: Louisiana State
        University.

Tinker, John N.
   1982 "Intermarriage and Assimilation in a Plural Society: Japanese-Americans in
        the United States," Marriage and Family Review 5, no. 1:61-74.

United States Bureau of the Census
  1966 Census of Population: 1960. Marital Status. Washington, D.C.: U.S.
       Government Printing Office.
  1972 Census of Population: 1970. Marital Status. Washington, D.C.: U.S.
       Government Printing Office.
  1984 Census of Population: 1980. Marital Status. Washington, D.C.: U.S.
       Government Printing Office.
  1985- Current Population Reports: Population Characteristics- Marital Status and
  1992 Living Arrangements, Washington, D.C.: U.S. Government Printing
       Office.

Weinberger, Andrew D.
  1966 "Interracial Marriage--Its Statutory Prohibition, Genetic Import, and
       Incidence," The Journal of Sex Research 2, no. 3: 157-168.

Williamson, Joel
  1980 New People: Miscegenation and Mulattoes in the United States. New
       York: Free Press, Macmillan.

Wilson, Barbara Foley
  1984 "Marriage's Melting Pot," American Demographics (July):34-37, 45.

Wirth, Louis and Herbert Goldhamer
  1944 "The Hybrid and the Problem of Miscegenation," in Characteristics of the
       American Negro. Edited by Otto Klineberg, 249-369. New York: Harper.

Woodson, Carter G.
  1918 "The Beginnings of the Miscegenation of the Whites and Blacks," The
       Journal of Negro History 3, no. 4 (October):335-353.

Wright, Richard R.
  1912 The Negro in Pennsylvania: a Study in Economic History. Philadelphia:
       A.M.E. Book Concern.

Biographical note

        ROBERT E.T. ROBERTS (1915-) is professor emeritus of anthropology
and sociology, Roosevelt University (Chicago). A native of Chicago, he earned his
B.A. (1936) in sociology and anthropology at Central Y.M.C.A. College
(Chicago), and M.A. (1940) and Ph.D. (1956) in anthropology at the University of
Chicago. He taught at Roosevelt University from 1951 to 1985, with the exception
of two years as visiting professor of anthropology at the University of Liberia and
two years as visiting professor of anthropology at the American University in Cairo
(Egypt). He was a senior Fulbright lecturer at the University of Rajasthan in
Jaipur, India in 1985-1986 and lectured in Papua-New Guinea and Fiji for the
United States Information Agency during 1986. Since 1937 he has conducted
research on interracial and interethnic marriage, particularly in the Chicago
metropolitan area.

CHAPTER 3

CROSS-CULTURAL MARRIAGE AS A LITERARY MOTIF IN AFRICAN AND CARIBBEAN LITERATURE

Charlotte H. Bruner

Definitions of a "mixed" or "cross-cultural" marriage involve considerations of a great variety of factors and values differently weighted in varying cultures. In the United States, for example, the term "mixed marriage" might immediately connote racial difference; whereas in other cultures race might not be a difference of note but geographic location, caste, or religious preference could appear to be insurmountable obstacles to a happy union. The recent history of Africa and of the Caribbean, with the confrontation of cultural differences present in colonialism, in neo-colonialism, and in civil wars of religion and political ideology provides personal traumas for many of the peoples there. Naturally, then, writers emerging from such cultural backgrounds do reflect in some of their writings these conflicts personalized. Using a Western literary narrative form, the novel, they may center a plot upon a love story or a marriage as basis for traditional plot development. However, they can also bring new insights through a portrayal of cross-cultural or mixed marriages. Sometimes such a portrait may be the main focus of the novel. Often such a fictional union may represent symbolically a union or reconciliation between larger opposing forces, Muslim versus Christian in the Lebanese war, for example, or Black versus White in apartheid South Africa. Sometimes such a portrayal is not the major plot interest, but provides the necessary motivation for action by one of the characters.

Critics may well question the authenticity of a thesis novel, protest novel, or propaganda piece as literature. Few would deny, however, that writers generally draw from their own experience and cultural backgrounds, even if they change, modify the image, and select what they wish to emphasize, as an artist must do. Often when contemporary African or Caribbean novelists portray a mixed or cross-cultural marriage in their fiction, they reflect either their own personal experience or that of their parents. Several of them, Albert Memmi, for example, devote a whole novel (Agar or Strangers) to the story of a wrecked cross-cultural marriage, but have themselves managed to make a successful one.

Since the milieu determines in large measure the nature of the conflict, it seems appropriate to mention several novels in geographical context in which the author has used such a marriage as a dominant theme for fiction.

In anglophone West Africa, race does not play a major part in the modern literature of mixed marriages. In fact, Fred Hayford, in his autobiographical Inside America: A Black Diplomat Speaks Out (Washington: Acropolis, 1972) says : "Had I lived in Ghana all my life, the chances are that I might have married a White girl without a second thought. After my American experience, the possibility is ruled out....in America...color immediately creeps into my mind. It's a sad, sad way of life" (15).

Efua Sutherland, also a Ghanaian writer whose own marriage to an American has proved eminently successful, makes a very positive endorsement of marriage to a stranger in her poetic short story "New Life at Kyerefaso." In this case a Hausa man from the north marries Foriwa, the Queen Mother's daughter, and brings innovation and prosperity to the village.

Ama Ata Aidoo is a Ghanaian playwright who has studied in the States. Her first play, The Dilemma of a Ghost (London: Longman, 1965) takes as its main theme the marriage of Ato, a Ghanaian been-to, to Eulalie, a Black American. They met at a university, but he takes her home as a bride. The most traditional objection to the match comes from the grandmother, who is scandalized that Ato could marry a descendant of former slaves. The dilemma--will or will not the marriage succeed--occurs because Ato has not told his family in advance of his marriage, and he has not really prepared Eulalie at all for the differing life style she will have to adjust to in Ghana.

A few years later, Daniel Jenkins went to West Africa and interviewed members of just such cross-cultural marriages. His Black Zion: The Return of Afro-Americans and West Indians to Africa, (London: Wildwood House, 1975) includes a compendium of actual documents by American partners who settled in Africa, mainly in Ghana, and wrote of their frustrations in encountering such problems as expectations of polygamy, sharing of concerns with members of an extended family and the resultant loss of privacy, conflicts in belief systems, etc. Many of the respondents made marriage work despite the cross-cultural barriers, but they did describe typical frustrations. Many did not succeed. The myth of a Mother Africa to whose roots her children may return, and the myth of a "savage, primitive" Africa both proved misleading. Present paradoxes also confuse the newcomer. "The family is in every sense a varied community with which the foreign wife must come to terms...she will be faced at all times by this every-present but non-absorbent social unit"(223). A West-Indian wife accompanying her Nigerian husband home described another paradox in Africa, after living there eleven years. "The veneer is really much more a thick crust of what you know...You're living on this crust that separates you from something sort of unspeakable. I've had this feeling when dancing with my husband. He'll be very intent on dancing, and I suddenly get this throw-back feeling... and he's like a stranger, at home in some extraordinary depths I can never know " (138). Since most cross-cultural marriages of couples in Africa involve mainly middle-class expatriate women, Jenkins devotes Part Six of his book to these wives' impressions of their experiences. He summarizes their "specific difficulties" as "a redefinition of the relationship with the husband on his home territory: a uniquely complex relationship with the husband's family, which may later give rise to disputes over the upbringing of children; and the living conditions themselves " (205). Further complications occur often because of the traditional African idea of the status of women, or the husband's own alienation from his culture if he is a been-to, and also the system of obligations to the extended family put upon the couple by traditional society. Many of the examples related by Jenkins' respondents occur also in the literature portraying such marriages.

Chinua Achebe used the marriage of Obi, a promising been-to, to Clara, an osu, member of a despised class. "It was scandalous that in the middle of the twentieth century a man could be barred from marrying a girl simply because her great-great-great-great grandfather had been dedicated to serve a god, thereby setting himself apart and turning his descendants into a forbidden caste to the end of time" (No Longer At Ease. London: Heineman, 1960. pp.72-73).

Five years later, a lesser-known Nigerian writer, Chukwuemeka Ike, wrote a short novel, Toads for Supper, (London: Fontana, 1965), based on marriage practices, particularly the traditional resistance to a union between an Ibo and a Yoruba. The hero's friend, Chima, advises Amadi on page one "That girl is Yoruba, you are Ibo. The twain cannot meet." In the course of the story, Amadi actually proposes marriage to three women, breaks all three promises, becomes reconciled with each, and finally ends in despair, mainly because he cannot resist the attraction the Yoruba Aduke has for him. He has made a death-bed promise to his father to carry on the marriage arranged during infancy to a beautiful young girl of his own ethnic group and village. Aduke goes mad.

Although the colonial atmosphere in West Africa in the English-dominated areas resembled in many ways that in the French and Belgium occupied territories, some differences in the European imposed value systems are markedly different in fact and in the literature. Obviously the training in the French language as a good in itself made a strong imprint not only in competency but in literary models on the educated elite of Senegal, Ivory Coast, the Cameroons, etc. Early, the only means for higher education for gifted students was by way of secondary school William Ponty on Goree Island and then university study in Paris. The chosen students, males, were therefore abroad at the usual courtship-marriage years. Naturally they met young French women as potential partners, and often married them.

Many of the educated elite of this generation also fought for France in World War II. Racial frictions during the war years intensified in Europe and in Africa thereafter. President Senghor was imprisoned in Europe as a prisoner of war--and met there his first humiliation as a black African among the French officers interred there. The consciousness of racial, Hitlerian-Aryan superiority hit not only Jews and Gypsies, but also Africans as well, and became a consideration in cross-cultural marriages. Sembene Ousmane's O pays, mon beau peuple, (Paris: Presses Pocket, 1975), somewhat autobiographical, is a fictional account of a Senegalese veteran who takes his French wife home. He is cognizant of problems, of course, but not fully aware of the burdens to be imposed upon his new wife by his own mother and all her in-laws.

Rene Maran was born on shipboard when his Guyanese parents moved to Martinique. Maran studied in a French lycee and served ten years in the Belgian Congo. He wrote a semi-autobiographical account of an almost failed cross-cultural marriage in Un homme pareil aux autres (Paris: A. Michel, 1962, c 1947). Here the black hero does ultimately marry a French wife, as Maran did, only after a period of upset and self-doubt provoked by the scorn of a white woman on shipboard who inadvertently reveals latent racial prejudice.

One of the earliest published writers of this generation, Guinean Camara Laye, however, in his allegorical Le Regard du Roi (Radiance of the King, Paris: Plon, 1956), shows a revolutionary reversal of this racism when his white hero, Clarence, is brought to abject humiliation upon the realization that he has been used to beget light-colored children, a curiosity prized by the subjects of the African King.

In Chiekh Amadou Kane's allegorical novel L'Aventure Ambigue (Ambiguous Adventure, Paris: Julliard, 1961), Samba Diallo, son of the Chief and future leader of his people, comes to Paris to gain a doctorate in Philosophy. He encounters Lucienne, daughter of a Protestant pastor. He is attracted to her for her blue eyes and blondness, but more for her idealistic commitment to communism, at obvious variance with her parents' beliefs. But Samba feels his mission to return to his country, to his religion, to his destiny, so strongly that he must reject Lucienne. Later he also rejects Adele, daughter of a Senegalese but born in Paris, because she can never be African, and he is as "at least a 'half-breed' only by his culture"(146).

By the time Mariama Ba received the first Noma Award, 1980, her second novel, Un Chant Ecarlate (Scarlet Song, Dakar: Nouvelles Eds. Africaines, 1981) was written but not published. It takes as major motif the failure of a racially mixed marriage between a European wife and a Senegalese husband. Although the main characters are stereotypic, and the husband's change-over from rational, idealistic lover to cruel and unfeeling egoist is unconvincing, the machinations of the African mother-in-law ring true in precise detail. Yaye Khady vows to break up Ousmane's marriage to Mireille from her first knowledge of it. Despite Mireille's conversion to Islam, her payment of tribute gifts to her in-laws decreed by custom, her attempts to learn Wolof, and her bearing of a son, Yaye Khady is implacable, making a meager celebration at the child's naming, spreading gossip and rumors, encouraging Mireille's rival Ouleymatou to seduce Ousmane in the hope of becoming his second wife. Ultimately, Ousmane's father, a holy man who had chosen to ignore the situation, can only reaffirm his faith in Allah. Mireille, in a fit of madness, poisons her child and stabs Ousmane, crying "the child "neither black nor white" has no place in the world." She is overpowered finally; Ousmane survives but the child dies.

In East Africa, literature written in English found international attention at least a decade after that of West Africa. Several contemporary novels treat of marriages between partners of differing backgrounds. In The River Between (London: Heinemann, 1965), James Ngugi's first novel, tragedy develops when two young people in love are separated by religious beliefs and tribalisms, not by ethnic origin. "The two ridges lay side by side....When you stood in the valley, the two ridges ceased to be sleeping lions united by their common source of life. They became antagonists." So on the two ridges, the peoples are divided, as one ridgesite has been colonized and converted to Christianity, and the other remained traditional. Waiyaki feels called to learn the knowledge of the whites and then to lead his people to their destiny. He falls in love with Nyambura, a Christian. Waiyaki wants to learn by education to reconcile the factions of his people, but he is forced into political action for land reform. He dreams of de-polarizing the factions, ever more antagonistic. He almost succeeds in convincing all the "children of Mumbi" to forget their differences, until his enemy confronts him with Nyambura, a Christian, and asks if he is truly going to marry her against tribal custom. When he affirms his desire, he knows that he is actually sentencing both of them to death from the action of the Kiama traditional judges.

The Sudanese writer, Tayeb Salih, used the cross-cultural marriage theme as his symbol for cross-cultural myths of misunderstanding in his Arabic novel, Season of Migration to the North (London: Heinemann, 1969). In this frame story a mysterious stranger in a Sudanese village tells his history to a been-to student. Mustafa recounts his own education in Britain, to which he had felt drawn by its mystery, its Westernisms, its mythical women. Mustafa has had many affairs with English women, who found in him the mystery of the unfathomable East. They succumbed to it, to him, and often to death by suicide afterwards. Ultimately, he married one of them, Jean Morris, an Englishwoman. This marriage was one of constant conflict and ecstasy, infidelity, reviling, and passion. Finally he stabbed her. He started to drown himself in the river, but, failing that, decided to return to the Sudan where he belonged, marry a local woman, and lead a traditional life. The whole is "an Arabian Nights in reverse, enclosing a pithy moral about international misconceptions and delusions" (cover).

Bessie Head, exile from South Africa to Botswana, provides in her writing a link between southern and eastern Africa. She is also the daughter of a mixed marriage. Her white, well-to-do mother married a black groom who then mysteriously vanished. She was confined to bear her daughter in a hospital for the insane. The mixed race child grew up in foster homes and was educated as a teacher. Rejected from her family and her society, she left for Botswana where she lived until her death in 1987. Head frequently exploits the theme of marriage and sexual encounters in terms of black and white, in images of Black Africa's domination over half-castes, like herself, in symbols of European infiltration into African traditional culture. She also uses themes of male dominance in marriage as representing political oppression by the powerful over the weak and downtrodden. "My revulsion for that particular sort of black person is simply because I have always belonged to the scum edge of life where the broad mass of people are."

Head's novel, Maru (London: Heinemann, 1972) features the marriage of Margaret Cadmore, of Baswara (Bushman) ethnic origin, and Maru, leader of a Botswana village. The success of this marriage can provide for all of the people a symbol of triumph over racism. "The Baswara myth is that they were the true owners of the land in some distant past, but that they had been conquered by the more powerful Botswana tribes and from then onwards assumed the traditional role of slaves. Baswara people were also abhorrent to Botswana people because they hardly looked African, but Chinese" (p.98).[2] Maru does marry Margaret, and they go off happily together to a distant cottage, surrounded by flowers. The Baswara people feel as though the cave they have been confined in has opened in a blaze of light.

In South Africa, almost all writing concerns apartheid. Naturally, the mixed marriage, illegal until most recently under the immorality (later the Conspiracy) Act, makes a startling and personalized literary motif for emphasizing inequality, caste privilege and blatant inhumanity all based on "color" differences. Even before the Emergency of 1960 when a notable crackdown after the Sharpville Massacre imposed even more oppressive measures than before, some writers had shown fictionally the problems of cross-racial unions. A very early novel by Peter Abrahams, The Path of Thunder (1948, just recently reissued, Cape Town: David Philip, 1984) showed a love affair between black man and a white woman. Alan Paton's Cry the Beloved Country (1953, which first appeared in 1948), was followed by Too Late the Phalarope, 1953 (New York: Scribners) which won much less recognition. It opens with several instances of legal action against contact between races, contact even with slight social or sexual implication. A young white Afrikaner asks a black girl for her name, and narrowly avoids punitive judgement because the magistrate only scolds him in secret. A farmer named Smith is sentenced to death because he and his white wife killed his black servant for fear that his sexual relationship with a black would come to light. The novel's main protagonist, Afrikaner police lieutenant, Jakob van Vlaanderen, rugby idol, "Lion of the North," church deacon, model family man, is brought down because he confessed to committing an offense under the Immorality Act. Throughout the novel, the conflicts are shown in the minds of the Afrikaner protagonists. The black victim, Stephanie, is portrayed sketchily only as a devoted mother willing to sacrifice to keep her child with her.

Lewis Nkosi, reknowned critic of African literature, was avowedly an idealistic student and then journalist in Johannesburg in the Fifties. A formative period, he recalls, in which "We had no literary heroes...we longed desperately for literary heroes we could respect and with whom we could identify" (Zell 1983: 435-436). He has lived abroad ever since he took a one-way exit permit to study at Harvard with a Nieman Fellowship. His early play, The Rhythm of Violence (London: Three Crowns, 1964) though tragic in its outcome, shows the idealism he referred to--the hope for romantic love between a white and a black, a hope Nkosi also lived when he married an Englishwoman. In the play, a group of left-wing students plan to bomb Johannesburg City Hall. Among the multi-racial student group is a new convert, Afrikaner Sarie, who falls in love at first sight with Tula, a Bantu, who returns her affection. The play ends in tragedy because Tula, discovering that Sarie's father had gone to the City Hall to break with the government, slips out to detonate the bomb, but dies in the explosion along with the father. Sarie is left to lament her and her country's loss at a failed understanding. More recently Nkosi has also explained the relative dearth of both novels and plays in South Africa due not just to the difficulty of survival, but of "the absorbing, violent and immediate nature of experience" there that makes prolonged reflection or extended artistic activity very difficult. Nkosi's novel Mating Birds, 1986, takes the sexual relationship between a white woman and a black man as its main theme.

More recently, a Capetown writer, Fatima Dike, resident playwright in the Space Theatre, produced her The First South African, 1977. Dike described the theme to interviewer Stephen Gray. "Based on a true story--about a man whose mother was black and whose father was white. Through some fate in the genes he was born white physically, blond hair and blue eyes...and was classified as a Coloured when he was old enough.... The question was: What is that man? That man is not white; he's the shadow of a black man. And he's not coloured...We had the father, who was a very passive black man who accepted what the system was doing had had no say. We had the mother, who was a very bright woman and fought for her son." Thus Dike says of her play that she tried to bridge a cultural gap for her audience in a single cast (Amelia House Checklist: Black South African Women Writers in English, Evanston: Northwestern Univ. Press, 1986). Dike has been able to publish only two of her plays. Of course, Athol Fugard in his play The Blood Knot shows the dissimilarity of two brothers. The apparent-white versus the apparent-black when they try to play these roles even in jest almost provokes fratricide. Fugard's play poses the same dilemma.

Nadine Gordimer is one of our finest contemporary writers. She has won international recognition and the Nobel prize for her many novels and short stories. Electing to remain in South Africa, she has moved to an increasingly forceful denunciation of apartheid. She has often written fiction predicting changes in the way of life there once Apartheid and its supporting government are terminated. In an early short story, "Inkalamu's Place," (Livingstone's Companion, New York: Viking, 1975), she portrays a cross-cultural marriage when the white narrator returns to the home of her childhood and revisits also the Scotch overseer's mansion of the estate. There she finds only Inkaluma's daughter by a local woman, who is tending a roadside stand. The old mansion Inkaluma had built British style with its fake pretentiousness is disintegrating at the end of the avenue. The visitor recalls: "My father and mother were white...and Inkaluma's wives were native women. Sometimes my father would pay a call on Inkaluma, in the way of business...but my mother never accompanied him...He gave us sweets while those of his own children who had slipped inside stood in the background. We did not feel awkward, eating in front of them, for they were all shades of brown and yellow-brown, quite different from Inkaluma and my father and us" (Unwinding Threads, p.121-122).

July's People is a fictional representation of the crumbling of the South African white government in the face of revolution, and the adjustment or inability to adjust of a white family caught up in the struggle. Gordimer's recent novel, A Sport of Nature (New York: Knopf, 1987), a main Book of the Month Club selection, shows South Africa during the life of the main protagonist, Hillela. She experiences the emergency at seventeen, and goes on to become a major force in the ensuing revolution and overthrow of the racist rule. Hillela, is a sport of nature-- and a hope for the future, uninhibited by caste, class or racial barriers. She lives in guerrilla territory, working underground. She marries Whaila Kgomani, a black rebel leader in exile, and works with him until his assassination. Subsequently, she travels and works abroad independently for her country's freedom. Later she remarries a Nkrumah-like black general, who becomes president of his own country. They form a happy union, albeit an unconventional one. She and he stand with her at the end when the flag of freedom rises above South Africa.

Amelia Blossom House, now an exile from South Africa, wrote a short story, "Conspiracy," as a part of her thesis at the University of Louisville in 1977 (Unwinding Threads, ed. C. Bruner, London: Heinemann, 1983). The plot is simple but telling. A young colored girl, Amy, and a Jewish boy, Saimon, meet as students and plan to marry as soon as they can escape from South Africa. Despite their careful plans, the night before their departure they are discovered together and sentenced to seven years of prison under the Conspiracy Act. South African playwright, Athol Fugard, bases his play, Statements after an Arrest under the Immortality Act, 1974, on much the same theme.

In the traditional Maghreb area of former French domination in North Africa, family, clan and village ties are particularly strong. Ethnic diversity is not featured in contemporary literature nearly as much as are schisms in religious or even sectarian dogmas.[4] Dichotomies between Muslim-Christian, Suni-Shiite, Western (French) dominance--Persian (Arab) control are strong, and even nationalistic patriotism may give way to the fervor of an all-encompassing Muslim religious state. Similarly, today Iranians may encircle Armenian Catholics, but seek to exterminate followers of their own "race" who follow Bahai.

In the soothsinger Kabyle Amrouche family, both a mother and her daughter wrote of difficulties encountered in cross-cultural marriages, some details reflecting their own experiences. Fadhma Aith Mansour Amrouche (Histoire de ma vie, Paris: Maspero, 1968) succeeded in a love match with her husband against much clan opposition. At sixteen she married him, a stranger, knowing only that he was kind. He had seen her working in a French missionary hospital and had fallen in love with her a year before, but his family had threatened to kill him if he married her--a bastard and a Catholic--even though her family was of a respected kinship tribe. The eighteen-year-old suitor had to wait a year, but did then marry her despite parental objection. Nonetheless, by Kabyle custom thereafter Fadhma was part of her husband's clan, subject to the whims and abuse of her mother-in-law, and allowed only three times thereafter to have contact with her own mother. She felt forever after a stranger.

Fadhma and her husband raised five sons and a daughter, although they had many tribulations, displacements and much poverty. Fadhma taught her children the folklore and songs of her Kabyle heritage, in Berber words and sound patterns, to pass on and preserve before the oral tradition could die out. The only daughter, Marguerite Taos Amrouche, studied in Spain, married a Frenchman, and lived in France. Several of her novels reflect her own cross-cultural upbringing, and some of the difficulties of cross-cultural marriages. (Several Maghreb writers seem to concentrate on such problems, even when they themselves have succeeded in surmounting the difficulties and have made successful marriages, generally, however, becoming expatriates in France.)

Marguerite Taos Amrouche's novel, Jacinthe Noire, La rue des Tambourins (Paris: Table Ronde, 1960) is partly autobiographical. It portrays women of three generations in a Kabyle family, the traditional Muslim grandmother, the mother, a converted Christian who dresses like a European, and the granddaughter, Marie-Corail, the odd one out who feels isolated from both worlds. Her fiance, Bruno, breaks with her. "Afraid of mystery; my origins, my past, the language of my ancestors, which he would never speak, everything that should have attracted him repelled him instead" (190). The story of this rupture is the theme of a sequel still in manuscript, Solitude, ma mère. A third novel starts similarly with the broken engagement of Amena, whose exoticism repelled her European suitor. Amena later marries Oliver abroad. He does accept her background and her differences. Nonetheless, their conflicting temperaments make their union an uneasy one. Finally, after a schizophrenic identity crisis, Amena tries to content herself with her child, and her journals, finding her solace in writing the Kabyle songs and folklore and thus preserving her ancestral culture (Jacqueline Arnaud review, Esprit, Jan, 1977 of L'amant imaginaire).

Albert Memmi of Tunisia has devoted much of his life and most of his writing, fictional and scientific, to a study of socio-psychological implications of humans' perceptions of their identities. An expatriate Tunisian Jew, married to a French woman, dean at one of France's great universities, he has personally felt and philosophically analyzed conflicts of colonialism, religious tradition, racial ambiguities, and psychic dependencies. Although in his essays, he avowedly distills his generalizations, removing from them personal human emotions, in his fictional portraits he gives a poignant and telling glimpse of many individual conflicts and crises of identity, often from his own personal experience.

In Memmi's first, semi-autobiographical novel, La Statue de Sel, (Pillar of Salt Paris: Gallimard, 1972) the protagonist Mordicai, is like his author, a young Jewish boy reared in a ghetto in Tunis. He wins a scholarship to study at a French lycee there, ultimately is inducted into the French army, and finally goes to South America. Mordicai's earliest years are complicated by a lack of communication and of common endeavor between his parents and their families as well. His mother is illiterate, a Berber woman, who experiences a peak of elation in performing a ritualistic traditional dance at a healing, exorcist ceremony. Her social life is mainly bound up with her family, who live in close juxtaposition to her and share gossip, hospitality, and close intimacy. It is the father, a Jewish shopkeeper, who presses for Mordicai's education and encourages him to seek wider horizons even beyond the ghetto in the alien French culture.

In Agar (Strangers, Paris:Buchet-Chastel, 1955) Memmi makes a cross-cultural marriage the main theme of his novel. A young Tunisian student studying in France marries a French girl and takes her back home. Despite their idealism and sincere mutual affection, the Mid-Eastern culture, embodied by his extended family, gradually ruins all chances for happiness for the "mis-matched" couple.

Memmi's clear realistic portrayal of resentments and misunderstandings occurring when the French wife cannot placate her husband's extended family does not mirror his own marriage, but does show his sensitivity and acuity in anticipating the many pitfalls possible in such marriages. Nor is Memmi alone in his concern for woman's subservient position in the Maghreb countries. With the peculiar flowering of francophone literature from the time of World War II up to and including the Algerian war of independence, several of the prominent male novelists of this period voiced similar concerns in their fiction about North African women who are subject to male dominance in word, thought, and deed. Often they drew on their mothers and their sisters in semi-autobiographical sketches, making a strong indictment of local customs. Like Memmi, Mohammed Dib of Algeria and Driss Chraibi of Morocco did marry French women and live in France today.

Another Moroccan writer, Abd Alkarim Ghallab, writing in Arabic, treats of cross-cultural marriage in his novel, We Buried the Past, (Beirut, 1966). The protagonist, Abd, loves and wishes to marry a French girl, but eventually his duty to his country and to his parents force him to renounce her. "My world is separating itself from the past and I cannot be allowed to take for myself a wife from a world behind this struggle..." (Evelyne Accad, Veil of Shame, Sherbrooke, Naaman, 1978, p. 88).

Critic Evelyne Accad finds a "striking cultural contrast" between francophone and Arabic writers in their frequent portrayals of the "European wife" motif. Accad claims that North African male writers generally describe the European woman favorably, even picturing her as a wife who easily adapts to Arab society as in Feraoun's works, and even Memmi's Agar. However, Accad also asserts that many Arabic writers justify the double standard of the Muslim world, noting that "the Arab male seems perpetually ready to have sexual intercourse with the alluring foreign female and he may even make a pretense of loving her, but he inevitably deserts her for the 'virgin back home'" (163).

Third-world women writers typically gain prominence and international attention much later than men do. The Arabian, Egyptian, and North African women writing today often are themselves products of cross-cultural marriages and international educations. By contrast, "None of the women writing in Arabic expresses the drama found in Taos or Debeche at being the issue of two cultures, at being taught two languages, at seeing two religions confronting each other within the same family" (Veil 163). The cross-cultural parentage in several cases made it possible for the North African francophone writers to find a European readership not available to the Arabic writers.

Just as earlier Fadhma Amrouche found personal solace in writing when she felt torn between cultures, families, religions, so some later francophone women writers have found creative expression possible and an audience abroad if not at home. Marguerite Taos Amrouche, like her Amena, did so. Andree Chedid, whose parents were of Lebanese-Syrian origin, considers herself an Egyptian writer, had an Egyptian passport, grew up in Cairo and attended the American University there. She married a doctor and now lives, writes, and published in France. Assia Djebar, Algerian Muslim, found a readership abroad in France and often an asylum there--because she communicated in French.

Evelyne Accad is of Swiss and Lebanese parentage. She built her first novel, L'excisée (Paris, Harmattan, 1982) on the motif of a mixed marriage. The protagonist, E. daughter of fundamentalist Swiss missionaries in a mid-eastern city, seeks escape and freedom from her puritanical father by running off with a Palestinian teacher, P. He has beguiled her with promises of working together to bring about a peaceful and non-sexist world, but once he takes her to his own home she must assume the veil and the docility of a traditional Muslim wife. For Accad, the traumatization, physical and spiritual, of female excision is a symbol for the horror of violence and war everywhere. In the tragic outcome of the novel, E. sacrifices her marriage, her unborn child, and her very life in trying to resist this practice.[5]

In recent literature of the Caribbean, the mixed-marriage motif becomes a predominant one. Portrayals are as varied as are the cultural and historic backgrounds of the several regions concerned. Not surprisingly, many degrees of color and of slave ancestry still mark differentiations in Haiti, where two hundred years ago legal status was determined according to 170 categories of black-white blood mixture. On the Corentyne coast of Guyana a different range of color-mixing sets privilege, and those of East Indian descent are lower on the social scale than those of African slave origins. In the French possessions, caste as well as color involves access to French education, French culture, and even life abroad. In Belize, the Latin-American citizen has a slightly higher caste than the English-speaking local black inhabitant. At least, these are elements in Caribbean literature visible and potent in contemporary writers' portrayals of mixed marriages there.

Maryse Condé, Guadeloupian scholar, critic, and novelist, married an African of Bambara origin, and, later, a white European. Her novel, Une Saison à Rihata, (Paris: Laffont, 1981) like all her works a study of power, politics, and cultural diversity, centers the plot on a cross-cultural marriage. Marie-Hélène, an Antillian, is involved with a pair of African brothers. She married Zek, the eldest, but took his brother, Madou, as a lover and father of her daughter. Zek and Marie-Hélène live in Rihata in an African country, resembling both Guinea and Senegal, where Zek is a minister of development. Marie-Hélène had met Zek in Paris where both were students, and had married him in spite of the skepticism of his family, who found her "white" because of her light color, and ever a stranger. She feels distanced from Zek's extended family, not only by her color and island origin, but also because she is one of the educated elite of her own culture and never feels she fits the mold of the typical African wife-mother-breeder they extol. When Madou comes to Rihata as a cabinet minister she has not seen him for some time. She feels awkwardly pregnant, aging, undesirable. She does renew an affair with Madou, which is cut short by his murder. Afterward, Zek, putting all rancor aside, reaffirms with her their marriage and their mutual affection. In this novel of shifting loyalties, political involvements, Condé traces without judging many aspects of struggle in this cross-cultural marriage. Family pressures affect both marriage partners. Zek's father uses Zek's marriage to an outsider to justify his own misprizing of Zek and favoritism of Madou. The cousin of Marie-Hélène,

Christophe, is uneasy in Africa or in France because of his color. He longs to go to Haiti to find the mulatto status a desirable one.[6]

Myriam Warner-Vieyra is also from Guadeloupe. In Le Quimboiseur L'Avait Dit (Paris: Presence Africaine, 1980, translated by Dorothy Blair As the Sorcerer Said, London: Longman, 1982) she shows the destruction of a young girl's sanity because her mother has formed a mixed marriage and tries to exploit her. The beautiful, ambitious mother divorced her local fisherman husband and married a white Frenchman. She brings young Zetou to France to share life in the new couple's household, planning to sell her daughter in marriage to an older French tycoon. Zetou in despair turns to her step-father for solace. He seduces her, with the connivance of the mother. The novel opens and ends as Zetou, not quite sixteen, is in a children's ward for the insane. The author's second novel, Juletane (Paris: Presence Africaine, 1982; translated by Betty Wilson, London: Heinemann, 1987) portrays a broken marriage between a West Indian woman and a Senegalese man. The wife, Juletane, is unprepared for a polygamous life when her husband takes her to Africa. Her frustrations and the death of her child are overwhelming, and she dies insane.

In Beka Lamb, (London: Heinemann, 1982) Belize's first novel, the author, Zee Edgell, juxtaposes two adolescent girls. Beka at fourteen is supported by an array of understanding and sympathetic relatives, from her great-grandmother on. But her friend Toycie, a brilliant seventeen-year-old student, lacks such support. Toycie loves and plans to marry Emelio, her classmate. Of Maya Indian and Spanish origin, he is above Toycie in social standing. Toycie becomes pregnant with Emelio's child. He virtually abandons her, as his mother insists he must go on with his education and attend university without being saddled with a wife. Toycie is expelled from her school, which alone could give her status and meaningful employment. She succumbs to disillusion, despair, madness, and finally death. The multi-layered society of Belize offers, with the hope of independence, a more equal opportunity for blacks, but only through education. At the vacation house Beka's family share on the caye with the rich Blanco family, Agency employers, "as is often the case, wealth, class, color and mutual shyness, kept the children of the two families apart, although they occupied the top and bottom of the same house" (51). So Beka's world is complicated by the strata of her society: whites, creoles, 'Panias like Emelio, and Caribs ("descendants of African slaves who escaped from West Indian plantations by paddling their way to St. Vincent. p. 68). "It was a relatively tolerant town where at least six races with their roots in other districts of the country, in Africa, the West Indies, Central America, Europe, North America, Asia and other places, lived in a kind of harmony. In three centuries, miscegenation, like logwood, had produced all shades of black and brown, not grey or purple or violet, but certainly there were a few people in town known as red ibos..." Nonetheless, "Each race held varying degrees of prejudice concerning the other," making cross-racial marriages difficult (11-12). When Toycie first confides to Beka her love for Emelio, Beka wisely says, "'Panias scarcely ever marry creole like we, Toycie" (47).

In Liliane Devieux's Haitian novel, L'amour, oui. La mort, non (Sherbrooke: Naaman, 1976) a cross-caste marriage is planned between high-caste Rachel, a "mulatresse fine," who is a medical student and who speaks French at home with her cultivated family, and Gabriel, a black social worker who helps his mother, a single parent and small shopkeeper, to raise the younger children. They speak Creole. Rachel and Gabriel meet surreptitiously. Idealistically, they plan to marry and work together to better the condition of Haiti's downtrodden masses. They both know their parents would try to forbid the match, Rachel's family from snobbery, and Gabriel's mother from her need of his economic support. Their idyll is interrupted when Gabriel must go to New York to get better pay, and then to service in the Vietnam War. When he is reported missing, Rachel has a nervous breakdown. Later, she continues with her education and afterward fulfills their common dream by devoting herself to give medical care to the impoverished. DeVieux here is affirming, like Gordimer, the possibility of a future without racial barriers when unlikes will be able to marry and work toward a free society.

A very complicated family structure involving mixed-marriages in yet another differently constituted Caribbean society forms the background for Edgar Mittel Hotzer's Guyanese novel, Corentyne Thunder (London: Heinemann, 1970, reprint from Eyre and Spottiswoode, 1941). Here the East Indian cowminder, Ramgolall, belongs to the lowest stratum of the local society. As an immigrant, he had worked out his indenture in the cane fields, but later acquired and minded his own cows. He sells the milk with the help of his two daughters, Beena and Katree. The girls are illiterate and so poor that each owns only one dress. In contrast, Big Man Weldon, the proprietor of a cattle ranch, is rich, and white. He lived with and later married Ramgolall's daughter Sosee, who bore him seven children. She "possessed a car and many jewels. She had done well in life and Ramgolall was pleased with her"(9). Weldon and Sosee have a son, Geoffrey, who is Weldon's favorite. He is light, seen as "white," and looks forward to an English education and all the prestige it conveys. Ramgolall's other child by his first marriage, Baijan, owns a rice mill in Essequibo. Baijan's elaborate and pretentious marriage points up the contrast with Beena's hopeless love for a married peasant, and Katree's pathetic, incestuous affair with Geoffrey. Geoffrey "has no roots, no responsibility," says critic Louis James (6). Distancing himself from his mother's world, he will never really fit elsewhere. James further claims that the generational difference affects marriage behaviors here. Weldon does eventually marry Sosee because he feels morally responsible for their large family. However, Geoffrey, who engages in his affair with Katree with no intention of marriage and no feeling of responsibility for their coming child is different. A child of a mixed marriage himself, he does not have the confidence or the authority of his white father. Though arrogant, he is unsure. He even foretells his eventual suicide, caught between cultures. Mittelholzer, "a dark 'throwback' in a 'white' family" actually did end his own life.[7] The novel is important for the presentation of a family dynasty with many varieties of mixed marriages, some successful, some not, against the background of Guyana's pluralistic society.

These fictional treatments of mixed and cross-cultural marriages represent an important theme in contemporary African and Caribbean literature. The theme is not new to literature. Problems arising from mixed unions have long been recognized. When Shakespeare wrote, "Let me not to the marriage of true minds admit impediments" he hopes not to permit or allow such thwarting of true conviviality. The Christian church has always sanctified marriage as primarily a spiritual union--"whom God hath joined together, let no man put asunder"--the spiritual above the corporeal.

In the main, the authors considered here seem to stress problems and subsequent failures of cross-cultural and mixed marriages. Nonetheless, there are also writers today who, somewhat didactically, do portray young couples working out their own such marriages and even convincing their communities of the rightfulness of their break from tradition. In <u>Honeymoon for Three</u> (East African Pub. House, 1975) by Jane Bakaluba, Niaga rejects a suitor chosen for her and marries Nuwa. She is a traditional animist and he is a Christian clergyman's son. Facing "apparently insurmountable obstacles, the young couple are able to bring together traditional and modern elements to society," and win over all family opposition (Taiwo, 39)[8]. Miriam Were from Kenya, in several of her novels, points out cross-cultural marriages where conflicts are resolved and the couple is recognized as a model for the future. In <u>Your Heart is my Altar</u> (Nairobi, East African Pub. House, 1980), "The love which gradually develops between Chimoli and Aluvisia is used to bridge the gap between people and religions, and to establish an enduring peace between two warring clans to which they belong...They show by their love for each other that ethnic hatreds need not be passed from one generation to another." (Taiwo, 175). Bakaluba and Were do write for young readers of their own countries, and may be seen as more idealistic than convincing.

Even the authors who themselves have made enduring cross-cultural or racially mixed marriages often in their fiction show marriages failing in circumstances similar to their own. Most writers, indeed, who treat this theme in their fiction <u>admit</u> and affirm the many impediments that do exist to unions of <u>minds</u> who seek to join without respect to color, ethnic, religious, or geographical barriers.

<u>Notes</u>

1   Betty McGinnis Fradkin, "Conversations with Bessie," <u>World Literature Written in English</u>, 17/2, Nov. 1978, p. 433.

2   Bessie Head, "Social and Political Pressures That Shape Literature in Southern Africa" <u>World Literature Written in English</u>, 18/1 April 1979, p. 21.

3   Hans Zell, <u>A New Reader's Guide to African Literature</u>, London: Heinemann, 1983, pp. 435-6.

4   Marguerite Taos Amrouche translated into French many of the Berber songs, proverbs, tales, and poems. "The Magic Pod" shows an evil Negresse who tricks the berber heroine, who subsequently wins out, has the Negresse dismembered and burnt. Similar racist references are frequent in this folk literature. A proverb: "Un nègre s'il est jaune est perdu," or, "Comme qui frotterait un nègre esperant qu'il deviendra blanc" (20, 156). <u>Le Grain Magique</u>, Paris: Maspero, 1969.

5   Etel Adnan wrote a novel in French, <u>Sitt Marie Rose</u>, (Paris: Des Femmes, 1978) about an actual Lebanese martyr who gave her life, serving deaf Palestinian children. A Christian, married with three children, she divorced her husband and lived with a Palestinian lover in Beirut. She was tried, tortured, and killed in front of her pupils in her classroom. One of her accusers in the Christian Lebanese army said, "She should not have had a Palestinian for a friend. She could have found someone better to sleep with. If she were my sister, I would have killed her long ago" (from Georgina Kleege translation, Sausalito, Post-Apollo Press, 1982, p. 60).

6   Conde's two-volume epic, <u>Segou</u>, instances many examples of cross-cultural marriages, but since it is historic in background rather than contemporary, they will not be delineated here.

7   Mittelholzer shows his attention to family history in his three-novel trilogy about a Dutch planter family in Guyana since the seventeenth century: <u>Children of Kaywana</u>, <u>Kayana Stock</u>, and <u>Kayana Blood</u>.

8   Oladele Taiwo, <u>Female Novelists of Modern Africa</u>, (N.Y.: St. Martin's Press, 1984).

CHAPTER 4

LITERARY IMAGES OF INTERCULTURAL RELATIONSHIPS BETWEEN WESTERNERS AND MIDDLE EASTERNERS
Christy Brown

In his Preface to The Colonizer and the Colonized, Tunisian writer Albert Memmi comments on Strangers, his novel about mixed marriage in Colonial North Africa:

> My hopes then rested on the "couple," which still seems to me the most solid happiness of man and perhaps the only real answer to solitude. But I discovered that the couple is not an isolated entity, a forgotten oasis of light in the middle of the world; on the contrary, the whole world is within the couple. For my unfortunate protagonists, the world was that of colonization.

He concluded that "to understand the failure of their undertaking," he first had to understand "the entire colonial relationship and situation." The relationship between Europe and, more recently, the United States, and the Middle East is the product of centuries of political strife followed by Western colonial and neocolonial domination which was reinforced by European images of the Orient in travelers' reports, art, and literature. The impact upon attitudes toward and the possibilities for successful intercultural marriage was enormous. We must view the portrayal of intercultural relationships in contemporary Middle Eastern literature within the context of Western hegemony over the Middle East which in turn shaped the portrayal of the Oriental man or woman in European literature.

Western culture claims its foundation upon Hellenistic culture (often handed down through Arabic translations), despite the fact that Greek culture is Mediterranean and thus in many ways was closer to Middle Eastern culture than Northern European culture. While the Greeks themselves felt an (unproved) superiority to the non-Greek world of Asia, Greek civilization was in fact "born in Asia" as a new "expression of the achievements of other, older cultures of the Near East and Egypt" and was oriented toward the East rather than the West (Baudet 4-5).

As Barbara Harlow points out, "Women have long been at the center of the conflict between East and West" (xiv). One of the most celebrated examples in ancient Greek literature of an intercultural relationship is the theft of the Queen of Sparta, Helen, by the Asian prince, Paris of Troy. Herodotus chided the Greeks for arousing the enmity of Persia by starting the Trojan War over a woman, arguing that "men of sense care nothing for such women, since it is plain that without their consent they would never be forced away" (3). The Asians, he said, never worried when Greeks "ran off with their women."

Euripides' Trojan Women concerns the fate of the women of the defeated Asian city who are treated as booty by the Greeks. While some of the noble women are married to Greek heroes, lower class women are to become slaves. Undoubtedly one of the commonest causes of intercultural marriage from foreign times has been invasion or occupation by a foreign army. Euripides stresses the women's uncertainty about their fate, their sorrow as they are forced to leave their ruined city, and their shame as they must submit to the conquerors who consider themselves superior.

The Greek prejudices against Asians and negative consequences of intercultural marriage for both parties can be seen in Euripides' treatment of the legend of Jason and Medea. Medea is an Asian princess who, made to love Jason by Hera, helps him win the Golden Fleece by betraying her father's secrets, and leaves her country as his bride. To defend Jason she not only kills his enemies, but her own brother as well. Forced to settle in Corinth, the couple live tranquilly, although Medea holds herself aloof from the local population. After several years Jason grows tired of his "aging Oriental bride," and in an attempt to improve his social status, arranges to marry the daughter of King Creon.

Euripides shows some sympathy for Medea, who by leaving her native country cannot depend on her family to protest Jason's desertion. When Medea complains to Jason he responds ethnocentrically that she is lucky that he took her from her "barbarian" country to live in Greece. Moreover, she is portrayed as everything the ideal Greek woman should not be: a slave to her passion for Jason, betrayer of her family, and a sorceress who revenges herself on Jason by killing their two children, Creon, and his daughter. The play suggests that the woman who leaves her own country to marry a foreigner is rather defenseless, while the Greek male loses social status by marrying a foreign woman, a sure-fire recipe for tragedy.

European ethnocentrism is by no means confined to the Greeks and does not diminish in the ensuing centuries. The division in the European mind between "West" and "East" was established with the rise of Islam in the seventh century, whereupon the Saracens became the "enemy." Penetrating as far as Spain and Italy, at one time the "Moors" threatened to devour the whole continent. Unquestionably the leaders in learning and the arts during the Middle Ages, the Islamic Empire was nevertheless portrayed quite negatively in Northern European.

In the anti-Islamic polemic, Muhammed was vilified as a sexual prolifligate bent on destroying Christianity through temptation (Kabbani 15). Middle English romances not only featured the defeat of Saracens by Christian knights, but the alienation of Saracen women from Saracen men. For example, the Saracen princess in "Sir Bevis of Hampton" is inherently lusty, and is willing to give up her religion if Sir Bevis will give himself to her. "He agrees with missionary zeal, and she becomes a 'good' Saracen when converted" (16). In another romance, the princess, like Medea, deceives her relations to help the Christian knight.

On the other hand, the Christian heroine is "self-sacrificing and virtuous." In The King of Tars a Christian princess sacrifices herself to save her people by marrying a dark, ugly Saracen king. When their deformed baby is baptized it becomes perfect and whole, whereupon the King decides to be baptized as well, and turns white (16)! Thus if the Muslim adopts the Christian religion and culture he or she automatically becomes "good," and the marriage is acceptable.

The image of the Muslim woman as lustful and attracted to European men and that of the male as unattractive, cruel, but always defeated in battle lasted for centuries and still exists in today's films and novels. I would argue that even today

Middle Easterners with more European features are thought more acceptable as marriage partners because they are more like "us."

Yet even when there is love between partners, social prejudice or political conflict can destroy the relationship, as with the marriage between Desdemona and Othello and the love affair between Cleopatra and Mark Anthony. In Othello Shakespeare drew upon Renaissance stereotypes of dark skin as ugly and North Africans as excessively jealous, yet Othello is presented as a noble person, in part because he is a Christian and serves the Venetian state. Still, it seems incredible to all but the fair-minded Duke (who also needs him to fight the enemy Muslim Turks) that Desdemona should fall in love with the black-skinned Othello unless she has been bewitched. Desdemona's and Othello's love transcend racial barriers, and it is largely though Iago's envy that the tragedy occurs. Yet bereft of her family's protection, Desdemona has nowhere to turn when Othello begins to question her chastity, implying that no matter how well-intentioned such a love is, misunderstandings may occur, so it is best to marry within one's own nationality and with one's parents' blessing. Yet according to the Earl of Shaftesbury, Desdemona's fate was not enough to deter succeeding generations of British women from romantic longings for African men; in 1710 he claimed that " 'a thousand Desdemonas' were so obsessed with stories of African men that they would readily abandon husbands, families, and country itself, to 'follow the fortunes of a hero of the black tribe' " (Cowhig 13).

In Anthony and Cleopatra Shakespeare drew upon Plutarch, conforming to the current view of the East as sexually unrestrained and opulently wealthy and decadent, as emotionally "feminine" as opposed to the masculine rationality, discipline, and order of Rome. Mark Anthony's tragedy is that he turns his back on his duty to his country and his Roman wife Octavia to indulge himself in the pleasure offered by the Eastern queen so "infinite in her variety." Yet the fact that Anthony and Cleopatra were willing to scorn the political repercussions and sacrifice "all for love" shows an attempt to overcome the limitations of their respective cultures, to value the personal over the political, to unite East and West, which has fascinated succeeding generations.

The translation of One Thousand and One Nights in the eighteenth century and its continuing popularity provoked a kind of love affair with the East itself. According to Henri Baudet, the eighteenth century witnessed the high point of European admiration and imitation of the Orient, partly in response to the idea of the "Noble Savage" with a correspondingly negative view of Europe's own corruption, seen for example in Swift's Gulliver's Travels. Mozart's favorable portrait of Pasha Selim in The Abduction from the Seraglio is a notable example (52). Pasha Selim pardons the European abductor of his beloved Constanze, but despite his magnanimity, the resolution pairs the European woman with a European rather than an Oriental male, suggesting that Europe was capable of importing coffee, tulips, ottomans, and carpets from the Ottoman Empire, but not willing to sanction intercultural marriages.

Europe's fascination for the Orient culminated in the Romantic period, during which the East was projected upon the imagination as an exotic escape from the mundane reality of newly emerging industrial culture. The dark, guilt-ridden, Satanic Byronic hero so attractive to women, while not always himself Middle Eastern, owes a great deal to Byron's and his imitators' fascination with the Middle East (Kabbani 33). Nineteenth century travelers to the Middle East were attracted to it as a space of sexual liberation from the inhibitions of European culture, especially during the Victorian period, but they did not forget their duty to Empire. The West's growing political and military power, which was exercised in the name of the civilizing mission and the "White Man's burden," along with ideologies which saw Europeans as racially superior to all other peoples could hardly encourage intercultural marriages between Europeans and darker-skinned people they had colonized, although they did not preclude liaisons between the colonizer and the local woman as long as the woman's inferior social status was clear.

The European male considered himself superior to the Middle Easterner and saw the Middle Eastern female as doubly inferior because she was a woman, a quite different woman from the chaste and sexless European (upper class) woman he placed on a pedestal. In general she was thought of as sexually libidinous, not fit to be a wife, but acceptable as a concubine if the required sense of superiority was maintained. Rana Kabbani points outs that as "part of the goods of empire," her supposed licentiousness allowed the European male to exploit her without guilt (50).

One interesting example of a European who actually married an Egyptian woman is E. W. Lane, an Orientist who authored Manners and Customs of Modern Egyptians, in which he portrayed Egyptians as "indolent, superstitious, sensually over-indulgent, and religiously fanatical," not to mention sexually promiscuous. In 1831 another European offered Lane a slave girl he had bought, Nefeesah. Lane made her his servant, put her on a diet and began to educate her (one thinks of Pygmalion or Prospero), reporting that "she is making satisfactory progress in reading and writing, as well as needlework; which, with arithmetic, are all the accomplishments I wish her to acquire" (Kabbani 45). Once "improved," but not to the point that Lane might feel threatened by her intellectual equality, and despite his contempt, he married her.

French orientalist Gerard de Nerval also married a Lebanese Druze woman after the failure of his relationship with his Egyptian slave (Harlow xv). For Nerval the Orient was "'le pays des reves et de l'illusion,' which like the veils he sees everywhere in Cairo, conceal a deep, rich, fund of female sexuality" (Said 182). He believed that to be part of the Orient he would have to marry "a guileless young girl who is of this sacred soil, which is our first homeland." He saw himself as the hero of his own drama; like Desdemona he was attracted to the idea of the exotic tale, which he wished to live for himself. Marriage to an Oriental woman was part of that story.

Gustave Flaubert was also attracted to the Orient, and while in Egypt met and slept with Kuchek Hanem, an Egyptian dancer and courtesan who became the model of his sensual Salammbo and Salome. Yet he wrote Lousie Colet: "the oriental woman is no more than a machine; she makes no distinction between one man and another man" (Said 186-7).

Similarly, Richard Burton, who made the East "his career," and while in India kept a female servant (coloured sister) who also served him sexually, noted "while thousands of Europeans have cohabited for years with and have had families by native women, they are never loved by them" (Kabbani 47). He attributed their indifference to the European males' inability to satisfy them sexually, without considering, as Kabbani notes, that the colonized woman's "emotional detachment was her only defense against total victimization" (48).

Yet the European literary image was romanticized and usually flattered the European male. In one of Victor Hugo's poems an Arab woman plaintively begs the "beau jeune homme blanc" to dream of the desert girls who "dansent pieds nus sur les dunes." French naval officer and novelist Pierre Loti's Aziyade was based on an actual affair he had with one of the wives of a wealthy Turk, but Loti embroidered the ending by having Aziyade die because of the risk she had taken for his sake (Blanch 129). Loti was a true Turkophile, and he valued the Circassian (hence white-skinned) Aziyade more than the Tahitian and African mistresses he met on his other voyages.

In Joseph Conrad's The Heart of darkness and Lord Jim European males are regarded as Gods by their Asian and African mistresses. In the former, Kurtz's sexual depravity with an African woman is contrasted with his pure, idealistic European fiance who waits patiently for him to return. But in some early Malay novels, Almayer's Folly (1895) and An Outcast of the Islands (1896), Malay women ill-used by European men curse them as liars and show a resentful attitude toward their claims of superiority (McClure 157).

Since British men and women lived in India in greater numbers for a longer period than in Middle Eastern countries, the subject of Anglo-Indian relationships arises more frequently in British literature. Kipling was the main proponent of the Imperial idea up to 1914; in keeping with his belief in racial separation, relationships between Englishmen and Indian women in his works "always end tragically" (Islam 6).

E.M. Forster's A Passage to India (1924) centers on the Muslim Aziz's alleged rape of the English woman, Adela Quested. In the novel it is clear that Aziz is not at all attracted to Adela; on the contrary, she is attracted to him. It is actually her hysterical reaction to her sexual frustration which causes her to imagine the rape. Forster is trying to counter the British view that all Indian males lust after British women. The British social snobbery even towards the most educated and wealthy Indians in the novel indicates the difficulty of maintaining even a friendship, not to mention a marriage, when one people is subordinated to another. In George Orwell's Burmese Days (1935) the protagonist is highly critical of British colonialism, but he leaves his Burmese mistress for a British woman who supports colonialism and believes in British racial superiority, indicating that even one who sympathizes with the colonized prefers a woman of his own "race."

Not until Paul Scott's The Raj Quartet, written decades after Indian Independence (1966-1975), does a British writer fully explore the barriers to intercultural relationships during the Raj. Hari Kumar is a British-educated Indian who feels himself to be "White," but to the British he will always be "Black," even though his upbringing is far "superior" to that of many of the British civil servants upholding the Raj. Daphne Mannrs wishes to get to know India, and she is attracted to Hari because of his Blackness, but as he has no truly Indian identity; she cannot find India in him (Tedesco and Popham 31). It is common in intercultural relationships for the person from the supposedly "inferior" culture to be attracted to someone from the "superior" race because s/he identifies with it, while the other person is a romantic primitivist who wants to reject his or her culture and is attracted to the "native" because he represents this cultural Otherness. Such couples are obviously at cross purposes. Before Hari and Daphne can doom themselves, their relationship and lives are destroyed by an attack on Daphne which is blamed on Hari.

Ronald Merrick, Daphne's British suitor, is the type of lower middle class administrator whose sense of racial superiority derives from the fact that he has more social status in India than he ever would have in England, because all British considered themselves superior to all Indians simply because of their skin color (Tedesco and Popham 23). His racial hatred is coupled with his homosexual desire for the Indian males to whom he is supposedly superior, a desire he resists but to which he ultimately succombs. Ironically, it is his relationship with an Indian lover which gives him "a brief moment of peace," the implications of which "appalled him" (242). For the racist, the despised Other is hated but also secretly desired, and the knowledge that a sexual relationship with him or her can bring happiness negates the ideology and hence the sense of superiority upon which the racist's life is founded.

Many writers and travelers have been attracted to the Middle East because of its greater sexual tolerance whether bisexual or homosexual: Byron, Oscar Wilde, Andre Gide, T. E. Lawrence. Homosexuality, punishable by death in England in Byron's day, was known to be tolerated in the Middle East, as was lesbianism, which was supposedly rampant in the harems. The Victorians condemned these practices, which made them feel superior to these other cultures; on the other hand, they were titillated by them. Richard Burton was ordered to disguise himself and make a report on India's homosexual brothels; the report later cost him his job, but furnished much material for his highly popular pornographic writings (Kabbani 58). But European homosexuals did not regard their Middle Eastern or North African love objects with any greater equality than did heterosexuals. For one thing, they were often very young boys and/or male prostitutes. Moreover, the European had to have the role of initiator; otherwise he would be demeaned. Thus T.E. Lawrence describes the trauma of his "rape" by a Turkish garrison commander at Der'aa (which according to his biographer never took place), but he himself loved the Arab Dahoum paternalistically, which was characteristic of his relationship toward the Arabs as a whole (Kabbani 111-112). Tennessee Williams remembered with nostalgia the "marvelous boys" he met in Tangier "years ago" (Choukri 36), and Michel of Andre Gide's L'Immoraliste loses interest in the North African children he observed voyeuristically on an earlier visit after they have grown up (Harlow xix). In Peter Weir's The Year of Living Dangerously the Chinese-American dwarf and moralist Billy Kwan condemns the American and British journalists in Indonesia for their fixation on "little girls" and "little boys," not because he is anti-sex, but because of the inherent exploitativeness of such relationships.

The British also occupied Egypt, of course, and in his Alexandria Quartet Lawrence Durrell uses Egypt as a backdrop against which his artist hero can explore his consciousness. Suffused in "androgynous" sexuality, his Alexandria "is the great wine press of love." The narrator of Justine, a British schoolteacher, has two affairs simultaneously, one with a rather pathetic Greek cabaret dancer, and one with Justine, the Jewish wife of a wealthy--and honorable--Egyptian friend. Justine represents the city of Alexandria itself, just as Cleopatra represents Egypt, but the weight of symbolism she has to carry deprives her of individuality. Durrell sees Egypt with the Orientalist eye par excellence.

One of the greatest ironies of the Colonial era was, as the French called it, the "civilizing mission," in which European men (and women) self-righteously preached against "barbaric" practices such as Indian suttee, female circumcision, seclusion, and the veil--Gayatri Spivak terms it "brown women saved by white men from brown men" (Harlow xviii)--while at the same time exploiting not only their bodies, but the idea of the harem and the Oriental woman as sexual object. Because European men could not penetrate the harem, painters and later photographers using paid models recruited from "the margins" of the colonized society (Aloula 17) created their own lurid and often pornographic image of what the harem was like, an image which bore little resemblance to reality. While "brown men" became more protective of women under colonialism, "white men's" exercise of power was circumscribed only by the harem, but while many Europeans fantasized about its supposed delights, so debased was the status of the Oriental woman in their eyes that few actually would have been willing to take the step of an honorable Islamic marriage.

What then of the European woman's view of intercultural marriage/sex? Several European women have written about their experiences in the Middle East and Colonial Africa: Lady Worthy Montagu, Isabella Bird, Gertrude Bell, and Isak Dinesen are only a few. Dinesen's husband probably contracted syphillus from Masai women he slept with (Thurman 137), but while Dinesen came to admire Islam, she saw her relationship to the African "Natives" (always capitalized) as that of a feudal overlord to her serfs. The higher the woman's social status, the more unthinkable the idea of intercultural marriage.

However, such marriages, while infrequent, did occur occasionally. One notable example is that between Eugenie Le Brun, a Frenchwoman, and Husain Rushdi, an upper class Egyptian who served as prime minister after his wife's death (Shaarawi 13). In the 1890's Le Brun began the first salon for women in Cairo, at which a wide range of women's issues were raised (143). As an insider in Egyptian society she was able to write a defense of Egyptian culture, Harem et les musulmanes (1902), to clear up many misconceptions Europeans had about the lives of upper class Egyptian women, and a second book about divorced women in Egypt which focused on the sufferings of pimarily lower class women in the Muslim divorce courts. Her attitude was thus neither to condemn Egyptian culture nor to idealize it, but to portray it as it was, without the sensationalism which attended so many other European accounts.

Egyptian feminist Huda Shaarawi, a close friend of Le Brun, records in her memoirs Le Brun's description of how her marriage came about:

> I married for love. I loved Rushdi very much and respected his fine character. My sister had married a man addicted to alcohol and gambling (I knew Islam forbade both). He squandered her fortune and ruined her life. I was sure Rushdi would never bring me to that end. My father, however, did not approve of the marriage. Fortunately, I had been raised by my grandmother who had encouraged me to think for myself. With support from my sister I was able to persuade my father I would be happy with Rushdi; coming from a well-to-do family, he could provide for me. My father reluctantly consented (81).

Despite her conversion to Islam and evident love for her husband, next to whom she wished to be buried in the Muslim cemetary "so we shall never be separated in this world or the next," she confessed that "marriage across cultures is a big mistake" due to "the constant strain of trying to live according to customs different from those one grew up with." She was also upset because no distinction was made between her and the majority of primarily lower class European women who married Egyptians (80-82). Le Brun seems to be the exception that proves the rule that most of those who married into colonized cultures during the colonial era came from classes in which they had less prestige to lose by marrying a man considered racially inferior, whatever his status in his own society.

The fictional relationship between Catherine Earnshaw and Heathcliff in Wuthering Heights (1849) confirms that racial and class barriers were seen by women as insurmountable. Because Heathcliff is raised with Catherine, he seems like her brother, but since he is actually an orphan her father has picked up in a Liverpool slum whose dark skin classifies him as a "Gipsy," Heathcliff represents the forbidden attractions of incest and racial miscegenation, extreme endogamy and exogamy, at the same time. He speaks "gibberish" and is described variously as looking like a Gipsy, a Lascar, a Spanish or American castaway. His dark skin and coal black hair leave little doubt that he is not British in origin. Although he has no name and therefore no social status, Nellie Dean advises him to construct an exotic identity as the son of the Empress of China or India. Catherine's reason for not marrying Heathcliff is the social and economic inferiority to which such a match would consign her, so she marries the wealthy Edgar Linton.

When Heathcliff returns from a two year absence attired as a gentleman, he becomes in Catherine's sister-in-law Isabella's eyes a romantic hero, which suggests how greatly the idea of Byronic hero--dark, inscrutible, and savage, with a definite Oriental cast, but princely, or at least aristocratic--affected the female imagination. Catherine and Heathcliff's mutual attraction suggests that the fascination for the "racial" Other was not limited to the male population, and Edgar Linton's dislike of Heathcliff is quite typical of the European male's response when a woman dares to love a non-European man. Heathcliff reproaches Catherine for throwing away their love for social position, but especially from the mid-nineteenth century, any "well-bred" European woman who married a non-European, even a "gentleman," was throwing away her reputation. Though motivated by the cruel treatment meted out to him, Heathcliff's spiteful marriage to Isabella and his savage treatment of her only reinforces the image of the non-European as cruel and savage, howsoever disguised as an English gentleman. Still, Catherine and Heathcliff's love suggests an underlying sympathy and yearning for racial unity which is cut off by European political and economic domination and their accompanying ideologies of racial and cultural superiority.

For most women writers, the Byronic hero is not a cultural "Other," although he might have links to another culture and thus an aura of exoticism. Emily Bronte's sister Charlotte's Rochester in Jane Eyre (1847), has spent time in the West Indies, and he disguises himself as an old Gipsy fortuneteller. Rochester is described as being so dark of complexion and close to Oriental in appearance (dark skin, "raven locks," and fine dark eyes) that his English origins strain credulity. Bronte's references to Byron's "Corsair" and the Middle Eastern costumes Rochester wears during charades at Thornfield display her desire to link Rochester with the Orient, but as a wealthy British gentleman, Rochester elevates rather than reduces Jane's social status when they marry.

The fact of slavery, servitude, or colonization reduced most men of color to inferior status in the eyes of middle class European women. But the Bedouin was another story because, although culturally "primitive," he was free and not subservient. E. M. Hull's The Sheik (1923), in which the aristocratic British heroine Diana Mayo is abducted by and falls in love with a bedouin Arab prince, popularized the by now cliche of Romantic exoticism:

> Her heart was given for all time to the fierce desert man who was so different from all other men she had met, a lawless savage who had taken her to satisfy a passing fancy and who had treated her with merciless cruelty. He was a brute, but she loved him, loved him for his very brutality, and superb animal strength. And he was an Arab! A man of different race and color, a native; Aubrey would indiscriminately describe him as "a damned nigger." She did not care...she was deliriously, insanely happy.

Diana Mayo's love is an act of cultural defiance, but Hull's portrayal of the Bedouin is more imaginary and stereotypical than real, providing the fantasy of primitive sexuality to be consumed by the hypercivilized, overprotected, sexually repressed European or American female.

In a similar but more recent fantasy the wealthy Northern Italian heroine of director Lina Wertmuller's Swept Away falls in love with the swarthy Sicilian deckhand on her husband's yacht with whom she is shipwrecked on a desert island. While they are in civilization the deckhand is the object either of her indifference or scorn; on the island, stripped of class differences he becomes a primitive hero who forces her to submit to his will. Both she and Diana Mayo are "swept away" by their desire to reject civilization in the person of a primitive, "uncivilized" male who treats them brutally but loves them passionately. This desire parallels the European male's longing for the sensual dark-skinned woman or youth, except that the European male desires to be the conqueror, whereas the European woman fantasizes that she is conquered, preferably by rape or abduction, so she doesn't have to bear responsibility for her fall. However, in this fantasy of rape or abduction she ultimately holds power over the brutal male because of his passionate love for her, a passion that European women might have felt missing in their socially approved relationships with European men (e.g. Desdemona's rejection of the "wealthy, curled darlings" of Venice for the "barbarian" traveler Othello).

Women who lack power within their own culture might also fantasize that they can achieve an alternative power, not social or economic power, but the power of defiance, through a "savage" male from another culture. The seeming domination belies an underlying primitive equality. Yet Wertmuller undercuts this fantasy when at the end of Swept Away the pair are rescued and the woman rejects her lover and goes back to her husband; in the real world, Wertmuller seems to be saying, social position wins out over passion; the socially/racially "superior" may fantasize about relationships with their inferiors or even take lovers, but marriage or long term commitment is rare.

Made into the film that made Valentino a star, The Sheik was one of many Hollywood films with Middle Eastern or North African settings, but most did not contain believable Arab characters and simply provided exotic local color for the European characters' exploits. In fact, in very few novels or films since the colonial period have non-Europeans been seen as fully developed, realistically portrayed characters (Mannsaker 117). In recent years since the Arab-Israeli conflict and Iranian Revolution have dominated the American political scene, the media image of the Middle Easterner has deteriorated to a new low. Despite recent attempts by the American Arab Anti-Discrimination Committee to protest the worst stereotypes of Arabs in film and TV, positive images of Middle Easterners in American films are practically nonexistent. Portrayed either as terrorist or as wealthy oil sheiks who ogle American women and lock up their own, Arab characters usually have minor roles, and the possibility of intercultural marriages between Americans and Middle Easterners is never even considered. In The Little Drummer Girl, adapted from a John Le Carre novel, the Iowa born heroine (Dianne Keaton) supports the Palestinian cause, but as soon as she has been abducted by a handsome Israeli agent posing as a Palestinian, she agrees to work undercover to catch a Palestinian terrorist. The terrorist is an unattractive, mindless rock music addict, but she must sleep with him to convince him of her loyalty.

In Half Moon Street, based on a Paul Theroux novel, American Sigourny Weaver works as a part time hooker to put herself through diplomatic school, and falls in love with one of her clients, a British aristocrat played by Peter O'Toole. Another, a short, fat, but charming Palestinian, lends her his flat in Half Moon Street. He turns out to be a terrorist, however, and she is nearly blown up.

These two films represent some of the most sympathetic portrayals of Arabs (at least they are portrayed as human beings), but in each the heroine sleeps with the man for money or duty, and is actually in love with an Israeli or European with whom she is reunited after the terrorist is himself blown up.

Greek filmmaker Costa Gavras, who is sympathetic to the Palestinian point of view, has produced the only major European film with a sympathetic Palestinian character, Hanna K., in which an American-Israeli lawyer falls in love with a young Palestinian accused of illegal entry into Israel. The peace she finds in this relationship is shattered by her jealous Israeli ex-lover. The Palestinian, played by Mohammed Bakri, is a tall, fairskinned Arab from Northern Israel who looks more European than Arab, so the sense of cultural difference is minimized. Nor is Selim's charcter developed to any great extent.

In Mexican novelist Carlos Fuentes' Hydra Head (1978), Sara Klein, a survivor of the holocaust, works as a teacher in Israel, but begins to question Israeli policy after she meets the Palestinian Jamil, who is later tortured and imprisoned. She says of her love affair with Jamil, "all the frontiers of my life disappeared...Along with Jamil, I became a citizen of the land we stood upon...I saw Palestine for what it was, a land that must belong to everyone..." (106).

Such an ideal of political reconciliation and cultural syncretism vis-a-vis the Middle East has not yet appeared in American films or literature. There is an obvious discrepancy between media stereotypes of -or silence about- intercultural marriage and the increasing numbers of stable marriages between Middle Easterners and Americans and Europeans which have occurred since decolonization began after World War II. Because of the long history of colonization and neo-colonialism, contemporary Middle Eastern literature also contains few instances of successful intercultural marriages, even though many Middle Eastern and North African writers are themselves (successfully) married to Europeans or Americans (for example, Palestinian novelist Ghassan Kanafani was happily married to a Danish woman, Sudanese writer Tayeb Salih married a Scots woman, North African writers Driss Chraibi, Mohammed Dib, and Albert Memmi all married French women, and the list could go on).

To understand the scarcity of successful intercultural relationships between Europeans/Americans in Middle Eastern and North African literature, we must return to Albert Memmi's statement in the opening paragraph of this essay. When Middle Easterners began to develop modern literatures based mainly on the European novel, one of their primary themes was a repudiation of colonialism and/or imperialism and the accompanying political, economic, cultural, and social inferiority to which Western domination had subjected them. Nationalist movements in Turkey, Iran, Egypt, and Algeria began by advocating Western reforms to modernize their countries and develop nation states in the Western sense, but another form of Nationalism asserted cultural identity in the face of Western attempts to subordinate or even obliterate colonized cultures. In Middle Eastern literature, Europeans and Americans alternatively represent exploiters or exemplify the Western values with which the writer's society is desperately trying to come to terms.

Particularly in North African literature written in French, but also in Arabic literature as well, the Western educated North African man or woman in a sense replaces a Western protagonist because the cultural struggle is felt intra- rather than interculturally. It is difficult enough for "Westernized" and "traditional" Algerians to harmonize their different values, let alone Europeans and Arabs. I myself have seen the difficulties faced by Arab women who grew up in the West and married relatively "Westernized" students from Arab countries they met at university. Moreover, there is the strain of intra-ethnic relationships as well, and many writers have expressed the difficulties between Jews, Christians, and Moslems (e.g. Memmi, Chraibi, Awwad, Adnan) as well as the bicultural strain of coming from a mixed heritage (Taos). The strain of biculturality has been one of the major themes of Middle Eastern literature. This strain has particular significance for men and women in relationships since differences in values, especially regarding the status and behavior of women, can be a significant cause of conflict.

One early example is Algerian writer Djamila Debeche's prerevolutionary novel Aziza (1955), in which the Westernized heroine, educated in French schools and employed by a French press agency, marries an Arab lawyer, Ali Kamal, who behind his liberated facade, is a traditionalist. Aziza refuses to play the role of traditional submissive wife, but when she returns to her former life, finds her French friends have deserted her because her Moslem marriage is regarded as "cultural treason" (Accad 35). Debeche portrays both colonizers and colonized as rigid in their beliefs, admitting of no compromise. Aziza is caught in the middle of two cultures, rejected by both. One theme common to many other works of Middle Eastern fiction is that of the male who accepts liberation for himself, but not wholeheartedly for women.

Algerian Kabyle Mouloud Feraoun writes of a marriage between a Kabyle man and a French woman in La Terre et le sang (1953). Amer returns to his village after fifteen years with his French wife Marie, who had been a prostitute in France. While Marie must adjust to restrictions on her personal freedoms, she gains respect and status because her blond hair makes her exotic. She feels comfortable, but she disrupts the tightly knit village society (Accad 64), and Amer's disappointed mother plots with his previous sweetheart to undermine his marriage with the foreign bride. This novel reveals how much status is granted to lower class European women who marry Middle Eastern men just because they are European, but also the difficulties which arise with family members, especially the mother. Even when the European woman is prepared to accept the new culture, she disrupts its homogeneity, thus confirming Memmi's contention that the couple cannot isolate itself from the social context.

In Lebanese novelist Suhayl Idris' autobiographical trilogy (1958-1962), the contradictions caused by cultural conflict are displayed by the Arab hero, Sami, who protests the sexual double standard of his society and defends his mother and sister. However, when in the second volume Al-Hayy al Latini (The Latin Quarter), Sami travels to France to study, he applies that same double standard to his relationship with a French woman, Janine. She had confessed to him she was not a virgin, so when she writes to him she is pregnant, he rationalizes that her lack of virginity absolves him of responsibility! After Janine has a near fatal abortion, a friend urges him to "face his responsibility as an Arab" and marry her, despite the fact that while he dates European women, he has previously sworn he would not marry one (Accad 141). Sami returns to Paris, but Janine has disappeared; when he finally finds her he does propose, but it is she who refuses. Idris is thus able to take the easy way out; his hero finally "faces his responsibility," but doesn't have to endure the consequences of marriage to a non-virgin.

Such contradictions are a standard part of supposedly "Westernized" Middle Eastern males' responses to both European and Arab women. In another example, in Moroccan writer Abd al-Karim Ghallab's Dafanna al-Madi (We Buried the Past), the hero 'Abd al-Rahman rebels against traditional culture and its restrictions on both men and women in choosing their own marriage partners. He opposes his sister's arranged marriage, but then proceeds to choose her fiance himself. He himself falls in love with a French woman, but breaks with her, partly because he fears what his parents will say, partly because he fears the marriage will not last!

R.K. Narayan, an Indian novelist who writes in English, provides a father's perspective on intercultural marriage in The Vendor of Sweets (1967). Jagan is a follower of Gandhi whose abstemious habits have allowed him to amass a large nest egg from his sweet shop. After studying in the United States, his son Mali returns a modernist, bringing with him a Korean-American bride. Mali's coldness and scorning of all things traditional alienate him from his father, who cannot comprehend his son's modern ideas and behavior. Grace is more sympathetic toward Jagan with her romantic view of Indian culture, and she tries to be a good Hindu wife, treating her father-in-law with deference. Mali has plans to start a business with a new technological invention, a storywriting machine, in which he wants to invest his father's savings, but Jagan, who would gladly give his sweetshop business to Mali, is suspicious of the project and refuses. Mali has little patience for his country's traditional ways, but Jagan sees no reason to change. When the business doesn't materialize, Mali and Grace drift apart, and Jagan learns they weren't really married after all. Feeling his house has been tainted by this unsanctified marriage, Jagan recalls his own traditional wedding.

Narayan satirizes cultural conflict, depicting the new generation who want to modernize India as having no soul, no poetry, and little practicality, while on the other hand, traditionalists are mired in arcane religious ritual and obsessive patterns of behavior. Narayan shows that the prospects for change in India are limited by centuries of tradition; he also points out that change may not necessarily be the best idea. After all, how can one write a story on a machine?

Another of Narayan's hilarious satires, The Painter of Signs (1977), concerns the mismatch between a "modern" Indian woman, a population control worker obsessed with limiting India's birth rate, and a sign painter she hires who has a romantic, artistic temperament. Raised on romantic images of inaccessible Indian females, he finds himself hopelessly in love with a hard-nosed independent woman who will let nothing, including love and marriage, stand in her way. As in previously discussed works of Middle Eastern fiction, it is intra- rather than intercultural conflicts and the personal tragedies that result that most concern Narayan. The Western wife is something that accompanies modernization and further disrupts society. Ironically, as in La Terre et le Sang, the Western wife may adapt to the culture better than the husband, but proves disconcerting to her in-laws.

One of the most positive portrayals of an intercultural relationship occurs in Syrian Halim Barakat's 1969 novel 'Awdat al-ta'ir ila al-bahr (The Return of the Flying Dutchman to the Sea), which was titled Days of Dust in translation. The novel concerns the Palestinian-Israeli conflict, a major concern of contemporary Arabic literature, and covers the six-day war of 1967. The protagonist is a Palestinian professor who watches the events helplessly from Lebanon. While the war is going on, he has an affair with an American woman whose husband has returned to the states. (The change from European to American represents the change in what Arabs see as the dominant neocolonial power in the Middle East, with the exception of Algeria, which is still very much tied to France.)

Ramzi admires Pamela's long blond hair, but he also admires her independence and freedom from tradition, comparing her favorably to his timid sweetheart, Najla. However, Pamela also symbolizes American oppression of the Palestinians, as she swoops down on him like the Israeli planes that bomb the West Bank. Barakat separates Pamela the person from Pamela the symbol of America though. She personally sympathizes with the Palestinians, and Ramzi contemplates marriage to her, but makes no decision by the end of the novel. Ramzi looks with satisfaction on the growing independence of Arab women students who try to help the refugees after the war.

Many Middle Eastern men marry Western women precisely because their society does not allow women to be emancipated, and they, having become emancipated themselves, prefer an equal partner. Such marriages, while beneficial to the man and more positive than those in which the man is ambivalent about cultural values, do not improve the condition of Arab women.

A recent novel by Egyptian writer Sherif Hetata, al-Shabaka (translated as The Net), shows that marriage to an emancipated Arab woman may not be enough to satisfy an Arab male who is attracted to an American woman. Hetata, who is married to well-known Egyptian feminist novelist Nawal Sadaawi, creates a parallel to his wife in the painter Amina, who marries political dissident Khalil Mansour. Despite their seemingly ideal relationship, Khalil drifts away from her and their infant son when a strike to prevent the takeover of his company by a multinational fails. He becomes obsessed with Ruth Harrison, née Gonzales, a mysterious American researcher, who like Pamela, is married, but to a wealthy businessman. Ruth proposes she use her husband's connections to find Khalil another job with a foreign firm, an idea which he finds repugnant but accepts. He sinks deeper and deeper into a morass of corruption from which he does not seem to care to extricate himself, until he learns that Ruth is actually a spy. Her employers turn on her, however, and she is mysteriously murdered before Khalil can learn whether she has been lying or sincere toward him.

The illegitimate daughter of a Latin American immigrant, Ruth has had to do anything to survive in the United States, including selling herself, and Hetata does not blame her for Khalil's predicament. Certainly Ruth has manipulated Khalil, but she is also a victim herself of a sinister multinational force which in its quest for profits will stop at nothing to penetrate third world countries and destroy the local industry and workers' rights.

The Net is a melodramatic allegory of neo-colonialism, with nearly every character save the heroic Amina caught in the corruption of the multinational intrigue during the Sadat regime. Khalil, representing the Egyptian intellectual, is portrayed as weaker than either his wife or his mistress, and quite vulnerable to the charms of Western women:

> These women from the West had a knack of playing on the imagination of men from the East like myself. We were easily seduced by their smooth white skin, their supple legs, and their long, silky hair (45).

The Western woman may herself be subordinated within a male-dominated society, but to the Eastern male, because she is part of a culture which threatens him with domination, she seems to have more power than he does. Both Barakat and Hetata feel threatened by the sexual power and threat of Western women; both see American women as sexually liberated from traditional morality, willing to commit adultery without guilt. Interestingly, they have reversed the stereotype held by Europeans about the Oriental woman, except that they see themselves as victims rather than conquerors.

But the source of this stereotype would turn out to be our own films and television series, which have been peddled throughout the third world. As Jagan's cousin says in The Vendor of Sweets:

> And the women are free...I have seen some of their magazines about films: their women mix freely with men and snap off marriages without ado, and bask in the sun without clothes (35).

It is this blend of attraction to the sexuality forbidden in their own culture, that which they desire and at the same time despise, and the sense of inferiority fostered by colonialism and racism which makes Eastern men's reaction to Western women so ambivalent.

No where is this ambivalence expressed with more shattering force than in Tayeb Salih's 1969 novel Mawsim al hijira ila al-shamal (published in English as Season of Migration to the North), which uses an intercultural marriage to symbolize the tragic confrontation between East and West, North and South, under colonialism. Salih rewrites Othello from an African point of view. Like Conrad's secret sharer or Marlow, the narrator, a Sudanese student recently returned from studying in Britain, becomes implicated after listening to the story of Mustapha Sa'eed, the first Sudanese ever to be sent to study in England. His mind "like a sharp knife," dubbed "the Black Englishman" by fellow students, Sa'eed is seen as Westernized in the Sudan, but as an African "savage" by his English mistresses. Sa'eed's game is revenge and conquest, a kind of reverse rape, and he deliberately cultivates their stereotypes of Africa and Arabia, which he combines in one person. These Desdemonas are not satisfied within their own culture, and look to him for fulfillment. Three of them kill themselves, but it is not Mustapha Sa'eed who is responsible, but the shattering of their romantic and primitivistic illusions of him.

But Jean Morris, however, outmaneuvers Sa'eed; she is a temptress whom he cannot conquer, and after pursuing her frantically, she demands that he marry her. But marriage brings no peace; she flaunts her unfaithfulness and goads him into violence, until he kills her in a ritualistic scene which symbolizes the inevitable violence that must accompany the subordination of one people over another. As Evelyn Accad points out, "The stress between their races and cultures...is too great to admit of a normal and tranquil relationship" (148). Unlike Desdemona, Jean is not portrayed as the innocent victim of primitive passions, but as a phantom whom Sa'eed can never possess and who carries within herself the death-wish of her culture. It is clear that Salih does not approve of Sa'eed's deed, but sees it as the inevitable result of colonialism in which cultures are portrayed as intrinsically all black or white, evil or good, inferior or superior, each having a false, stereotypical view of the other.

Sa'eed is sentenced to only seven years, after which he returns to the Sudan and marries a girl from the narrator's village. Sa'eed imparts to Hosna an air of foreignness, and after his death, she refuses to marry a seventy year old man who asks for her. She is forced into the marriage, however, and makes good her threat to kill both the man and herself. The narrator who has witnessed the events in horror realizes that his society will never be the same.

Season of Migration to the North reveals the strains upon the third world individual's personality from colonialism and modernization as well as the difficulty of overcoming the obstacles to intercultural relationships within a framework of cultural, political, and economic domination. Salih, who is married to a Scots woman, does not write of the individual couple so much as how the situation affects individuals on the level of what one might call the collective unconscious. Similarly, Algerian Kateb Yacine's Nedjma (1956) allegorizes the colonial situation through the difficulties of mixed marriage (Harlow xx).

Perhaps because Iran was never directly colonized by the West, the subject of intercultural relationships occurs very infrequently in Persian literature. In Gholam-Hossein Sa'edi's "Dandil" (1977), Iranian villagers pandar the most beautiful virgin in the village to an insentive American sergeant, who does not even pay them after he has deflowered her. The story obviously refers to the American influence in Iran under the Shah; the young woman is Iran, deflowered and exploited by the American presence. The naive villagers are to be blamed for expecting the American to remunerate them for what they offer him.

Jalal Al-e Ahmad's Gharbzadegi (Weststruckness) appeared in 1962, and despite the fact that the SAVAK (secret police) prohibited its distribution until the revolution in 1978, Al-e Ahmad's thinking was influential in provoking the anti-Western attitudes which helped produce the Iranian Revolution. Al-e Ahmad criticized the wholesale adoption of Western attitudes and technology which he felt were a facade of democracy and development when the infrastructure needed to sustain them was not there. He saw Western values alienating the people, especially the bourgeoisie, from their own culture. On these grounds, Al-e Ahmad opposed the growing number of marriages between Iranians (primarily those educated abroad) and Westerners, saying:

When the basis of the Iranian family with a close and familiar wife and husband is falling apart, of course it's obvious what must be happening in this sort of mismatched family. These young people and their families are like homing pigeons with two roosts. They are the ultimate human results of Gharbzadegi. To solve the domestic difficulties of a family like this is itself enough of a problem. This group of young people has neither the ability nor the ambition to solve the external, or social problems (156).

Al-e Ahmad classifies Iranians who marry Westerners into three groups: 1) those from poor families who studied in the West and want to improve their social standing by a marriage with a European or American, 2) those who "settled" for a Western wife or husband because of marriage restrictions in Iran (arranged marriages as opposed to freedom of choice), but who come back to Iran finding the restrictions eased, and therefore needn't have married out of their culture, and 3) those who became sexually debauched and/or lost their religion and couldn't be satisfied with an Iranian spouse. He does not consider the possibility that these Iranians fell in love with Westerners and married for love, despite the cultural differences.

Al-e Ahmad's worries that those Iranians who marry outside their culture will be more likely to stay abroad, creating a "chronic manpower shortage" (157), seem legitimate. He raises important questions about the impact of intercultural marriages, especially among the most educated sectors of the population, on a relatively small country trying to sustain its cultural identity. In such cases the more powerful force of Westernization can lead to cultural schizophrenia and loss of identity and direction. He does not consider the possibilities of cultural syncretization as benefitting Iran, perhaps because the cultural forces are not competing equally.

A single example of an intercultural marriage in a novel by an Iranian appeared in English in 1978. Nahid Rachlin, an Iranian woman living in the United States and married to an American, is an example of the "loss" of manpower to which Al-e Ahmad refers. Unfortunately, that loss has only continued on a much broader scale since the Revolution was supposed to restore Iranian and Islamic culture. Rachlin's Foreigner (1978) is the story of an Iranian woman who exemplifies the loss of cultural identity that Al-e Ahmad speaks of. Estranged from her country for several years, Feri returns to visit her family. She had studied in the United States, become a biologist, married an American, and seems to be living "the American dream." We learn, however, that she is deeply hurt by a miscarriage and her husband's adultery. Feri's identity had been shattered in childhood by her separation from her mother, who had run off with another man and was prevented from seeing her daughter. Although feeling ill, Feri sets out to find her mother, and discovers her living in poverty with her blind uncle. Her lover had deserted her.

Feri has developed an ulcer, as the handsome young Iranian doctor tells her, "a Western disease." Feri is attracted to this man, who has also been educated in the West, but who has returned to Iran to better conditions there. He loves Iranian culture and takes Feri to visit some monuments. Receiving Feri's urgent telegram, her husband Tony arrives to take her back to the U.S. He shows no interest in Iranian culture, and continues to work on a paper, ignoring her family gathering. He feels superior to her step-brother's macho attitudes. Feri obviously feels estranged from him, and decides to stay in Iran with her mother for the time being.

Rachlin's portrait of the American male is unflattering, but not inaccurate. Tony is aloof and unemotional, devoting most of his energies to his work, and committing adultery casually, all complaints American women have made about American men. Feri's brother is a typical uneducated Iranian, hot-tempered, jealous, concerned about honor. The Iranian doctor represents a syncretization of Iranian and Western culture; he combines the technical skill and rationalism of the West with an Iranian warmth that Tony seems to lack. He therefore seems a better match for Feri, who resents Tony's obliviousness to her culture. Rachlin seems to suggest that such syncretization can occur within the bi-cultural individual, and might provide a better solution than rigid adherence to either culture.

Some of the most interesting work regarding intercultural relationships has recently come from ethnic minorities living in Europe and the United States such as Rachlin. It is no wonder, since they themselves are bicultural. French Algerian Medhi Charaf's Tea in the Harem and the better known My Beautiful Laundrette, screenplay by British Pakistani Hanef Kureishi, both deal with the racial and cultural conflicts between Europeans and racial minorities in Europe.

Tea in the Harem concerns the friendship between Majid, the son of an Algerian worker, and a French youth, Pat. Both are part of the underclass in French society, and are thus shut out from the hope of advancing within the system. Majid idealizes Pat's sister who supposedly has a "good" job as a secretary, until he learns she is actually working as a prostitute. She too is doomed by the economic system. Majid's mother tries to discourage his attraction because she thinks it will weaken his adherence to his Algerian heritage. The relationship between the two friends dominates the novel/film, however, with Majid's buddy leading him deeper into illegal activities, while his mother, representing his Algerian roots, cautions him to get a job and face up to his responsibilities to his family. We note her frustration as we see her slipping further away, rejecting Arabic and his culture. The film shows how the "beurs" (North Africans living in France), essentially shut out of French life save for the most menial of jobs, can turn to petty crimes and an aimless life of instant gratification and cultural disintegration.

My Beautiful Laundrette shows a similar situation among the Pakistanis living in London, except that the Pakistanis in the film are from a wealthy and influential background in their own country. In England they are despised, and they turn to drug dealing to make it in Britain. Omar's uncle is a ruthless business man and slum landlord, while his father is a communist intellectual who wants his son to have a university education. His uncle seems to be winning out, however, since Omar sees the possibilities of rising as a businessman, which is anathema to his father. Omar's uncle has a daughter, Tanya, who would make an obvious choice as a wife for him, but Omar's friendship with Johnny, a working class schoolmate who once marched with the fascists in an anti-Pakistani demonstration, becomes a love affair. Johnny takes a job helping Omar renovate a laundry owned by his uncle, and has to fight off his working class friends who see his action as racial betrayal. A conflict between the fascists and Omar's corrupt cousin Selim end in the destruction of the laundry.

Tanya, rejected by Omar and Johnny, leaves the family, presumably for independence. Omar's father seems about to die, and with him his communist ideals. His uncle's Pakistani wife puts a curse on his English mistress and she breaks out in a terrible rash, thus forcing the end of the relationship. But Omar and Johnny are left happily together amidst the ruins of the trendy laundrette.

So ironic is this film that it is hard to draw any definite conclusions, but it seems that the relationship between Omar and Johnny is supposed to represent a new generation of cultural syncretization. Even though Omar wishes to repay the humiliation he has felt from British racism by forcing Johnny to work for him, their relationship, with the possible exception of Omar's uncle's love for his British mistress (also based on her financial dependence on him), seems to be the only glimmer of hope of overcoming the racial conflict plaguing Britain. Yet the corruption and hostility surrounding the couple suggests that our society is no more ready for intercultural than homosexual relationships than it was when Forster wrote A Passage to India.

My Beautiful Laundrette is exceptional in that Middle Eastern homophobia makes it practically impossible to express homosexual desires in the Middle East (another reversal of Western stereotypes is that Middle Easterners see homosexuality as another example of Western "decadence"). In "Al-Muwa" (The Meowing), a short story by Syrian writer Ghada al-Samman, an Arab woman studying in London, who misses Arab men, "'real men' in contrast with the effeminate British," has a vaguely homosexual encounter with a British woman, which shatters her gender identity. As Evelyn Accad points out, it is not easy "for a person raised in a traditional culture to adapt to the mores of a libertarian culture where 'all things are permitted'" (114-115).

While Western and Eastern cultures share some of the same stereotypes about each other's men and women, while both are ethnocentric, and while conflict over women represents a struggle for dominance between these two patriarchal cultures, the reasons for the failure of intercultural marriages in the literary works differs profoundly. In Western literature intercultural relationships represent a romantic escape from "civilization" which usually ends tragically. A major barrier to intercultural relationships is the "inferiority" or "barbarity" of the Middle Easterner or North African. In contemporary Middle Eastern literature intercultural relationships appear threatening because the Middle Easterner fears cultural, political, and economic domination, and the Western male or female represents the powerful forces of modernization and the perceived loss of identity accompanying it, which even Middle Easterners who accept change see as threatening. Especially threatening is the loss of the strong family Middle Easterners value and the prevalence of individualism and egotism in the West. It is not clear whether this picture will improve so that constructive cultural syncretization can occur and intercultural relationships can flourish.

I believe this will happen when and if Westerners begin to feel less superior and Middle Easterners begin to feel less threatened, which depends largely on a shift in the balance of political, economic, and cultural power. If any writers can now bridge the gap they are those who have lived on the margins of their own cultures and are truly bicultural; they are more likely to be Middle Easterners than Westerners.

References

Accad, Evelyn.
  1978 Veil of Shame: The Role of Women in the Contemporary Fiction of North Africa and the Arab World. Sherbrooke, Quebec: Éditions Naaman.

Al-e Ahmad, Jalal.
  1982 Gharbzadegi: (Weststruckness). Lexington, Ky: Mazda.

Allen, Roger.
  1982 The Arabic Novel: An Historical and Critical Introduction. Syracuse University Press.

Alloula, Malik.
  1986 The Colonial Harem. Trans. by Myrna Godzich and Wlad Godzich. Introduction by Barbara Harlow. Minneapolis: University of Minnesota Press.

Baudet, Henri.
  1965 Paradise on Earth: Some Thoughts on European Images of Non-European Man. New Haven: Yale University Press.

Blanch, Lesley.
  1983 Pierre Loti: The Legendary Romantic. New York: Harcourt, Brace, Jovanovich.

Choukri, Mohamed.
  1979 Tennessee Williams in Tangier. Translated by Paul Bowles. Santa Barbara: Cadmus.

Cowhig, Ruth.
  1985 "Blacks in English Renaissance Drama and the Role of Shakespeare's Othello" (1-25); McClure, John. "Problematic Presence: The Colonial Other in Kipling and Conrad" (154-167); Frances, Mannsaker "The Dog that Didn't Bark: The Subject Races in Imperial Fiction at the Turn of the Century" (112-134); In The Black Presence in English Literature. Ed. David Dabydeen. Manchester University Press.

Herodotus.
  1942 The Persian Wars. Translated by George Rawlinson. New York: Random House, 1942.

Hetata, Sherif.
  1986 The Net. London: Zed.

Islam, Shamsul.
  1979 Chronicles of the Raj: A Study of Literary Reaction to the Imperial Idea towards the End of the Raj. London: MacMillan.

Kabbani, Rana.
  1986 Europe's Myths of Orient. Bloomington University Press.

Memmi, Albert.
  1965 The Colonizer and the Colonized. Boston: Beacon.

Narayan, R. K.
  1983 The Vendor of Sweets. New York: King Penguin.

Popham, Janet and Janet Tedesco.
  1985 Introduction to the Raj Quartet. Lanham, MD: University Press of America.

Said, Edward.
  1978 Orientalism. New York: Vintage.

Shaarawi, Huda.
  1986 Harem Years: Memoirs of an Egyptian Feminist. Translated by Margot
    Badren. London: Virago.

Thurman, Judith.
  1982 Isak Dinesen: The Life of a Storyteller. New York: St. Martin's.

PART II :

ADJUSTING TO RACIAL AND CULTURAL PLURALISM

CHAPTER 5

RACIAL PLURALISM, RACISM, AND EXILE FROM AMERICA

Bolaji and Jeanne Bamijoko

We met in 1957 in Ohio, my brown skinned husband and I. Our courtship wasn't a long one for right from the beginning we felt that we wanted to be together. Our ideas, values, and opinions seemed to click and I guess we could say it was love at first sight. Of course, the fact that we came from different races was a factor to be considered. However, we decided after due consideration that the decision to marry despite racial differences must be within ourselves. We first had to recognize ourselves to be as we really were, a man and a woman. The real issue of a mixed marriage is a psychological one. If a couple regard themselves as a mixed couple first, and knowingly feel they are doing something that's taboo, they are doomed before they begin, for, if they feel this way, how will the world feel about it?

In 1957, civil rights groups were just beginning to surface and America's conscience was forced to admit that a real racial problem existed in the society. There were 16 states in America at this period of time that didn't recognize mixed marriages and in some states the participants of mixed marriage could be criminally prosecuted. This was the situation when we married.

Ivan insisted that we go to my hometown, Rochester, Minnesota, so I could inform my mother about our marriage. She really surprised me. I had always viewed her as a liberal thinker, however, when I told her, she refused to meet Ivan. She also warned me about telling my father. He had very reactionary feelings towards Jews, Catholics, and Blacks.

We were quite depressed when we left Rochester. Still, we realized that family attitudes could change in time, and we were determined to try and achieve this through patience.

We went on to St. Paul and spent several hours looking for a room. We had almost given up when we spotted a rooming house called Mamies. An old woman answered the door and invited us in. She agreed to give us a room with kitchen privileges. We stayed there a week and Mamie became our friend. We had something in common with her. In 1935, after the death of her first husband, she met and fell in love with a black man. This affair and marriage had at that time caused her and Daniel, her husband, a lot of heartache and sorrow. Mamie had been committed to an insane asylum and Daniel had gone to prison. However, at the end of their imprisonment, they had gone away together and spent some 20 years finding happiness. Mamie at 73 was looking forward to joining Daniel in the next world, as she put it.

We had found a pioneer in this thing called mixed marriage, and throughout our life the courage and dedication she had displayed gave us the inspiration to go on.

At this time, after much discussion, we decided to go out into the world and see what we could find. Since Ivan was a musician, it would be an interesting experience to see other places and meet other people. He would have a chance to learn other music. So began our nomadic life of 14 years, traveling through over 20 different countries.

Our first stop was Mexico City. It was obvious to us from the beginning that Mexico had very strenuous laws regarding musicians. The musicians union there had a policy of exchange, and if a Mexican musician wasn't allowed to work in America, then the American musician wasn't allowed to work in Mexico until an exchange could be arranged. However, there were some clubs that by-passed the law, and Ivan found one of those clubs and began working. He played the piano and sang at this bar, and was exploited because of his lack of working papers. Our accommodations were terrible, and the pay was worse. We actually had to sneak away from the place as we found out that the owner was a small time gangster. We met an American man, Jack Dyer, who thought Ivan's talent extraordinary. We went on to Acapulco, and although many clubs liked Ivan and wanted to hire him, the union wouldn't allow it. After Acapulco, we went to Veracruz only to find the same situation. It was then Jack decided we should go on to Guatemala. We got as far as the last town in Mexico, Comitan. When we got ready to cross over, we found that our visas weren't valid and the authorities arrested us. After much discussion, we were allowed to stay in a small hotel because Comitan was very small and only had one jail for men. The people in the town became very interested in us. They decided to help us in any way they could. The head of the village opened the old movie theatre which had a piano and let Ivan entertain the public. The funds they raised came to us to help us with our expenses. The Mexican people are very romantically inclined, and they talked of nothing but the negrita and the blanco, the black and the white. They thought our romance was wonderful. Although we were allowed to stay in the hotel, we had a guard on the door constantly. The sheriff was a big, tall man with a handlebar moustache. He used to come to our room with his guitar and play romantic ballads for us.

The Mexican officials in Mexico City had to be notified that we were in Mexico illegally, and then they had to decide what to do. It was going to take weeks as Comitan had little or no way to communicate with the outside world. Jack decided that we should go on, into the interior. The guard had long since been removed. So, that's what happened. We packed our things and one night, we just walked out of the village into the interior. Jack hired horses for us further on in the interior, and our next adventure began. We went up mountains, into swamps, and on to the highway that led to Guatemala. We went through a bandit village, where bandits from both countries lived together away from any authority. They treated us with respect, and helped us in any way they could. It was quite an experience. We went on to Guatemala.

Before we could regulate our papers in Guatemala, we were picked up. Ivan had been working about a month, and the hotel had promised to fix his papers, but they hadn't done it. We had made some friends, but none influential enough to help us. In Guatemala, it's the Napoleonic law. You are guilty until proven innocent, and Ivan had to spend 9 months in the penitentiary leaving me alone to stay with some Guatemalan family who treated me like their own. It was surprising to find out how much the people there knew about racial discrimination and about mixed marriages. The newspapers tried to help by writing articles about us. The immigration decided that when Ivan was let free, we could stay in Guatemala and make our life there. That's the way it happened. We stayed in Guatemala about two years. Two of our daughters were born there, Sheila in 1960, and Laura in 1961.

The political situation in Guatemala, like so many Central American countries, changed constantly, and after the Bay of Pigs invasion when Guatemala was holding its breath waiting for Cuban retaliation, we decided to go back to Mexico.

This time, the union allowed Ivan to work. He worked in a very exclusive night club, Chipps. He also made a long play recording. The album was titled, "Vin Morris Canta por Los Enamorados," "Vin Morris sings for lovers." Yes, the recording company decided for commercial reasons to change my husband's name and he became Vin Morris.

The Mexican people never showed us any discrimination. They treated us like we were one of them. That is, until the government decided they couldn't allow us to stay in Mexico anymore. Our third daughter Robin, was born in December, 1962 and it was at this time we received an expulsion order. Vin's name was on the marque of the biggest theatre in Mexico City, "The Blancita", but he wasn't allowed to perform. He was heartbroken.

Vin Speaks :

All my life I had been reminded in one way or the other that I was a second class citizen and as such, I should appreciate any opportunities that came my way, and not in any way fight back to obtain better conditions. We blacks in America in the forties and fifties had our own racism going, and it all evolved around the color of our skin. We light men were scapegoats for both the black and the white. I could not begin to count the endless times I was accused of thinking I was smart just because I was a little lighter than the rest. After a while I just thought to hell with it, and went about doing the best I could do. I missed many chances because I wouldn't conform to the norms set out by both the whites and the blacks. When I met Jeanne, I was at a low ebb in my life and she gave me new hope and love that I knew would never die. I figured the best thing to do would be go out and see the world, and find out if the same type of racism existed everywhere. Mexico and Guatemala were our first experiences in other worlds, and although we didn't find the die hard racism of America, we found that each place had its own type of problems all based on either race, color, or creed. We had some bad times and some good times in these two countries, and each experience helped us find ourselves, and brought us closer together as a couple.

We decided at this time to go to Europe. During our stay in Mexico, Vin had met some of his old musician friends from the states, and they all said Paris was a swinging city for night life, and that if we ever got the chance to go there we should go. It wasn't going to be easy with three small daughters, but then, since we had the opportunity, we decided to take it.

We arrived in Brussels, Belgium and had a night's stop over. It was cold and dreary after the balmy weather of Mexico. The woman receptionist found us a room for the night. The next day, we took a short flight to Paris, and then our problems began. When we landed in Paris, the receptionist there began calling around to different hotels in search of accommodation for us. It took her about five hours to find one. The Parisians apparently didn't like children in their hotels. She finally found a temporary place, and we went to the St. George Hotel to settle down.

The European attitude towards babies was completely opposite from that of Mexico and Guatemala. In Central America, they had a very reasonable attitude to babies crying. In Paris, it was exactly the opposite. People complained constantly about the noise the three girls made. There was a knock at the door or a tap on the wall every five minutes. It was a nerve-racking situation. We did our best to keep the children quiet, but our best most of the time wasn't good enough.

Vin heard that Kenny Clarke, the American drummer, was playing at a club called St. Germaine Des Pres on the left bank, and so he took his album and went to see him. Two days later he had a job singing with Kenny. We found alternative accommodations in a smaller hotel, and life continued.

Paris was a very cold city, weather-wise. Even in July and August, by noon time the air would turn chilly, and by night it was cold. There didn't seem to be any summer. The people were very nationalistic, and French was the only language they seemed to understand. If they knew how to speak English, it was hidden from me. Don't misunderstand me the French didn't bother us; they just ignored us. This was soon after the Algerian conflict, and they were very bitter about the outcome of it. Vin was often mistaken for an Arab and constantly harassed when he was alone on the streets. Once somebody threw a stone at him from a passing car and it hit him in the face, just missing his eye.

The children and I hardly left the hotel. We didn't have the money to go out anywhere. I would keep the children as quiet as I could in the mornings so Vin could get some sleep, as he worked until 4 or 5 o'clock a.m.

We were really discriminated against when we got a small car. We couldn't go two or three blocks before we were stopped by the gendarmes and our papers checked. It got to be very embarrassing.

Vin Speaks :

> The time we spent in Paris was very hard on us all. Although I worked every night, I felt very sorry for Jeanne and the girls because they were so isolated from everything. I was getting the exposure I needed to further my career, but was it worth it? Kenny Clarke was a great name in jazz, and with his endorsement I could go far. He, however, felt I should send Jeanne and the girls back to the states. This contention made me really angry. I felt I had enough talent to make it, and Jeanne was willing to wait, so why should we be separated. Several opportunities came my way, but Kenny would always say I owed him as he gave me the first chance. I just kept on working, and hoping that things would change, and when they didn't, I knew it was time to go on to some other country. I knew I could make it wherever there was a jazz club, and there were many in Europe.

> After the children were born, my mother began to write to us. We sent pictures to her, and she was very proud of her lovely grandchildren. My father, on the other hand, had written to me early in my marriage and told me he didn't want to hear from me again. He said that as far as he was concerned, I was dead. That

was really hard to take. I really felt sorry for him, for he was missing the love of some very nice grandchildren.

Friends were something we didn't have many of. Kenny's wife, Daisy, a Dutch woman, asked us to her house for dinner one Sunday. Unfortunately, the baby, Robin, was having a difficult time adjusting to Paris. She cried constantly. On that Sunday, the situation was no different, and before we'd even had dinner, Kenny began to fidget. The crying made it impossible for us to eat in peace, and we soon took our leave. That was the first and last time we were invited there. One of the band members was married to a German girl, and when she arrived from Germany, she came to see us several times. That, however, was the extent of our social life. I didn't have time to be lonely, but occasionally like every woman, I dreamed of a day of rest.

We left Paris, went to the south of France, and then on to Switzerland, Germany, Copenhagen, Denmark, and then to Norway.

In Copenhagen, Vin found another of his friends from the states, Dexter Gordon, the saxophonist. He got Vin a job in the best jazz club there, the Momarte. We found a nice apartment, and life smiled at us for two months. The Danish people were open, friendly people, and they accepted us like we were one of them.

From there we went to Norway, another lovely country with very friendly people. During our stay there, Vin made another recording, this time a 45 recording with only two songs. We rewrote the words of the songs, calling one of them, Sheila Baby. It was quite a success, and Vin and Sheila did a T.V. show to launch the recording. The girls weren't so much trouble then, as they were slowly growing up to be smart, quiet little girls. We made friends in Norway, spent our Sundays hiking and drinking coffee in friendly homes.

We finally left Norway and went back to France. We stayed only a short time, and then went on to Spain. Work was seasonal there, and Vin got a good job working with some well known Spanish musicians. It was at this time that our two sons were born. First, Eric was born in February, 1965, and then Ivan, Jr. in December, 1966.

Spain is a very religious country, Catholicism being their faith, and they take their faith very seriously. They have great love and respect for the family unit. The common person who makes up the biggest portion of the population is hard working, God fearing, has many children, and little money. They believe in hospitality, and are willing to share, no matter how little they have, with anyone who needs help. They love children, all types of children. The following story is an example:

The off season came and work in Barcelona was scarce, so we decided to go down the coast to Malaga where there were a lot of clubs that had business year round. Vin found work in a small club, and the man in charge gave us a small apartment to stay in during the off season. I was pregnant again and not too happy about it. I had been to one doctor in Malaga, but he had gone away, and so I was trying to wait until he returned. Sometimes the children and I would go for walks near the beach. The village people always greeted us and would stop to play with the children. Little by little, we made a few friends.

Labor started in the evening of February 6, 1965. All we could do was wait until morning, for our house was about 20 miles from Malaga. In the morning we went to town by taxi and found a hospital that would accept me. Before noon, our first son, Eric, was born. Vin was elated, at last a boy.

Eric was a long, lean baby who didn't like to eat. He was very calm, crying only rarely, and would spend his time just looking around. The girls were entranced by their little brother. However, money was very scarce, and the clothing I had for Eric was very inadequate. We came home the third day. Early in the evening, the door bell began to ring. Our village neighbors had come to see the new baby, and each and every one of them brought gifts for him and the family. They brought clothing for the baby and the girls too, toys, and foodstuffs of all kinds, dresses for me, and many other items they felt we might need. Before they left, they all prayed for us, and then they continued coming back to visit until we left the apartment. They were really some gracious, Godly people, and they were the nicest people we have ever met.

We traveled back and forth between France and Spain. Since the work was seasonal, we had to go where the work was.

In Barcelona, on the 1st of December, 1966, our second son and last child was born, Ivan, Jr. Vin now had two sons. We had been thinking about going to North Africa. Vin met an old friend from the days he had worked in the clubs, Mr. Lopez, and he agreed to help us go to Africa.

Our car was an old citroen. We had bought it in France for fifty dollars, and it looked just like the old packards used in America by the gangsters in the 1920s. We headed for Algerciras, the port in Spain. It was Christmas eve when we got there and lined up like the other vehicles to await the coming of the ferry. The headman inspecting the vehicles wasn't very impressed with ours. In fact, he told Vin we couldn't pass. Vin went inside to talk to the man, and returned with him to the car. The girls were standing with me watching the approaching ferry. Eric went to stand beside his father. As the man approached the car, the baby began to cry. The man shook his head.

"Anymore," he asked?

I shook my head. The girls were standing beside him by then, smiling up at him the way children do.

He smiled slightly and said, "Here is the pass. Go on and Merry Christmas to you."

Several hours later we arrived in Spanish Morocco. It was near midnight, and the church bells were singing out their Christmas message. We parked near the churches, watching the merry church goers. Around three o'clock a.m., a priest who had seen us sent food to the children for Christmas.

We spent time in Morocco, Tunisia, and eventually moved on to Algeria. It was very lonely in those countries because they are completely Muslim and adhere to the traditions of the staunch Muslims, particularly the women. They never appeared on the streets unless they were covered with the traditional shrouds. Only their two eyes showed, and there were parts of Morocco where only one eye was allowed to show. The Arab women felt that their western counterparts were allowed too much freedom, and it was unusual to find even one woman who would greet a westerner. The following story is an example:

Vin had met some Arabs who enjoyed his singing, and they had asked him to bring his family and come to their home for lunch. We went, the children, Vin, and I. We were all seated around a large table. When the men had seated themselves, I looked around wondering where the women would sit, as there were no vacant places. When we were settled, the women emerged from the kitchen carrying the food to the tables. They were dressed in the traditional style, and they didn't say a word, simply placed the food on the table and went back into the kitchen. I was stunned. The girls and I were the only females allowed to eat at the table with the men, as tradition forbids the woman to sit down with the men. She eats with the children in the kitchen.

Vin worked in Morocco and Tunisia, and then we went on to Algeria. The French-Algerian war hadn't been over very long, and the people of Algeria were very nationalistic. Most of them didn't like foreigners at all. The government, on the other hand, felt very differently about foreigners. There were many black governments in exile in Algeria. They helped us a great deal, finding work for Vin in the radio station. He was put in charge of foreign music, and each week I helped him plan two programs. The programs were translated into French before being presented. We stayed over two years in Algeria.

During our stay in Algeria, we didn't have many Arab friends. People of different nations grouped together. During the Pan African Festival held in Algeria, we met Stokely Carmichael and Miriam Makeba. Eldridge Cleaver, one of the leaders of the Black Panthers, came to Algeria and set up a party in exile. Stokely suggested we go to black Africa, Nigeria perhaps.

During the festival we also met a young French philanthropist, Serge Bard. He had brought an entire movie company to Algeria, planning to make films in the Sahara Desert. He liked us immediately, and he especially liked the children. When he found out we were going to cross the Sahara in our old citroen, he decided to give us an old army van he had with him, a 1956 Dodge ambulance, 7 tons with a large wheel base. We made the back into living quarters, setting up a place for everyone to sleep, and space for cooking. It was like a small trailer. Then, with five children in tow, we crossed the Sahara desert.

It would take me pages and pages to relate the trip across the Sahara. It took us over 14 days, and it was a really eventful trip. We received some help from English and Scotch people, and we were turned down when we requested water from some of those same people. It had nothing to do with being a mixed couple, it was only a struggle for survival in a vast desert. We landed in Niger, went on to Dahomey, now the Republic of Benin, and then to Ghana, back to Togo, and we eventually reached Nigeria. There we began a very different life, for upon arrival, Vin was claimed by a Yoruba family to be the long lost son of one of the Royal families there, Mrs. Esther Adefolaju Bamijoko.

It began like this. The Nigerian civil war hadn't been over long, and people with American passports were being turned back. Vin decided to go to the Nigerian Charge D'Affairs and see if he wouldn't give us a visa. We went. There we met a very enlightened, intelligent, Charge D'Affairs. After much discussion, he agreed to give us a 72 hours visa. However, he told us that we should explain everything at the border and he was sure they would give us an extended visa for at least two weeks. Then, we could arrange our situation. This we did, and the customs people took us to their compound on Harvey Road in Lagos. It was there that the newspapers picked up our story. Several weeks later, we moved our van to a private compound and it was there Mrs. Bamijoko came to claim her long lost son,

Bolaji. That day marked the beginning of our new life, a life we have lived for the past 23 years.

The old woman told a remarkable story, and topped it all off by identifying a mark on Vin's arm, a mark that he hadn't been able to identify his entire life. Even before he left the states, he had told me of his dreams of Africa. He couldn't understand it. There had been a woman in it, and she always seemed to be calling him by a strange name. He even heard African drums, and he always awoke with a sad, melancholy feeling engulfing him.

We now entered into a new culture. We were introduced to the different local foods, given African names and African clothing to wear, taught African customs. Everyone from Mama Bamijoko's village came to Lagos to pay tribute to the return of Bolaji Bamijoko. Day and night the house was full of visitors. They stayed for days, cooking, talking and praising mama for finding Bolaji. Everything in this new culture was different, the diet, the people, the climate, the customs, the language, and the mode of dress. Perhaps the most difficult thing to get used to was the lack of privacy. People were at the house visiting us every minute of the day and night.

Several weeks later, we were taken to a village outside Lagos to meet Baba Bamijoko. This was a special event, and preparations went on for weeks. We had to take everything with us, including food and drinks. We went there in a car borrowed from mama's cousin, a big chevrolet, a rare oddity in this society.

The old man was pathetically ill, sitting propped up in a big stuffed chair. He smiled tiredly when he saw us, and beckoned Bolaji to sit down beside him. They talked privately for an hour, and when they finished the old man accepted Bolaji as his long lost son. Festivities followed, traditional music, drumming, eating, and drinking, and when it was finished, Bolaji was proclaimed an African prince.

<u>Vin speaks</u> :

> I had found a new family at the age of 43 years old. Mama was a very determined, self-reliant woman. She was a victim of her own society, as she was extremely superstitious and believed in her traditions. Still, who am I to say she wasn't right. It was amazing to find myself a prince, and I decided then and there to never mislead the people around me, and to set a good example of anything I did, as I found out at the beginning that the people watched me and would copy many of the things I did. The American experience is a hell of an experience to forget, everything moves so quickly and so smoothly there, and everything in Africa seems to be the opposite. However, what can a person expect, we've only had our freedom 33 years, and they have been turbulent years. Still, it's difficult to slow down, even after 36 years.
>
> Jeanne, on the other hand, finds the society a challenge. She relates to the people well, in fact, most of them call her mama, a very respected title for an older woman, and a rare title for a white woman. Most white women are regarded as madam. She's very proud of her title, and helps out in the society whenever she has a chance.
>
> Our marriage has been a successful one mainly because we really love each other. The necessity to protect one another from outside criticism brought

about because of our racial differences has drawn us closer together. To be considerate of each other's opinions and to encourage each other in all our different endeavors has been one of the policies that has helped us through many rough places. We have been able to meet the challenges of life head on, because we have done it together.

God has been the principal concept in our lives. Pantheism is our religion. It simply means we see God in everything in the universe. We try to preach love and devotion here because brotherly love is lacking in this society. Tribalism and nepotism have separated the people, and a more united society is needed to head off all the problems present in a developing nation.

Our children have always been the focal point in our lives, and that's what makes it so difficult to understand them. Our young women have always felt very victimized because they are mixed. They seem to bathe in the chaos of self pity, never wanting to accept who they are. There is some degree of discrimination in Nigeria, but they have always been special to the people here because of the story that follows them. At an early age they learned the language, and have always been able to communicate with the people. As they grew older, we have always felt it was their inability to accept themselves that divided them from their African counterparts, and diverted their attention to the white side of their being. The black feeling of inferiority has reversed itself, and it is the girls who feel they must exaggerate their ideas and achievements to find acceptance in either race. Two of our girls have married mixed Nigerians, and we can only hope that their attitudes will change as they grow older, and they will learn to accept themselves for what they have achieved in life and not for what they are. The third girl left Nigeria several years ago and went to America.

The young men on the other hand have tried to make the most out of who they are. They don't dislike their African heritage. They speak the language fluently, without accent, much to the delight of most Africans. They attended an all black school, have many, many, African friends and aren't in anyway worried about their mixed status.

We are known by many Nigerians as mama and papa. We have been in drama here, one very special serial written by a Nigerian. We have toured the country with a Nigerian comedian. Bolaji and Sheila have made a recording, and they have performed in several musical shows. In 1983, Bolaji and I wrote a book, dedicated to Mama, who passed away the same year, and titled it, From the Bottom to the Top. The title has only one meaning. Nobody can argue with us concerning the black man's status in America. He is definitely on the bottom as far as education, job facilities and housing. When he comes to Africa, if he can accept his roots, he is on the top for in Africa he runs everything. The book has had a moderate amount of success and would certainly have had more if it hadn't been for distribution difficulties. Several teacher's colleges have used it as a text book, and several universities also. The common person likes it very much, as the letters we have received prove so. Someday we hope to be able to distribute it abroad. We have tried in our small way to show the world that mixed marriages are here to stay. Bolaji and I believe the mixed marriages are God's way of stopping the terrible diseases called racism and discrimination.

CHAPTER 6

UP FROM THE FIFTIES

Donald R. and Blanche O. Hill

Both Don and Blanche:

Although we've been married for 32 years and continue to love each other today, ours has not been a textbook case of "the happy marriage." Through the years, even though we have gained a lot of strength from each other, the marriage has had its ups and downs. At times we have each thought seriously about divorce. But today, with one grown adopted child and two 'successful' professional careers, and with discrimination against middle class blacks and interracial couples less severe than when we were first married, our marriage remains strong.

Blanche is black and was born Blanche Olivia Taylor. She has no siblings. She was born into a middle class family of some note in Greensboro, North Carolina, in 1939. Her father - himself one of five sons of a prominent Washington D.C. minister - was the first black to graduate with a master's degree in Fine Arts from Syracuse University. He had settled in Greensboro, where he married Lelia Sharpe. She was from Leakesville, North Carolina. Her father was a mill worker and her mother took in washing. Blanche's mother, her younger brother, and her sister all became school teachers. On her father's side, Blanche's uncles, aunts, and cousins are teachers, musicians, doctors, ministers.

Don is white, the third son of Lowell and Rosamond Hill. He was born in Long Beach, California, delivered as the family story goes, by his obstetrician uncle. His paternal grandfather was once registrar at Berkeley, and both grandfathers were also superintendents of school districts in California. Both grandmothers were "housewives," as was his mother. His father was an obstetrician. His oldest brother was an orthopedist before his death of leukemia at age 39. His other brother is a manager at the Budweiser brewery in Williamsburg, Virginia, a strange irony for a teetotaling upbringing. Most of Don's relatives are teachers or medical doctors.

Don:

Blanche and I met at Fisk University in Nashville, Tennessee where she attended school and where I was an "exchange" student from Pomona College in California (I have always thought there was something strange about that term, "exchange," as if I were visiting a foreign country and needed smallpox shots or something). The year was 1958, one year before Fisk was to play a major role in the "sit-ins." We were peripherally involved in "the Movement" and counted as friends some of its leaders.

Outside meeting Blanche, the most significant thing for me during these years was the gradual development of my interest in folk music, an interest which would eventually lead to a career in anthropology.

It was during this period that Blanche and I were dating, but not yet married, that I had an experience that I will never forget. A white friend and I were in Clarkesdale, Mississippi, attempting to record folk music. We had become friends with a black barber, Wade Walton. He tried to help us by taking us to meet blues singers and by singing and telling old stories himself. A day or two after we arrived in Clarkesdale we attended Wade's church. Upon leaving, we were arrested by the police. After being taken into custody, but before being searched by the cops and the FBI (they were a sort of tag team then), I had the good sense to eat a picture of Blanche which I carried in my wallet. People have laughed at me when I tell this story - I say that Blanche is close to my stomach, not my heart. This was a couple of years before the Freedom Rides in Mississippi, and I'm convinced that we were not taken to be the threat as we might have later.

Blanche:

At Fisk, Don sat in front of me in sociology class, always surrounded by smoke from his pipe. We started talking to each other primarily because we shared this class and shared a mutual love for folk music. He was an intellectual snob. Initially, he had never seen a black person with red hair like mine. It was on this auspicious occasion that we began a relationship that has lasted more than thirty years to date.

Don and I courted that term with the help of the local movie theater and restaurant. We toyed with the thought that we were more in love with the idea of interracial relationships than each other. Our friends thought otherwise. The semester ended with Don informing his mother, on a tape recording no less, of his interest in me ("Hello mom; I've got a girlfriend here at Fisk." "Well, bring her home and let me meet her.")

Don:

Telling my mother about Blanche was quite unusual for me. I rarely discussed my girlfriends with my mother; it seems that she would make me very nervous with her nettlesome inquiries. It is interesting to note, however, that all my "serious" girlfriends came from backgrounds other than my own: my first "girl" was Jewish. In high school I had a Norwegian girlfriend (her father was a business man stationed in the United States), and another who was half Italian and half Swedish (she was American). Then, in college the only person I dated before Blanche was a Japanese-American. I didn't "seek out" women from such diverse backgrounds, it was just the way it was (this is probably the reverse of the supposed preferences Jewish men have for Wasp women and black men have for white women!)

Blanche:

When Don returned home from Fisk, his parents had him psychologically evaluated by experts ranging from ministers to marriage counselors. In the end of the psychological probings Don went to Europe, where he wrote me a rather strange letter about the talents of the American composer, Charles Ives.

Don:

I know what I like in Ives. It is his composition which musically depicts a parade from the vantage of a spectator. The spectator hears one band pass, another approach, and then both bands at the same time, each playing a different tune. Finally, the onlooker hears only the second band. Now that I think of it, this sure sounds like a metaphor for an interracial marriage!

Blanche:
        In that same letter Don professed his love for me. And so we kept in touch through letters, tapes, telephone calls. Eventually, we each graduated, me from Fisk and Don from Pomona. I went to Tuskegee Institute and Don went to New York.
        Don left New York and brought an engagement ring to Tuskegee, Alabama. I discussed our possible marriage with a few friends. They offered no opinions one way or the other.
        Nevertheless, when I left Tuskegee to join Don in Monterey, California, my family and friends were surprised. My family doubted that we were really married; that is, they thought it was not possible that a white man would marry me! Don's parents were not told for a while. Then, on an occasion after fixing our house up for our meeting with them and still, he didn't tell them, I gave him an ultimatum. Either tell them or it is "goodbye." So, he told them.

Don:
        After graduation, I hung out in New York City for several months and Blanche came to visit me. Those were halcyon days. We looked up old friends from Fisk, and we made the clubs of Harlem and the Village. Soon, however, Blanche had to go to Alabama to teach summer school at Tuskegee Institute. I stayed on in New York, living in the lower East Side and working a pushcart off a delivery truck. I was thinking about Blanche a lot; I checked into going back to school at City College in education, but that wasn't what I really wanted. I phoned Blanche often, and then, suddenly, I decided to return to California, by way of Tuskegee and Blanche, and then join the Army. This would help me decide my part as to whether we should marry or not.
        Blanche and I spent a week together in Alabama, which was a bit unusual in those days (1961). We wanted to marry, but we weren't sure.
        Back in California, I joined the Army and was soon at Fort Ord in Basic Training. Then I was stationed at the Presidio of Monterey so that I could take a year of the Korean Language at the Army Language School (now called Defense Language Institute). During this time Blanche and I spoke frequently by phone, and after a few months, we decided to marry. She took the train to California after she finished her year at Tuskegee Institute. We got our marriage license in Pacific Grove and were married in Seaside by a preacher Blanche had met on the train.
        We lived in Monterey (in a neighborhood described by Steinbeck in Sweet Thursday) for six months. These too were very happy times. Being at Language School and in the Army Security Agency was about the closest one could get to being in college while actually in the army: there was very little military drilling. One's entire time was spent learning a language.
        Weekends were filled with parties with army buddies, all of whom were in the same class as I (I think there were 16 of us, all services and many different ranks, in two rooms, learning Korean six hours a day, five days a week, for one year).

Cops regularly came to our door or to the houses of our friends, wherever we were partying. Thinking back on this it seems clear that we were protected by my being in the service. Since I am white, discrimination did not fit into my job (I was surprised that my romance and marriage to Blanche did not harm my top secret security clearance, but it didn't: I think that the army was one of the fairest environments for us then).

The only ill effect of these six months in Monterey was my own doing. I was very much afraid of my parents, especially my father. To some extent, I had bought their threats of impending disaster in the family if I were to marry Blanche. My father said our marriage would kill his father; my brother said it would kill my father; my father said that he would disown me. My response to these threats was not to tell them that we were married. It was Blanche - actually she said that she would leave me if I didn't tell them - that eventually got me to tell my parents that we were married.

And when we did, they seemed very shocked. But, almost instantly, they said that they would back us. My father and mother, both liberal Republicans in a conservative Republican milieu, had always fought discrimination up to a point: they talked liberalism but went along with the system. So although they accepted us (they visited frequently over the years and even came to see us in the Caribbean), we got the feeling that it was partial. For example, although we visited them on occasion, those visits were always more tension filled than their trips to where we lived. While they like to see us, they seemed tentative when we entered their world.

Blanche's mother - her father had been dead some years by then - accepted our marriage, but again, this had a racial component. As a light-skinned 'black' once married to a brown-skinned man she tended to prefer light-skinned over dark-skinned people. Over the years we have gradually become aware of the fact that Blanche was a double victim of racism: first, the national, white American racism and a derivative racism from the home.

Blanche:
        Eventually, Don's parents were very supportive, but his paternal grandparents were not told of our marriage. His maternal grandfather was told; Don's grandfather hoped that we would raise another "Ralph Bunche." It was felt by Don's oldest brother (the one who died) that there would be negative repercussions from the community. He questioned Don's motivations for such a thing. To this day Don's widowed sister-in-law and her three children have no communication with Don. The other brother has expressed fears throughout the years, that we would "pop up" at his home in Virginia, and embarrass his in-laws. We exchange Christmas gifts with this family.

Don:
        As I said, once they knew we were married, my parents gave us their 'qualified' support. My brother, however, never spoke to me until the day he died in 1973. Through the years I have attributed this to his own problem, but recently, as I am becoming closer to my relatives, I am entertaining the idea that his resistance was more my sister-in-law's idea than his. My brother had only one girlfriend in his life, really, and it was her. They had gone together since each was sixteen, married at 21 and stayed married until he died at 39. I've known Pat since

I was 11 years old; often she came along with us on family vacations and she was always over at our house. I was like a little brother to her.

When Lowell died, I flew to California from New York for the funeral. I have only seen Pat once since Blanche and I were married in 1962 and it was at Lowell's funeral. When she saw me she cried (later my mother explained that I looked like Lowell to her). Except for a few pleasantries, she has only spoken to me once since then, when she called at Christmas, 1986, at my mother's request to tell me that my father had died.

Similarly, I never saw my paternal grandparents since we were married. And, my maternal grandmother was already dead. My maternal grandfather and my multi-divorced uncle kept in touch with us. My grandfather was especially helpful with advice and with money to help me through graduate school.

Blanche:

We left Monterey: Don went to Korea and I to Gary, Indiana. In Gary, I spoke with Don's mother over the phone on several occasions during which she kept reminding me that Don might not return for a variety of reasons: the main one was that he would probably re-enlist.

Don:

I was in Korea for a year and so, just six months after our marriage, Blanche and I faced a lengthy separation. We wrote each other nearly every day. I had a large picture of Blanche which I put next to my bunk. I knew that her picture would draw comments as there were few black men in our unit and it seemed that most of the GIs were southerners. Perhaps it was the fact that no American women were allowed where we were stationed and therefore many of the soldiers informally lived off base with their Korean girlfriends, I don't know. While I do recall many racial slurs addressed to Koreans - even to one's own girlfriend - I don't remember any racially motivated attacks made to me, except whispers and curiosity. These reactions, of course, were nearly as offensive. I suspect that reactions would have been much more severe had I been black and Blanche white. My point in this discussion is this: for whatever reason - probably both because I am the white partner and because of my own personality - from the time that I was in Korea on it has always been easier for me to deal with the wider society than it has been for Blanche.

Blanche:

In spite of the "warnings" from his mother, Don did return and we lived in Washington, D.C., ten blocks from the White House. Don was stationed at Fort Meade, Maryland, at National Security Agency.

While in Washington, Don was introduced to most of my relatives on my father's side. Most accepted us with one uncle saying, however, "If Clint (my father) had lived, this marriage would have never happened. But he seems to care about her and that is important."

Don:

Our Washington experience was something like our lives in Monterey in that we had many GI and school friends in the area and Blanche had many relatives there. Nevertheless, for me, that was one of the loneliest periods in our marriage.

I hadn't definitely decided what I wanted to do for a career, although in Korea I had gotten the idea that I might like to be a folklorist or an anthropologist.

We did get to know some of Blanche's relatives. One especially comes to mind now, although he's been dead for over a decade. We shared interest in music and in politics. He seemed to accept our marriage, although I have since learned from Blanche that he had some negative thoughts about it.

Blanche:

We left Washington and moved to San Francisco, a very idealistic environment in those days. After about a year, we settled down in the Haight-Ashbury district with other "flower children." One block from our basement apartment was a "Peace Garden;" around the corner usually parked was the psychedelic bus of the Grateful Dead. There it was "in" to be "out."

While we had the usual problems finding housing in San Francisco, we had jobs and friends and life was good. But then, there were the stares. One friend called it "negative celebrity status."

During the Watts riots and subsequent fall-out we frequented Mexico for "R and R" trips. In Mexico the responses were, "You are too young to be married" and the only stares were from the American tourists.

In San Francisco, I was constantly reminded of difficulties similar to my childhood days. I was raised in the south before the 60s, with a history of rejection from my family and from the environment. Both have to do with the color of my skin. My skin is brown, but my mother's skin is white and there were chronic tensions around this difference. To cope with these bad feelings I would "disappear" a lot in movie theaters and libraries. In San Francisco I resorted to these same defense mechanisms: the movies and the library. I would "disappear" when newcomers would come to the house to see Don.

This was just a pattern when I was younger: black members would stay behind while the lighter members would go and get services. That is how it worked. For example, when my mother wanted to try on a dress, she said, jokingly, "You walk behind me." But I would walk behind her.

Don:

Of all the places we've lived in - at one point in our marriage we had lived in thirteen different places in eleven years - San Francisco was one of my favorites. I had received an early discharge from the army to go back to school, although we were both a little apprehensive that I would be called back because of the increasing American involvement in Viet Nam (it was the fall of 1964).

I attended San Francisco State College. It took me three years to get my Masters degree in anthropology because I hadn't taken many anthropology courses as an undergraduate and I needed a full year of school before I would qualify for their two year masters program.

I found anthropology to be very rewarding. I soaked up school like nothing I had ever done before. My grandfather had given us some money and that, together with what Blanche made as a bank teller (she was in the first group of black tellers at Bank of America in fact) supported us. After the first term, I got a part-time job which also came in handy.

Some of our friends from the army days lived in the Bay area and we gained new friends, mostly people I met in classes. Indeed, during those volatile times we had a group of friends we hung out with. It was an interracial group and everyone's politics ranged from liberal to radical. We marched against the war in Viet Nam and were active at State to "reform" college. But as it was at Fisk, the major confrontations in San Francisco were to come after we left the city.

San Francisco was the first place we lived in a primarily Black community - the Fillmore District. By now Blanche and I had developed an adjustment to interracial living that has lasted until this day. After a year there we moved to the Haight-Ashbury, which seemed integrated. In fact, it seemed to become less integrated as blacks moved out and hippies moved in.

Blanche liked to go to movies, especially drive-ins. Neither of us liked being stared at and drive-ins afforded us a night out with minimum hassle. We also went to plays, art movies (at the sort of movie houses that serve coffee). We began to develop separate identities. I got plenty of socializing in at school: for example, every Friday afternoon the anthropology department at State had wine and cheese buffets for graduate students and faculty. Sometimes Blanche would attend, but usually I'd go alone. I found anthropology and the people I met through this field very exciting.

The results of these differences has been that I often beg off everyday social activity, and when we do decide that it is time to do something together, Blanche has tended to be very selective in the social events in which she would feel comfortable to participate. Nevertheless, over the years she has expanded the sorts of activities she likes and although we don't "go out" as much as some other couples, we are going increasingly to more things.

Blanche:

In California, I eventually came out of the closet and we had a very supportive group of friends. But we had to leave California for Bloomington, Indiana.

I had a lot of reservations about this move, but Don silenced them with the following observation: "They have a lot of African students there, and therefore they are bound to have a lot of white girlfriends." He was saying, in effect, that we would not be unique.

Our new home in Indiana had KKK members marching down Main Street, robes and all. After the one and only black-owned book store was burned to the ground, I went back into the closet.

I came out of the closet to find a job at the university in one of the departments and also downtown, but I was told I couldn't get the job because I was too qualified. I said to myself, "OK, I'll be a mother."

My constant dream was to be another Josephine Baker, not the singing part but the mother part. Josephine Baker had nine adopted kids from all races. With no more thought of motherhood than my wanting to be like Josephine Baker, we adopted a child.

The fears that I had previously about our marriage were now compounded with the normal responsibilities of parenthood. One of our weapons before parenthood in fighting racism and the possible repercussions of an unsupportive environment had been our ability to be selectively quiet about our marriage. Parenthood put a stop to that.

The most frightening time in Indiana as parents was not because of overt racism. For this kind of racism is easier to deal with. But covert racism is a little more difficult. One incident involved simply getting gas in Spencer, Indiana. Nothing was said to us by the station attendant and nothing was done. But a kind of sixth sense told us to get out of there as quickly as possible. It was near there a few years later that a black door-to-door saleswoman was killed and the white man that tried to help her was ousted from town.

<u>Don</u>:

I had decided to go for a Ph.D. in anthropology, and so we moved to Bloomington, Indiana where I attended Indiana University. I was very "preoccupied" then (as Blanche might put it). Blanche was unable to find work, even as a clerk at the university (she was always "overqualified"). We adopted our only child in Bloomington, Tony. He both increased the happiness in our lives and was a new source of friction between Blanche and I, and between us and the outside world.

We developed some new friendships in Bloomington, some of which would last for decades. Although I was busy in school we attended parties given by other graduate students. Blanche liked our social life in Bloomington, but because I was studying all the time she wanted to do more things than I did. I loved the life of a graduate student. I enjoyed the courses and the excitement of learning a profession.

After living in Bloomington for a year we decided to adopt a child. In those days white social workers were practically giving away black or mixed kids. We expressed a desire to adopt a child, one whose color was between ours (this was more Blanche's idea than mine and it probably was a good one since in the U.S. this would bring less hassles.) We had no trouble at all qualifying and in a couple of months or less, we were told that our child had just been born.

We were in Bloomington just six months with Tony before we moved again. Blanche and I shared all the things one does with a baby: changing, feeding, holding. Often I would put Tony in a back-pack and traipse around campus. In some ways the presence of a child put a wedge between Blanche and me. Instead of centering attentions on each other it seems that there was always something to do for Tony. Even so, he was a welcome addition to our household.

Tony was six months old when I had finished my course work and comprehensive examinations and it was time for me to begin anthropological field work. I selected the Caribbean largely on the advise of Dan Crowley, for whom I was a teaching assistant in our last summer in Bloomington. I had specialized in Afro-American cultures and the culture of the Caribbean island of Carriacou was surely both African and creole.

<u>Blanche</u>:

We were in the Caribbean for three years, a place where Don was anxious for me to experience how races get along together. The first night we were there, in our cabin in Carriacou, Grenada, a truck drove by and shouts of "Black Power" were heard. That made me feel that I was back in the United States and nothing had changed. I was proved both right and wrong for there is a form of racism in the Caribbean, but not as blatant as in America.

Don:

Carriacou is a very small island in the Lesser Antilles with a population of about 5000. For the first time since San Francisco we lived around black people: sometimes there were one or two white foreigners living on the island in addition to me, sometimes there were no others. But strangely, here is were we learned another lesson about color. These rural West Indians and I had more in common than they did with Blanche. After all, I was there to learn about their lifeways. Blanche assisted me, but she did not share that anthropological interest.

I felt lonely and out of place the first year in Carriacou and to this day I am thankful that we were able to stay long enough for me to get used to the islanders. It was during the second year that I discovered my "mask," that is, my work. I was a veritable "anthropological machine" and would always go about with camera, tape recorder, and note pad. Some people thought I was a tourist on an extended holiday, others thought I was a priest. One lady even thought that Blanche and I were brother and sister: that opinion sunk in and showed me how widely color perceptions can vary.

Now I'm the kind of person who is highly self conscious, hardly a likely candidate for an interracial marriage. Furthermore, I used to faint easily, purely for psychosomatic reasons. I was so nervous in my first experiences at anthropological fieldwork at San Francisco State that I sometimes felt light headed. This lengthy, but leisurely fieldwork in the Caribbean allowed me to escape these humbugs and helped me relate to people with confidence and singularity. I still have some apprehension in social situations at times, but it results more in a positive excitement in whatever I am doing rather than in a debilitating nervousness.

Thus, while in that second year in Carriacou I gradually became comfortable in most any public setting, something which was quite new to me. Both the interracial marriage and the fieldwork has helped me to control this social phobia.

Blanche:

We lived in Carriacou for two years and then we moved to Trinidad where we lived for one year. I felt that I had been sent to Siberia at times during these three years in the Caribbean.

Don:

The two years in Carriacou were followed by a year in Trinidad. Again, I was preoccupied as I was writing my Ph.D. dissertation (I thought, why write it in Bloomington when I could do the work in Trinidad just as well).

We lived in a highly integrated neighborhood: there were Trinidadians of all sorts and descriptions; our landlady was Chinese. She had a white roomer. Most of our neighbors were black Trinidadians but, less than a block away creole families became less frequent and East Indian ones more numerous.

Considering the fact that on most days I "holed up" in my room writing, we did a lot in Trinidad. We went on weekly rides on the motorscooter we had brought from Carriacou. We went to movies and to concerts in Port-of-Spain. We attended carnival events, although that was the year of the delayed carnival and the subsequent carnival rains (1972).

As luck would have it Trinidad was in turmoil then, and there was talk of black power. The island was tense, not like the idyllic situation in Carriacou at all. We both were affected by occasional shouts sent in our direction. Some of that social comfortableness was washed away and it took me a few months to regain my public persona. We were in Trinidad on tourist visas and I did not have permission to conduct anthropological fieldwork.

After a year we left Trinidad for an annual convention of the American Anthropological Association, in order to give a paper and to try and find a job. After the convention we returned to Bloomington for a few months while I finished up my dissertation.

Blanche:

The one thing that kept me going was that our plans were to go anywhere but the United States when Don finished school. This was not to be. Instead we went back to Bloomington, Indiana, where our son, Tony, almost died from some mysterious virus. His behavioral problems started to surface at this time as well. We were all physically, emotionally, and financially spent.

Don:

Ever since I began fieldwork I had tried to find work, especially in Canada where we had felt more comfortable as an interracial couple. But during the three years we were in the Caribbean the job market for academic anthropologists had dried up almost completely. I would have been better off getting a job with my master's degree, as it turned out. I tried as hard as I could, but I couldn't land a job at a university in Canada or in the few places in the United States we felt that we could live happily. So when I got an offer to be a curator at the American Museum of Natural History I convinced Blanche that New York was quite cosmopolitan and that the place would be OK for us.

I was not secure in my position at the Museum: I was one of two curators in the Education Department, a half research and half departmental appointment. My boss wanted me to generate creative educational programs; I wanted to complete work on a book on Carriacou. After a few months on the job the budget crisis of New York hit. Rumors had it that many lines at the Museum would be lost. After about a year I was told that my contract would not be renewed when it expired in about two years. In fact, my line was "abolished" along with me.

For the rest of the time we lived in New York I was more or less looking for a tenure track line in a college or university. We had placed restrictions on where I could look: Canada, the northeast except for Boston, the northwest (from San Francisco north).

After my contract ran out at the Museum I was unemployed for about six months. I had anticipated this and so I had inveigled extra time by building up paid leave. By the time my boss got wind of what I was doing I had built up more than six months beyond my three year contract. This, together with the unemployment checks was a nice cushion while I searched for a job. Then, one week before the fall term was to begin I got a part-time job at Hunter. And, a couple of weeks into the term, it turned into a full-time appointment. As good as this job was, I was always a temporary employee. So I kept looking and, I left Hunter in the Fall of 1978 when I got the tenure track position at the State University of New York at Oneonta, where I am now.

Blanche:

New Jersey was to be, by far, the most cosmopolitan home we'd had, including the Caribbean. It was a veritable United Nations. I gave piano lessons to blacks, whites, Filipinos, Cubans, and played for a Presbyterian Church with a Korean minister and mostly Korean congregation. We were in this town, West New York, New Jersey, for several years while we both worked and while Tony was in school.

Family problems centering on the marriage and on Tony's behavior erupted during this period. Subsequent unemployment cemented the despair.

Don:

The anxiety of these years affected my family and our marriage. After a few years Blanche went to work, making good money as a "report typist" (almost as much as I) for some international advertising agency: they did market research and among other things made Trinidad safe for a particular brand of toothpaste.

The agony of the job search was almost unbearable: one place had 240 applicants. I must have sent my vita to over a hundred schools, and I interviewed about eight times, but no appointment resulted.

This took a toll on Blanche and Tony as it seemed that for years, every evening we would discuss my application to some university. We argued a lot, and developed a "style" of disagreement in which we shouted at each other, called each other every nasty name we could think of, and then made up.

When Blanche suggested that we all have therapy I was reluctant. But with both of us working, we had the money. Eventually we each had individual therapy and then family counseling. I got so involved in my neofreudian therapy that I took two sessions a week.

When we realized that our therapists were nuttier than we were, we were on our way toward improvement. (I'm not just going for a cheap laugh here - I honestly believe that at the very least most therapists are even more strange than I.)

It was at this time that Tony developed a pattern of not doing any work in school and being disruptive. It was years before he was off the medicine for his mysterious convulsion, but eventually he recovered completely. His attention span was short and, after we moved to Oneonta he began a pattern of failure in school which lasted through his early teen years. Mostly to try to figure out what was going on with his problems, I became the parent representative for the local school board on the Committee For Handicapped Children. This was an enlightening experience as the good people in the school system struggled to help kids who did not respond to the usual school situation. Whereas in New York we lived in a Latin neighborhood which, in American terms had a majority of "whites" but was integrated, Oneonta was almost all white (the only black people in town in 1978 were either the handful of professionals associated with the colleges or were very poor). Thus, schools consistently misread the behavior of black kids and I'm afraid they were fast to blame the kid and/or his parents rather than look at some of their own practices.

Today, I am happy to report that Tony has passed through his major crises. He has graduated from high school, is currently working at a ski resort during winter break, and is enrolled in college.

Gradually our lives improved in Oneonta. One reason for this was probably due to the better environment for middle class blacks in the late 70s and early 80s.

But most was due to our own growth. Blanche - although a talented pianist and able to teach music education in the public schools - decided to undergo a change in career. She returned to school and obtained a Master's in Social Work.

Both Blanche and I are successful in our professional careers now. We have found that our arguing has eased as Tony is finding his way and as we gain more respect for each other's "space." In recent years, I have felt less guilty about doing things I like - such as attending conferences or going to do research in the Caribbean - on my own. At the same time, Blanche is doing more public things as she gains confidence in her social work. I love her, but it is not the sort of "lightning bolt" love that I once had. Although we have discussed divorce from time to time, I know now that we will remain married.

Blanche:

We finally ended-up in a small college town in upstate New York, not unlike a vision one of Don's professors (Harold Driver) had said of his desires, "a college small by a waterfall." It is in this town, Oneonta, New York, that our non-traditional lifestyle has been challenged the most.

One criticism of interracial marriages has been, "What about the children?"" I was reminded of this comment again by a social worker who told us, when Tony was having some minor difficulties in school: "People don't know how to deal with your son because he is neither black nor white." And again: I went to my front door one day where the janitor from the neighborhood school was standing angrily. He said that it was reported that Tony had put graffiti on the main door to the school and that he, the janitor, was going to call the police. At this time, Don came to the door and the consequences for the graffiti shifted almost immediately. Instead of calling the police now, the janitor only requested that Tony, and his white helper in crime, clean up the mess. Message: black kid, criminal activity. White kid, childish prank. When Don came to the door, Tony became white.

Don's Reflections:

I think that it is a mistake for an interracial couple to confuse the cultural differences between them, or the way society perceives them, with the everyday necessity to relate as a couple aside from these differences. Although family, friends, cultural differences, or the social environment may cause a marriage to fail by driving a wedge between the partners, a marriage can only succeed if there is a strong personal relationship between the two. Surely Blanche and I have such a relationship. We know each other very well indeed, with the kind of knowledge that can only come from a long life together. This sort of intimacy surpasses even primary family relationships: after all, over our lifetime we have seen more of each other than anyone else, including relatives and friends. With this knowledge comes a kind of security which can override the difficulties of an interracial relationship.

But although our personal bond is close, there are elements in our friendships and in the social environments in which we have lived which have been clear assets to our marriage. Both of us live like very ordinary members of the American middle class. However, mentally we are both bohemians. We like to surround ourselves with interesting friends and live in an interesting environment. Sure - there was an escapism to our many moves through the years - but no one can deny we've lived full lives to this point, and have seen a good deal of what there is to see. Being an interracial couple "fits" with these bohemian notions as well as with the lifestyle of a cultural anthropologist and a social worker. These positives from our social environment more than offset the negatives that we have encountered, and have allowed us to grow in the love and respect we have for each other.

Blanche's Reflections:

As a social worker I see interracial marriages as possible only if given certain kinds of resources. Along with resources, personal and financial, one needs a similar outlook on where they are going and how they are going to get there. Without these ingredients, these kinds of marriages can be devastating to the people involved. This is so because the people involved in interracial marriages have to be bicultural. You are in the black culture and you are in the white culture, usually simultaneously. If your environment supports this philosophy, then there are no problems. This country's philosophy does not support that. Instead it motivates one to choose one or the other. This is where the problem begins, particularly for parents.

If your ego is in good shape (personal resources, comfortable finances) then the periodic negative experiences will be blunted. This was brought home to me vividly while viewing a film based on Oscar Lewis's book, The Children of Sanchez. For as the father's resources grew, so did his patience for family idiosyncracies.

It is true that opportunities for a variety of goals are here in this country. However, interracial couples or families have to make their own alternatives, for they are not as yet a part of the fabric of this society. Interracial couples, like all minorities, are peripheral. That is a myth though, I think. In my way of thinking, they have to have dual cultures. Because of this, each partner requires a wealth of self esteem, information, sensitivity, and adaptability. For example, if you know that you are going to be in a questionable neighborhood, racially speaking, you go in unobtrusively. If on the other hand, your partner says, "Why should we have to do this?" you have problems. We all have to bend, not just minorities. Some of our greatest problems, for example, have come from our different childhood backgrounds. These include tradition, manners, and family postures. When I would tell our son Tony to 'dress' before speaking with a neighbor, I was speaking as a southerner! Don would disagree because he came from the west where dress is informal. While the goal is to adapt to your community, it can sometimes get lost in the ways you want to achieve that goal. The goal is just to develop as a responsible human being. Therefore, interracial couples must be unrelenting in their appreciation for their differences as well as their similarities.

CHAPTER 7

THE IMPACT OF THE PEACE CORPS ON AMERICA

Patricia and Kevin Lowther

We shared three things in common on the day that we met: We both had
been born in 1941, had "summered" in New England in our early youth, and had
served in the Peace Corps. Of course, Kevin's summers in Vermont were full of
fun and sun at a lake. Pat's in the Berkshires of Western Massachusetts were
devoted to helping her mother housekeep someone else's vacation home.

Kevin, obviously, is white and was raised in the upper middle class
bastions of Westchester and Fairfield Counties. Pat is black and grew up in
segregated Aiken, South Carolina.

There was no magic in our meeting. The Peace Corps had brought us
together, following our service, to be recruiters. It was just after Christmas 1965,
and we took an instant dislike for each other. Pat saw Kevin as a smug Ivy
Leaguer; Kevin saw Pat as shy and uncommunicative.

Within months, we were deeply in love. Marriage was never proposed, but
assumed. However, Washington, D.C., where we both continued to work, was
still very much a southern city. The flustered Catholic priest we approached could
not bring himself to ask our respective races as he filled in the church forms. He
asked instead for our "nationality," and when we confirmed that we were both
Americans, he suggested that we might have to get married in Maryland. We
assured him that interracial marriage was legal in the District of Columbia, but the
good father from Holy Comforter was never comfortable in joining us together.

It would be tempting to say that race did not affect our early relationship,
that we were just two people truly meant for one another. We were surrounded,
however, by supportive friends and workmates, including some who clearly saw
us as symbols of the new era in race relations which appeared to be emerging from
the crucible of the civil rights movement.

Not long after we had been married in mid-1967, for instance, we were
attending a reception at the Lesotho Embassy. Kevin's boss, who was black, was
having an animated discussion with a white South African diplomat when he saw
us passing. He pulled us over in a transparent attempt to confront the South
African with flesh-and-blood evidence that white and black can make it together.
The South African was prepared. "I know you are trying to embarrass me," he said
goodnaturedly, "but this (meaning us) simply wouldn't be possible in our society."

There were certainly some in our universe of friends, acquaintances and
family who would have said in 1967 that our own society was not yet ready for
interracial marriage. As Kevin's father expressed it, upon learning that his son
might marry a "negress"--like the priest, his vocabulary was not yet ready to cope
with the situation--marriage was difficult enough without adding the burden of
being mixed. What he may also have been saying is that they were going to lose
some friends if we married, and they did.

During our courtship, we certainly considered the consequences of being an interracial couple. Kevin was the first to recognize that the relationship was becoming serious and was committed to sustaining it, come what may. Pat, having been raised in a rigidly segregated environment, was more acutely conscious of the lines we were crossing. She also had had a sheltered Catholic upbringing and schooling. To be involved quite unexpectedly with a more worldly and non-Catholic white boy seemed too improbable, even threatening, and there was a brief attempt on her part to persuade Kevin that they should break off, that "it" just could not be.

It was too late for second thoughts. We were in love. But we might not have married, much less fallen in love, had it not been for a number of factors which helped to bridge the socio-economic gulf between us.

Neither one, to begin with, brought to the relationship negative stereotypes of the other's ethnic group. We can thank our parents for that. We did not grow up in homes where ethnic jokes and racial epithets were common fare. When it came time for the "look who's coming to dinner" phase, Pat's mother and Kevin's parents opened doors and hearts which hid few fears or deep-set prejudices. Kevin's family initially expressed strong concern, then proceeded to fall in love with Pat as well. Her mother, meanwhile, betrayed nothing more than parental anxiety over the morals and manners of her future son-in-law. She had taught Pat to judge people on their merits alone, and Kevin easily met her high standards. It may also have helped that he showed a healthy appetite for southern cooking, soul food and a sweet potato pie served by an old family friend.

Positive "role models" may also have pre-conditioned us to be open to an interracial relationship. Although Kevin barely knew a single black before he went to Africa in the Peace Corps, he has no trouble recalling the three blacks who made the greatest impression on him as a boy: Jackie Robinson, his Brooklyn Dodger teammate, Roy Campanella, and Alvin Childress, who played the strong and sensible Amos in the television version of "Amos 'n' Andy." Each man displayed the quiet pride and dignity that comes from knowing who you are and what you stand for. That each was black did not then mean much to Kevin, who was only vaguely aware as a child of the country's racial heritage.

Pat's childhood recollections of whites are more complex, and more vivid. She can remember watching the Ku Klux Klan riding round Aiken's black neighborhoods. Her mother made her watch, determined that she should not grow up afraid of cowards. She also was raised on an integrated block, where white boys played ball with blacks in the park, and where country and western music blared from the home of poor whites across the street. She likes C and W to this day.

There were also the stern Irish nuns who taught and disciplined her, and a priest, who linger prominently in Pat's early memories. They were white, but in the natural order of the segregated South, they occupied an accepted niche in the small black Catholic community. It was their qualities, and not their complexion which impressed Pat.

Peer support was another crucial contributor to the development and consummation of our love. To friends and associates, we were a very special couple. Whites and blacks accepted us in equal measure, but living and working in a predominantly black milieu gave the black community the greater opportunity to shape--or destroy--our relationship. Without exception, our black friends and associates welcomed us into their world.

That Kevin was secure living among black Washingtonians, just as Pat would later feel at home in a small New England town, strongly suggests that our Peace Corps experience prepared us to adapt to dramatically different cultural surroundings. Each of us graduated from college with limited horizons. Kevin knew little of life beyond surburbia and New England before landing in Sierra Leone to teach school. It was Pat, however, who consciously determined to complement her Catholic heritage by going to live in a Moslem society--Turkey, as fate would have it.

One final circumstance, having nothing to do with race or culture, family or friends, may have had the greatest impact on our getting married and on our staying married. As Peace Corps recruiters, we spent much of our first six months traveling and working together. This provided an unusual chance to get to know each other well and to determine whether familiarity might breed contempt. When we took more stationary jobs in Washington, we conspired to live close enough that there was little free time we did not spend together. Having seen the best and worst of the other for the better part of a year, and still being in love, we concluded it was safe to marry.

We entered marriage with few long-term expectations, which may partly explain why it has endured, at this writing, for 26 years. We were absolutely fearless in terms of the racial and social challenges that might lie before us. But given the cocoon of support and acceptance in which our relationship had evolved, we could blythely ignore that racism was--and remains--a strong force in the United States. Being an interracial couple, we decided, might be a problem for other people, but we would not allow it to become a problem for us. In any case, we assumed that we would always live in a community where we would be accepted, as a couple and individually. We have yet to be disappointed.

Our marriage has been successful because we chose it to be. We have been fortunate not to be faced with serious stress, such as economic hardship, which might have undermined its strong foundation. But the simple and abiding fact is that we wanted the marriage to last. That has meant internalizing the frustrations which afflict the happiest of couples; and it has meant compromising one or the other's desires on occasion.

The one reef on which we might have foundered was religion, not race. It is probably just as well that Kevin was not raised in any church. Otherwise there might have been an inherent conflict with Pat's Catholicism, especially with regard to any children. In what was probably our first compromise, Pat did not insist that Kevin become Catholic and Kevin agreed that the kids could be raised in the church. Over the years, Kevin has engaged selectively in church-related activities, attended important religious services and became good friends with our parish priests.

There has been little conflict, as well, in establishing a viable balance of responsibilities within the marriage. There has been a tendency to share chores, burdens and experience. This has ranged from Kevin's helping with housework (which amused and scandalized people when we lived in male-dominated Africa) to his participating enthusiastically in the natural birth of our two daughters. For her part, Pat has played an important part in Kevin's professional work in international development, particularly for the five years that we resided in Lusaka, Zambia. Her cultural sensitivity and sincerity was instrumental in our establishing close personal and working relationships with Zambians. Ours became an African household in the sense that people knew our door was always open to unannounced visits, that we appreciated and practiced the African tradition of hospitality.

Wanting a marriage to succeed guarantees nothing in a society where divorce is commonplace. All the support mechanisms and the willingness to compromise would have been worthless had we not preserved the most vulnerable bond between any two people: trust. We have spared each other real or imagined infidelity. This innocence may strike outsiders as naive and incredible. However, we did not take each other's faithfulness for granted.

Pat's cultural roots may have had something to do with this. As he came to know her mother and friends in South Carolina, Kevin was impressed by the wholesomeness of Pat's native surroundings and her extended family. She had not emerged unscathed by segregation, but she had survived with a firm and well-defined moral code. Meanwhile, although Pat harbored qualms about Kevin's real intentions (Was he merely on the make?), a mutual colleague--a more experienced black woman--convinced her that he did love her and that good men are hard to find. Doris McGruder, wherever you are, thank you.

We can also be thankful for what might be called "community support." We have lived in all-black and semi-ghetto areas of Washington; in a working-class neighborhood of an all-white New Hampshire town; in a cosmopolitan African capital; and most recently in a prosperous Northern Virginia subdivision which is visibly losing its white complexion as black and immigrant families move in.

We have felt secure and at home in each of these settings, but nowhere did we feel stronger, or a more unexpected, sense of belonging than in Keene, New Hampshire. We bought our first home there, on a street of modest woodframe dwellings, where people worked "down to the Peerless." We made friends slowly but surely in the Yankee way and discovered hospitality no less genuine than in Africa. Neighbors did not burn a cross on our lawn when they discovered who was living at Number 11. They didn't welcome us with homebaked bread, either. But when it came time to leave for good, many years later, we left behind the truest sense of community we have ever known. It was not easy to leave, and it was hardest of all for Pat, the black southerner.

Born as we were to a society and a world in which race and ethnicity are omnipotent and divisive, we can be grateful that we and our children have been allowed to live and love in peace. This is, after all, the same society which did not permit Pat's mother to vote until she was 50, and the same world in which 30 million white and black South Africans are violently estranged by apartheid.

We have beaten the odds, perhaps, but it is also true that our marriage has coincided with what may be the start of an era of greater racial reconciliation, amity and amalgamation. When a sage friend of Kevin's father learned of our relationship, he assured him that in a hundred years Americans would be completely homogenized racially. One might dispute the timeframe, but not the ultimate achievement in America (and the world, given a few millenia?) of a genetic "rainbow coalition."

Is this the subliminal image that we convey to others: the happy prospect that we are not doomed to racial armageddon, that in the end there will be no white and black, only cafe au lait? We met and married at a time when urban riots, kindled by the civil rights movements' unmet expectations, revived Thomas

Jefferson's prophecy of fireballs in the night for his slaveholding nation. We must have seemed to some a sign that Jefferson would be proved wrong and that he and Sally Hemings were simply born 250 years too soon to celebrate their love openly and legally.

And what must we have seemed a few years ago to the students of a rural black secondary school in the South African "homeland" of Lebowa? Never mind how we came to be there. We were as unlikely a pair of visitors as two Martians, but the students kept their wits and went straight to the heart of the matter. "How did you fall in love?" they asked, all smiles.

It was simple, Kevin responded, using romance to make a political point. We were allowed the random chance to get to know each other, naturally and as two human beings. He did not have to state the obvious: that apartheid leaves little to chance.

We make no special claims about our marriage. We have seen too many good marriages and good friends--mixed and matched--split apart to think that we are different or better. Our union has lasted 26 years, but will it last 30, or 35? It will if we want it to, but either way our being an interracial couple is irrelevant. Others may choose to see something special in us because we are mixed. That is understandable. But if we are special at all, it is because we have remained true to our marriage vows and because our children know that we love each other and therefore must love them.

CHAPTER 8

INTERRACIAL OR CROSS-CULTURAL?

Carlie and Gary Tartakov

Interracial or Cross-cultural?

They wondered: Interracial or Cross-cultural? It depends on the side from which you look. From the outside it's interracial, as simple as black and white. And at first, when we were on the outside ourselves, that was what we felt as well. But then there was being married, and from here, on the inside, the interracial aspect of our marriage has turned out to seem less important and less interesting than the cross-cultural aspects.

We were both born in Los Angeles and raised in California, and neither of us has had any confusion about our own races - as race is defined in the US. Though it turns out that we defined them differently. In simple, it is Carlie Black and Gary White. But life in these United States isn't simple. As several members of Carlie's family pointed-out in their first questions about him. "Is he White or Jewish?" Gary is a Jew, and to them that wasn't quite White. A surprise to him. One that made it a little easier, but a little more complicated too. Being a Jew isn't exactly being White to the Black community. The Black community sees a good many gradations of race missing in White consciousness.

In the White community racial gradations don't count for much. Things are more often than not crudely simple: Black or White, by the one drop test. And if Jews aren't seen as exactly "normal" their abnormality isn't racial. They are White. Or that's what Gary thought.

No one would call Carlie anything but Black, but she's relatively light. That too has different weights in the Black community and in the White community. And those differences are significant. However amorphous in reality, these are distinct communities in practice. For all their interaction, interdependence and actual interrelation our Black and White communities have long and continuing histories of separation as well as different cultural roots. And culture is a matter of roots and continuities. If one says, "My grandparents were all East European Jews who immigrated here at the turn of the century," the other answers, "Most of my ancestors have been here for generations, and some forever. Only one, that I know, was a Jew from Europe."

These cultural differences are most clearly understood, and easily read, in the difference between the Black and White communities, but that caricatures them as much as it clarifies them. In America interracial is, in important ways, also cross-cultural.

And why would her family ask? Because to them it made a difference. Their division of the "White world" into Jews and Whites had visible social consequences for them. Jews in the US have seen themselves as excluded in many ways from Gentile society, and they have identified and sympathized with Blacks in that, while Blacks have, since the time of slavery's Christianity identified with the

Israelites of the Old Testament. And these identifications have led to practical outcomes. Black enclaves in the northern cities have come to be called ghettos, after the term of Jewish enclaves because Blacks found it possible to move into Jewish neighborhoods when others were more restricted. And Jews stood out in the White community of the north, as willing to do business with Blacks, so nexuses have developed between them - symbolized more-satisfyingly by somewhat more widespread familiarity and intermarriage and less-satisfyingly by the Jewish businesses in ghettos they have since abandoned.

Why and How did you Enter a Mixed Marriage?

She said: When we married, in 1973, it was my second racially mixed marriage. I had previously been married for 13 years and I brought two children from that marriage with me. Gary had been married before too, and brought a son with him. The children's ages at the time of our marriage were 12, 13 and 5.

I come from Afro-American families that have crossed over racial and cultural lines for some time. I see myself as Black. But my family is not simple. One of my great grandfathers was a German Jew, another English. Native Americans are there and Irish. Within my immediate family, my mother married and had children by men of diverse backgrounds. One of my brothers had a Native American father, the other's grandfather came from Haiti. My father was quite light. My mother is dark, though the German Jew was on her side. These various mixtures are not unusual within the Black community. And within mine, neither race or culture existed as a taboo against entering into any relationship.

If anything, the members of my family welcomed and supported each other in life choices involving different backgrounds. With both of my marriages, their concerns centered around what kind of person this was: supportive? nurturing? provider? positive? Things like that. Or so it seemed. They have never expressed disappointment to me, that I didn't marry Black. With one exception, they didn't seem to interpret my choices as rejection or denial of my race. The exception was when one of my brothers responded to my second marriage by asking me what that meant that I was again marrying a man who wasn't Black. When I said that Gary was the one who was there, he understood.

I realize my family's openness isn't standard in the greater society. In general, I think they feel as I do, that crossing racial or cultural barriers has its problems, but there are bigger problems than those. I would say that crossing class lines or religious lines can be more difficult.

He said: From the beginning I was surprised less by how important race was than how important it wasn't. On one hand, it didn't seem to matter that much. On the other, where it did matter, it seemed positive. Living in a relatively cosmopolitan, New England college community, in the 1970's, we met no real impediments. That might not be true of the more uniformly White, mid-western community where we live now. Few seemed to take much notice of our relationship, and when someone did it was usually positive. We both had multi-racial circles of friends, that included mixed-race and multi-cultural couples. And we both had involvements in progressive social and political activities, where racial and cultural understanding were sought after and respected. It wouldn't be wrong to say they were even admired. If we had reasonable expectations that some people would be surprised or annoyed at our relationship, those were people we didn't know, or want to know. The people we did know and respect, shared with and depended on, were all supportive.

I'd been married before, and that match would seem sociologically more appropriate. We were both of the same age, religious and social backgrounds. We'd grown up in the same community and attended the same high school. And it hadn't worked. In spite of our relatively equivalent expectations and backgrounds, our marriage collapsed, out of an inability to cooperate. And now I was getting to know someone who, for all our differences in background, I seemed to cooperate with intuitively. If socially surprising, the match was personally satisfying.

The fact is, despite the obvious social impediments, or maybe because of them, interracial marriage may be as attractive to some as it is threatening to others. When there is not enough pressure to make the interaction difficult, then some people will, for all sorts of cultural and aesthetic reasons, seek out people who are different from themselves. Maybe it's not so different from the different sexes' interests in each other. The real reasons for people of the different communities to have an interest in one another are the same as those for members of the same community. Growing up in total separation from Blacks, I had a certain curiosity about them. It wasn't very large, but it impelled me to seek Black acquaintances in college, where I first found myself around them. But then, I made Asian acquaintances at the same time. If asked, I think I might have said that I found interracial couples interesting.

When I was in junior high school and the other sex started to replace sports at the center of my consciousness, the music I listened to was, partly by accident and partly because of the times, an urban mixture of White and Black. That was in the early 1950's and in LA along with the four or five "regular" pop music stations was one Black station, that I remember, and one whose Rhythm and Blues was predominantly Black. My junior high had only one Black kid in it, and the only other Blacks I ever met before college were men or women who worked for my family.

I knew who and what Blacks were in American life. And you didn't have to be a sociologist to know their official status and the treatment expected of and toward them. My family was liberal. I was never encouraged to be with or appreciate Blacks, but I was taught that prejudice against them was wrong. So I was open. Growing up at the height of the civil rights movement certainly gave one a view of Blacks in American life.

One other factor in an explanation of my development is my professional development. In college, I ended up studying culture and Asian cultures in particular. This has led to spending much of my adult life studying or living in India and other non-European cultures, and exploring those cultures and our interaction with them. This provided me with an appreciation and a fascination for the diversity of human culture. Jews are used to being different, seeing different alphabets, hearing different languages. I grew up with Hebrew and Yiddish as well as Spanish and English. And I enjoyed the differences, and found a career in studying them. So, long before we met, cultural differences had become one of the focuses of my life - and most, if not all, of what we call race in America are just that.

As we became close, these differences became questions, because of their degree of deviation from general social expectations. Why was I interested in someone so apparently out of the ordinary for me? The answers, I think, were surprisingly simple. In reality, Carlie wasn't at all out of <u>my</u> ordinary. On one hand, we weren't as unusual a couple in our local social world as we might appear elsewhere. We lived, and continue to live, in an academic setting, where a greater than usual percentage of the people were not members of the majority. We both had good friends living in mixed relationships. On the other hand, there were a number of factors to whet my interest in a woman of another culture or race.

Why did I ask her out? Because she looked so good to me. Why did I get to know her so well? Because our values were so complementary. And why did I want to marry her? Because, to me, she was so fine. Race? It wasn't an issue for us. Until we thought about the wider community, outside of our circle of friends. And on that, second, thought we realized that we were safe enough in our personal situations to not be coerced. As far as we can tell, we do not seem to have suffered for it.

<u>She said</u>: Why has my second marriage been successful, after my first marriage failed? I believe the success or failure of my marriages has had less to do with race than class and perceptions of sex roles. Maturity, political and social attitudes, and the supportiveness of our families and the communities we identify and interact with, have played a part too.

I married Gary because of the kind of person he is: his intensity, openness, intelligence, sense of romance and daring. Also, his strong commitment to others, and in particular his commitment to social change, and his clear direction and sense of who he was and where he was going appealed to me.

<u>He said</u>: My first marriage lasted as long as Carlie's, and it ended about the same time. Its failure was a matter of inequality. My first wife and I liked each other well enough, but we had such unbalanced abilities and interest, that as husband and wife we were in constant conflict. One was always carrying the other, or pushing them, or frustrated by the other's inability to do a fair share. That weighed on my mind when I considered marrying again. Carlie and I are more even matched in our abilities and expectations.

<u>They said</u>: The major characteristic of this marriage has been its equality and sharing. We don't do the same things or spend much time on wondering who is doing enough. We have, from the beginning, both felt willing to do whatever needed doing, without fear of getting an unequal response when we needed support. We've shared household work and the children, career development and friends, in a continually satisfying way. And when one can't get there to make an appointment, or can't cook, because something has come up, the other takes over. And when things get out of balance, there is no fear to say so. Competition over roles and careers were weaknesses in our previous marriages. Perhaps their failings taught us something. A conscious striving for equality has replaced that competition.

<u>Class and Gender</u>

<u>They said</u>: The past twenty years have revealed gender and class as bigger issues than race in our marriage. Issues of race are obvious, particularly to those on the outside, but they seem less central to what has gone on inside. Race became an issue when we had to consider a move to a new job. There were places we eliminated from consideration. But on deciding who does what work around the house, choosing wallpaper, making career decisions or arguing-out the inevitable

misunderstandings of daily life the major fulcrum of difficulty (beyond the essential one of being different individuals) comes from sex roles and different economic backgrounds.

He said: I was raised in a household where what I got seemed to be largely a matter of what my parents agreed to provide. "We can't afford that," is not a phrase I remember as important. I grew up in single family houses, where most of the time I had my own room. I always had jobs, working for my father or my uncle. I had to save most of the money, and had to account for how I spent what I did, but that left me free to buy a car at 16, and to dress as well as anyone in the fairly affluent suburb where I spent my late teens. I worked while I was at UCLA.

When we have disagreements about how to spend money, how and where to save it, I think this becomes an issue. I am much more interested in buying things than Carlie is, but she'll go out to eat more quickly than I will. On the other hand, I will take chances with my job over political issues, where she would not. Both of these differences seem to grow out of the financial security I grew up with, and she did not. She, on the other hand, will spend more freely on clothes than I am sometimes ready for, while it was I who pushed for a new sound system and a micro-computer for word processing. It is she, who will spend on air tickets to visit the relatives, mine and hers. A good deal of this is certainly a matter of gender.

Stability

She said: Stability and commitment. We are committed to making our relationship last. Trust. We know that we can depend on each other. I'm there for him and he's there for me. We are each other's best friends. And most important, maybe, is that we share the same vision of how we think the world should be and our place in it. We also share friends and activities. Our styles of communication are different. But we do communicate. We work on our problem areas.

We moved from a community that was relatively open and tolerant of mixed marriages to one we perceive as not. We feel that people who are unaccepting of our relationship are suspicious of our motives. A certain amount of disrespect is shown.

Its not always easy to live in both the Black and the White communities. We've known couples where one member gave up their community to live more or less exclusively in the other, which is not something we want. We have retained our individual identities. Neither expects or desires that the other live solely in one or the other. Because of the kind of support offered by our families and friends we've been able to move in many different communities. Traveling in Asia has broadened our perceptions also. We feel enriched by the different communities we've shared. "A world full of vanilla ice cream only, just don't make it!"

It's not always been without anxieties for the children. Their struggling to find their identities has been, and will probably continue to be, difficult. Living in two such separate communities can be trying. Where we first lived there was a sizable mixed community, but most places there isn't. And then, as now, we find ourselves shifting back and forth among separate camps. And that can be more interesting than convenient. Fighting to hold on to both does not allow for real comfort with either.

It has affected our choices of place to live, schools for the children, where we prefer to travel, and who we want to be associated with,--not to mention jobs and their location.

What's the impact our marriage had on our friends? It's hard to say. I doubt it has affected them much. Neither was able to put up with the sort of people who wouldn't be comfortable with us together. Our friends have been positive. I suppose no one who'd be uncomfortable with us would be attracted to many of our friends and interests. I can't think of friends we lost by getting married. Whoever would be threatened by our relationship would be threatened by us individually.

Personality

He said: We've not tried to homogenize our backgrounds or bury them. In fact, I'd say we've been both respectful and celebrators of the differences. I've spent my adult life studying cultures, but it was not until I met Carlie that I realized White European-American culture was just another culture. Perry Como and Christmas aren't natural, they are learned. Baptisms and Bar Mitzvahs are already different. So if I could grow up enjoying mayonnaise as well as horseradish (probably more), and learn in India to enjoy curd and curries, it was not a big deal to try grits.

Most of Black American culture was vaguely familiar to me, as it is to most non-Black Americans. And it was intriguing, and attractive. I knew White Rock & Roll comes out of Blues; then I learned about Gospel. When, during the course of our marriage, Carlie got involved in singing Gospel music, I learned to love it. I already knew some, as everyone in America must. I didn't have to become a Baptist to enjoy it. And none of the deeply religious people in her choirs expected me to. As with many things, we've found that the key has been acceptance and respect of each other's interests, not conversion.

If anything, our personal cultural interests have grown somewhat, out of interest in not losing touch with our own histories. I've gotten interested in Black history and culture as I never did before. And that led me to an interest in my Jewish heritage I didn't have before. When I finished Roll Jordan, Roll, the World the Slaves Made, I went on to The World of Our Fathers.

Children

She said: Certainly it has created anxieties for the children. Their struggling to find their identities has been and probably continues to be complex, and at times painful. Especially my children, since their outward appearances are somewhat white and ambiguous. At times, trying to meet the needs of families, friends, and different communities is a serious strain on them. Fighting to hold on to both does not allow enough time for exploring either.

When you live in a world where there is a demand that a person pick sides, you are either one thing or the other. There is a message that says you must choose and value your mother's or your father's heritage. Fortunately, in our family and the community we have lived in, there has been some mixed community where we fit in without comment. Our children have refused to internalize much of the common oppression of our racist society. They define themselves and their heritage as mixed. Though, when forms require a choice, they refer to themselves as Black.

Mixed, what we all really are, is not a viable spot on government forms yet. Our daughter tells me that being mixed is for the most part wonderful. Any identity quandries, awkwardness, and even the odd insults are far overshadowed by the sense of pride and insight. She has always felt proud of her mix of heritage, and feels that the biggest problems have been fighting the rigid roles that other people want to put on her. She resents being labeled Black, or assumed White, or being told how "cute" mixed offspring are.

Everyone is mixed to her way of thinking. We all bear the heritages, stigmas, and mannerisms of our many ancestors, as well as our environments, cultures, and countries. She only truly adjusted to herself, she says, after a memorable occasion on which I testily said that she was Black and denied her father's heritage. As her dad had sullenly insisted she should accept the fact that she was White. She feels she can be neither. Though she's said it would be easier to be darker, in order to simplify things.

The Impact on the Larger Society?

<u>She said</u>: It's hard to say. I doubt it has affected the behavior of our friends. If they are our friends, then positive. I suppose as a couple we attract those who are more open to diversity. The other side of that, of course, is that we probably won't know who is threatened by our relationship.

<u>He put in</u>: We do have a lot of friends and acquaintances. Carlie in particular spends a great deal of time on friendships. Most of these we share, though she is often more active than I am. And we both take part in a good number of political activities, around which many of these friendships tend to be arranged.

<u>She goes on</u>: I think that some people look at mixed marriage as interesting, some as strange or curious. Some as undesirable and unnatural. Their viewpoints on mixed marriages are different depending on their relationship to it. Some ask, what does this mean? Are these people rejecting their backgrounds? Is this marriage an attempt to escape? (Escape? From or to.) What kind of statement are these folks trying to make? Are we defying authority? Rebelling? Others respect us for being willing to live our lives as we wish. For the most part, I don't think most people give it that much concern. We're about as interesting as a new hem length worth a comment at first encounter, and not much more.

The first time we enter a new community - regardless of its make-up - the fact of our mixed marriage draws a response, and people make assumptions about us. That can create barriers and it says, we or they may be asked to prove something: that we're ok, or they're ok. Who can be trusted, respected?

In some parts of the Black community, the assumption may be that I am an oreo. And there I feel I am more criticized than my husband. I feel I will be given the cold shoulder in the Black community, faster than he. People in the White community may assume the same, but it doesn't hurt as much. I don't expect as much from them, since I can never be accepted as White, not that I want to be, or that Gary wants to be Black. There are times that I feel banished to a never-never land momentarily...when I refuse to be locked out of the rich experiences I need. The nature of the activities I engage in continually pulls me towards the Black community.

I really feel that my life would not be much different if I had married Black, or if I hadn't married at all. Married or not, I would be drawn towards a multi-cultural society. Tasting the richness of varied cultures in this country has been my way before and since my marriage. I imagine that I would have married someone very similar to those men I married in the first place, that our vision of the world would be similar, our values the same, our concerns about our children also the same. In some ways, some of our struggles would have been easier. The need to explain oneself would not be as necessary in terms of motive. I would have seen less curious, hostile, and rather stupid stares, and remarks. But...as my son, Erik, said, the problems the (American) world gives us stem more from being Black than being in or from a mixed marriage. I suppose that Gary has to deal with a few more things than he once did. Some things he may not even be aware of (losing some White male privilege). Though I don't think that he really buys into the mainstream enough to care.

He said: Being in a mixed marriage is remarkable, but so are lots of other things. A generation ago it was much more problematic than it is today. When we married I supposed it could be a weak point for us. It had the potential for social sanctions that could come between us, and differences of personality that could lead to conflict.

But the US has grown in the last twenty-five years, as it has continually since the Civil War, slowly in the direction of a society in which the personal equality of our public statements is realized. We have a long way to go, but we have come a measurable part of the way. Interracial marriage is no longer against the law. And in a number of regions, even our small mid-western college town, it is no great impediment to a reasonable life. It wouldn't be so easy anywhere else in the state, but in most big cities it would go largely unnoticed.

The mixture of our backgrounds has turned out to be a strength rather than a weakness. Part of this may be because of our very direct interest in the social world around us. We are both activists. Instead of accepting what our communities have had to offer us, we have been involved in shaping them ourselves, by working in progressive political and social groups. Our marriage has been an opportunity of which we are making the most. Its the best thing in our lives.

CHAPTER 9

THE OTHER SIDE OF THE COIN

Richard W. Wilson and Myoung Chung Wilson

After being happily married for two years, we moved to Korea. This gave us the opportunity to assess a different kind of reaction to a mixed marriage. As might be expected, it was a response with its own unique features. What we will do in this brief essay is to describe how a mixed marriage is perceived in an Asian society.

Before we begin we wish to set forth, very briefly, who we are and the reaction that our marriage aroused among our American friends and family members. This may help to place the Korean response in comparative perspective.

Myoung, originally from Korea, has lived in the United States for twenty-five years, is an American citizen, and has adjusted to almost all aspects of American life. Two of her sisters live in the New York City area, while another lives in Canada. She works as a reference librarian in the main social science research unit of the Rutgers library system in New Brunswick, New Jersey. Dick's parents were naturalized American citizens from England. He was born and raised in America and is a professor of political science at Rutgers. The marriage is Myoung's first and Dick's second.

When first asked to write this article, we talked about it with several people. This was in America. The phrase we used to describe our project was "interracial marriage" and the response we received, without exception, was, "what's interracial about your marriage?" Indeed, one of the people with whom we spoke, an American Jew raised in New York city and married to a Scottish Presbyterian, made so bold as to claim that his was a far more interracial marriage than ours. Interesting. Have Asians disappeared, so to speak, in American life, or does this view of interracial really mean intercultural? And if it does mean cultural, is the implication that Myoung is now completely Americanized or that Asians in general are? Or perhaps it means only Asians who live near New York, Los Angeles, or San Francisco? After all, any good American history book will recount the racial discrimination that Asians in America were once extensively and openly subjected to. We don't pretend to know the answers. We do know that with only one exception, a drunk in a New York city cafe, we have never experienced the feeling that our marriage is singularly unusual, and certainly not that it is despicable. A trifle exotic for some, perhaps, but that is a different thing. Three huge bloody wars in Asia in the last fifty years, of course, may have changed American attitudes in any number of ways. Or perhaps it is simply the uncomfortable realization that Asians are mounting the most effective technological and industrial challenge to Western supremacy that has ever been seen.

Koreans do not use the term "interracial" or "mixed" marriage. For them, as is the case generally in Asia, the term is "international" marriage. Coming from a society that is remarkably homogeneous in language and traditional culture, they are acutely aware of the Western impact and of the way that their traditional values have

changed. Christianity now claims as adherents over 25% of the population. A
more or less permanent American army has been stationed in the land, and
thousands of Korean women marry these and other foreigners every year. The
society has changed explosively with aspects of material well being now reaching
virtually everyone. Still, this has not kept Koreans from migrating. It is said that
over 350,000 of them now live in the Los Angeles area alone. At the same time,
anti-Americanism is on the rise, although still largely a minority sentiment and non-
violent in form.

Korea, it seems safe to say, is a society characterized by ambivalence
regarding Americans. On the one hand, American values are admired and emulated;
on the other, they are derogated and feared. The marriage of a Korean and an
American is viewed with a similar ambivalence. It is in the untangling of these
contradictory sentiments that we can best understand Korean feelings regarding
intimate relationships with foreigners.

What makes people in general nervous about an international marriage?
Why should it be a matter of concern to anyone except the two who are actually
involved? The answer, of course, is that marriage never was and is not now
(romantic myths notwithstanding) a matter that concerns only two people.
Families, neighborhoods, and others may all be involved and their attitudes, values,
and expectations regarding the marriage are often critically important. Different
societies have different ideas about what marriage is and who should be
appropriately involved. Many of these feelings and expectations are implicit. What
an international marriage does is to make them explicit.

For Koreans, race as such is not a major issue, although it would be foolish
to say that race does not intrude into marriage questions. Racial consciousness,
however, is generally of the "blood is thicker than water" variety rather than the
crude racism of vulgar Darwinism. Koreans resent racial slurs, but their worst
historical experience with "others" has been at the hands of co-racials, the Japanese,
who attacked Korea brutally in the 16th century and governed it with a mailed fist
as a colony from 1910 to 1945. As a consequence, race tends not to be an
overriding or primary issue, but is, rather, one that is mixed in subtle degrees with
other concerns. The raw crudity and brutality of race relations as they historically
existed in North America, and currently so in South Africa, is absent. So also is
the sister crudity of religious bigotry and intolerance. Koreans of different faiths
live amiably side by side. There is no cleavage such as exists in Northern Ireland
between Protestants and Catholics, or in India between Hindu and Muslim. As a
devoutly anti-communist country, however, anyone wishing to marry an avowed
Marxist (a rare find, in any case, outside of university student circles) would likely
risk community aversion. In South Korea, a political dissident on the left has no
comfortable home.

This intolerance of political opponents, and the inevitable Romeo and Juliet
type enforced separation as regards marriage choices, is fostered by political
propaganda in schooling and in society generally that depicts the left as evil. There
are, of course, people who can attest first hand to the horrors they experienced at
the hands of the communists in the Korean War. Such memories help polarize
political viewpoints and provide a rallying point for nationalism and social identity.
In fact, South Koreans are nationalistic, with great pride in their history and their
current accomplishments. Curiously, however, with the exception of the anti-
communism issue, they lack the intense socio-centrism of the Japanese and

Chinese. It is hard to think of Koreans describing Magellan's circumnavigation of the globe as one Chinese elementary teacher did to her class. Magellan's trip, she said, had proven many things, but of these the most important was that China could be reached from the east as well as the west. Perhaps Korean exposure to almost all of the worst aspects of Japanese nationalism provided them with an example of the difference between justifiable pride and unjustifiable arrogance.

Exposure to hostile outsiders has certainly given Koreans the opportunity to project undesirable characteristics of the self onto others. Both the communists and the Japanese are viewed as highly aggressive. Americans, on the other hand, are nervously liked, but the question is often asked whether they are powerful enough to serve as guides and protectors. Is there some weakness in American society, and do Americans have enough strength of character to be dependable allies? Are they morally corrupt and sexually lax, the main victims of a worldwide AIDS epidemic that is somehow symptomatic of deep flaws in American society? The projective quality of such sentiments is clear when it is kept in mind that Korea is a society where prostitution is widespread and police brutality (and arrogance) a common feature of the social landscape.

If Koreans project undesired characteristics on to others, it is also true that they have positive views as well. Like Asians generally, they laugh at the Chinese joke about the four goods and the four bads. The four goods are an American salary, an English house, a Chinese chef, and a Japanese wife. The four bads are a Chinese salary, a Japanese house, an English chef, and an American wife (one Japanese who heard this story earnestly tried to explain that Japanese houses really are not that bad - he did not disagree with anything else). These are stereotypes, of course, negative and positive, and from an Asian perspective they contain a "kernal of truth." The point to be made here is that in an international marriage, the foreigner may be the recipient of this kind of mixed stereotyping. The American, for example, sometimes referred to neutrally as a Yankee, may be considered well-paid, smart, friendly, and privileged. On the other hand, he or she may be derisively termed a meikooknom (or meikkookyeun for a woman) or "american slave," and be looked upon as a self-indulgent, unreliable, pampered slob. Which will it be? Much depends on the context, of course, and the previous experience that any particular Korean has had with Americans. Exposure to the American armed forces network, a regular channel on Korean network TV, may also have a bearing. Geared for the young American serviceman, the evening programming is heavily slanted toward shows like Miami Vice and Dynasty, and especially toward sports. It is difficult (nay, impossible) for us to state the exact nature of the impact that such cultural exports have. What does seem clear, however, is that without any additional data, such as might come from a trip abroad, the image of America that is portrayed is itself largely a stereotype.

In our essay to this point we have mentioned a number of factors that we believe pertain when assessing Korean's attitudes about international marriages. They are not, we feel, usually the crucial factors, but each has its role as part of a broad context of evaluation. Clearly, enough has been pointed out to show that Americans, at least, are the objects of complex and often ambiguous judgments. Sometimes viewed positively, they are at other times viewed negatively. In no sense are they simply seen as a kind of industrious and law abiding "model minority," a term that has become popular in America to describe its own Asian citizens. Americans do not universally exemplify the virtues that Koreans hold dear. Sometimes they do, sometimes they do not. This means that the view of the international marriage is often ambivalent and assessed in terms of the personal characteristics of those involved.

Marriage is a contract involving, among other things, an exchange of advantages. The classic case is the one of "beauty for bucks," the universal story of the ugly rich man who marries the poor but beautiful woman (or the other way around). Although couples and their families often strive for status congruity, this objective is not always achieved. If status incongruity pertains, what can be offered by the inferior side to bridge the gap? What presents must be given, what slights borne, what hopes of future expectations fulfilled? These are the kinds of questions that are asked in traditional contexts, meaning those where the prospective partners and their families know each other's histories and share a cultural framework of evaluation. But this is precisely the problem with the international marriage. The partners may know a great deal about themselves but others, and especially their families, may not know the other side's history, nor share a common cultural framework. From the families' standpoint the contract has blind spots; the assessment of relative advantages can only be made by crude indicators. International marriage is thus a worrisome and potentially undesirable thing.

For some Koreans, of course, what matters most is escaping their own history. Korea may be rapidly becoming a developed society, but there are still many whose lives are mired in poverty and whose life chances are slim. With no firm knowledge about specific instances, many Koreans believe that those who marry American servicemen generally do so for monetary reasons. These women are considered to be low status by the very act of their fraternization. As such they become branded with the derogatory title of "Yangkongju" or "Western Princess." Although love and affection may be present in the relationship, it is widely assumed that what the young woman really wants is a life of greater material comfort and the possibility of extending some of those benefits to the family that has been left behind. The bargain is assumed to have been agreed to by the woman's family in the hope that one member of the family, and perhaps all, will gain a tangible benefit. In such instances, the American is of some limited use in promoting the family's collective "face" and in elevating perceptions of the family's social status. For only when these conditions are fulfilled does a marriage truly have worth.

Korean society is not one that glorifies independence. Individual merit and achievement, while applauded, are not the sole criteria for judging a person's worth. Rather, the social context is one of intense interdependence. It is important, therefore, that an addition to the family be a person who will assume family obligations of reciprocal care and assistance. The ability of family members to fulfill mutual obligations, in fact, is a major component of the collective judgment of the family's worth. Just as important, a prospective addition to the family by marriage should ideally be an individual who has status assets that are valued in Korean society and that can maintain or improve the family's net standing. Small wonder that arranged marriage was the universal pattern historically.

In our case, we met and courted outside of the Korean social context. Myoung's sisters, as would be expected, made known their judgments; these were, happily, positive. So too did Dick's family. We were, of course, older than the norm at the time of our marriage, and by that fact alone, free from some of the constraints that younger people face. There were no plans for children and we were well matched in terms of educational background and income level. We also have compatible dispositions and interests.

In Korea, these attributes have made us acceptable -- if novel -- to a range of acquaintances who in general share the same background characteristics. The primary difficulty is not status, but rather bridging a language barrier. Indeed, because being a professor has very high status in Korean society, much higher than in America, our tenured faculty positions at Rutgers insure the family against loss of face. Myoung's father, who warmly supports the marriage, was once asked if he would have these same feelings if Dick were a laborer rather than a professor. Rather forthrightly he stated that it would have made his support more difficult.

Even an international marriage such as ours, however, does not fit in Korean society without friction. The importance of face and fulfilling obligations as criteria for the acceptance of a couple presents difficulties for those with other values. Women, for example, are second class citizens in Korea, expected to provide support for males rather than assert themselves as individuals. Myoung cannot return to that. When she is with her Korean friends, she often feels that a gap has grown between her and them. She feels liberated from the constraints that her friends accept and in what sense she is viewed as an anomoly. In return, they are, in her terms, in a Korean box.

To an American, Korean social relations are not simply interdependent, they are excessively intermeshed. The placing of obligations on others and the expectation that these will be paid off in the future assumes for Dick (and Myoung, too) a burdensome quality. The necessity of constantly thinking about others in terms of the long and short term utilities of relationships, and most important in terms of one's own and one's family's face, are calculations that Dick stumbles over (despite the fact that such calculations are not entirely absent in America). Going "dutch treat" with one's colleagues at lunch, for example, is never acceptable; the slate in relationships is never clean. More to the point, it is not expected to be clean.

In America, a recent poll found that American men now prefer Asian women as wives over all others. In contrast, in Korea, American men (and women) are not the first choice as marriage partners. Not the least of the reasons for this are extended family concerns. For the Korean family, the international marriage is still a gamble.

PART III :

BECOMING A MINORITY THROUGH THE STUDY ABROAD EXPERIENCE

CHAPTER 10

ALIVE AND WELL IN LOVELY LAGOS
Tolani and Judy Asuni

Learning from Jimmy and Rosalyn Carter's experience, we decided to write separate accounts and stay happily married. The first section is by Tolani, a Nigerian psychiatrist trained in Dublin and London. The second part is written by Judy, an American sociologist trained in the US, Nigeria, and the UK.

Tolani's Account

My Background

My early childhood experience of interracial relationships was during the colonial era when anything from Europe, especially Britain, was the ideal. The white person held superior positions in government and the private sector. Yet I had the good fortune of interacting with whites on an informal level. Some of my respected and adored school teachers were missionaries. My cub master was also a delightful Englishman, who was a civil servant. Before going to Ireland to study medicine, I worked in the civil service for a couple of years during the Second World War. I met some young British soldiers through the British Council, and we interacted socially. They visited my humble home, and we had dinners together in a popular hotel. The myth of the superiority of the whites was considerably watered down by these interactions.

As was usual in any culture, my parents and paternal grandmother had some words of advice to give me a few days before my departure to study medicine in Ireland. I was twenty-one. They asked me about my thoughts of marriage, as I would be away for at least six years. My response was that I had a Nigerian girl friend whom I was leaving behind but who was also likely to go abroad for post-secondary education. In any case, there are many slips between the cup and the lips and my relationship with this girl might not develop further. At this stage the question was asked if I was going to marry a white girl. I then explained that since I would be away for at least six years, I would be meeting and interacting with Irish girls. If I was going to live a normal life and make friends, it would not be right for me to draw a line in the development of my relationships from the beginning. This would interfere adversely with spontaneity and openness which are necessary for genuine friendship. With this explanation, the matter was closed.

As it turned out, I was away for nearly eight years, and I did not marry a white girl. My Nigerian girlfriend indeed went abroad and in fact went to the same university with me. The relationship did not develop for religious reasons. I am a Muslim and she a Christian, and she would not go against her parents' wish not to marry a Muslim. This was a time when the Muslims in Nigeria were generally not exposed to European and Christian education and consequently were not holding positions of power and influence within the country. Thus they were looked down upon.

I started my sojourn abroad among whites with an attitude that I had to find my socio-cultural level. The first girl that I dated was one I met at a dance hall. During our first encounter I found out that she worked in a laundry, presumably as a laundry hand. Even though I was pleasant to her, I made up my mind that she could not be the type with whom I could develop a deep relationship, as I equated her with girls in Nigeria doing comparable jobs with whom I would not associate -- not because they were not human beings but because of the wide differences in our educational, social and cultural levels. When I reported my experience and decision to my fellow Nigerian student friends, they asked what type of girls I would date. I told them that there were girls in the university, meaning Irish girls as there were considerably fewer Nigerian female than male students. They commented that my lecturers and professors would not like that, and this would adversely affect my academic progress. My response was that it could only deter my progress if I were on the borderline, not if I were scoring high marks.

As it turned out, I struck a friendship with a female medical student from England, who was doing her clinical in the same hospital where I was doing my house job. This relationship developed to the point where I spent a few days in her home in London during a vacation. I was warmly received by her parents. I was surprised when her father invited me to dinner in a restaurant when next I was in London. I wondered why he invited me to dinner in a restaurant and not at home. My suspicion was confirmed when he explained that he did not want to appear to his wife to be encouraging the relationship between me and their daughter. He said that he had no objection to the relationship, but since I had been away from home for six years, he suggested that it might be wiser for me to return home and see what home was like. The alternative was that he could send his daughter to Nigeria for her to see what environment she would be living in if she married me.

I told him that I was not ready to return home and that Nigeria would not be the same for his daughter without me. We left the matter undecided and I thanked him. When I reported the meeting with her father to my girlfriend, she suggested our getting married secretly. I told her that it would not be fair to her father to take such a step. Our relationship continued until I returned home. We exchanged frequent passionate letters, and I called her on the telephone a few times. Then one day, I received a letter from her, telling me that her love for me lacked the vitality on which marriage should be based. That was the end of the relationship at that level, although we are still friends.

After I got over the feeling of loss, I started opening up to establish new relationships, including renewing the relationship with my former Nigerian girlfriend. Each time I came across the same religious barrier. On each occasion I was expected to convert to Christianity. With my first wife, who was a Dutch widow of an Englishman and living in Nigeria, the issue of religion was not a barrier.

One big lesson I learned from that marriage is that it is not enough to fall in love with a woman. It is vital to know her background, especially her intra-family relationships, interaction, and communication. This is indeed one of the kernels of marriage institutions in my community--that not only the union of two individuals but also the establishment of relationships between the two families. Unfortunately, I did not meet the parents of my first wife until after our marriage, and when things started to fall apart, she had not developed the awareness of the usefulness of reporting the situation to my family of orientation. They could have intervened in a constructive manner, especially as she had been truly accepted by my family, she had admirably adjusted to the culture, and most importantly, she had children by me.

The success of my second marriage to a white American is partly due to some of the lessons I learned from my first marriage. In fact, even though I had met my wife in Nigeria and known her for about a year, I did not decide to ask her hand in marriage until I had visited her in the US with her family. I was impressed not only with her nuclear family relationships but more so with the extended family interactions. I met uncles, aunts and cousins. In fact, she was surprised when the tone of my letters changed after that visit. Of course, I explained that seeing her with her family had convinced me of her suitability as a wife in the Nigerian context.

I had been separated from my first wife for 8 years before marrying Judy. Before doing this, I had discussions with my children about my intention and the difference it would make to our lives. I explained to them that when I married there would be a mistress of the house who would be in control of the household. In addition to the expected practical changes, they would understandably resent my wife consciously or unconsciously, because of the notion that she had come to displace their mother, even though the latter had left the country five years previously. I told them that I would not want to be put in a situation of having to choose between them and my wife. I had a similar discussion with Judy, calling her attention to the possible resentment which she might receive from my children. I must admit that one of the factors that facilitated this move was that my eldest son had asked why I did not marry again, as he did not think it good for me to continue to live alone with my cook-steward running the house with an apparent lack of companionship. At this stage of my professional career, I was the boss and living on the grounds of a psychiatric hospital which was isolated from the small, provincial town. As the head of the hospital, I had to keep a respectable social distance from my staff. This accentuated my apparent loneliness, even though I spent most of my time working.

My expectation of marriage was formed from my own idealism and my observation of successful marriages during my sojourn in Ireland. This expectation did not conflict with my concept of traditional marriages. I looked for companionship with someone with the same or similar intellectual range, someone on the same wavelength with me in many respects. Living in small towns away from my extended family in Lagos allowed me to fashion my life with little or no interference from other members of my family, who respected my lifestyle on occasions of their visits to me. My wife, on the other hand, knows what is expected of her in terms of looking after them when they do visit.

My idea of marriage was that it should not alienate me from my friends and particularly my own family. It was for me to ensure that my relationship and interaction with my friends and family did not interfere unduly with my life and my relationship with my wife. I also expected my wife to be accommodating and hospitable to my friends and family, and if their demand was too much for her, or their pattern of behavior was disturbing her, she should tell me, and it was for me to shield and protect her from whatever I consider to be too much, while at the same time encouraging her to be more understanding and tolerant as the occasions of such interactions with them are sporadic and short.

I also expected members of my family, especially the females, to guide my wife as to what was expected of her, bearing in mind that she might not be able to go along with them all the way. If she found herself unable to comply with their guidance, I expected her to tell me and it was for me to explain her stand and if necessary, make excuses for her. This has worked out well because of my respected position in the family.

The Mixed Marriage

The major factor that has contributed to the stability of our marriage is the various personality traits of both Judy and myself, which are complementary-- rationality, tolerance, flexibility, and compassion--to name some. These personality traits have made it possible to develop conscious and unconscious mechanisms which have sustained our marriage. One area which distinguishes our marriage from those that are not mixed is the fact that Judy does not have her own relatives in Nigeria and therefore does not have the same family commitments and support outside her marriage. I am always conscious of this, and she on her part keeps regular contact with her family by correspondence. She writes to them almost every week, keeping them informed of her activities. They also write regularly.

There are differences between our cultures. Most people in developing countries eat to live while many in developed countries live to eat. It is a common practice for Americans to go out to eat, while Nigerians usually eat at home. In developed countries, there are many social services--old age pensions, welfare services, council houses, unemployment benefits, education and recreational facilities, etc. Most of these services are not available or very limited in Nigeria. This contributes to different attitudes to life and planning for the future. Another difference is that in Nigeria, domestic staff are still available. Judy and I view and treat the staff quite differently. She is more egalitarian and trusting than I am, and this has led to minor arguments.

Yoruba culture has naturally affected our lifestyle and interaction. While I do not share the Yoruba concept of sex role totally, I still hold on to some to a limited degree. I believe in consultation, but I also believe that there cannot be two captains on a boat. I believe that male and female sex roles should be complementary, each carrying equal weight, especially when husband and wife are both working.

Even though Judy is a Christian and I am Muslim, neither is ritualistic and both practice the main tenets of the two religions which are not dissimilar.

The aspects of our two backgrounds which have facilitated our adjustment have already been mentioned, as have areas of cross-cultural conflict. The fact that my own family accept Judy and hers accept me is a very positive factor.

What may be the weakness/constraints of our mixed marriage can also be the strength/advantages, depending on how one looks at it, and the socio-economic circumstances of the couple. The fact that Judy's and my families are thousands of miles apart can be a disadvantage, but it can also be an advantage in that it eliminates conflicting interferences, such as in-law problems.

The Mixed Marriage and Society

There are so many mixed marriages in Nigeria, especially in our socio-economic stratum, that they do not seem to make much difference to the wider society. There have been ministers of state and high ranking politicians and government functionaries with foreign wives, and a few highly placed Nigerian women with foreign husbands. There have not been any palpable societal influences with which we have had to cope. While our children are being brought up as Nigerians, they also know that they have connections with Judy's country, and they know all their maternal relatives and interact positively with them during their annual visits to America.

The social climate towards mixed marriages is one of acceptance from our experience. I would not be surprised, however, to be told that some people have strong objections to them, but we do not come across such people. Even if we do, it does not make any difference to us, as such people do not matter, nor can they do anything to jeopardize our happiness.

Sometime ago couples of mixed marriages, essentially black and white, were rather isolated socially, especially during the colonial era in Nigeria. There were few of them. But there are so many now, and the foreign spouses have adjusted better than before. These couples are no longer isolated. This is due partly to the whole social change in the country where the white person is now seen as an individual and does not represent the colonializing power.

If I had married someone from my background, my perspective of life would have been very limited, and I would not have developed the capacity to be flexible and understanding of other cultures.

Judy's Report

Mixed Marriage and Me

"For a happy marriage, marry someone of your own race, religion, and background," advised the well-meaning Baptist minister. I often wonder what he would think if he could see who I did marry, for I am a white American from a respectable Presbyterian middle-class family who married a black Muslim Nigerian 23 years my senior. The poor man would probably turn over in his grave. A long time ago I decided that if I did marry, it would have to be exciting, and I think that I got my wish.

What brought a girl from a small town in upstate New York to Africa? Somewhere in teenage my excessive childhood curiosity was diverted away from exploring dangerous places and things to exploring other people and the way that they think. My international life started when, at 17, I was one of the first exchange students from my school to Latin America. In spite of the fact that we were totally unprepared for what we would meet, my summer in Nicaragua and subsequent stays by other exchange students at our home whetted my appetite for the foreign life. Coming to Africa was really by chance. My sister was unable to take me to Europe in the summer of 1967 as planned, so I looked around for alternatives. One noontime for want of anything else to read, I retrieved from the dustbin a brochure from Operation Crossroads Africa, which I had discarded upon noting the fee of $1000. More thorough reading showed that there was a Cornell

University Crossroads Committee which could help prospective volunteers, and I was on my way. A summer in Niger gave me a desire to return to Africa, which I did in 1969 as a teacher in Ghana under the Teachers for West Africa Program. After the two-year contract, I decided to stay in West Africa and study sociology, so I came to the University of Ibadan, with some Nigerian friends. Three years and many adventures later, I met Tolani. In the meantime, I had already accepted a job in the US, so returned there for one year. After several visits from Tolani, we decided to marry and I returned to Nigeria in 1975. After three children and 5 years with the UN in Rome, we are now at home in Lagos.

In discussing our intercultural marriage, it must be emphasized that ours is different from most mixed marriages between Nigerian men and foreign women. I came to Nigeria as a free choice, liked the country and stayed. Most expatriate wives marry abroad while the husband is studying in the wife's country. Many such wives, upon coming to Nigeria, feel trapped here by marriage and children. I did not. This freedom of choice has contributed greatly towards the success of our marriage. Tolani is also an unusual Nigerian husband, in that he had a foreign wife before and has learned from that experience. Although we had to make the normal adjustments in any marriage, our cultural adjustments were not as great at those of many mixed couples.

Which is not to say that the cultural differences do not exist. Because I had lived in Nigeria for a number of years before marriage and, as a sociologist, had studied the Yoruba family, I was somewhat familiar with what I was about to experience. However, I think that we all have unconscious expectations, based on our own family experiences as children and siblings. I came from a solid family-oriented rural area and my own father played an active role in childrearing. Being bigger and smarter than most boys, it never occurred to me that girls were in any way inferior. Attending a very liberal university in the activist era of the late 1960's reinforced this sense of equality. Therefore, the Yoruba strict division of labor and social interaction between men and women came as an unpleasant surprise to me. Nigerian men spend a great deal of their free time together in warmer, deeper friendships than most American or European men. They are also expected to spend a great deal of time and energy on their extended families in social visits, advisory sessions and financial obligations. At the same time, the Nigerian woman is involved in similar ways with her own family, friends, colleagues, schoolmates and a host of other social contacts. The expatriate wife, without this built-in social network, often feels isolated and left out. This division of social life is exacerbated in our case by the great difference in ages between Tolani and myself. Most of his female friends are at a very different stage in the lifestyle than I, so we don't have much in common. Luckily I am independent and outgoing, so between my friends from my single days and new friends made through the children and interest organizations, I have built my own social network. I am happy with my present social life and feel that is is more realistic than the Western ideal of a spouse fulfilling all, or most of the other's needs. However, this cultural difference required considerably initial adjustment.

Probably the biggest adjustment that I've had to make in our marriages is that although Tolani plays a more active role in raising our children than most Yoruba men, it is still less that I had expected. Although intellectually I knew that mothers bear the brunt of childrearing in Yoruba land, unconsciously I expected a family life similar to that of my parents. It is also especially difficult to socialize children into patterns that are not completely familiar. This personal need partially determined my choice of a Ph.D. topic on the changing patterns of Yoruba childrearing. The lesser participation of Yoruba men in childrearing, coupled by Tolani's frequent absences during his stint with the UN, have meant that I've made the majority of decisions about the children. Now, that Tolani travels less and the children are older, he is able to take a more active role with them.

These cultural factors have required difficult adjustments on my part. There are other cultural aspects which bother some expatriate wives but not me. One is the demands of the extended family. Some husbands are expected to financially support or house either older or younger relatives. I am lucky that Tolani's family is generally able to take care of itself, and he takes a firm stand against supporting lay-abouts. My own family is very close and visits to all of the extended relatives are an integral part of any trip to my home area. Therefore, I automatically expect our active participation in Tolani's family events. Many foreign wives find it hard to adjust to the lack of privacy, the high noise level, the frequency of visitors, and the general lack of services and amenities in Nigeria. I had adjusted to all of these differences before marriage, so my role as a new wife was easier than for many.

An intercultural marriage can present many problems. Its success or failure often depends on the personalities of the parties involved. Both must be mature, flexible, tolerant and understanding. I would say that the brunt of adjustment lies on the part of the spouse living in the other's culture (Tolani might say the opposite!). For a spouse coming to live in the Yoruba part of Nigeria, s/he should also be independent, resourceful, and resilient. It has often been noted that the person who makes the most successful adjustment in a foreign country is the one who comes from a stable background and has inner security that allows that person to weather storms. The foreign wife who has no strong roots in her own country is more likely to feel that she belongs nowhere, then the one who feels at home in both places. Before marriage, I had lived in several countries. After meeting Tolani, I went back to the US for a year, so I could evaluate what I would lose and gain by marrying a foreigner. My security is also increased by my family's acceptance of Tolani and our marriage. Although my parents, being strong Presbyterians, initially resisted my older sister's American Catholic boyfriend, they have moved with the times and liberalized their views. Their four sons-in-law now include an Irish Catholic, a Nigerian Muslim, an American Jew and an American Unitarian! We joke about our cultural differences and live happily as a mini-United Nations.

In spite of our obvious differences in ethnicity, race, age and religion, Tolani and I share some basic values that hold our marriage together. We are in fundamental agreement about our lifestyle. Neither of us is very materialistic or ostentatious. We value ideas and reading. Family and children are important to us. Our big luxury is yearly trips to Europe and America, to keep in touch with family and the world outside of Nigeria. We have the advantage of being economically comfortable without being too rich. Although we have our minor financial differences, we basically agree on where to spend and where to save. Both of us enjoy working hard, receiving friends and relaxing quietly. This basic consensus on how to live mediates our differences and external problems.

In summary, our marriage has several things going against it, principally ethnic and age differences. Religion could also be a divisive factor if we allowed it. I come from a strong Protestant background and was very active in church work up through university. Over time I have come to see that Christianity does not have a monopoly on truth. The concepts of a supernatural being and good will towards others are found in all the major world religions. To me, these similarities should be emphasized over the differences. Although Tolani is a practicing Muslim, he does not insist that the children follow his ways. We've agreed to teach them about both Christianity and Islam and let them choose their religious affiliation when they're mature. In a similar way, we try to expose them to both of our cultures and take the best from each, rather than emphasizing one and negating the other. In this way, we try to diminish our cultural differences. Even where these differences do exist, our consensus on basic values has enabled us to build a workable marriage.

The Mixed Marriage and Society

As Tolani has said, mixed marriages in Nigeria are very common today. I belong to an organization called Nigerwives, which is dedicated to helping the integration of foreign wives into Nigerian society. We have members from almost every country of the world, and represent thousands of expatriate wives of Nigerians. Thus, our marriage is not unusual in the society in which we live.

I am used to being called "oyinbo"--white person. What is ironical is when the children are called oyinbo in Nigeria and black in America, although the girls' skin color is closer to mine than Tolani's. I find that people tend to classify someone slightly different in the opposite category to themselves. Our girls have developed ways of dealing with this, emphasizing the fact that they are Nigerians but with a uniqueness. Nigerians note a difference, not necessarily a negative one. We've never had any bad experiences in the US, perhaps because we're not looking for them. Spending 5 years of childhood in Rome was a good start for the girls, as Italians do not have a colonial heritage of racial discrimination and indeed look upon someone a bit different as beautiful. I even became super-saturated with complete strangers stopping on the street to remark on the beautiful children and ask about their names and origins. The Italian preoccupation with tanning gave 5-year-old Bolanle the confidence to tell our pediatrician that she would be more beautiful than Mummy because she already had a tan and curly hair, so didn't have to work for them.

Being part of a mixed marriage puts all of us in an international situation, which we might not otherwise enjoy. For example, I have friends of a dozen different nationalities; our daughters go to school with a mixture of children ranging from Chinese to Kenyan to Polish to Brazilian. Kofo's teacher is Indian, Derin's is English, and Bolanle's is Jamaican. All of these contacts add depth and interest to daily life, which we would not have enjoyed if we had married within our own ethnic groups. Of course there can be problems, such as offending a Saudi woman by trying to shake her hand or being too blunt with a Japanese friend. However, the advantages of this cross-cultural contact outweigh the disadvantages.

In analyzing the effect of our marriage on our associates, it is hard to balance the ethnic versus the age difference. When I first became serious about Tolani, my mother could accept the fact that he was black and an African and a Muslim. What she found hard to take was that he is only 3 years younger than she is! Quite objectively, Tolani and I are a most unlikely pair and this has caused considerable surprise in people meeting us for the first time. Someone meeting either of us singly usually expects a spouse that matches the first. We've had a number of amusing incidents with dropped jaws and stunned silence. Considering that Tolani has a completely black son and white stepdaughters from his first marriage, our family dynamics are slightly confusing to the outsider. We take all of this in a light-hearted, good-natured fashion, and our daughters quite enjoy being part of an unusual family. Having siblings who are 25 years older and different colors than they are adds to the interest.

My favorite parenting book, The Mother's Almanac, advised every day telling your child that s/he is beautiful. We've tried to give our children this basic security and feeling of self-worth. And it seems to have paid off. Although our three daughters are only 16, 14 and 10 and have not yet encountered all of the traumas of teenage, they have been able to successfully cope with a number of changes in their lives. Bolanle was 3 and Derin a baby when we moved to Rome, where Kofo was born. After 5 years in Rome, the adjustment back to Nigeria was probably hardest on Bolanle, who had very fond memories of Nigeria but found the present reality quite different. I was pleased to read one of her more recent letters to a friend abroad, which said "Mummy used to say that I would learn to like Nigeria. I didn't believe her, but now I do. Now I know that Nigeria is the best place to live." We have tried to give the girls good feelings about Nigeria and about themselves, emphasizing their uniqueness. When we first returned to Nigeria, after being in a small school in Rome where no nationality predominated, the girls had difficulty finding their niches, as their school tends to have English, Chinese and wholly Nigerian groups, with a sprinkling of other nationalities. Over time, they have made their own friends, and are able to mix with kids from all of the groups, without being limited to any one.

In the same way, the girls are very flexible in adjusting to each new culture when we travel. After a few hours in London, or Ireland, or Rome, or New York, they feel at home. Even their accent changes. However, they have a basic identity as Nigerians. After seeing other mixed children who feel homeless or pulled apart, Tolani and I have agreed to raise our children as Nigerians. We want them to feel that they have a strong base, from which they can launch out as citizens of the world. We have tried to combine the best features of American and Yoruba childrearing. For example, we play down the ostentation and the bad attitude to work found too often in present-day Nigeria. On the other hand, we don't accept the extreme individualism of many Americans. Instead we try to strike a happy balance of teaching our children to be independent while still caring for others.

Concerning the society's response to mixed marriage, I believe that you find what you look for. I have never had a truly negative reaction to my marriage--surprise yes, but real rejection, no. I had been working with older people in the US when I decided to marry Tolani and was a bit worried how they would take this news. They were sad to see me go but did dislike the actual marriage. Of course, times had changed a lot in the US by 1975. I was told in all seriousness by an otherwise nice 85-year-old man that I shouldn't go to Africa in 1967 with Crossroads Africa, because in Africa they tie you down and jump on your stomach until you're dead. Hopefully these preconceptions are passing into oblivion.

Our experience has of course been affected by where we've lived. Living in a cosmopolitan city like Lagos is very different from living as a foreigner in a small village in northern Nigeria. Our years in Rome were within the United Nations community. At one not unusual gathering, we discovered that only 2 couples in a roomful of people were married to spouses of the same country. In this way, the acceptance of our marriage has partially depended on the cosmopolitan circles within which we've moved. However, I remember a basic principle from a university course on racism: action can change ideas. Put into an uncomfortable situation and expected to perform well, most people will rise to the occasion. We have expected acceptance and have found it. Those who cannot accept us are not usually worth worrying about.

What would life have been like if I'd married a nice white American protestant university grad? I'd like to think that we'd have a happy, expensive home with 2.1 children and good jobs. We'd probably take yearly vacations to the Bahamas or camping in Colorado. I'd be putting away the nest egg for the 2.1 kids' college education. Unless of course, I was the 1 out of 3 who was divorced, in which case the picture would be less rosy. I wouldn't spend my annual 3 weeks in the US frantically buying computer parts, or do a Ph.D. long-distance to the UK, or have to worry about daily power and water shortages. I wouldn't lead a Brownie troop with 10 different nationalities or have friends from a dozen countries. I wouldn't have any aunties-in-law with whom we share no common language. I might even understand my husband so well that I could anticipate his every thought and action. Wouldn't it be dull?

CHAPTER 11

CROSSING RELIGIOUS LINES IN AMERICA
Christy Brown and Ayoub Farahyar

Christy Brown

I was born in Los Angeles, California in 1949. My father was the son of Swedish immigrants; my mother's parents were of Scotch and German ethnicity. Both families were relatively well off during the depression, and my parents grew up with typically WASP prejudices against Blacks, Jews, Hispanics, and even Catholics; in short, against any non-Northern European people. I attended virtually all-white schools in the San Fernando Valley. When I was in high school my parents looked down on my Italian-American boyfriend whom they tolerated but hoped I wouldn't marry.

My first husband was from an Irish Catholic working class family, but he was getting an advanced degree, so my parents accepted him. I had always felt that there was something missing--call it feeling perhaps, in my Protestant heritage, and I converted to Catholicism in the wake of Vatican II.

But it wasn't until I returned to Indiana University in 1978 to finish my Ph.D. in English Literature that I became close friends with people from cultures radically different from my own. My values had gradually changed during the eight years between my marriage and separation, and I think I was looking for something beyond what might be called the American dream, which seemed shallow and empty. The striving to survive on a limited income, the political infighting at my husband's college, my lack of identity without a career were all beginning to create a sense of rebellion in me.

As a single woman in Bloomington I had much more exposure to people from different cultures and ethnic groups than I had as a married graduate student eight years earlier. I renewed and deepened my friendship with a brilliant Black American graduate student in literature who was interested in African literature, film, and politics. I met and became friends with students from many different third world countries, but especially from North Africa and the Middle East. The Iranian Revolution had just begun and Camp David was also underway, and Iranian and Arab students were politically active on campus. I became acquainted with the political struggles in Third World countries and eventually became active in Solidarity work in Central America, South Africa, but primarily the Middle East, as well as in the Women's Movement.

The international students I associated with formed a cosmopolitan group whose outlook was generally "progressive." They were from India, Taiwan, Nigeria, Iran, Palestine, Afghanistan, Chile, etc. We shared each other's food, customs, music, and ideas, and seemed to have more in common with each other than traditional or conservative students from our own countries. These students favored modernization, but wished to maintain their cultural identity, and they were generally opposed to U.S. intervention and what they considered exploitation. Most planned to return to their countries and help the people through education.

I had long term relationships with three Middle Eastern/North African men and experienced the difficulties of intercultural relationships; at the same time I felt I learned a great deal about how the rest of the world thinks. In seeing American culture through these men's eyes I could never again take any behavior or way of thinking for granted. I also began to realize one cannot "know" a culture through a single individual, especially when cultures are going through a process of modernization which affects individuals differently depending on their class, country of origin, political ideology, etc. All the men I dated were very different in their behavior and some were much more liberal in their attitudes toward women than others. In general, I found that men who identified with the left were more likely (although not always) to have open-minded attitudes toward women which approximated Western radical views of sexual equality. Educated men from Iran, Lebanon, or Palestinians seemed more "Westernized" than men from North Africa, Saudi Arabia, or the Gulf States. However, a religious Iranian could be more traditional than a leftist Saudi.

Many of my friends were also involved in intercultural relationships and/or marriages; in several cases the American spouse like me, had political sympathies with the Middle Easterner. I could compare these relationships with marriages in which both partners were from the Middle East, and try to understand the advantages and disadvantages of each.

I also became close friends with several Middle Eastern women, who were very supportive while I was going through a difficult period after my divorce. I saw male-female relationships between Middle Easterners from both sides and began to understand the difficulties such relationships entail for the educated Middle Eastern woman, who is expected to conform more to traditional patterns of behavior than an American woman married to or dating a Middle Eastern man. My female Middle Eastern friends expressed the most anger about the double standard applied to male and female behavior in their societies.

The division between traditionalists and modernists in Middle Eastern societies created almost a kind of intracultural split in itself, so that it might be harder for a Westernized Iranian woman, say, to marry a traditional Iranian male than an American. And one Lebanese professor who had married an American told me he preferred American women because he felt alienated from women from his own culture.

I had relatively little contact with fundamentalist Muslim students, most of whom were married, although I did get to know some single men. (Degrees of adherence to and interpretation of religion vary, so I am talking about a continuum more than a black-white division.) The students I associated with did not get along for the most part because of their radically different lifestyles and ideologies. Muslim fundamentalists on the whole were more resistant to close contact with Americans, and when I or other American women dated fundamentalist men, we noticed that they often felt guilty, which wasn't a pleasant situation for the women. They sometimes tried to hide their relationships from married or even single friends. Those few American women who married fundamentalist or more traditionally minded men found that they were under a great deal of pressure, even while in the United States, to adopt their husband's lifestyles; to wear "hejab" (Islamic modest dress, unlike the veil the face is not covered), to stay in the home, and to avoid speaking with men. Most were not prevented from continuing their education, but unless one was prepared to convert to Islam, these conditions must have seemed nearly intolerable.

I had no interest in adopting a traditional Muslim lifestyle, but I was interested enough in Middle Eastern culture and politics to think I would like to teach in the Middle East, and I believed marriage to a professor from the Middle East might be more feasible than marriage to an American man who did not share my interests. However, I did realize that the wife of even a non-religious Middle Eastern man can have difficulty adapting to the cultural differences, especially different expectations of women, and even more so if she lives in the Middle East. I noticed that even men who are sincerely interested in modernizing their societies, and condemn the oppression of women, cannot change their behavior and cultural assumptions overnight. While Middle Eastern men are often extremely charming and courteous in casual conversation, their expectations of a wife or even a girlfriend are different from a casual acquaintance.

Most Middle Eastern men come to the United States with no idea of American dating practices; in their cultures it is extremely difficult even to talk to a woman, and men are expected to contract arranged marriages with very little knowledge of the woman other than assurances that "she's a good girl." (For example, my brother-in-law saw his future wife on the street several times and liked the way she looked, so he sent his mother to ask for her hand.) Therefore, they often rush into relationships with American girls in the same way they would contract an arranged marriage, then later find the cultural differences too great to overcome.

On the other hand, men who come to this country at a younger age and stay longer adapt much better to American dating practices. Yet I have heard some of the most seemingly sophisticated men express the fear that a woman who "has been around" (a typical American woman), cannot be trusted in marriage. One supposedly "progressive" Iranian told me women were like cars, and who would buy a used one if he could have a new one? But he eventually married a divorced American woman who was over thirty!

Middle Eastern men who fell in love with American women (often despite their intention of having a temporary relationship only), were almost inevitably faced with the obstacle of parental pressure to marry a girl from their country, preferably a cousin or close friend of the family. Relatives often visit the man and try to dissuade him, or, when he returns home on vacation, they pressure him into an arranged marriage, leaving a broken-hearted American girl to wonder what happened. However, in some areas it is a sign of prestige to marry an "Aroos farengi" (foreign bride), especially if she is a blonde.

Most Middle Eastern men I met were also afraid that their American wife will not be able to adapt to living in their country, even if she wishes to go with him, but those who plan on remaining in the United States at least semi-permanently often feel that an American wife will be an asset in helping them to adjust.

The "green card" syndrome is one reason any American woman who dates Middle Easterners (and other non-Americans) learns to distrust them. I have heard Middle Easterners not married to Americans remark (mistakenly of course) that the only reason a Middle Easterner would marry an American is for a green card. Because the political and economic situations in many third world countries are so volatile, many men and women are desperately trying to achieve some kind of security, and since marrying an American is the easiest way to obtain permanent residency in this country, and since in many ways it seems similar to contracting an arranged marriage, many Middle Eastern men try to contract marriages of convenience. From the American point of view this is a disgraceful way of using a woman, but many Middle Easterners don't see anything wrong with it if the woman agrees and is fully aware that the marriage is temporary. They believe that with the high divorce rate in the United States, most women do not care if their marriages are permanent or not, (sometimes I get the impression some Middle Easterners cannot conceive that Americans have any feelings at all). I objected to men dating a woman ostensibly to have a relationship, then suggesting that a temporary marriage be arranged. However, from the man's point of view, a woman he didn't know well could try to bribe him or enforce community property laws going beyond the sum of money originally agreed upon. The problem is that from the American side its very hard to tell motivations for marriage and how much the desire for the green card is entering into the man's decision to contract even a permanent marriage. I think if it were easier to stay in the United States and work without permanent residency this problem would not be so widespread.

Given the potential for misunderstanding, or worse, tragedy, involved in relationships with Middle Eastern men, one might wonder why I chose to enter into such a marriage. One American male political activist I knew asked me how I could consider myself a feminist and date Middle Eastern men. At the time this seemed evidence of a prejudice that many Americans shared, assuming that just because a man was from the Middle East, he was automatically an extreme chauvinist. Of course, many radical feminists believed that marriage to any man would be a compromise, and in my experience, many of the same problems regarding sharing housework, etc., would exist in a marriage with an American man. If I had taken that extreme view I doubt I would have been able to marry at all. It might have seemed unrealistic to some people, but I can say that I expected that if I did marry a Middle Eastern man, he would also be a feminist and would not impose any limitation on my lifestyle based on the fact that I am a woman.

I believe a woman must have at least some interest in Middle Eastern culture to make such a marriage a success. When I met my husband, I was literally caught between two cultures. Not only because of the differences in culture, but more because of the familial and political barriers to intercultural marriages. I felt that the likelihood of meeting the kind of person with whom such a marriage would work would be almost as hard as finding an American male who would share my interest in Middle Eastern culture and/or political radicalism. The kind of progressive, feminist American man I held up as an ideal against all the difficulties I had encountered with Middle Eastern men did not seem to exist, or at least was not there when I might have been receptive. But the main thing that was missing was the emotional warmth I felt most Middle Easterners brought to relationships. My Scandinavian background did not prepare me to respond spontaneously and affectionately as my Middle Eastern male and female friends did. I felt they supplied something that was missing in American culture. And whereas most American men seemed like buddies, Middle Easterners almost always respond to a woman as a woman, even to a friend or acquaintance (I don't mean by this they have designs on every woman, or that American men don't, but they respond with greater warmth to women). Also, after having relationships with Middle Eastern men I became more attracted to their darker coloring, slimmer builds, aquiline noses, etc. American men seemed unnaturally tall and fair, their noses undistinguished, their faces and accents too bland, (ironically, many Middle Eastern men and women I know are more attracted to Americans for these very characteristics).

Since I had decided the personal price of "success" is too high in our society, another thing that attracted me to Middle Easterners was their emphasis on people. The Middle Easterners I knew liked to spend time together, eating and drinking coffee or tea, having heated discussions about the latest political development. I could drop in on someone frequently, without notice, whereas most Americans had to plan meetings far in advance. While some Middle Eastern men and women complained about the lack of privacy "back home," they also commented that they felt Americans to be alienated from each other; I agreed.

Since I had begun doing research on third world/Middle Eastern literature, I had become interested in living in a Middle Eastern country. I was offered jobs in Saudi Arabia at very good salaries, but I was finally hesitant to take them because I didn't want to leave my friends in Bloomington at that point. I was offered a job at the University of Cincinnati, which was only a three hour drive from Bloomington, a position which I felt would be better for my career. After I accepted the job, I received a job offer from a university on the West Bank for which I had applied several months earlier and had no response. I had to refuse that job, which meant that when I applied again I was turned down, so for various reasons I was not able to determine from first hand how I would like actually living in a Middle Eastern country.

At the beginning of my second year at Cincinnati I met Ayoub at a demonstration against the U.S. invasion of Grenada. He was a new Ph.D. student, and seemed to be interested in radical politics. When I found out he was a Kurd, I told him I had a Kurdish friend in Bloomington, and he was surprised, I think, that I knew as much as I did about Kurds. My friend in Bloomington was also a leftist who had married an American feminist leftist, and Ayoub reminded me of him.

Ayoub and I began to see each other frequently. Many Middle Eastern men I had met like to cook, and Ayoub was no exception. Ayoub began to cook meals for me, and even to bring them to my apartment in large pots. He helped me with my political activities, but I sensed he was not as interested in them as in me. However, he did more work than others who were supposedly organizing the activities. He always seemed to be there when I needed him, so I began to depend on him. Over Christmas we drove to New York to visit some of his friends, and I was very impressed with what nice people they were. I also introduced him to friends of mind, a Palestinian couple, and they got along very well.

Even though I had several Iranian friends, I knew more about Arabic culture and history, and had taken a course in Arabic, but I didn't know any Persian. I was resistant to learning Persian because I thought the difficulties of learning Arabic were enough, but I soon began to learn some Persian, and I also found that Persian cooking was quite different from other Middle Eastern cooking. Otherwise, I found that a major difference between the Iranians I met and Arabs was a somewhat smoother, more polished manners, and more Westernized attitudes. I will say that Kurds like Ayoub, although he was also Iranian in attitude and behavior, seemed less urbane and closer to peasant culture. This is not an insult; it means he was less pretentious, more open, honest, egalitarian, and hospitable. He got along very well with my Palestinian friend's husband because they were both from this type of background, and had not adopted Western fashions and consumerism as many upper middle class Iranians had. Ayoub had an expression for these Iranians-- "sissool"--which I guess roughly translated would mean sissy.

I felt that Ayoub was very involved with me, but he seemed confused about marriage. He had visa problems, and he suggested we get married a few months after we met, but I told him I didn't want to get married to solve his visa problem, although I was sympathetic to his plight. We shared an apartment for five months after that, and got married in May in a civil ceremony. Because we were afraid of how our friends and parents would react, we were somewhat secretive about the marriage. To us, marriage was somewhat of a formality, and we weren't interested in a celebration (I had gone through all that once before). Although we have had problems related to cultural as well as individual differences, Ayoub has been a very committed, caring person and any doubts about the relationship I had at the beginning have not been substantiated.

In many ways Ayoub was more open and flexible than some Middle Eastern men I had met, and I therefore felt our relationship would have a greater chance of success. While many Middle Eastern men express sympathy about the plight of women in their country, they still apply a double standard when it comes to sexual equality. Ayoub seemed to consciously try to adopt a single standard regarding sexual behavior as well as women's right to work and sharing of housework. Since educated Middle Eastern men generally marry women about five to fifteen years younger, with less education, when I found out that Ayoub was several years younger than I, I was doubtful about the possibility of our relationship working out, but he seemed quite interested in continuing the relationship. He had been engaged to a woman in Iran who had been attending medical school, and he had no sense of inferiority because of my higher degree. He also told me he believed women should work because staying at home would be frustrating and would limit one's growth as a person.

Ayoub and I also shared a common political outlook, although we did have some political differences. Many successful marriages between Middle Easterners and Americans, I have seen, have been based on political and/or cultural sympathies on the part of the American, although one does not have to marry a Middle Easterner to support his political cause. However, like most other Iranian students on the left, Ayoub was extremely disillusioned by the reactionary turn of the revolution and the suppression of all dissent in Iran, and pessimistic about the possibility of change in the future. Ayoub's activism seemed to depend on the level of activism around him. When he spent time in San Diego where there are large Kurdish and Iranian communities, he became more politically involved than he had been at Iowa State, where I taught after I left Cincinnati. My activism spanned a wide range of interests, and while I worked on the Institute on World Affairs, for example, Ayoub was less interested than I was in that kind of educational work. He often had a pessimistic attitude, as if he considered any kind of political work a waste of time in Reagan's America. However, like many Iranian leftists he is not politically parochial; he is an internationalist, and like me is interested in politics on a global scale.

Neither Ayoub nor I nor our families are religious, which is another potential problem we didn't face. Ayoub's family also was more receptive to our marriage than the families of many other couples I knew. Ayoub's mother came to the United States for the first time the summer after we were married. He met her in New York and took her to visit his friends before coming to Iowa to meet me, but she kept demanding to get to Iowa as fast as possible because she wanted to meet Christy. I was extremely nervous, and I invited another Iranian woman over for moral support. Ayoub asked me to cook a Persian dish, but since he did all the cooking for us, I didn't know how to cook it very well, and nobody ate much of anything. Despite this failure, my mother-in-law liked me. My extreme nervousness helped, because she assumed I was shy, like an Iranian girl. But as an "Aroos Farengi" (foreign bride), she allowed me freedom of behavior which she did not allow Ayoub's brother's wife, who she seemed to have a grudge against.

Ayoub's mother brought me wedding presents: two beautiful Kurdish dresses with matching scarves, a handmade nightgown, a gold necklace, two Kurdish rugs, pistachio nuts, Isphahani picture frames, a samovar, a beaded belt made by prisoners with a 007 belt buckle, and many other items. She refilled her enormous suitcases with presents to take to every relative and friend imaginable, and I gave her some of my old clothes to take to some relatives who were less well off.

Although Ayoub's mother had never been out of Iran, she was very open-minded. She even tried to go swimming, wearing one of my bathing suits! It was too much for her though, and she preferred walks after dinner. She made herself right at home, rearranging my cupboards and furniture to suit her convenience. Every night she made an absolutely delicious meal which was ready as soon as Ayoub and I walked in the house after classes, and then we would have tea and chat with her and Ayoub's brother, who had accompanied his mother on the trip. Later we might visit friends. I felt that Ayoub was very close to his mother and brother, even though he had not seen them in seven years. But I was glad the visit lasted only a month because being polite all the time is rather a strain, even if you like the person.

I felt sorry for Ayoub's mother because she had rather a hard time of it with his father. When she was younger she had tried going back to her family, a common way of solving marital difficulties. While Ayoub was in the United States his father had married a second wife (the first wife's permission was required before the revolution, and Ayoub's mother had been too proud to refuse it). As the eldest son Ayoub had taken his mother's part and protested. His father had quickly tired of the second wife, since he had married her mainly to spite Ayoub's mother's indifference, so he divorced her and was now back with Ayoub's mother, but she complained about his temper.

While she was there I noticed that she used direct and indirect strategies to circumvent Ayoub's authority, such as when she wanted to go to a garage sale and he told her to stay away from the "junk," she communicated to me in Farsi (she didn't know any English except "Tank you," "Stand up," and "Sit down" which she reversed), that I should go with her. She refused to use the washing machine, even though they had two in Iran, and washed all the clothes by hand, hanging them to dry on our front porch. When she wanted to buy a more expensive present for her nephew than her niece, Ayoub told her she should treat them equally, but when Ayoub, who has a streak of his father's temper, got very angry with me because I didn't want them to cut up the carcass of the lamb they had just bought from a local farmer on my Chinese rug, she scolded him, saying that he was behaving just like his father.

Ayoub broke down and cried after he returned from taking his mother and brother to the airport. The fact that I haven't learned enough Farsi to communicate well with her over the phone makes our relationship difficult, but she continues to send me dresses and other items through people traveling to the United States. I have many hilarious mother-in-law stories to tell involving my friends, but the most tragic is the story of a dear friend whose Iranian parents objected to his lovely American girlfriend because she looked too old, and didn't have enough education. He didn't want to cause a break with his family, so he broke with the woman instead. The parents of Middle Eastern women who marry American men are even more likely to object to their marriages; an Arab woman friend of mine's mother has still not spoken to her daughter since she married an American professor, although her brother attended the wedding. Since the family is extremely important in Middle Eastern culture, it's very important for parents to be supportive of the intercultural marriage, and they can make or break the marriage, unless the man or woman refuses to bow under parental pressure and the family is forced to accept the situation.

On the other hand, parents on the American side can also make things very difficult, especially when the girl is relatively young or from a religious family. My father was not happy when Ayoub came to visit as my boyfriend. Seeing every kind of (to him) undesirable immigrant pouring into Los Angeles has made my father extremely paranoid. His attitudes have changed little since the forties. Ayoub sat politely listening to my father, trying to avoid discussing politics, but things ended up badly, and Ayoub avoids visiting my parents because my father has a heart condition and he doesn't want to cause problems. My father also disagrees with me politically, but I suppose because I'm his daughter he has decided to tolerate me. So my parents and I have an uneasy truce about the situation. From my perspective, living far from either in-laws has made our relationship much easier.

Marriage between an educated, "modernized" Iranian and an American woman is not as different from an American marriage as one might think. Cultural differences may be less important than differences between individuals. For example, Ayoub is an engineer and has less interest in art and literature than I do, but that is not a cultural but a professional difference.

Some cultural differences seem fairly superficial: different tastes in food, entertainment, etiquette. But they can cause problems and misunderstandings. For example, most Iranians like to eat raw onions, and Ayoub is no exception. The smell of raw onions on Ayoub's breath can make me nauseous and so I complain to Ayoub, but he doesn't want to give up one of his favorite foods. I don't think he eats raw onions as much as he used to, but he still does on occasion.

Otherwise, I like most Persian food very much (if I didn't I would be in trouble), although it can seem too greasy at times, and I occasionally get tired of rice and stews. The good thing about Persian cooking is that it uses fresh, natural ingredients. Iranians also like to eat fresh fruits instead of sweets. However, since Ayoub cooks, I don't often eat food prepared "American style." Unlike many people from the Middle East, Ayoub likes pork, but he doesn't like mashed potatoes and gravy, roast meats (especially if they are rare), most canned or prepared foods, seafood, orange juice for breakfast, scrambled eggs, desserts, etc. Sometimes it's a matter of the hour of day when one eats something: Ayoub will drink orange juice at night, and he usually likes dessert with tea at four o'clock. On the few occasions when I do cook, Ayoub has a habit which really irritates me of "supervising" my cooking and trying to change the way I'm cooking a dish to his method. Ayoub also likes to go grocery shopping, and since he cooks, he selects most of the food. Occasionally he objects to my buying one of my favorite foods, which also irritates me, but generally I will buy foods like orange juice for myself.

Most Middle Easterners I've met do not enjoy going to restaurants as much as Americans, and don't have the same concept of gourmet food. They believe one can prepare better food at home for less money. They prefer to go out for tea or coffee only, or when they are traveling and have no other choice. Ayoub and I compromised and agreed on going out once a week, but Ayoub, like other Iranians I know, prefers buffet chain restaurants like Bonanza which are moderately priced but not known to Americans for the quality of their food or their atmosphere. We both like to go to ethnic restaurants, but the only time I can go to a "quality" restaurant is when I'm attending a conference or having lunch with a friend because Ayoub absolutely refuses to try these restaurants.

Most Middle Eastern men I know like soccer and basketball, but few like football or baseball. They spend far less time than American men going to sporting events (except soccer games) or watching sports on TV. Ayoub does not watch any sports on TV, but he does like jogging, exercising, and occasionally swimming. Having spent many holidays subjected to noisy football games on TV, I find American men's obsession with sports extremely boring, and I find the peace and quiet refreshing.

Although I have had some Middle Eastern friends who like movies, most don't like them as much as Americans. They prefer to watch TV or videos. Ayoub likes political documentaries better than other types of films, and usually when I suggest going to a movie he usually says he prefers to stay home. Now we rent videos fairly often, which is a fairly acceptable compromise.

Most Middle Easterners I know enjoy visiting each other's houses for dinner and conversation, or having picnics or barbecues in parks or at lakes. These are very enjoyable occasions, and the only problem I have is that sometimes people forget to speak English to me, which is understandable but can be boring.

"Tarof" exists in Arabic as well as Persian and Kurdish culture, but I don't know if it has a name in Arabic. It is a whole system of etiquette which one must follow, and is very internalized behavior that can affect Middle Easterner's responses to Americans without either even knowing it. The primary rule of "tarof" is self-abnegation. The person who can do the most to help someone is considered most prestigious.

Even Iranians can find tarof bothersome at times and complain about it. The younger generation of Iranians living in this country usually dispense with the more constrictive aspects of tarof. For example, they might not insist so stridently that one should overeat. But when they are around older people or strangers they usually revert to more formal behavior because they don't know how the others will react.

I am often afraid that I will unknowingly make a faux pas and then be condemned in absentia. For example, at dinner parties I am expected to force my way into the kitchen to help the hostess, and she will protest vigorously that she doesn't need any help, but I am supposed to insist. I have been at my own sink washing dishes, only to have an Iranian woman bodily push me out of the way so she can do my dishes. One of our friends' girlfriends offered to do the dishes after his mother made dinner and was told to sit down, they didn't need any help. When she did just that, they criticized her for being lazy.

Other rules of tarof I have observed are as follows: one must always offer to share food from one's table, or even one's plate; even if a person refuses food or drink, the hostess must insist because she assumes the guest is refusing out of politeness; one generally offers a house guest one's own bed; a younger man must allow an older man to precede him through a door or into a car; on the rare occasions when Middle Easterners eat out, they must argue over the bill (dutch treat is considered vulgar and selfish). Usually one man will grab the bill from the waitress, refusing to accept any money from the others. A man never lets a woman pay for herself, even if he is much poorer, and she has eaten more.

One example of Ayoub's use of tarof with me is that he used to offer to do the dishes, even though he had cooked, or alternatively tell me he would do them later. I found that he had no intention of doing the dishes (I was not supposed to accept the offer), but was offering out of politeness. But when I didn't do the dishes, he would accuse me of not doing my share. He always refuses when I ask if I can pay for something, but then he might later accuse me of not paying my share of the bills. I tell him he has to be direct with me because I won't know if anything is wrong unless he tells me, but he can't seem to manage it.

In my experience, a common reaction to any injury or insult on the part of both Middle Eastern men and women is sulking. The generally warm person becomes cold as ice. Sometimes it takes a long time to pry the problem out of the person. These periods of sulking can last a few hours, or days, and are very painful to Americans who are not used to such indirect communication. Moreover, things that seem trivial to Americans can seem major to Middle Easterners. For example, one of my friends had an American male friend and she became angry with him because he didn't offer me dinner when I visited their house. She became very distant with him, and he could tell something was wrong, but had no idea what it was. Later she complained about what happened to me and I told her he probably was unaware that he was doing anything wrong. Her response was that he should have known he was being rude. I tried to tell her that Americans are not under obligation to serve dinner to drop in guests who are leaving soon anyway, and that we usually function through more direct communication. Still, it was two days before she decided to forgive him.

Ayoub was much less given to sulking than some other Middle Eastern men I had known. He never holds a grudge for very long, but very occasionally he can get very upset and behave in this way. Like other Middle Easterners he finds it hard to tolerate anger in women. Middle Easterners are generally polite even when they are angry and they try not to show anger or raise their voices, but I think if women raise their voices or show anger it's considered more inexcusable and insulting than in men. Middle Eastern men, including Ayoub, get angry when women cry, but its generally the only way to get them to realize one is seriously upset or hurt. Saying that one is sorry or didn't mean the offense, or arguing rationally does not help, but if one cries, they will usually soften.

Part of traditional cultures is a strong patriarchal family. In general, Middle Eastern men are good family men. Once they settle down with a wife or girlfriend, they are extremely domestic. They are usually quite devoted to their families and do not consider divorce as an option except as a last resort. To American women who find American men's lack of desire to make a commitment frustrating, a relationship with a Middle Eastern man can seem more stable.

I also think Middle Eastern men are more interested in children than American men, and care for their children deeply for the most part, although they can be strict disciplinarians. Ayoub likes to play with his friends' children, and he gets along well with my son from my first marriage, although at first he thought I didn't discipline him enough. While in Middle Eastern society it is customary for a couple to have children as soon as possible, Ayoub is very unusual in that he is not really interested in having his own children.

Some Middle Eastern men I've known leave their wives at home and go to bars and nightclubs with other men; some American men do the same, although there is more of a double standard in Middle Eastern culture. I had one Arab boyfriend who would stay out with his friends quite late, but was quite suspicious of my friendships with other men. I did not think he was seeing other women, so I didn't mind him going out, but I resented his blaming me for any advances other men may have made to me. On the other hand, Ayoub rarely goes out with his friends to bars, and when he does he always invites me to come, nor has he shown any jealousy about any of my many male friends and acquaintances, even though he doesn't have many female friends. If he did, I think I would be more inclined to be jealous than he is. I've found that Middle Eastern men are not suspicious of their own friends, and one can be good friends with them without one's boyfriend or husband batting an eye, which gives one a certain interesting freedom of behavior with men without the threat that there might be sexual interest involved.

The devotion to family is the positive aspect of Middle Eastern culture; the patriarchal aspect I find less appealing. Middle Eastern men have strong personalities and well-developed egos. They have to compete with other men in their society for dominance, so they must develop assertiveness. This assertiveness may seem overly aggressive to Americans who don't understand how their personalities are formed. Middle Eastern men often appear to be confident and self-assured, asserting things as matters of fact, even if they know little about the subject or are completely wrong. They are not afraid to question or contradict salespeople, doctors, professors, or anyone else. They are often the first ones to ask questions at public lectures, and their questions sometimes sound like speeches. When I visited Jordan and the West Bank in 1985, I noticed that not only do women defer to men, but younger men defer to older men. Foreign women and professional women are treated more as equals, however, as if by virtue of our education we are no longer women!

I am rather timid about asserting myself and I find I've developed a kind of dependence on Ayoub to stick up for my rights for me. However, sometimes he pushes me to do things I don't want to do, such as to bargain with salespeople or make a complaint. And I can tell him something which I know is true, but if he thinks otherwise he will insist on his opinion. The other day I told him the heater in my car was not working well, but he insisted it was working "perfectly" until he saw for himself that it did not work!

But the Middle Eastern women I've known also have strong personalities; they have to in order to stand up to the men. They generally try to assert themselves in any way they can, and are not afraid of arguing with their husbands. Traditionally, women do not speak much around men; sometimes an extremely dominant man can talk so much no one can get a word in. But when they are with other women, Middle Eastern women also talk a great deal; one of their favorite topics is complaining about their husbands. I usually talk more than Ayoub around men and women, and I have always assumed that I will be treated as an equal, and when we visit educated people I have never noticed that women's ideas are not respected. As a matter of fact, I have several Iranian women friends who have Ph.D.s and are supporting their husbands (and also cooking and doing housework), one of whom is a very strong feminist and is not afraid to argue with any man. I think I am at somewhat of a disadvantage compared to Middle Eastern women because I don't have a strong enough personality to stand up to Ayoub when he opposes something I want to do, or perhaps I don't know the best way of doing it. I think Ayoub's tendency to try to make decisions for me is more or less unconscious; it's the way he was brought up, and it's very hard to change. Of course in traditional society I would make all the decisions regarding the household, but in our case these roles are blurred, and as in American society, there are no longer any rules to go by.

Another area of difference is in clothing and body language. I know that this can cause a lot of conflict because my Arab boyfriend would frequently object to my clothes (I think this was an attempt to exert psychological control over me), but Ayoub and I have very few problems. In Middle Eastern culture, men and women, even if they are married, do not touch each other in public. We were walking in the mall together when we first met, and Ayoub had his arm around me, but he immediately moved away when he saw two Iranian friends of his. I did not feel offended because I know it is just an instinctive reaction.

99% of the time Ayoub doesn't care how I dress, but the bottom line is that no matter how westernized, most Middle Easterners really don't feel comfortable wearing shorts or going out with wives or girlfriends who are wearing shorts. I also know some British women who also don't feel comfortable wearing shorts, so I'm inclined to believe that wearing shorts is an American custom. Once we were going to Ayoub's friend's house to go swimming and I wanted to wear shorts; Ayoub was afraid his friend would be offended. But when we got there his friend was wearing shorts himself!

Ayoub's style of dressing derives partly from his "peasant" background and partly from his leftist ideology which scorns paying attention to how one looks. Whereas some upper middle class urbanized Iranians dress very fashionably, Ayoub's way of dressing is closer to that of most people from the Middle East (other than those who still wear traditional clothing). He wears long-sleeved shirts, always buttoned, and conservatively cut pants, and he doesn't care if his sweaters or pants match. When he's not working, he generally doesn't shave and he wears old clothes. I have tried to suggest that he pay more attention to his appearance, but have had no success. On the other hand, he doesn't like me to wear make-up, and he doesn't pay any attention to my clothes.

The biggest conflict we have is over our spending habits, which I think is partly although not entirely related to differences in culture. Interestingly enough, I had an Arab woman friend who was hesitant to marry an American because she felt he was too cheap. She insisted that Arab men (whatever their shortcomings) were generally very generous to their wives. On the other hand, I have found that while extremely generous to guests, Ayoub is obsessed with saving money. My American friend who is married to a Kurd once commented that Kurds must be the Scots of the Middle East. I think we can start with the assumption that Middle

Easterners in general, men and women, are inveterate bargain hunters. You will find them in discount stores, farmer's markets, at the buffets in Las Vegas hotels, anywhere prices are lower. This is a very good characteristic, especially since paying retail prices these days is difficult even for most Americans. Middle Easterners help each other with finding bargains as well. Ayoub has a friend in San Diego who buys repossessed late model cars at auctions, repairs them, and sells them. Ayoub bought a car from him about two thousand below the list price.

My family, however, shopped in "name" stores and valued "quality" products. I was never taught to conserve energy, and sometimes I would rather sacrifice savings for convenience. I believe in spending money for enjoyment now, rather than saving everything for the future (although I do have savings). Most of the Iranian families I know are much closer to Ayoub's way of thinking about spending money than I am, so I would assume Ayoub's practice is cultural, but there are variations, with some people spending more and some less. Ayoub has gradually stopped protesting about everything I buy, especially since his income has increased, and I have become more conscious of saving, but we still have serious differences. I think for me the most serious consequence is when Ayoub objects to my spending money to buy books, go to conferences, or to buy a PC, because these things are connected to my work. I earn enough money to buy these things and should be able to make my own decisions about what to buy, and Ayoub cannot really stop me. Thus I have bought everything I need, but Ayoub's objections create a psychological pressure, and I must spend time justifying my purchases which would be better spent more productively. Some Middle Eastern women have told me that they face these objections from their husbands and that I shouldn't feel intimidated because they will eventually agree to the purchase.

I think some of the differences I have with Ayoub relate more to male-female differences in general than cultural differences per se, or else to the differences in our professional interests. Both my American friends married to Americans and Iranian friends married to Iranians sometimes complain about the same problems. Even though my first marriage was to an American, I can no longer imagine what it would be like married to an American. I remember that during my first marriage I did all the cooking and most of the housework, and that when my husband went to the grocery store with me he complained that he was bored and had no idea what we should buy, and that he got mad at me if I lost one of his socks. My problems in my first marriage seem to have been related to the fact that I didn't have a job and felt I had no identity apart from my husband, and from my husband's own problems with his career. But I was a different person then. Now Ayoub's culture seems like second nature to me, and I don't really think of our cultures as that different.

Ayoub Farahyar

I was born in 1957 in Sanandaj, Iran, the capital of Iranian Kurdistan. My father is a Kurd and my mother is a Lur--two nationalities living in Western Iran, so I myself was the product of an intercultural marriage, although these nationalities were very similar. One difference is that Kurds are Sunni Moslems whereas Lurs, like most Persians, are Shiite Moslems. However, my mother was not very religious, so there was no religious conflict in my family.

My father used to pray five times a day, but later he started drinking and gave up praying because drinking is not permitted in Islam, and he had to perform complicated ablutions every time he prayed after drinking. I went to Koranic school and learned to read the Koran in Arabic; my reading was so good I was called upon to read on special occasions. But my father did not force me to pray, and I also began to question the contradictions I found while reading the Koran. As early as high school I was attracted to leftist ideas and I began to reject religion.

My father's parents believed education was the work of the devil, so they did not allow him to go to school; he finished primary school by going to night school after work. He wanted me to get a good education and he worked very hard as a tailor so I could go to high school in Tehran. Later he began to invest in real estate during the boom before the revolution and became quite prosperous. He was working about sixteen hours a day, and when we did see him he was rather cross and tired, so I was closer to my mother.

My mother had worked for a feudal family before her marriage and had learned Persian cooking, which is more elaborate than Kurdish cooking. She also worked as a primary school teacher during the early years of the marriage, but while she was teaching she would leave lunch cooking on the kerosene stove, and one day a fire started, so my father asked her to quit work and take care of the house.

My mother used to take me to the public baths until I was about fourteen, when the other women protested that I was too old. She replied that I was still too young to know anything, but I was actually curious about women from a very early age. I used to play house with the neighbor girls, but after we became teenagers we had very little opportunity to talk to girls, and if we did have an opportunity we were very shy. Of course we were very frustrated.

At home we spoke Kurdish, while in school we had to speak Persian because the central government wanted us to consider ourselves Iranian rather than Kurds. At school in Tehran I was somewhat "Persianized"; however, Iranians regarded us as somewhat more "uncivilized," but also admired us for our courage and later for our resistance to the central government.

After I finished high school I went to the technical university in Tehran to study engineering. The two most prestigious occupations in Iran are engineering and medicine, and one has to study very hard to be admitted to these fields because the competition is very stiff. I became politicized as early as high school; with so much poverty in the midst of the oil wealth, it is hard not to question the system and want to improve the lives of the people. Many of the best writers and teachers and least corrupt people in the country were leftists, and so many idealistic young people became leftists. The technical university was the most radical in the country, and we could see the SAVAK (Shah's secret police) spying on university students and arresting them. During my sophomore year the school was practically closed down because the teachers and students were out on strike against the government. I felt my chance for an education was growing dimmer, so I decided to come to the U.S. to study. I didn't know that the revolution would take place just a few months after I left.

In Tehran, especially among the middle and upper classes, the separation between the sexes was becoming more relaxed. I was very much in favor of more freedom between the sexes; men did not like arranged marriages any more than women because we had no chance to get to know the woman we were going to marry. I developed my ideas about men's and women's sexual equality from the leftist groups who saw women in Iran as oppressed but also saw Western women as treated as sex objects and not truly liberated. One women who was a leader in a leftist guerrilla group escaped from prison where she had been raped and tortured; she was a heroic figure in our eyes. Many women also participated in leftist demonstrations, but it was hard to talk to them because Moslem students would accuse us of having a relationship. I was impressed by an Iranian woman poet, Forrugh Farroukhzad, who wrote about woman's sexual and social liberation. I showed her poems to my mother, who said she liked her poetry, but didn't approve of the fact that she had left her child and husband.

While I was living in Tehran I became interested in one of my friends' sisters. I used to visit my friend's house in hopes that her sister would be there. She was attending medical school and was very serious about her career. Many men admired her because she was so serious and worked very hard. Very few women were studying engineering and medicine, but I think, especially in the case of engineering, the percentage of women studying in Iran was higher than in the United States. It was quite acceptable for women in the middle and upper classes to be professionals, but they had to take care of the house and raise children too. They could usually leave their children with their mothers during the day, but they worked very hard to maintain a career and a home at the same time. The girl I was in love with was a year older than I was, and she wanted to finish medical school before thinking about marriage, but when I left for the United States we had an understanding that we would marry when we finished.

In Iran we had formed stereotypes about American (and European) women from American films and TV series which showed women to be sexually available to the hero. James Bond films, for example, were quite popular in Iran. I was expecting American women to meet me at the airport and take me home with them. In Iran the only way to have a sexual relationship with a woman before marriage was with a prostitute. But the houses of prostitution were dirty and crowded, and seemed demeaning to both the women who work there and to the men who are forced to go there. The whole idea of prostitution and pornography and even make-up disgusts me because it reminds me of those places.

It is therefore hard for us to understand the idea of women who are not prostitutes being able to have sexual relationships. I found the sexual morality in New York to be very liberal when I arrived in 1978; however, after studying at SUNY Buffalo and Virginia Polytechnic, where I got my master's, I realized that sexual behavior varies according to the region of the country and the individual values of the person. I never judged a woman according to her sexual morality, however, as some of my friends did, because I considered it hypocritical to have sexual experience myself and then expect to marry a virgin.

When I came to the U.S. I really had no intention of marrying an American woman because I was planning to return to Iran after I finished my education. For one thing, I was studying very hard, twelve to fourteen hours a day, and I didn't have time for a serious relationship. Then, especially at first, my English was not very good, which made it difficult to communicate beyond a superficial level. The anti-Shah political groups I was involved in in this country also discouraged us from anything so superficial as dating.

I did date several American women, but not longer than a few months. Most of the women I met did not share my interests or political views, and sometimes cultural differences got in the way. Most women did not even know where Iran was or what language was spoken there. Some women were prejudiced against foreigners, especially dark-skinned foreigners, and during the hostage crisis men's and women's prejudice increased. However, American women were much more open-minded and easy to get along with than American men, who I found unfriendly, chauvinistic, and boring. Even men in American leftist political groups, although more open-minded than most, were often unfriendly.

Many American women seemed very nice, but also very naive about (or uninterested in) politics. Younger women (undergraduates) seemed to be more interested in having a good time than a serious relationship, and seemed much more immature than Iranian women of the same age. Women in graduate school and women over 25 seemed more serious; they often talked about the problems they had in relationships with American men. I became rather close to an American woman graduate student, but we had some cultural differences and the relationship didn't last. One problem was that she would call me up and ask if she could come over. In our culture we will not say no to this kind of a request, even if we had an exam the next day, but when I called her up and asked to come over she would refuse, saying she had work to do. I didn't want to continue such a one-sided relationship.

After I had been in the United States for four years my girlfriend in Iran finished medical school and my parents tried to arrange an engagement between us. My parents didn't want me to come back because of the war and because the Kurds were opposing the Khomeini government. Several of my friends who had returned after the revolution had been imprisoned or killed. Not only was I eligible for the draft, but it was also hard to get a job unless one was religious. My girlfriend would have come to the United States to do her internship and we would marry, but she couldn't get a visa. I wrote her that in that case she shouldn't wait any longer because she was already 25 and would have a harder chance getting married if after I came back (and there was no telling when that would be possible), we found that we had changed and no longer cared for each other. So she married the next man on her list (several men had asked to marry her).

When I came to Cincinnati to do my Ph.D. and met Christy, all my plans had changed. I didn't know when I could go back to Iran, I didn't know if I could even stay in the United States because I, along with many other Iranians, was having trouble with my visa, and my plans for marriage had been given up. I was still not really thinking about marrying an American woman, but I did feel the need for a more serious relationship, especially if I was going to live here for an indefinite period of time.

Because of Christy's political views and knowledge of Middle Eastern culture, I felt really comfortable with her from the beginning of our relationship. She was attractive and she seemed much younger than she was. She was also the most intelligent American woman I had met. She also did not care how much money I had and did not want to go to expensive places like some American women I had met. Of course, I didn't mind that she had a career, since I had been encouraging my former fiance with her career plans. I also didn't care that she had been married before or had had other relationships because as I said I rejected the idea of a double standard.

I began to want to spend most of my free time with Christy, which was difficult because we both had roommates. I thought it would be a good idea to live together because we could see if our relationship would work. I was not thinking of marriage right at first, because I felt as long as we got along and were satisfied with living together, marriage wasn't a big issue to me. But later I began to get more attached to Christy and I decided a permanent relationship could work.

Of course, we did have some problems, even from the beginning. Christy was somewhat disorganized when I met her. She had a hard time taking care of her bills and her car. I remember she had over two hundred dollars in parking tickets. She didn't eat well, and I began fixing dinner for her. She also was involved in several political groups and activities, and she would periodically drop everything and work on this conference or that event, which bothered me because she would leave everything in a mess. Finally, she seemed to spend too much money and save practically nothing.

I don't think one can ever explain why one loves another person, because love is an emotion, but I felt closer to Christy than anyone else I had known, and as I knew her better I felt more and more attached, so I began to think about marriage. It might have seemed more logical to marry an Iranian girl studying in this country, so there would be no cultural problems, but since the restrictions between Iranian women and men existed even in this country, it was much easier to meet American women and get to know them. Then also, one has to overcome the resistance of the Iranian girl's family, who expect her to marry someone they know. A few of my friends have married Iranian women, but most of them have married Americans. Generally, the American women they have married have been very nice, with a few exceptions. The marriages that have worked out the best have been those in which the woman was interested enough in Iranian culture to learn some Farsi, and liked or at least tolerated Iranian food and customs.

If I had married an Iranian woman, even a professional woman, she would automatically cook and take care of the house (although I would help her). She would probably be more sexually conservative than most American women, but she would probably want to have children immediately, and she would be very close to her family.

My father had always thought that the advantage of marrying an American woman was that she would not be as attached to her family as an Iranian woman, who often care about their families more than their husbands. An Iranian woman would be able to speak Persian with my friends and my mother, whose greatest fear about my marrying an American woman, aside from the fear that she would leave me and get a divorce (a common assumption about American women), was that she wouldn't be able to communicate with her daughter-in-law.

Actually, around the time that I met Christy my mother was suggesting that I marry a woman I knew from my home town; her only objection was that the woman was too old--she was my age. I was a little hesitant to tell my parents about our marriage, although I told Christy I didn't think they would object, but my friend's mother had had a heart attack when his brother told her on the phone that my friend was serious about an American girl. But when they found out one day when Christy answered the telephone, my mother was quite excited and pleased because she wanted me to get married very badly.

My friends who are married to American women tend to have an easier time assimilating to American culture. Christy has helped me a lot with my English, has helped edit my papers, resumes, etc. But Americans have some habits it is hard for us to get used to such as going out to eat, going to movies, and celebrating holidays such as Christmas and Thanksgiving. For example, we don't have Christmas trees, and we don't give each other gifts, so Christy gets rather upset when I don't get excited about Christmas, even though her own family doesn't really celebrate it extensively.

Christy has pointed out many of the areas of cultural differences, but I think the main difference is a sense of caring about people which makes Iranian culture more humanistic. Men and women who sacrifice a lot for their families are greatly respected in Iran. In the United States, people seem to be more concerned about themselves, and tend not to help each other out. I know at work some of the American engineers are very unfriendly and won't help me out when I ask them. I get along better with foreign engineers. The system of tarof Christy was writing about, to us, is a way of showing we respect each other. I know as an American, Christy cannot be expected to understand these behaviors, but sometimes I really wonder how Americans can be so impolite as to eat in front of people without asking them if they want to share the food for example. I have helped Christy a lot by fixing her car, driving her places, etc., but when I ask her to help me on my resume, sometimes she says she has work to do.

Christy has pointed out to me that she doesn't feel that she is as warm or affectionate to me as I am to her. This is true, but this is a part of the person that can't be changed. I don't think it's because she doesn't care, but just because she hasn't learned to express her emotion. I notice she also finds it difficult to kiss Iranian women on the cheeks as is customary, but most of my friends like her very much because of her interest in our culture and because she is very nice to them in general.

But as Christy says, the biggest disagreement I have with her is with Americans' consumerist mentality. American society wastes so much compared with other countries, so much electricity, gas, food, etc. Christy likes to leave water running, lights on, etc., when she could so easily remember to turn things off. She also likes to buy a lot of things she doesn't need. For example, she doesn't need to belong to a health club to exercise when she can exercise outdoors in the park. Things like exercise clubs are marketing strategies designed to make Americans spend unnecessary money. I realize that she has her own money, but since we are sharing life together, and I am trying to save money for both of us, when I see her spending a lot of money on clothes, for example, when she already has a lot of clothes, I get the feeling that why should I be willing to sacrifice when she isn't? Most of my friends married to American women have the same conflicts, although maybe about different items, but we usually feel that we cannot change the person so we just give up trying and accept their buying whatever they like.

Christy is also afraid to ask her employer to give her money for conferences, moving expenses, or to xerox materials for her. She would rather buy a book than get it from the library. All this is hard for me to understand.

Another difference between Iranians and Americans is that Americans tend to follow rules much more than we do. They are afraid of breaking even minor rules, yet wealthy Americans often get away with breaking laws with very little punishment. Ordinary Americans are sometimes naive about how much rule breaking goes on in this country. For example, we know that hiring an immigration lawyer who in turn bribes immigration officials is sometimes the only way to get a visa to the U.S. In Iran we couldn't survive if we followed all the rules, and thus we are much more cynical about the motivations for enforcing the rules, and feel less guilty about breaking them. Christy and I sometimes have differences in this area.

Another difference is between American and Iranian furniture. We usually eat and sit on the floor. We put a "soufre" (tablecloth) on the floor and sit around it. We also sleep on cotton mattresses. I find it very hard to get used to box springs, and I don't like sleeping so far off the ground. Christy does not mind eating on the floor, and I don't really mind eating off a table, but she didn't like sleeping so close to the ground. We solved the problem by getting a platform bed with a mattress and no box springs.

As far as having children goes, I think my generation of Iranians, especially educated Iranians, was slowly changing from wanting several children to wanting families of just two or three (now that Khomeini is in power I've heard that the birth rate has gone up a lot, however, because birth control is hard to get and because there is nothing else to do for fun). So I don't think I'm that unusual in that I'm not that interested in having children. Having children in the United States seems more problematic than in Iran because there's very little job security. With Christy working, I worry about who would take responsibility for the child. If we were in Iran my mother could take care of the child, but that's not possible here. Those of my friends who have children usually complain about how much trouble they are, especially when both people are working.

Over all I think the problems in our marriage have not been that significant and we both have been able to adapt to each other's cultures enough to get along. Perhaps if I had married an Iranian woman who did not agree with my politics, for example, we might have had more differences than I have had with Christy.

Conclusion

Since the Iran-Iraq War has continued, Iranians studying in the United States have been forced to try to either postpone their studies indefinitely or try to find employment here. Many are in very precarious economic and psychological circumstances, not wanting to return to Iran until the situation improves, but not really feeling part of American society. Ayoub decided it would be hard to get an academic job as he had originally planned, so he tried to find an engineering job in California, where he had many friends and there was a lot of work. Despite an excellent academic record, he was looking for work for eleven months, because although he had a green card, he did not have U.S. citizenship, required by most of the largest employers. He finally got a good job for one and a half years working on the space shuttle in Utah, but recent budget cuts have made his position uncertain.

I was able to get a job, but I think both of us feel rather culturally alienated here. We both miss our friends in various parts of the country. Neither of us has the time, and this is not the environment for political activism, and it seems that as Ayoub becomes more "Americanized" he is moving in the direction of the same lifestyle I rejected several years ago. Ironically, I would have more opportunity to travel to the Middle East if I were not married, and so I have once again postponed the idea. If the Iran-Iraq War ever does end, I am not sure Ayoub would really want to go back to Iran, except perhaps for a visit. However, if we did, I am sure that I would have to make a much greater adjustment in terms of culture than I have had to married to an Iranian living in the United States. I'm not really sure how I would cope, which is why it would be challenging to try.

It is strange how politics can change people's lives completely. Neither of us could return to the perspective we had before we encountered each other's culture, but hopefully we can syncretize the two cultures in a way that can satisfy each of us.

CHAPTER 12

DIFFERENCES CAN BE STRENGTHS

Judith and Walton Johnson

Writing these thoughts about our marriage was not easy. We procrastinated. In the end, we wrote separate pieces rather than struggle to do something jointly. Our individual statements follow as we wrote them. Upon reading each other's statement, we were frankly relieved and amused to see how many of our most crucial views and descriptive imagery were similar.

<u>Judith</u>

Why did I marry someone of a different race? Why not?! It seemed like a good idea. As most young women of my generation, I was expected and indeed expected to meet, fall in love, marry, and live happily everafter with some eligible male who would sweep me off my feet. Nobody every told me about the rider that said an eligible male is someone of your own race, your own class, your own religion, and preferably your own countryman. The interesting question is not why I married outside of my group, but why my instincts for survival or self preservation were so poorly developed to allow me to do so. Where were my pack instincts?

I don't think I ever decided to enter an interracial or intercultural marriage. I met a young man who I thought was wonderful, who was noble, valiant, and stood head and shoulders above the rest of the other young men I had met. He was bright and charming, came from a good family, had good prospects--why not marry him? If you had asked me as a teen-ager what my ideal husband would have looked like, I would have described someone tall with light brown or blond hair and blue eyes. That would have been logical since all the photos in the family album of my assorted beaus, of whom there were quite a few, looked like that. Who would have thought that my destiny would turn up in the guise of some brown skinned, kinky haired, baggy-eyed, button-down collar, black American. I was hardly aware that there were such people. After all, Hollywood of the 50's didn't reveal that side of the USA, although I had seen Dorothy Dandridge in Carmen Jones and I was vaguely aware of Jim in Huck Finn or was it Tom Sawyer.

My family was middle class from the North of England, not professional mind you - hard working, lower/middle management. I grew up amongst a contented and maybe self-satisfied people. We come from a part of England that is wild, beautiful, and in parts pretty. I knew every inch of the West Riding of Yorkshire. There were Sunday rides, school trips, hikes, and days at the coast; there were history lessons on Roman York with walks on the Norman walls, and field trips to plot the historical development of the woolen industry; there were geography lessons on the millstone grit and the limestone karst scenery at Malham, and in English literature we would read the Brontes and visit Hawes. We were secure. The winds of change had not yet blown and upset our ordained destiny;

unemployment hadn't shaken our self confidence and soured our generosity. Why should we perceive other countries or cultures as threatening.

I was not brought up to be wary of or dislike people of other backgrounds. Why should I be? We were all the same; there were no other groups around to dislike. I suppose if we had really been into this "We & They" mentality there were always the Jews and the Irish, but in my family, which was apolitical and non-religious, they were not a subject for humor or dislike.

My father used to visit the docks in Liverpool for receptions organized by his freight agent. He used to bring home souvenirs for his only daughter and postcards of the boats. I used to get the stamps from his overseas correspondence and look up the countries in my atlas. From him I learned that the world was exciting and interesting. We weren't part of the British raj or Colonial administrations, we were in the mills and down the mines.

My father was the Works Manager for a heavy engineering company. In the States and maybe in England today they would have given him a fancy title, but he was the top management person in charge of production. His cousin was the shop steward, and his brother-in-law a contractor who used to maintain the furnaces for him. I never felt nor was I taught that we were better than others, nor was I taught that others were better than we were. When I came along, I was able to benefit from the postwar labor government's educational reforms and be the first of my family to go to university. The system opened up for us. We were the brightest. The local corporation schools had the best pupils. It took only one generation to change all that. The crop was creamed and now we are back to the old boy school system. But, for a brief time the kids from the local grammar schools thought the world was their oyster.

So here was this cocky little Yorkshire lass down in London, pretty to boot, who didn't know the definition of an eligible male, but who had the confidence and love to think that the world would change.

I doubt if my parents thought my future husband was the most eligible of males; being wiser and more experienced, they were probably very apprehensive, but it was too late. As the song from South Pacific goes, you have to teach them to hate when they are young. It was too late to teach me lessons that they had never learned themselves, and when the time came, they were respectful of me and have always been loving and supportive of my family.

I think you would describe our marriage as stable, and I would say successful. Last week if you had asked me, I would have said just the opposite and probably next week will again. After 31 years we are still talking things through, gnawing on the bone, and he still stands 7 feet high. I suppose that is success.

It has not been an easy relationship. I would say that I am primarily responsible for our successes except for those occasions when he is. We are rather like two bloodied contestants on their hands and knees holding on to each other with one arm while flailing away with the other. But should a misdirected blow land, the other will be there to administer first aid until the contestants are able to flail some more. We argue, we fight, but there are rules - we are never destructive, we leave space to maneuver, and instinctually know that when things are really down, somehow one of us can rise to the occasion and save the day, can replace our marriage on its pedestal, battered, bruised, but hardy. You may say sentimental HOG WASH!!! It is; but if you don't have romance and a commitment to a grand love, life can be long, lonely, and boring. It works!! Our sense of ourselves as individuals and within our marriage and our family continuum allows of nothing else and so it succeeds. The question then may seem - "Why bother?" Why!!! Because we are gloriously successful except for when we are miserable failures. We are only children, and therefore siblings, but these are personal details of a relationship. The dynamics of keeping a relationship alive and vibrant doesn't really have anything to do necessarily with its being interracial or intercultural.

So what is the racial component? In truth, I do not think that between the two of us it exists. There is an intercultural dimension, but that is limited. I don't think that either of us is a culturally tied person. I am English, he is American and you can be whatever you are - that's OK. Where it does come in is as individuals and couples relate to others. We are all conditioned by our experience. We expect to be perceived and relate to others in certain ways. The dynamics of any marriage involve a reconciliation or acceptance of these expectations. How this plays out in society at large varies.

In an interracial situation there are three major sets of relationships. The first is how you relate to other members of the racial group into which you married, then how you relate to society at large, and then how you relate within your immediate family.

For my husband's immediate family, I believe that they have absolute faith that I will take care of the best interests of their son and his children, and so what better basis for a relationship? I would have liked a closer relationship, but that it isn't has nothing to do with my being white or from a different country.

I don't really separate myself from black America. As far as I am concerned, I chose to be black unlike black America, and so I don't have to justify my white self, and I don't have to take a lot of nonsense. When the chips are down, there is no doubt which side I will be coming up on, and similarly I expect that support as my right. What does it mean in everyday terms? Well for a start, I don't think that I have to like everyone and everything just because they or it is black. However, I do feel that I have the responsibility of acting in accordance with my political beliefs and racial identification. Of saying "No, I disagree with that or your assumptions are wrong!"

On the whole, I would say that I have found black America quite accepting of myself and certainly my family. When I was first married there might have been some tensions between myself and black women my age. In retrospect, I think that was because I was seen as an intruder who had absconded with a valued possession. I think that this perception is valid since eligible professional black males are at a premium, and the response seems legitimate. Now, however, my family and the length of my involvement and commitment legitimizes me. I am not seen as someone engaging in a temporary incursion into forbidden territory who will quickly retreat when the going gets tough. I'm here to stay!

I don't spend very much time worrying about other people's response to our marriage. If you disapprove, that's your right and not my problem; however, if you impinge on my rights just a fraction and I have the means of redress, then I'll respond. It is not a chip on the shoulder, it is a matter of assuming the responsibility for change and realizing that most blacks don't know their rights, and those who do for the most part won't, cannot, or maybe fear to take action or are just too demoralized. It is a matter of assuming the responsibility. At the same time, we are not conducting an introductory sociology course in race relations, and

I do not wish to be used to work out other's developmental problems. The issue in truth is not so interesting.

There were events or happenings in my early marriage which did have a profound effect on my thinking and attitudes. That they occurred early on is significant since they served to mold my attitudes and define the parameters of my relationships. Today I would not be so vulnerable or innocent. The incident I recall most vividly was when my oldest child was about two years old. She was as cute as could be and she was running along in front of me as I went to the local supermarket in New York. She was adorable, laughing and bubbling along, and I was trying to catch up with her, a sight that any adult enjoys with a smile as you remember your children and the sheer joy of infancy and young motherhood. An elderly woman swept her up in her arms and smiled at her. She reminded me of my grandmother or yours. She was talking to her and as I went up to retrieve my daughter I realized with horror what this woman was saying. She was saying, "I don't blame you darling, its that !!!!!!!!!!! of a mother." I swept Kimberley into my arms and took her home. I was very upset. When I told Walton he was furious, but there was not much he had not experienced in American race relations. For me it was the first time that I had ever experienced malevolence, and I was completely unprepared. That I could be the subject of such an attack was amazing - after all, didn't everyone like me? Wasn't that approval my right? That the attack could come from some little old lady who looked completely innocuous and benign was a shock, but that the attack could come through my children, that they were vulnerable was terrifying.

Perhaps everyone has to lose their innocence sometimes, and maybe that I had held onto mine so long was startling. I had always thought that people were good and kind; that is not so. Since then I have learned, not always in a racial context, that people are stupid, greedy, selfish, and, yes, malevolent. It's an act of faith to assume anything else, and so I tend to distance myself and ask the question "Who are you?" Most of my friends would describe me as outgoing, sociable and friendly, and I am, but I am not foolish. Another observation is relevant and was made to me by a black American woman friend who I would see at different predominately white occasions. She observed that whereas her husband would be greeted and fussed over by the white ladies thereby acknowledging him as a sexual being, black women in similar situations are forced into an asexual sterile role. I have found that as a black man's mate, in similar situations I am also forced into this role. This phenomena is peculiarly American and does not obtain in other countries either with black Americans or the black nationals of those countries. This experience has particular relevance for one's black daughters. It is pervasive, but most prevalent, in affluent, professional, liberal, white circles, and less so in working class ethnic groups, although my knowledge of these groups in the States is limited.

Do we live life as black or white Americans? The answer would be neither. Black or white America or England for that matter is too confining. We have spent many years overseas, and those we are most comfortable with have a similar experience. There are a lot of rolling stones in this world, and so I see myself and my husband as picking a bouquet of flowers. I like this one and that and don't forget -------! I love going home and immersing myself in my family and Yorkshire bonhommie. Southern family Christmases with collard greens and chittlings and sweet potato pies are wonderful. We have friends in Philadelphia that go back to teenage days, and in England too. So, we pick and choose and travel. We have been fortunate. That we can do so with relative ease is I think a reflection of the security of our home environments.

We have three children who have been brought up as black Americans. They are not half English, they are not half white, they are 100% black American. It was not in their interest to be anything other. It was not always easy, particularly for me, and I had to have complete confidence that we were right in bringing them up this way. I wasn't sure, but I was certain that bringing them up as anything else was wrong. I also trusted my husband, after all he knows how to be a self assured black man in America, which is a difficult act to pull off. How can you have the confidence to sally forth in the world if you don't have a sense of who you are and your history. They are perceived as black by society, so why prepare them to be any other? So they learned to be black American, warts and all. What we have tried to teach was for them to assume the responsibility for being black.

Our older two children are female. The teenage years were for me at least the most difficult. They ran into the problem that I have observed earlier - the asexual treatment of black females. Their interaction with white, middle/upper class youths was not conducive to a positive self image. At a time when adolescents are questioning their appeal to members of the opposite sex, the majority of their white classmates were seeing them as neuters. This tended to reinforce their identification with black America. That, I think, was a healthy response to an unhealthy condition; however, black America itself is a similar response. It is only as they have developed their sense of themselves as black Americans that they are able to deal with America in a healthy fashion, having defined their space and existence.

Our son is in his teenage years, and I hope that this will be easier since he does have a successful role model in his father. Although my friends tell me that these are hard years for black youths. In the end you cross your fingers, pray, trust your instincts, and give out a lot of love, which is true of all black parents, white parents, and any other combination of parents.

What we really want for our children is for them to be successful as people, in harmony with their world. If they have some material success, good, but I would not want that as a goal.

Walton

Growing up as a black person in America was a major factor in my marrying someone from a different culture, though I don't think it accounts for my marrying someone from a different race. During my youth, I was subjected to institutionalized segregation and debilitating personal discrimination. Retreat into the black community is a common and natural response to this experience. I was not inclined in that direction however. I had the feeling that retreat into the black community would be constraining. Middle class socialization prevented me from considering retreat into the black proletariat and, at that time, I thought the tiny black middle class was too parochial. Not that I knew then what I was searching for, but, in retrospect, like other adolescents, I was trying to carve out my own individual identity.

It was in this context that I was interested in moving out from the black American community. I went to Oberlin College, a predominately white, liberal college, where important friendships with whites - male and female - developed.

Yet, quite obviously, even had I wanted to, I could not have found a satisfactory identity in white America. Even in liberal circles like Oberlin, white America is so fundamentally racist that it was of no use to me.

Non-American cultures therefore were attractive to me. I first went to Europe just after graduating from college. I worked for a year in Germany and France. I found learning and communicating in other languages exciting. Like other black Americans, I also discovered that Europeans viewed me in a different light. This was great for my sense of self as an individual, and my sense of self as a black person. After 22 years of American racism, the new sense had a liberating effect.

As a part of my exploration of other cultures, when I was 23 years old, I went to Sierra Leone with Operations Crossroads Africa. Until that time, I had had no special interest in Africa and, indeed, would have just as eagerly have traveled to Asia or Latin America. But as luck would have it, I found myself in Africa.

Here my interest in other cultures was deepened. Aside from the excitement of seeing a continent enter a new era, and the stimulation of Africa's cultural and physical beauty, it was fascinating to get to know black people whose culture was so different from mine. They also saw me in a different light - different from racist America and different from chauvinistic Europe.

When it came time to choose a field for graduate study, therefore, I chose African Studies. I went to the School of Oriental and African Studies in England because the field was so much further developed there, and because I had learned to like being in foreign cultures. When I met Judith in London, I was already programmed to accept and enjoy persons from different cultures.

I do not feel I was particularly attracted to people of different races. In fact, given my previous experiences, I suspect Judith's being white was more of a negative factor for me. But, having fervently acquired the 1960's ethos of nonracialism and multiculturalism, I did not focus on our racial differences. I wanted to marry her for the same personal and private reasons any other two individuals want to marry. The different culture was definitely a plus - exciting. The different race was ignored.

On the whole, cultural differences between Judith and me are not great. We speak mutually understandable languages (sometimes) and are native to an Anglo-European culture. Generally speaking, our respective role expectations have been borne out. Relations with in-laws have been good and surprisingly unaffected by cultural or racial differences.

Marriage was not a relationship that I had thought much about. I must have internalized ideas about marriage roles from socialization, but had not elaborated conscious convictions of my own. Looking back, I suppose the role women play in black America was the role model which most influenced my expectations of marriage. Wives shoulder much of the burden in black America. They are super efficient as housewives and mothers, and they bring home wages from employment. Given my needs as a young, insecure black man trying to make it in white America, I most certainly over-focused on these attributes.

My images clashed sharply with Judith's in this regard. She had learned that a husband was the exclusive provider, the protector, the anchor for the family. A wife was the 'little woman' who filled in the gaps, providing the mortar which cemented the family. Major family responsibilities fell squarely on the husband's shoulders.

The sharpest conflict in our marriage has probably had to do with these roles. We each demanded from the other in accordance with our culturally based expectations. The success of our marriage is due in part to each of us, with considerable bludgeoning, being molded into the other's expected role. It was difficult though. Meeting Judith's expectations of a husband generated fear, anxiety, and some bitterness in me. Similarly, I think Judith felt anxious, insecure, and overwhelmed by the 'super woman' images she found in the black American sub-culture.

But while they may have created some problems, I am certain that cultural differences have increased our marriage's ability to survive. Most importantly, the awareness that we come from different backgrounds has added a perspective to the normal marital give and take, and has made it a little easier to find tolerance when stresses emerge.

But, cultural differences have been a strength in other ways. Like most other people, we would like to think that there are many personal, idiosyncratic reasons why our marriage has survived - our love, our patience, our commitment, our tolerance. In fact, however, we probably have no more of these qualities than many other couples. Certainly there have been trying times in our relationship. But just as the cultural differences between us have constituted a paradoxical kind of strength, so too have the cultural differences between each of us and the cultures in which we live. Here, in the United States, Judith derives considerable social benefit from America's general eurocentricity and, in particular, its anglophilia. Post 1960's, Walton gets social kudos by virtue of being a 'buppie'. But neither of us is indigenous to the majority culture in the United States - nor are we seen to be. This common estrangement from mainstream white America has been a powerful bond in our marriage. We can only look to each other for support vis-a-vis this outside world.

This curious dynamic has been most evident during our years of living abroad. We spent three years in Zambia in the late 60's during the early years of our marriage. The environment was hospitable to both of us. Judith was highly regarded because she was white and British. I was highly regarded because I was a skilled black engaged in nation-building activities. Nevertheless, neither of us was Zambian or even African. So we had something in common which bonded us vis-a-vis the 'others'.

Ten years after returning to the United States, our marriage was greatly refreshed again by a two year sojourn in Zimbabwe. As in Zambia, Judith, being white and British, had high ascriptive status. Being a professional black in a 'helping' role, I also had high ascriptive status. And once again, our common estrangement from the indigenous culture, the white settlers and the diplomatic corps pushed us together psychologically and emotionally.

I see the African sojourns as having introduced a special adhesive into our marital relationship. But, this same positive force of common foreignness exists to a lesser extent in the United States as well. Though we have lived for some time in Britain, and though our relationships in the United States are often in the black community, had we conducted our marriage entirely in my culture or entirely in her culture, the danger of it coming unstuck would have been much greater. We would not have had a common estrangement to bond us together.

It is difficult for me to place our marriage in the context of wider society. Inside the marriage, we relate as an ordinary couple. We are not constantly conscious of being an interracial couple or an intercultural couple. Without always having those antennae up, therefore, it is difficult to know how others view us. Clearly, society notices and attaches much more importance to the interracial and intercultural character of our relationship than we do. These are minor attributes for us, but, for others, they are often the only attributes.

When we were partying together in England, few people thought it was a lasting relationship and were surprised when we married. Arriving in the US in the mid-1960's, in the heat of the civil rights tensions and intense black nationalism, society definitely noticed us. It's hard to say what they thought. We were certainly a novelty. No doubt, many whites objected. Many blacks objected. Many were just curious.

Unquestionably, being an interracial couple is part of our identity. Contact with us has visibly broadened the horizons of our family, friends, and associates, but I don't think knowing us changed any ideas. On the whole, we have not experienced difficulties in these relationships. Here again, everyone's awareness of cultural differences probably reduces tensions by putting conflicts and differences in a more objective, less personal, context.

During the 1970's, I did sense curiosity and confusion among the black students, particularly black women students, at Rutgers. Seeing me teach in a 'black studies' department and observing my commitment to giving students information about Africa and Afro-America which would enhance their black pride, many of these students, I felt, found it difficult to understand how I could be married to a white person. It was not a situation of competition, or me representing a scarce resource which was alienated from the community, but rather how the ideology of blackness squared with marrying a white person. For the past fifteen years, I have detected less of this.

We consciously encouraged our children to identify as black. In our view, this simply was the social reality in which they had to live. However, they have also been encouraged to have high regard for their English background and to be active members of the family in England. This appears to us not to have posed a problem for them. The absence of problems is largely due to the willingness of the parents and in-laws on both sides to accept, identify, and interact with the others. The children took their cue from the adults.

As young children in Princeton, a small, affluent, predominantly white university town, race was not at all a problem for them. They had friendships which bore little relationship to race. As male and female relationships assumed greater importance during the teen years, however, race became more of a force in their relationships. The broader society defined them as black, so they identified and behaved as blacks. It was easier, safer, and offered more opportunities for meaningful social interaction. As far as we can tell, this was also not a problem for them. Here too I suppose they took their cue from the adults - the parents. Race was not an issue in the marriage. Both parents loved and accepted the children. The children acknowledge being 'half white', but recognize that in this society they are considered black.

While the psychological and emotional benefits of this posture have been substantial, I have felt one major problem. The problem is how to allow the children to accept and respect themselves as blacks without their falling victim to the negative socialization this society imposes on blacks. American culture, and the school systems in particular, fail to instill confidence, self-esteem and positive self images in children it defines as black.

Having spent her junior year in London (Kings College), Kimberley graduated from Rutgers and went on to University of London and then to veterinary school at the University of Pennsylvania. Krista majored in international relations at John Hopkins, spent her junior year in South Africa, and has now begun her PhD studies in Political Science at Northwestern University. Despite this respectable showing, I am still deeply distressed by the up-hill battle with regard to America's negative socialization of blacks. Jamie, who is 20 years old, passed through this crucial period with our support. He spent his ninth grade in South Africa followed by a voyage around the globe on the Semester at Sea, and has now begun his undergraduate studies.

We hope our influence has been some help, but the most important force in giving different images to the older children has been our travel. In Africa, there are different (though not always positive) images of blacks and of black Americans. Living and going to school there gave the children a different view of themselves. Moreover, living among their 'white' relatives in England, who saw them as relatively well-off, middle class Americans, also gave the positive ideas of themselves. We do feel however that we have vigorously struggled to fight adverse socialization of our children by American society.

CHAPTER 13

The CAMEROON-IOWA CONNECTION

Ajaga Nji and Katherine Langhurst Nji

Introduction

One of the consequences of the rapid social change that is sweeping through many societies is the phenomenon of social mobility. Right on the heels of social mobility comes the search for identity. The common denominator for these social processes is status-seeking and status-change. Many people who seek social mobility do so in a conscious effort to move up the social ladder: to move from an ascribed social status to an achieved status.

Marriage is one way by which role and status change take place. When a person leaves the country of origin/birth to another country to study, or when another person leaves a town or city of origin/birth to another one for the purposes of education, such persons do so because they want to improve their social positions through education. Thus the school not only serves as an institution of socialization, but also as a vehicle for the interplay of many social and psychological forces, particularly the development of many social relationships.

The origins of the unions of many young couples can be traced to happy encounters at elementary school, high school, or college. The relationship which we discuss was developed and consummated in college. First on the pews of Ames Collegiate Presbyterian Church, then on the reading tables of Iowa State University Library, and finally on the banks of Little Wall Lake, about 35 miles north of Ames, Iowa.

Dating or Not to Date

On that Sunday morning in November 1977, I sat beside this beautiful WASP sophomore in the Collegiate Presbyterian Church in Ames, Iowa. I had never met her before, so I didn't know her name, who she was, or what she was doing in Ames. She picked up the hymn book and asked me to share it with her in singing a congregational hymn. I did so with pleasure.

The Minister announced that there was going to be a social evening for all new and old students in the Church at 3:30 p.m. that Sunday. I asked the girl who had invited me to song and prayer if she was a student, and whether she would come with me to the social evening. She said yes to both questions.

We agreed to meet at 2:25 p.m. at the corner of Sheldon Avenue (midway between her dormitory and my apartment). I didn't ask her name until 2:25 when we met again --- for the second time!

Katherine and I attended the social evening of punch, cookies, and games which we both enjoyed. We met several times afterwards in the library and in the Computer Center, but neither Katherine nor I was quite sure at that time about dating each other. In fact, we were both naively unaware of the permanent relationship which was dawning on us through what may be superstitiously called "destiny."

One Sunday, after another worship service, I asked Katherine formally for a date, which she accepted with pleasure. Our friendship grew into a mutually beneficial relationship day after day for several months. When I asked Katherine six months after we first met whether she would marry me, her reply was "maybe."

Breaking the Barrier of Racial Stereotypes

Katherine comes from a rural farm family background, the epitomy of deep-rooted moral values. Born in a community of less than 1,000 population, all white, and deeply rooted in the American value system, Katherine's decision to marry a black man from Africa (of all places) was to be influenced by his parents, grandparents, and brothers.

The decisions to date someone from another racial background was tough enough. Deciding whether or not to marry the person was even tougher. The trump card for the decision was in the hands of her parents (particularly her grandparents). When I discovered that her greatest obstacle lay in breaking the racial barrier, I encouraged her to work through a process which would enable her parents to look at the positive side of the relationship, rather than concentrate on the negative connotations of racial stereotypes.

Congruence in Perceptions

At this stage, it became more and more obvious to me that for Katherine, as for me, marriage was not just a union of convenience for two isolated individuals, but a social bond that ties two families together. Both of us were influenced by our "significant others" (Henslin, 1975). I was concerned, in the same way that Katherine was, about the possible reactions of our parents and friends. Thus, while Katherine worked out her way through the social web in Springville during weekends and school holidays, I tried to convince my parents and friends in Cameroon by letter about the merits of my decision to marry a white American woman. This perception of congruence in significant others was, to me, an important factor that reinforced my relationship with Katherine, and justified, in a way, the rightness of our decision.

My family was divided almost 50/50 on the issue. On Katherine's side, the situation was similar each time we met to compare our "opinion poll" results. It was interesting for me to watch how opinions shifted in my family. At the beginning, many people were in disfavor of our marriage, but the rate of approval increased as the relationship lasted.

From the Cameroon side, their main concerns were whether: (1) Katherine would like to have children, if she could; (2) I would return to Cameroon after the marriage; (3) Katherine would accept the social and cultural environment of rural Cameroon, or the Third World in general; and (4) Katherine would be willing to do the things generally considered as woman's work (child rearing, cooking, care of the home, and farming).

I invited my family and friends to state the reasons for their refusals; and after analyzing all of them it became clear that they were not in disfavor of Katherine as a person; they were more concerned about the social structure, the value system and the impact of cultural (structural) forces on marriage as an institution. One of the reasons my family was in disfavor of the union was that the experience in Cameroon with mixed racial marriages has not been as positive as that of local marriages. It was perceived that the divorce rate is higher among the former than the latter, although no empirical tests have been conducted to affirm or deny this assumption scientifically.

In one of the letters my father sent to me from Cameroon, he lamented:

> How can you marry a wife who will not understand our language? How will I communicate with her when I speak no Whiteman's English? Will that white woman accept, receive me in your house when I come to visit you? Won't she want me to send a letter first, asking whether I can come? Why, my son, do you want to put me into such isolation? Why?"

In the same envelope was a letter from my step-mother in which she unleashed her skepticism about "white wives" (literally translated "red women"). She moaned:

> Do you think that that woman you want to marry will regard your mothers[1] and sisters as human beings? We live in dust, we sleep in dust; we cook with firewood with lots of smoke in the kitchen; we wear no shoes. Will a "red woman" stand to all these inconveniences? Will she eat the food I cook or even enter my smoky kitchen? I am illiterate, how shall I be able to teach "my wife"[2] the culture, songs, dances, and folklore of the village? How, how, how shall I play my role as a good mother-in-law? In what language shall we communicate?

The opinions of female members of the family are very crucial in all kinds of marriage in Cameroon. And generally, their questions, queries or concerns go much deeper than the men's. They are concerned about the woman's capacity or general attitude towards the family institution, the home, children, the farm, and social relations. The letter from my step-mother expressing uncertainties about Katherine's reactions on these issues was quite incisive:

> My son, I am not saying that you should not marry. I am concerned about how the woman will take care of you. Will she cook? Most white people do not like to cook, wash clothes, or care for the children. They like to employ servants instead. Will you have the money to hire all these people? We live on hills, we work on hills. Will that woman accept to come and live in this hilly country of ours even for one day? We work on the farm every day. We come back dirty. Sometimes I may come to your house with dirty feet. Will that your white woman not roll the carpet under my feet? I don't know. Please don't bring us another Maggi .[3]

Expectations Fulfilled

I expected to marry a woman who would love me and all my children and family equally. I also expected my wife to recognize the beauty of good, friendly relationships, and the harmony of a quiet and genuine life.

The six months during which I got to know Katherine well were six months of real loving and caring. I was convinced from this experience that while she may not fit into the ideal images of all the members of my family, she was, to a large measure, the ideal person with whom we could raise a family of love, compassion, and hope.

The fulfillment of "traditional marriage roles" by Katherine was crucial to me in the decision making process. I expected "my wife to be" to be a loving friend, mother, and a daughter-in-law who cares about my parents and other members of the broader society, regardless of sex, religion, race, or nationality. On the other hand, I expected my "wife to be" not to disobey or disregard the counsel of her parents and family. I expected her to be able to weave both families into a united, coherent whole with minimum discomfort or perceived disdain on her side.

The basic assumption about the family appeared to be a common normative postulate for me as well as for Katherine. We sort of "sized up" each other on key issues: marriage itself, divorce, sexual relations, children and childbearing, abortion, the family, work, and money. I probably did more sizing up of Katherine than she did of me, perhaps because I felt that in the final analysis, I would be the one to bear the consequences of our union. I believe that if the results of our self examination were not mutually satisfying, we never would have entered into a marriage contract with each other.

Factors That Contribute to the Stability of Our Marriage

Cultural Consistency

Although my cultural background is not white middle-class, I shared the same social values as Katherine, which are also the cultural expectations of my kinship, the Metta clan of the North West Province of Cameroon.

Perhaps some of these values have been reinforced over time by my education in the United States prior to our first contact. But it remains true that elements of cultural consistency between Katherine and myself conspired to provide the foundation for a stable marriage.

In-Law Relationships

One of the sources of strain in a marriage is "parental interference." I discovered this soon in our dating relationship, and drew my then-girlfriend's attention (now my wife) to that possible source of conflict. I remember to have asked Katherine one evening as we mooted the possible outcomes of a unilateral marriage: "Don't you think your dad would pull the trigger of his short gun on me if we got married?" I asked her. "No, no, no, Ajaga; no way can he do a thing like that," Katherine retorted. I had been so used to trigger-happy Americans that I was forced in my turn to lavish a cultural stereotype on Katherine's father.

I remember that Katherine returned from Christmas vacation in 1977 and told me that her mother was "somehow supportive" of the whole idea, and that she (her mother) had taken upon herself to sound the opinion of her own mother (Katherine's maternal grandmother). "The what?" I asked.

"Grandma seemed to come down on my side too, and I am so delighted about her support," Katherine replied. I was quite conscious of the influence of in-laws because in Metta Clan, one's in-laws can make or mar a marriage. The problem is even more acute in Africa because of the obligations a son-in-law has to fulfill in an extended family system.

By taking such a precaution, I managed to avoid the in-law syndrome, a major source of marital conflict and source of marital breakups in American marriages. I was convinced that the kin network was as strong among rural Republican Iowa farmers as they were in the villages of Cameroon. Thus I was able to avoid or preempt a possible threat to the stability of our union.

Age At Marriage

I remember Katherine to have told me (when we decided to go ahead and see the Minister to announce our decision to be married) that we should plan our wedding after her 21st birthday. That was in April and her birthday is in May. Her rationale was that at 21, she would have attained legal maturity to decide what is best for herself. We got married on June 3, 1978. To our surprise and satisfaction, among the signatures in our guest book were those of Katherine's parents, three brothers, and a sister. While Katherine celebrated her twenty-first birthday, I was seven years older than she. In my opinion, then, we have been able to sustain our marriage because we were both mentally mature at the time we decided to live together in union with each other, regardless of the impact of parental pressures.

Trust and Truth and Love

We began our relationship in complete trust of each other. I opened my heart to Katherine and she opened hers to me. She had never traveled out of Iowa until I met her, except for a few trips with her parents to Canada. So I opened her mind up with the realities of poverty and misery in Africa. I showed her the worst possible pictures of Africa and narrated Tarzan-like stories to give her the celebrated picture of "Africans living in trees" as many social science teachers in the United States believe. Even with all that, Katherine decided to love me, to trust me, and believe in the truth of the social reality of Africa. The combination of these three factors, probably more than any other, is the driving force behind our stability, since Katherine has been able to discover for herself that things are not as bad as the media portrays them.

Since we have been married, our relationship has been strengthened by our children. They have provided the point of convergence for our love, trust, and hope. And the circumstances under which each of them was born gives us more room for love for each other. For example, Akwi was born in the middle of my qualifying exams. I drove from Ames to Iowa City Hospitals and back within 24 hours to write my qualifying exams the following day. Afor was born in a government hospital in Dschang with the barest minimum of hospital equipment and personnel. The midwife and myself single-handedly delivered our second daughter.

Differences

We have experienced and continue to be influenced by different expectations in our two cultural backgrounds. We differ somewhat on principles of child rearing. I believe in physical punishment when necessary, Katherine does not. I believe in the development of individual personality characteristics in our children. In other words all children cannot have the same personality traits. Katherine would like to see the children develop a homogeneous personality as much as possible. We both tolerate conflicts and occasional bickering between the children for that's what makes them human, different but alike. I believe in the variability of cultural patterns, although Katherine would like to see everyone think and behave in a <u>predictable</u> way.

In spite of all these differences, we respect each other's views, live a harmonious relationship, and share the joys and displeasures of struggling to lead a decent and honest life. That is the cement that holds our relationship together.

Benefits of Culture of Residence

Two years after we were married, we moved to Cameroon where we have been living since 1980. Katherine has come to know about other ways of life (e.g. polygamy, the extended family) without accepting them wholesale, of course. But these experiences help to reinforce and enrich each of our experiences.

None of our social values has changed greatly since moving to Cameroon, except that Katherine probably misses the goodbye kiss in public <u>a l'Americain</u>. But we have also found that our slight divergent backgrounds complement each other. I like to fix things, but I neither have the patience nor the time to read complicated instructions (e.g. for new equipment and drugs). But Katherine has a tremendous capacity to hold herself down and read each word in an instruction booklet. She does the reading, while I follow her instructions about installations or dosage. With regard to child rearing, Katherine has a lot of patience and capacity for sitting and talking to the kids. I do not. I travel a lot because of my work. Her job as a High School teacher rarely takes her out of town. We complement each other in a great way.

Since settling in Cameroon, the concept of our "family" has taken on a different meaning. We have moved from a small nuclear family to a large extended family system. We have my sister and two other relatives living with us, and people stop over for a night without notice. We have come to realize that the visitors cannot help but stop over without notice because the communication system is undeveloped and life in Cameroon, like in most developing countries, is unplanned but very eventful. The road network is poor, the telephone system is inefficient and the postal system suffers from several handicaps. The health system is chaotic and social services rudimentary.

All these factors affect our marriage in one way or the other, but we still hang together as if nothing is happening, because we know that there is no society nor union without its own peculiar problems and circumstances.

The Mixed Marriage and Society

In 1979, when the late Professor Bernard Fonlon, a witty Cameroonian philosopher-thinker-scholar visited Katherine and me in Ames as a Fulbright Scholar, he had this to say as he held two-month old Akwi in his hands: "There is a new marriage phenomenon emerging in Cameroon about which many people don't seem to be aware. It's not the British-Cameroonians; It's not the French-Cameroonians either. It is the American-Cameroonian generation."

Dr. Fonlon was referring to what he perceived as an increasingly high rate of mixed marriages between Cameroonians and Americans of both sexes, and going in both directions. He mentioned Cameroonian females married to Americans and living in the United States as one group, and those Americans married to Cameroonians and living in Cameroon as another group. "This is a new generation of Cameroonians coming up," he said, without casting any verdict on the future consequences of such a relationship.

The children born to racially mixed couples are very light-skinned. In Cameroon, people on the street refer to them as "metis." And since light-skin is fast becoming a status symbol, the offspring of mixed marriages (light-skinned children) seem to influence the excessive use of body bleaching creams and hair dying techniques that change the color of the skin and hair from "ebony black" to "half baked metis."

As I see it, this is a serious social problem which results in an identity crisis for many young Cameroonians. Because of their fair skin and long hair (Katherine calls them mops), our girls are often the object of attention for other children. In Dschang, I was strangely surprised when two children passed by our car as our two daughters sat in the back seat waiting for a treat of "soya" (barbecued meat). I heard the passing children say in the local dialect "Ndege."

Akwi made a funny face at them, and when I asked her what "Ndege" means she said it means "whiteman." Although such labels may not have been made to insult our daughters, the girls get quite defensive on the sound of the word "Ndege" by other kids. Our children are very well integrated. They identify with me just as much as with Kathy. But since they do not speak the dialect yet, they tend to communicate with other children in English only. This reduces the circle of friends they can play with, but that does not present a major problem. However, Mommy is always the nicest person in the family because "she bakes the birthday cakes, buys the Christmas toys, and plays with us. Daddy buys clothes instead of toys, and is always gone."

Mommy Listens, Daddy Yells

There are times when I feel terrible about social relationships even with my own brothers or sisters. But Katherine cools it all off most of the time. Consequently, the children tend to go to her more of the time to get their problems solved than they come to me. And if a relative has a tricky request to make (such as borrowing money), they go to her rather than come to me. I believe that Katherine's congeniality has less to do with her gender and more to do with her personality.

I think that my life would have been different on the negative side if I were married to someone else. I have developed personal values which are not very consistent with my traditional culture. The society in Cameroon, as well as in the United States, is accepting mixed marriages more than before, and this creates a good climate not only for mixed couples and their children, but for humanity as a whole. Perhaps one day, mixed couples will provide the bridge for cultural integration among the races of the world and pave the way for international peace and justice.

Notes

1 Any woman in the African village who is of the same age-group as one's mother is labeled "one's mother."
2 The wife of an African is culturally labeled "my wife" by the mother of the African male spouse and other elderly women in the compound or homestead.
3 Maggi is the name of a girl friend (Cameroonian) with whom I had three children prior to going to the U.S. in 1975. She was the stereotype of a "white woman who does not work." Although Maggi and I knew each other between 1973 and 1975, we were never married. My dad dislikes "these book women who cannot bend their backs or soil their hands" when they have to.

References

Bott, Elizabeth
    1957 Family and Social Network. London: Tavistock Institute.

Duvall, Evelyn M.
    1954 In-Laws: Pro and Con. New York: Associated Press.

Henslin, James H.
    1975. Introducing Sociology. New York: The Free Press.

Landis, Judson T.
    1947 "Adjustment After Marriage." Marriage and Family Living 9 (May): 32-34

Rockwood, Lemo D. and Mary E.N. Ford
    1945 Youth, Marriage and Parenthood. New York: John Wiley and Sons.

Simpson, George E. and I. Milton Yinger
    1958 Racial and Cultural Minorities. New York: Harper and Row.

Thomas, John L.
    1953 "Marital Failure and Duration." Social Order 3 (January): 24-29.

Young, Michael and Mildred Geertz.
    1961 "Old Age in London and San Fransisco: Some Families Compared."
    British Journal of Sociology 12 (2): 124-141.

CHAPTER 14

THE LURE OF GREAT BRITAIN

Pamela and John Rooks

In some ways, we feel that our inclusion in this study is semi-fraudulent, since the differences in our native cultures are less extreme than is the case with many of the other couples represented. Certainly, there are significant differences between America and England, but they are more difficult to define and perhaps easier to bridge than those between, say, America and Nigeria. In addition, it is difficult for us to say with absolute certainty which of the differences and similarities between us can be traced to our respective cultures, and which to our individual natures. Certainly, we are each regarded as eccentric in some of our views by some Americans and some Britons. Since we have each lived for some years in each other's homelands, and for two years in Nigeria, which differed radically from both America and England, it is all the more difficult to state categorically that this or that notion springs from this or that cultural predisposition.

To begin with common ground, before launching into our individual narratives, we are both white, and were raised as not particularly committed or sectarian Protestants. Neither of us was the first in our families to get degrees (although we are, so far, the only ones to have advanced terminal degrees); there is teaching, of one sort or another, on both sides of the family tree.

Perhaps because we both were raised by working mothers, both of us have always assumed that we would each work. Moreover, we value our own and each other's careers equally. We've been fortunate enough to avoid any of the wrangling about cooking, cleaning, and child-care that seems to plague some working couples--we both like cooking, we both accept the necessity of cleaning with some consistency but without fanaticism, and we both find spending time with our daughter at least as interesting as spending time with students or in libraries.

Pamela

In a third grade autobiographical composition, I described my maternal grandparents as having been in their youth a nomadic people, but civilized. The same formula might be applied to my husband and me, although our peregrinations have been as scholar gypsies rather than as vaudevillian actors. Our joint wanderings have taken us thus far from England to America, via Africa. In America, we've taught so far in Michigan, Iowa, and Georgia--three fairly distinct regions in the supposedly homogeneous culture of the USA. Before meeting my husband, who is English, I'd already left my native America to do a BA in Canada. We met while we were both doing our doctorates in English literature at the University of York, England, and married there. Faced with the near impossibility of finding suitable academic work for one, let alone both of us, in the UK, we accepted two-year contracts at the University of Sokoto, Nigeria; after completing those contracts, we came to America, first teaching for one year at Eastern Michigan

University in Ypsilanti, Michigan (where my mother also taught, in a different department), then doing three years at Iowa State University in Ames, Iowa, where our daughter, now nearly eight, was born. We then left for Statesboro, Georgia, to teach at Georgia Southern College. Whether we settle for a long time or not will depend on our career development.

All of this moving about, while not altogether voluntary (John, indeed, grew to man's estate without any particular inclination even to vacation abroad, and regards his recent wanderings with a certain bemused incredulity), has definitely had some effect on us. For the purpose of this study, perhaps the most relevant effect has been to cause us, not altogether consciously, to create within our marriage the kind of rootedness--the cultural identity and security, as it were--which might otherwise have grown out of staying in one place, amongst one stable group of people. Having forged the roving Republic of Rooksland over the past fourteen years, we, like Gypsies, carry our home and our culture within us.

I went to England as a graduate student brimming over with an anglophilia which had been primed and fed by the number of English friends whom I'd had in Canada. I'd lived for two years with an Englishman, who returned to Britain to begin graduate work at the same time as I did, though in a different subject at a different university. After about a year in England, we broke up. By the time John and I met, I had lived amongst the English for long enough to have outgrown my adolescent romantic infatuation with things and folks British in general; this generic and uncritical fascination needed, I think, to be worked through before I could be sure that I was marrying a particular man rather than an Englishman. I suspect that cross-cultural marriages which are based on an uninformed love of another country (which love is often based on an informed dissatisfaction with one's own country) are less likely to be stable than those which are based on a love for another human being who happens to be from another country.

Although John had never been to America, he had had some other American girlfriends; also, by the time we met, I had been in England for a few years (and had had exposure to the English during the four years in Canada) and so appeared less exotic than if I'd been straight off the plane. Like many Englishmen, he quite liked Americans as individuals even before he met me, while retaining a certain good-natured contempt for America (and, indeed, any place that wasn't England). What he liked best about Americans was what he perceived as a refreshing quaintness of expression, which has continued to provide him with a rich vein of amusement in me and in other American friends.

I have always been more Anglicized than he has been, or is ever likely to become, Americanized. For example, I am prone to echo the accent of the region I live in--after living in England, I sounded, at least to Americans, English (I had no doubt that I would pick up a charming drawl in Georgia). Indeed, I was something of a surprise to the British friends that John had made in Sokoto during the six months that he was there while I was in England finishing my dissertation. When he told people that his wife was American, they formed a stereotypical notion of what I would look like and sound like and think like, and were both disappointed and relieved to find me just a regular (i.e., more or less English) person.

My family, although they approved of my doing my graduate work in England (my mother has some degree of anglophilia in her, which may be where I got it from) were somewhat disturbed by this chameleon streak in me, and took pains, particularly when we moved back to the States, to remind me of the

American names for things which I had fallen out of the habit of using ("we say 'trunk', not 'boot'; that's an 'elevator', not a 'lift'..."). I think that they became worried that my prolonged absence from America (nearly thirteen years), and my marriage to John, would mean that I would never come back to America again, and that I would be in some vital way lost to them. Certainly, the Nigeria years were a terrible strain on my mother, who found it a constant torment to have me living in a place with no telephones. (It irritated me too, but less so--after all, I was there, so I knew that I was all right.)

My family perceived John as Foreign in a way that I never have. Perhaps expecting him to be unaccountable they found him incomprehensible, feared that he would never be able to teach in the States and would carry me back to England or keep me confined in the remotest corners of the British Commonwealth. It must be said that his accent is regional (Americans often think him Australian or Scottish, although the Manchester accent sounds nothing like either) and does not carry the Oxford-BBC recognizeability or cachet. It must also be conceded that (consciously or unconsciously) he acts more the daffy Englishman when he is abroad, has always liked to tease people by saying outrageous things (some of which he means) and has more than his fair share of his national characteristic--irony. For example, when my mother, shortly before our wedding, asked him if he would look after me, he replied certainly not, that I should look after him. It was also hard on my parents not to get a chance to get to know John--they flew to England only a few days before the wedding--until we'd been married for a few years. Also, their first vision of him was perhaps a worrying one, since he had very long hair and a slightly disreputable look (what they fortunately didn't know was that it could have been worse--he had only recently acquired a pair of clear glasses in honor of their coming--having broken his other pair some months before, and being short of funds, he'd been making do with a pair of prescription sunglasses).

John's family accepted me more easily than mine did him. Again, it is difficult to offer any one simple explanation for this. It was probably a combination of things; they were marrying off a son rather than a daughter, and the fourth and youngest child rather than the first and eldest; we were living in England, close enough to visit frequently and spend time with them, allowing the initial tolerance to ripen into a real affection; they already had a daughter who was married to a Canadian and living in Canada; I was perhaps more eager to please them than John was to please my family; they were certainly easier to please.

We both would have been quite happy to settle in England, had there been suitable work for us there. We hadn't really planned on Africa; our time in Nigeria was more the result of a series of coincidences than of a passionate political or missionary interest in the Third World. John's supervisor at York had spent six weeks in Nigeria for the British Council and returned full of enthusiasm about the cultural Renaissance that seemed to be taking place. A York couple were already in Sokoto-and so, the seed was planted. When, a couple of years later, we were looking rather desperately for work, applying to America and England, we saw an ad in The Guardian for university jobs in Nigeria, and sent letters as a sort of jeu d'esprit. When, some months later, we were invited for interviews in London, and offered two jobs, we weren't really in a position to turn them down; nothing had come through in England or America, and we were ready for an adventure.

The time in Nigeria, though difficult in many ways, served as a useful bridge between England and America, especially for John. Had we gone straight from England to America, he probably would have suffered more from culture shock than in fact he did. As it was, after Nigeria, America seemed quite homey; the luxuries of hot and cold running water, consistently efficient electricity, and fully equipped supermarkets were more than enough to ease any difficulties in making the transition from one world to another. Perhaps most importantly, his mother died while he was already in Nigeria, although I hadn't gone out yet. His father being already dead, there were no family ties to feel guilty about leaving behind. A chapter in his life seemed to have closed and he was ready to start another.

This is not to say that John feels fully at home in America. He told me once, when we were still living in England, that he had the curious feeling that if he went abroad, he would never grow any older, since nothing that happened there would seem quite real. There's a certain truth in this fanciful notion, for him. It's certainly true that he takes America less seriously than I take it (or indeed than I take England). He disapproves of much about the politics here, as do I, but he doesn't disapprove passionately, as do I; his attitude is more dismissive, more what-can-you-expect. The only real newspaper in the world, as far as he is concerned, is The Guardian; The New York Times doesn't count for much. He is somewhat irritated by minor things; for example, he feels deeply nostalgic about roundabouts, finding stop signs a poor substitute.

He distrusts the medical community in general, but regards the American system as less moral than the British. It seems to be the case that a common cultural prejudice is in favor of one's own medical system. When we were in Nigeria, an Egyptian friend assured us that a certain eye doctor was completely reliable, since he was Egyptian--this didn't have the same immediately calming effect on us as it might have had on another Egyptian. We came to trust, more or less, the Polish physicians in the community, since they were the only medical personnel in the area who were European. I realized, when I was pregnant, that I was much happier to be having our baby in America than I would have been in England.

It wasn't really that I would have been concerned about the competence of the English doctors, but that I found the system here more reassuring. For example, I was glad to see the same doctor every time I went in for examination, and to know that, barring some unusual crisis, that same doctor would deliver the baby. In England, one goes to the pre-natal clinic, and then into the hospital, dealing each time with whatever doctor or midwife happens to be on duty. Of course, the National Health makes it affordable to have a baby (or any other condition requiring medical attention!) in England even without the insurance that only a job can make affordable in the USA.

John was amused on his first visit to our obstetrician to see the luxury of the waiting room, and commented that each potted palm would represent an extra few hundred unnecessary dollars on our bill. For himself, he sought out an Army-trained physician whose waiting room was shabby and full of people hawking and spitting. He said it was more like home. Of course, it made no difference in the bill, but it seemed to make him happy.

Speaking of babies, our daughter Elinor, as the first real citizen of Rooksland (apart from the founding father and mother) represents an important change in our lives. We are no longer as willingly peripatetic as we used to be; although we would like, at some time, to spend a few months teaching in Ghana, and Poland, we'd be less cavalier about making a decision to go someplace where we weren't absolutely certain of being able to get whatever she might need in the way of medical attention, schooling, and food, and we feel (probably mistakenly) that her needs are less flexible than ours. She makes us, too, more hungry for a house and yard of our own, and for the security of knowing that we have work not only for this year, but for next year, and the next twenty years.

Even so, we hope that she won't spend all of her life in one place, and that it will always strike her as rather comical that she should have been born in Ames, Iowa. We want her to be a traveler as we are travelers--not restless and rootless, but able to make her home wherever she may find herself. She will probably grow up in America, but we would be very sorry if her perceptions were limited by the American tendency to be not only ill-informed about, but unaware of and unconcerned about anyplace else. We hope that we will be able to forestall such blinkeredness in her--deliberately, by doing such things as taking her with us where we go (certainly, with frequency, to England--she's already spent five weeks there); and also, less systematically, simply by our living example.

Our anecdotes and traveler's tales, as well as the differences between us, should help her to recognize that not everybody looks and sounds and thinks alike. Also, we tend, by some sort of osmosis, to attract people from different places, so that our friends represent a fairly broad spectrum of nationalities, races, and backgrounds. Since this tendency is likely to continue wherever we live, she should grow up with that combination of open-mindedness and fiercely smug personal pride that we feel distinguishes us.

John

Leaving home is one thing; being banished is quite another. Of course, banishment means that you cannot return and thus promotes a sense of loss and feeds, without chance of release, any natural nostalgia. But, more than this, it suggests that you didn't develop as you should given the stock from which you grew and the soil which nourished you. You are a briar rather than a rose, and the careful gardener prunes you off the stock.

It doesn't really matter whether you are driven out by an angry medieval king or a twentieth century government that removes your means of livelihood: the effect is the same. Had we removed directly from England to America when we finished our doctoral work, Pamela would have been coming home and I would have been coming into banishment.

Since there was no reasonable chance of finding suitable work in England in 1981, and no prospect of our ever being able to do so, we simply had to leave if we could. We could, because we had America. But, under such circumstances, our choice would have been constrained; we would not have been acting freely. America would have looked like a bolt hole where convenience obliged us to seek immediate refuge. Whether we should have stayed or not, I cannot tell. But I suspect I should have made efforts to find some acceptable third country which we might both have chosen as our new native land.

As it happened, I was not banished from England nor was I constrained to flee to America. I was given a period of grace in Nigeria and this allowed me to choose. I chose to be an expatriate and should remain one, paradoxically enough, even if we returned to England to live.

What I learned in Nigeria was very salutary. In the first place, it quickly became evident that national origin was not a personality trait, or even a bundle of behavioral dispositions. Knowing that someone was British, American, Nigerian, Ghanaian, Polish, or what-have-you did not allow you to predict whether they would be decent companions or whether they would help you out in difficulty. It seems strange, now, that I might ever have thought to the contrary. Perhaps I saw myself clinging to the little British-American community (longing nostalgically for a red coat with brass buttons, murmuring "steady, lads") and was surprised when this didn't happen.

I was certainly surprised when, after my first day's teaching, I was invited out for a drink by a Ghanaian and a Nigerian teacher whom I had never seen before. At the end of an evening talking literature and philosophy, I realized that (my English acquaintances notwithstanding) I'd just made my first two friends and had had the best conversation since I'd left home six weeks previously.

Yet more remarkable was the second lesson. At the end of the first year of our tour of duty, we took Christmas leave in the States. Primarily this was to look for some work that we might take up when we'd finished our contracts in Africa. It was good to be in a land of running water, electricity and general physical ease. But I was homesick for Nigeria--for our house, our jobs, our friends, our independence. On our return to Sokoto, after an interminable drive up from Kano, the huge, absurd, orange concrete fish that served as a sign for the Sokoto Hotel at the edge of town was a sight more dear than the Houses of Parliament or the Statue of Liberty.

Thereafter, wherever Pamela and I had jobs, a house, and friends would be home.

The third lesson was that, to make it a permanent home, all that was required was that our work should be secure and fulfilling. Since it is not possible to be an effective scholar in our fields without access to proper library facilities and a study with a tolerable temperature, this narrowed down our choice quite considerably. And America, if it would offer us work, seemed to fit our needs very well.

The fourth and final relevant lesson was that I had the patience to be a successful expatriate. In England I had no patience whatsoever with shopkeepers, transport officials, electricians, restaurateurs, with anyone. Abroad, I have the patience of a saint. And this is essential for, otherwise, you quickly come to blame the buffets of daily fortune on foreignness rather than humanness and want to leave. Even England, when I last visited, seemed far less exasperating than I remembered.

If you're living in a foreign country, it helps to be married to a native. As once I felt both thrilled and smug to be in Dosso negotiating in French with a Niger security guard, so now I feel a surge of excitement and self-satisfaction at finding myself in Chicago or Kansas City, Seattle or New York--places I'd heard of as a child but never expected to visit. If I'm there on my own, it's sufficient to drive round the Loop or visit a local market to feel my sensibilities quite electrified. But Pamela is less easily impressed, so we actually get to visit some museums and see some theatre.

Beyond that, of course, she is showing me her New York, her mother's Chicago, her sister's Indianapolis, her brother's Denver and their familial Michigan and North Carolina. Because of their associations with her, these places have a worth and a solidity that they would not otherwise possess. The Rockies exist in my imagination not because they look like pictures in a calendar, but because I infuriated her brother by not being able to distinguish between Pike's Peak and Cripple Creek.

Most importantly, she is a constant reminder that my children can grow up here and still be the sort of people I'll want to have dinner with. Perhaps I shouldn't need reminding for, true to my Nigerian lesson, I am not aware that our friends are American and, I hope, they are not aware that I am British. But perhaps one of the things I value in her is that she, too, was and could be again, an expatriate. Probably I rather hope that my children will regale me with absurd and touching stories about Malaysia and Brazil when I visit them in Lancashire or Oregon--or somewhere else that has electricity, running water, and decent libraries.

When we married in England in 1979, it was our dream or, rather (given the unemployment situation that already prevailed and was drastically to worsen), our fantasy to divide our working lives between England and the States. Had that come to pass, our cross cultural experience would, I suspect, have been very different. We should have been lifetime tourists: each country would have remained forever new but perhaps our vision would have narrowed, as it seems to with tourists, to the condition of the bathrooms and the quality of the beer.

John and Pamela

When we told our bank manager in Michigan that we were moving to Iowa, she threw back her head and roared with laughter. After three years in Iowa, students were still asking us why we were there, and seemed a little hurt and disappointed when we said that we came for the jobs. Few people seem satisfied with the explanation that we went to Nigeria to practice our trade and earn some money; that we weren't motivated by Christian concern, Marxist solidarity, post-colonial guilt or neo-colonial cultural imperialism.

In a different world, our wanderings might have taken us to the same places for different reasons, or to quite different places for the same reason. But in this world, since we started to work, we have followed the lodestone of employment. We each wanted a career as a professor of English; we were not prepared to live apart during the working week; and if you want to obtain two university jobs in English in the same location, you've got to cast your net wide. And you've got to be lucky: we have been delighted by the great good fortune that has kept us employed in the same departments for the last twelve years. Long may it continue--here, or there, or elsewhere.

So much for where we live, but surely that has very little to do with whom we married. Surely we didn't marry because we each had a commitment to English literature and a background in philosophy. Not altogether, but that was a large part of it. Initially, we were much more surprised to be marrying someone in the same discipline than to be marrying a foreigner. Our work is also our fun; of course, we gossip and chit-chat like everyone else, but over breakfast, after dinner, in the car, in the pub what we talk about is most likely literature and philosophy--or, in a lighter vein, our students. We disagree on just about everything except the fundamental moral values of these concerns, and so we can argue endlessly and creatively. Now, what you learn very quickly as a university student is that it is extremely difficult to find a partner who wants to share that kind of fun and is sexy too. So, you date a classicist or an economist and keep the academic talk for your colleagues. Our fates were finally sealed one Saturday afternoon by an argument over aesthetics while in a small railway station in West Yorkshire. For the first and last time in eight years, John conceded defeat and proposed a week later.

So, is it just that our domiciles and nationalities make us cross-cultural while our marriage is emphatically mono-cultural? Not at all, for Pamela's approach to literature and philosophy is very much in the American-Continental tradition while John's approach is rooted in British empiricism. The two traditions have very little to say to each other and the wonder is that our dialogue has proceeded so cheerfully. Of course, it is attended by our love and respect for each other and it takes place on our true common ground--our love and respect for ideas about the human experience.

Given our interest and our fondness for arguing about them it seems, with hindsight, that we were bound to marry into another culture, or another sub-culture, if we were to be truly happy. Given the nature of our work and our desire to see each other suitably employed, and the times into which we were born, it seems inevitable that we should move into and across cultures different from our own. However, since we know how very nearly we did not come together before Pamela had retired back across the ocean (she had been planning to return to the States in December to finish the thesis there; we married in January) and John had retired into his British insularity--probably never, even, to visit France--it all seems less a matter of cultural imperatives and more a matter of love conquering all.

CHAPTER 15

BEYOND THE HOMELANDS: A EURO-ASIAN MARRIAGE IN AFRICA

Leendert Jan and Mady Slikkerveer-Oey Kiat Lien

Despite the fact that both of us were born on two islands of the Indonesian Archipelago, Java and Sumatra, we came a long way from different Chinese-Indonesian and Frisian-Dutch cultures to meet and marry in the Netherlands. In addition to reflecting on the position of the mixed marriage within the cultural context of either one or the other partner, we will also focus on the interaction of our love match with a third "culture of residence," namely Sub-Saharan Africa.

Our experience has shown that the initial Dutch and Indonesian reactions to our mixed marriage differ considerably from the responses of African society where we have lived periodically for quite some time. How did the perceptions of our "new" community in East Africa differ from those of our relatives and friends in the two homelands, and what impact did they have on our relationship?

Mady, the second child of the third generation of Chinese immigrants from South China to Indonesia, was born after the Second World War in Bandung. Her father, a stern lecturer at the Universitas Padjadjaran, considered cultural enrichment of highest importance in his life and that of his family. As part of the local elite, most Chinese intellectuals associated easily with the Dutch ruling class in the colonial Dutch East-Indies. This interaction - apart from its economic considerations - resulted in serious interest of many Indonesians in Dutch culture. As a consequence, Mady and her brothers and sisters became well-acquainted with Dutch culture and language amidst the process of "Indonesianisation" which took place as the post-war society evolved into the independent Republic of Indonesia. Mady's bi-lingual and multi-cultural orientation paved the way for her further academic education in the Netherlands, where she presently is completing her Ph.D. dissertation on Languages and Cultures of Southeast Asia and Oceania at the University of Leiden.

Her strong Chinese identity, her participation in the emerging Indonesian consciousness, together with her familiarity with Dutch culture certainly influenced her to marry outside the traditional Chinese environment.

Immediately before the outbreak of World War II, Jan was born in Padang, Sumatra. Almost immediately after birth he was taken as a baby into a Japanese concentration camp together with his sister and mother. His father, who had come to Indonesia during the early twenties as a schoolteacher, was imprisoned for four years in another concentration camp for males on the same island. Despite incredible hardships and suffering, they all managed to survive the camps and after liberation, the family reunited and resettled in the capital of Batavia, now Jakarta, until 1950. The environment of the camp provided Jan with the opportunity to meet other children from different cultures. The camp experience fostered a strong, restless frontier spirit in Jan, generating an interest to reach out into other circles and cultures, to meet people of other backgrounds, and to learn about their views and lifestyles.

In addition to his strong alliance with his native land, where he regards himself almost as a "White Indonesian from a Dutch Tribe," his early confinement has certainly contributed to the urge in his later life always to go beyond "the fence" and meet with people from the other side.

His primary school years in Jakarta brought him into close contact with children from other ethnic groups, cross-cultural experiences which enriched his early childhood in a rapidly changing society in the tropics. After repatriation to Holland, the family moved several times, creating other opportunities for Jan to meet and make friends in both rural and urban post-war Dutch society. After his secondary education and compulsory military service, he traveled throughout Europe and the United States before entering into the study of anthropology and development sociology at the University of Leiden.

While his sister Anneke and her husband emigrated to the West Cost of the U.S.A., Jan began to develop a keen interest in Africa, particularly East Africa and the Horn of Africa, where different groups and cultures have been living on the cross-roads of Asia and Europe. It is therefore not surprising that immediately after receiving his M.A. in 1974, he took the challenge to leave for field research in Ethiopia in the medical social sciences. Although the country went through great turmoil in the 1974 revolution, he managed to complete his work among the Muslim Oromo, and to continue his Ph.D. research among different ethnic groups in the Ogaden Desert, only interrupted by short visits to Leiden to lecture and perform his duties at the university.

We first met at a workshop on Indonesian languages at the University of Leiden in 1973, giving us the opportunity to exchange our common Dutch-Indonesian experience. Most remarkably, however, we both rather quickly noticed our inclination to search beyond that experience, and dream to enter into other worlds.

Within the academic environment of the university, and especially within the circles of both the Faculty of Letters and the Faculty of the Social Sciences, intensive contacts among students - whose interests were first and foremost overseas-oriented - were not only rather common, but added to the special cosmopolitan feeling among the staff and students. As the Departments of Anthropology and Southeast-Asian Languages were located in the same university building, its members often got together for coffee or lunch, and discourses on Asia and Africa were common.

From within this canteen niche we started to develop a personal, mutual affection. Over time this flourished further within the students' brown cafes which made Leiden so popular among young intellectuals in the seventies. When Jan left for post-graduate training in the U.S.A. at Florida State University in the field of environmental studies and the medical social sciences, Mady entered into the study of classical Arabic. Their separation seemed to strengthen their affection. Jan sent his diary back home to Mady, and his exciting experiences of the post-powerflower era in the States prompted Mady to visit her cousin in New York. They enjoyed the feeling of multi-cultural communication across the Atlantic Ocean.

After several years of close friendship, strong personal affection and love, and a steady sharing of work, hobbies and lifestyles, we decided to pursue a marriage bond in the Netherlands. The initial decision to enter into a cross-cultural marriage forced us to reflect on the general hesitation among traditional Dutch groups towards "gemengde huwelijken," religiously mixed marriages between Roman Catholic and Protestant partners. This attitude influenced the post-war attitude of Dutch society towards Indo-European marriages. The strong cohesion and closed character of the Chinese community abroad also affected our case. The long-term cross-cultural communication between us and between and among our parents, relatives, and friends elicited not so much the differences in our background, but on the contrary focused on the common aspects of our background, paving the way and even encouraging our matrimony.

As regards the religious element in our relationship, we have different backgrounds. While Mady's family had become Roman Catholic in Indonesia, Jan's family had been Protestant from the early days. Religion played an important role in daily life in both families. There was a steady ongoing process of secularisation in Dutch society after World War II. A growing tolerance towards non-Chinese religious traditions emerged in the Chinese community. The humanistic world view which Jan's parents had developed also facilitated the intermarriage for both family-groups.

Our mixed marriage thus confirmed a feeling of positive, cross-cultural identity, which became an instrument for forging a strong bond and even a feeling of a "special unit" in our everyday life.

Mady's father considered intimate friendships for his children as a threat to their intellectual development. He was also inclined to accept a son-in-law of Chinese origin. Quite surprisingly, he never objected to our friendship and eventually envisaged the marriage. Certainly, both our academic careers contributed to his approval of a non-Chinese partner for his daughter, taking into account his own academic work in Bandung and his appreciation and esteem for a life dedicated to science. Her mother, whose gentle character successfully guided the entire family's life both in Indonesia and in Holland, had put the personal happiness and fulfillment of her children in the first place. She never insisted on an in-group marriage, and in fact supported our relationship from the very beginning.

The mother of Jan involved herself very much with the education and socialization of her children after the miserable experience of the concentration camp. Like Mady's father, she adhered to the idea of an in-group marriage, based on her Frisian-Dutch roots and her social position in the colonial Dutch East-Indies. However, the first meeting with her future daughter-in-law, carefully arranged by her lifelong friend, proved to be a great success from the very beginning. Mady's bilingual orientation enabled her to adapt completely to the Dutch way of life, while retaining an Oriental dimension. This appealed very much to Jan's mother, who immediately sought to accentuate our common background re-associating herself with her "past culture" of the Dutch-Indonesian society, in which she had lived for more than a quarter of a century.

Jan's father, who had learned to appreciate the intellectual dedication of local elites in Indonesia, was pleased to respect his son's choice of a partner for life from a Chinese background. It seemed not only contributive to Jan's personal happiness, but also to his wider intellectual development. He was proud of our friendship, and saw a fortunate combination of appreciation of our common homeland with spiritual ambitions for our future.

The reactions of our wider family circles and friends, for whom the announcement of a formal wedding did not come as a surprise, were very encouraging, despite the fact that mixed marriages among our friends were the exception. Although we had tried to keep the actual wedding ceremony confined to stylish simplicity in a snow-covered Wassenaar, a tremendous party eventually inaugurated a new and challenging era in our life.

Our mixed marriage life has been characterized by extensive travels within Europe, and due to our professions, by different longer sojourns in Asia, Africa, and the United States. Apart from our short-term reunions with relatives in the homelands during fieldwork carried out in Sulawesi and West Java in Indonesia, and regular visits to our relatives in the U.S.A., we wish to focus next on our experience with the African "culture of residence," where we have stayed together for almost a year in East Africa.

In East Africa, in particular Ethiopia and Kenya, mixed marriages are still the exception rather than the rule. In Ethiopia most mixed marriages with foreigners are well-accepted, and mostly consist of Italian and Armenian husbands who married women predominantly from the Amhara ethnic groups. In Kenya, we met mixed marriages between British, Italian and Dutch men and Kikuyu women, but these were very few.

As in most African societies, <u>one</u> specific type of man-woman relationship does not exist in either Ethiopia or Kenya. Generally, the population differentiates between two variants of marriage, whether mixed or homogeneous: the harmonic and the disharmonic marriage. These variants have been described by anthropologists such as Epping (1975) and Jongmans (1978).

The harmonic marriage is described in both the Bible and the Koran, but it is difficult to assess in its African context because of its highly private character. In the Koran, the Prophet accentuates the respectful, sexual relationship between partners, which forges mutual confidence beyond sexuality into daily life. The woman, respected in her sexual rights at night, will comply with her daily duties, as her husband will accordingly respect his wife during daytime. Discussions and consultations in bed on important matters between husband and wife will continue in daily life, enabling the husband to combine authority with respect. This respect often includes his attitude not to interfere with her household matters, finances, preparation of food and shopping. In situations of conflict, reproof, sexual abstinence, and eventually involvement of the partners' mothers and fathers will provide a beneficial therapy for the harmonic marriage, on which the blessing of God rests, and which richness and social respect awaits the future.

The disharmonic marriage, which is characterized by an often imperious husband, who treats his wife with no consideration and who expects his will to be law in the family is sometimes easily stereotyped. However, it is generally accepted that such a husband's position is merely based on superiority, power, and intimidation. In such disharmonic marriages, affection and love is lacking, the wife feels herself an object, and the marriage is a potential danger to the order of the community. This particular type of male dominance in marriage, described for Africa and the Arabic world, links up with the widely recorded machismo-complex referring to a sexually active husband and a passive, submissive wife.

During our stay in Africa we felt that - in contrast with our European and Indonesian experience - our mixed marriage was not so much assessed and evaluated according to intercultural or interracial factors, but rather according to the harmonic or disharmonic characteristics of a marriage between members of a different culture. There were several cross-cultural and interracial marriages within

Ethiopian and Kenyan society, in which Christian, Muslim and indigenous African religions were united in marital relationships. Cross-cultural marriages existed between Oromo, Amhara, Luo, Kikuyu, Swahili, and even Arabic partners. Although in-group marriage was still favored for obvious cultural, socio-economic and political reasons, the mere fact of inter-ethnic marriage has socially been well-accepted for several decades.

In this context, mixed marriages have generally been viewed from the in-group perspective. Behavior towards individuals has indeed been regulated from a point of reference, if that individual is - or can become - a member of the in-group. It comprises respect, considerate behavior ("proper conduct") and is based on exchange of services and (sometimes) goods.

The out-group refers to the lack of a viable relationship, one without behavior-regulating rules, and characterized by negligence and rivalry. Interestingly, the reaction to our mixed marriage has lacked such in- and out-group reference: we both come from different non-East African cultures and by consequence belong to the out-group. We, however, have undergone a rather intimate in-group acceptance within our neighborhood, especially in terms of abundant help, understanding, and exchange of services and goods, where we were expected to comply with proper conduct and in-group behavior, as far as our interaction was concerned.

From such a tolerant community, we experienced most positive reactions to our mixed marriage. Although we ourselves regarded the love-basis of our relationship pivotal, and by definition an example of a harmonic marriage, our African social environment based its assessment more on both of our individual attitudes and behavior. Our neighbor's expression, "if you're dominant in life, you're dominant in marriage," approaches the type of marriage from the outgroup-perspective. In most Asian and European societies, the type of marriage is chosen on the basis of the inner relationships within the family. By consequence, Mady was always treated with respect and admiration, which was expressed in recurrent appraisals of her "white skin," her "beautiful jewelry" and her "good cooking."

We feel that our experience in the predominantly rural society of East Africa has enriched our personal perceptions of a mixed marriage far beyond the appraisals we received in our homelands. It exceeds the very popular and complimentary reactions we enjoyed from the international diplomatic and business community with whom we socialized in the capital. In fact, it gave both of us a very special African dimension to the classical expression in anthropology: "by looking to other cultures, one learns more about one's own."

PART IV:

IMMERSION IN A NEW CULTURE: LIVING AND WORKING ABROAD

CHAPTER 16

THE GHANAIAN-NAMIBIAN CONNECTION IN ZAMBIA
Leslie and Elizabeth Bruce-Lyle

Leslie

We first had initial difficulties in that Elizabeth belonged to a liberation movement, SWAPO, which actively discouraged marriage of their womenfolk to male non-Namibians who were generally described as foreigners! Many obstacles were thus placed in our way but that probably strengthened our relationship.

Our marriage was only possible because it took place in Ireland and is accepted by both our parents and our friends which is what matters to us. The attitudes of people from both our countries who were against marrying from a foreign country have, since the marriage, come to accept it and have been quite supportive.

Since we are both black and have the same religious beliefs with a similar culture, we really do not see our marriage as a mixed one! People meeting us at first glance will also not know of it being a mixed marriage until we start speaking to each other.

Since we speak completely different languages, we communicate in English all the time. There were initial difficulties at first since it happens to be Elizabeth's third language learned only a few years before we met in 1979. She has now become so proficient in expressing herself that difficulty no longer exists. One change in attitude has been for all our visitors from either of our countries to always speak English when we are both present rather than lapse into each other's own languages.

Our attitudes to types of food has had to change and in that we have coped quite well. I come from a part of my country where food is tasteless if it does not have really hot peppers. Also, coming from the coastline we tend to enjoy and eat a lot of fish. Elizabeth on the other hand comes from a part of her country where the main emphasis appears to be on milk, yoghurt, meat and maize meal. They cannot stand anything hot or spicy! I have learned to be tolerant of the occasional meal without pepper and she fortunately has learned to cook all the kinds of food we eat in my country.

In both our cultures, in spite of education and some influence of the western way of life, the traditional role of the male has been as the breadwinner and that of the female has been to look after the home and children which should not be unduly negatively affected even if she has a job as well. This has been the case in our situation.

One pattern since our marriage has been the chance of meeting many couples of cross cultural marriages. We seem to have made many more friends from foreign countries and very few new friends from our own countries. This is probably because one becomes more easily acceptable to people from other countries and vice versa when it is realized that you actually live together with someone from a different country. This was especially evident to us during our almost three year stay in Ireland. Mixed marriages in Ireland tend to be between Protestant and Catholics. They can be fraught with immense difficulties for the couple due to the very strong influence of the Catholic Church. Indeed I found that an interracial marriage between a black African and a white Irish girl was much more easily acceptable to the society if they were both Catholic than the aforementioned case.

However, once the Irish realize that two people from different cultural backgrounds were living together they felt they could trust you to accept them as friends rather than as just people whose country you lived in. Some of our most true and trusted friends to this day are from the Emerald Isle.

For most cross cultural marriages we have come across, one important point seems to be whether to live in the husband's country or the wife's country. This was especially evident in marriages between Ghanaians and Nigerians and there was a more difficult problem if both the partners had a profession. On the other hand it also gave the partners (as it did us) a more global outlook to life enabling one to make small sacrifices to live where it suited both partners especially where schooling is involved.

Having lived in Ghana and Zambia and being separated from my parents 80% of the time except when I went to work in Zambia for five years, I have been prepared to live anywhere that suited me professionally. However, my wife has only recently come to grips with the idea of having to live far from home since she is of the opinion that the borders of her country may soon be opened so she can go home and see her mother! For that reason she would prefer that whenever possible we live close to Namibia so she can slip over easily from time to time!

What languages are the children to speak at home? I know one couple where the mother spoke one language to the son while the father spoke his. The son thus speaks two different languages to both parents. We are aiming to do the same to our son (18 months) when he first picks up the English language fluently! That will probably ensure I'm home more often to keep my language up!

Things one takes for granted such as naming of children suddenly could become a problem. A Ugandan friend of mine who happened to be Muslim and his wife Catholic named his two sons after his side of the family while the daughters were named after the wife's family. However, the two sons were made Muslim and the two girls Catholic. My side of the family will name the sons and my wife's will name the daughters, if we have any!

Part of the reason for our coping well is that cross-cultural marriages are nothing new in my family and are quite common in my country. My grandfather (paternal) was a white Scotsman and my grandmother (paternal) a coloured Ghanaian. I therefore grew up in an environment where this was nothing strange. One of my cousins who was in the army married a Japanese lady. Until their divorce two years ago my own sister was married to a Sri Lankan and their divorce was more due to a disagreement over my sister's career than any problem to do with cross-culture or different race.

Personally my perception of a cross-cultural marriage (and I stand accused of being prejudiced!) is that although there may be difficulties in understanding certain attitudes of behavior in the two different families, I find this easier to handle than an association from one's own country. In such a situation both families tend to think they know too much about each other and with this familiarity comes a contempt and unnecessary meddling in the couple's affairs. Cross-cultural marriages when accepted by both families brings with it a familiarity but at a respectable distance thereby leaving the couple to get on with their own lives.

I also feel from personal experience and from what I have seen of a few interracial and cross-cultural marriages is that both parties must be very honest about their cultures and if possible seeing it at first hand before plunging into it.

I have known some Irish women who think they are marrying Nigerian or Ghanaian princes only to be shocked when they get back to Africa and return badly traumatized. This has led to a change in attitude of white girls who now take every tale of 'being the son of a chief' with a pinch of salt; and rightly so!

Elizabeth

I left Namibia about 19 years ago. It was quite hard for me to make such a decision. At the end I felt that I had finally made up my mind, even though I had to leave my family behind; my mother, my three sisters and two brothers. We are six children in the family of which I am the fifth.

Such an idea came to my mind when I listened to Radio Namibia every Sunday afternoon that was broadcasted from Zambia. I then heard voices of some people whom I knew who left the country a few months earlier. Stories were told around that those people were dead. Surely if they were, how come some of them were able to speak on the radio, telling us in the country to go and join them? If they were dead, then what I heard over the radio were ghosts' voices. That did not change my mind a bit; it rather encouraged me to get going.

The day I left I felt very sad that I really had to leave my family behind, especially my mother whom I had not seen for four years at that time, in total now for 23 years, because I lived with my elder sister in Windhoek and my mum lives in the north in Ovambo where we were born. Our father died quite long ago. I was very young at that time and cannot remember much about him. I left with a lady whom I knew well. She is my aunt. Her husband was involved in organizing SWAPO political meetings, and he was arrested several times by the South African police. At the end he felt that his life was in danger and had to leave the country. Later on his wife also decided to make a move to escape some kind of harassment from the forces. She then asked me if I was interested to leave the country. We kept it a secret because during that time you could not trust anybody, as people were reporting those who gave the impression of wanting to leave the country to Zambia. I told my sister because I trusted her. She thought I was joking and did not take me seriously. I told her a month in advance before I left. I had even obtained a permit that I was going to visit my mum in the north so that when we pass at the gate in Tsumeb, we wouldn't have problems.

I never said anything to her since. At that time I was then staying at the nurses' hostel because I had just started a nurses' training course and went home only on weekends when I was off. The day I left I wrote a letter to my sister telling her where I'd gone so that she wouldn't be worried and left it with one of my friends. I told my friend that I was going to Walvis Bay for a day and that she should give the letter and my room key to my sister when she went to work. My sister also worked in the hospital as a registered nurse, so it wasn't difficult for my friend to find her. In the letter I also asked my sister to take the rest of my stuff home and leave the key in the room; otherwise, she would be in trouble if the authorities found out that she knew where I'd gone.

I left to go to my auntie's house with my small bag. It wasn't too far, only ten minutes' walk, and nobody suspected anything because it was my day off and I was due to start my night shift in two days time. As soon as I got there, the car was ready. My aunt had told me that we'd travel with some other people. We left as soon as possible heading north. We drove through the night up to the borders of Namibia and Angola. We off loaded our luggage and crossed into Angola. We had to be careful then because South African soldiers patrolled along the borders. We were very lucky. We didn't come across the soldiers. We walked till we came to a small village where we were provided with shelter until the next morning. We felt safe and were relieved, because once you'd crossed into Angola no one can bother you. The people in the village told us where to catch the bus that would take us to a town. They seemed to know a lot as they had helped many others through the same route. We went to wait for the bus that took us to a town called Ongiva. We found many Namibians there who were waiting for transport to be dropped at the borders of Angola and Zambia. We were put up in a hostel. It was then UNITA who was in control at that time, and we received help throughout our stay there. They helped us in terms of food and accommodation which were provided free. This was quite a great help because many people, especially the youngsters, had no money to buy food.

When the day came when we were to leave, everybody was happy because we thought we were going straight to Lusaka, the capital city of Zambia. In fact, people who arrived in Angola before us told us that we'd be dropped at the borders of Angola and Zambia. From there we would then travel by air - BOEING 707 - to Lusaka. I couldn't possibly tell you who told them all this. I was so excited by the idea of travelling by air because I've never been on a plane before.

We got into trucks about eight in the morning. It took us about four to five hours to reach a small town where the trucks left us. We had lunch and got into other trucks which took us up to the borders. We arrived there at six o'clock in the evening. We were told to get down and off load our belongings. The soldiers told us that they can't take us any further; we would have to continue our journey by foot into Zambia. They off loaded boxes and told us they contained biscuits, tinned food and tablets. The tablets, as we were told, were for diarrhea in case anybody got it. Some people then had the courage to ask about the Boeing 707 which was supposed to have been there waiting for Namibians travelling to Zambia. The soldiers told us that they never heard of the Boeing 707. Most of us were so disappointed, because we really looked forward to boarding a plane for the first time in our lives! Never mind, we just forgot about that and were then thinking about the journey ahead. None of us had any idea how long it would take to reach Lusaka. We started sharing the food which was left for us by UNITA soldiers. They told us that we must get going because nobody knows when the plane would come if there was any.

We set off and walked for about three or four hours before we came to a village. We met a man with a gun who asked us where we were going. We told him we were going to Lusaka to join SWAPO. He spoke our language, which was Oshiwambo. He told us that he belonged to SWAPO and that he would take us to a house where we would spend a night and also have something to eat. The owners of the house were Zambians and were very kind people. They gave us food and after the meal we dropped to sleep since we were very tired. The following day the gentlemen who brought us to this house told us that many people passed there daily and that we should all follow one road that would lead us to where the rest who left the country before us were. He said they were all well looked after.

We walked for about two and half weeks before reaching the place. Throughout our journey we got a tremendous support from the Zambian villagers in terms of food, water and shelter. Often, some of those who had many things like clothes had to give some to the villagers in exchange for food. Since we were a large group, they could not really feed all of us. Also, people who had a lot of things such as clothes helped those who didn't have anything to buy food. They had to do this because their luggage became too heavy. Nobody expected to walk, and many people had their cases full of clothes and other goods.

We walked throughout the hot day. Anyone who felt tired could sit down under the trees and continue again after the rest. There were families with small children who needed to be carried. They could not go faster, so I personally walked with them because I couldn't keep up with the pace of some of the people who were so anxious to get to Lusaka first, not knowing that the capital was nowhere near. If it got dark and we were unable to reach a village, we often slept under the trees in the middle of the jungle. When we met villagers, some people would ask how far Lusaka was. They'd say about 200 or 300 metres. Some of us didn't understand because English was quite Greek to us, especially to me. Those who understood a bit of it told us that it wouldn't be too long before we reached Lusaka. They we realized that the villagers didn't have a clue how far Lusaka was. We just forgot the idea of distances they told us. It was actually the same answer we got from everyone we asked along the road.

When we finally came to a lake and saw many people and washing hanging on bushes, we knew that we'd reached the place the gentleman had told us about earlier. We were so delighted and relieved that we'd finally reached somewhere. Of course, we had to cross this lake walking, but that didn't matter any more. It wasn't that deep because the water just came up to my waist. I was about 5'3" during that time. When we crossed, we met some of the people we knew right there. They either came to have their bath/wash or just to wash their clothes. We were taken by two men to the place where the others were. They said that there were always people at the lake waiting for the new arrivals.

When we reached the place, we were asked to put our names down. When we had done so, we went for a meeting to a quiet place under one of the trees to be filled in with the rules of do's and don'ts. We stayed here for about three months before moving to another place. This took longer because people have to be moved according to groups. Those who arrived first were taken first and so on. When the time came, I joined a group of about 80-90 people to another place where I stayed for two years. I'd learned a lot of things which completely changed my lifestyle towards almost everything in life. It is a pity that I am unable to discuss all I had done during the two years because of some circumstances beyond my control. One morning I was called and told that there was an English test to be taken in a few days time and that my name was put down. I was quite frightened and kept on asking myself what kind of questions would be asked. I didn't know English at all, because back home we were taught in Afrikaans, and we had only half an hour of English grammar periods daily. You couldn't really learn proper English from that apart from nouns and plurals, or filling in missing words such as is, was and so on.

Finally the day came, and I went and sat for the test with many others. We were told that those who pass the test would be going to join the United Nations Institute for Namibia in Lusaka. The test was quite tough for someone of my standard as far as the English was concerned. But, what really made my legs go jelly was when we were asked to write an essay about "Why I want to go and join the Institute for Namibia". The word Institute itself made me crumble. I just didn't know how to start, even though the person who conducted the test did everything he could to explain. Well, I got on with it. I can't quite recall what I wrote that day. When the results came, I was among those who made it. I just couldn't believe my ears when the news came.

Now I was rejoicing in my heart. At least I was going to see Lusaka which I've heard so much about. The day of the journey to Lusaka came, and we set off. It was a long journey, but that didn't matter as long as we were heading towards the capital. We finally arrived in Lusaka in the evening. We were then taken to our rooms and afterwards to a dining room. The next morning we proceeded with the formalities such as registering, followed by a meeting where we were filled in with the rules and regulations of the Institute. After all these, some friends and I decided to go and have a look at the city. It was very near the Institute, so we didn't need transport.

The first thing that shocked me was when I saw black and white people entering through the same door into the post office. I completely forgot that I was no more in a colonised Namibia, but in an independent country. I also saw coloured people who wore long dresses, but not really dresses. Apparently they were Indian women wearing saris. I then thought, what kind of coloureds they were. I asked some one who told me that they were Indians. I had never seen an Indian before. There were none in Namibia at the time I left, and if they were there, they probably were in other places in the country, but nobody ever talked about them. I began to discover many things that were new to me and took me a long time to accept that there were actually countries that have their own black leaders. I have learned quite a lot since them.

It was then when I was at the Institute that I met Leslie. We had been dating for five years before we finally got married. There were quite a lot of problems during those years from my side; not from my parents or relatives, but from my Namibian colleagues. The problem was that Leslie was a "foreigner." That put a lot of pressure on me, but at the end I didn't mind any more. I'd say that made our relationship even stronger. The day came when he proposed marriage. I was overjoyed. This happened when we were in Ireland, where I was doing a health administration course. He also came over to do postgraduate studies in Ophthalmology. That made it possible for us to have the ceremony.

I then wrote to my mother to tell her about it. She already knew about him while we were still in Zambia. She and my elder sister wrote back on behalf of my entire family confirming that we could go ahead with our plans. I was very happy that I got my family's blessing to enter marriage.

Our cultures are quite similar even though from different countries. The only difference is about food preparation. At first I had to prepare two separate meals. The reason being that he eats very hot food, these being stews. By hot I mean that the stew has to be prepared with plenty of chili powder or with fresh chilis and other spices. I was not used to that because back home we don't use hot spices, but now I'm used to it and enjoy it very much.

We have been happily married for three years now and have a lovely little boy who is nearly eight years old. About the naming of the children, I don't quite mind, because in my country it is the man who normally names the child. So it is up to my husband to decide.

CHAPTER 17

THE BRITISH-BARBADIAN CONNECTION IN AMERICA

Hugh and Maris Corbin

We are both individualists, taking pleasure in being different, in doing unusual things, in exploring out-of-the-ordinary byways. Perhaps this trait arose because we were both raised as members of a minority, but a minority with a strong group identity, and a certainty of its own values.

In Hugh's case the group was West Indian, specifically Barbadians who had emigrated to New York in the twenties and thirties but retained their own cultural identity, speech patterns, church affiliations, family ties, and their commitment to as much education as possible. They were proud of their island heritage and of its relatively tolerant, multi-racial society, and they thought always of Barbados as "home." Although they lived in the Black ghetto of Harlem they considered themselves to be first and foremost Barbadians. They worked hard and saved money to buy their own homes and to pay for a good education for the next generation. Their culture was more British than American, most were Episcopalians, and their educational standard tended to be higher than the Black Americans around them; therefore it was easy for them to maintain their separateness and a feeling of the rightness of their ways, and from their secure base it was easier for them to go out into and identify with the White American society.

In Maris's case the group was a religious one: British Quakers. The Quakers are a tiny minority in England but they tend to be well-educated and reasonably affluent, and to form a close-knit group with a sense of mission to assist those who are less fortunate, of whatever race or nationality. Their traditions date back to the seventeenth century, and include a belief in the worth of every human being, and in pacifism. During World War II, Maris's father was exempted from being conscripted into the armed forces because of his occupation. Her mother would have had to do some kind of war work, but because of her pacifist beliefs felt that her time would be better spent in studying to become a doctor. Maris was sent to boarding school at age eight, and her mother eventually obtained her medical degree.

Hugh's background and Maris's, therefore, had certain things in common. Our families both saw themselves as middle-class and financially stable. We came from closely-knit minority groups which were secure in their own traditions. We were used to being different, but had been raised with a sense that our ways were good ways. Both in Barbados and among Quakers there was a multi-racial tradition--a sense that each person was an individual whether Black or White. Neither of us had been conditioned to an awareness of racial barriers, and we were used to doing things which would be considered unusual by the majority. And yet on the surface, in matters of everyday living, both we and our parents have tended to conform to our surroundings. To our colleagues and neighbors we have appeared to merge into the background because we have followed an anonymous middle-class lifestyle, in clothing, housing, cars, United Way drives, bake sales, and so on.

Our school experiences added to our sense of being in a minority and different. Hugh's parents felt that the best elementary school education available in Harlem was in the Catholic parochial schools, and although he was not Catholic they were able to enroll him in a nearby one. From there he went on to the Bronx High School of Science, where he was the only Black student in his year and where his interests were in the arts and not at all in science. Since the school was almost all Jewish, his friends were Jewish, and at one point he developed an interest in the Ethical Culture Society and attended some of their activities for high school students.

Maris went to an English girls' private school with its dedication to team sports, which she thoroughly disliked and was hopeless at, and she was the only Quaker. Once or twice she attempted to present the Quaker pacifist position on war--this was during World War II-- which was naturally received very negatively, and she gained a reputation as an eccentric.

On leaving high school in the early fifties we each followed unorthodox paths. We were both idealists who were discontented with the social and political events around us.

Hugh spent two years in college, then became a part-time student at various institutions, including the New School for Social Research. While at college he joined an Episcopal discussion group because he was exploring the possibility of becoming a minister. But he was plagued by extreme idealism which finally led him to move away from the Church and to join pacifist and non-violent action groups. He lived for short periods in two intentional communities and traveled through the South with an interracial student group in 1956. The longest and most satisfying association was with the Quaker American Friends Service Committee.

Maris worked for a time as a nurse's aide in a hospital in England, lived with a family in Austria, worked as a secretary and then became articled to a lawyer in London. She lived in a Quaker international center in London, where her friends included a Ghanaian and a Pakistani. She participated in political demonstrations, and during vacations took part in voluntary work camps, run by the Quakers and other groups, in a number of European countries with participants from all over the world. Finding herself unable to comprehend enough about Trust Accounts and Bookkeeping to pass the mandatory exam, she rather thankfully gave up her legal training and headed for a secretarial job in the United States. She had met so many Americans in the European voluntary work camps that she wanted to experience their country for herself.

We met in East Harlem, New York City. After arriving in New York, Maris had started to participate in weekend work camps run by the American Friends Service Committee in Spanish Harlem. The weekend work camps were successful and the AFSC decided to sponsor a group of young people who would actually live in the East Harlem area, thus experiencing the problems of a slum neighborhood at first hand, and who would spend their free time in helping local people to work on the problems. Hugh learned of the group through his volunteer work with the AFSC. We joined the group independently, and both found it an extremely rewarding and enlightening experience. After about eighteen months we decided to get married, and we left the group a short time later.

East Harlem, whose inhabitants were mainly Puerto Rican, was an ideal environment for nurturing an interracial marriage. We were living surrounded by people of every possible skin color, with the Spanish tradition of being non-judgemental as to racial appearance, and who in any case had far more serious problems on their minds, such as how to get the landlord to provide heat, or how to get a decent job or to learn to read English. The Quaker group was also very supportive of our relationship.

The reaction of Hugh's family was positive towards the marriage because Maris was British and well-educated and thus an affirmation of West Indian-American values and goals. Maris's family was initially reluctant because they realized their daughter would be living so far away, but they soon came to accept the situation.

We were married in 1959 in the Episcopal cathedral by the priest who had known Hugh well in the college discussion group, and who valiantly quelled his rather obvious doubts about the long-term viability of such a marriage in his counseling session with us. He must also have been doubtful about performing the ceremony since neither of us any longer attended any church; also Maris was to be given away by a Quaker and our best man and bridesmaid were both Jewish. But Hugh's family was there in force and they were Episcopalian.

While we were with the group in East Harlem, Hugh had taught in a local public school, and he has remained a teacher on various levels ever since.

After our marriage we lived in a racially mixed area of Manhattan until the birth of our first son, when we moved to a small town in Vermont--where race was certainly not an issue. In fact, the town was absorbed in a struggle between the long-time conservative residents and the more recently arrived liberals and radicals from urban areas, and it was totally irrelevant that there were three interracial families (and only two Black ones) in the town. We sometimes had the impression during our years in Vermont that we were invited to gatherings not so much for ourselves as for the liberal seal of approval which the presence of an interracial couple gave, and that people were pleased to be able to show whose side they were on in the Civil Rights struggle. Perhaps this also applied in some small measure to the conservative Vermonters who were struggling to keep control of an area with so many newcomers. Our three closest neighbors were the postmaster, a retired farmer, and a storekeeper, and all of them were unfailingly friendly and helpful to us as neighbors.

Towards the end of our time there, a group of local mill workers put up a large sign on the main street which read "Commies, Pinks and Pacifists not wanted here--Vermont KKK." We were assured by responsible community leaders (who quickly had the sign removed) that the mill workers did not know what KKK meant, but knew only that it represented a reaction to liberal change, the thing which they were struggling so hard against. Our younger son, Marcus, was born in the town, and the older one attended first grade without ever being made to feel that he was in any way different.

Apart from one summer of leading an AFSC project in the Black ghetto of Los Angeles, we began to feel that our lives were out of touch with the problems of the wider world and the ideals we had tried to follow in our youth. This feeling, together with the climate of conservatism in the Vietnam War era--and a dislike on Maris's part of the long, cold Vermont winters!--decided Hugh to apply for a teaching position with the African-American Institute in an African country. In all, we spent eleven satisfying years in Zambia, Uganda, and Nigeria (with a break of three years while Hugh obtained his doctorate and another break of a year when we had to leave Uganda).

We found the expatriate communities in those countries to be completely accepting of interracial families--in fact there were so many interracial families it would have been hard to exclude them. (Many of the couples had one partner who was Black American and thus had a particular interest in being in Africa.) Perhaps it would have been different among the White settler farming communities of Kenya, Rhodesia, or even Zambia, although we were certainly welcomed by the equivalent stratum in the mining highlands of Nigeria. The Whites who were living in Nigeria and Uganda and Zambia at the time we were there, after independence, had largely come to terms with Black power and government, and the Black Africans seemed able to accept expatriates as temporary advisors and visitors, whether Black or White. There was no longer any official color bar anywhere.

We knew a number of expatriate couples whose marriages did not survive their time in Africa, usually because one partner enjoyed and adapted to the experience much better than the other, or it transpired that their expectations of expatriate life had been different. As far as we could see, this did not appear to be more of a hazard for interracial couples than for others. There were sometimes much more serious strains apparent in marriages where European or American women had married Africans and were trying to adjust to an African way of life on a permanent basis. Of course, we also knew of many successful such marriages, for instance the two British women married to a Nigerian Moslem dentist in Lagos.

Our decision to leave Nigeria and return to the United States was made on two grounds: the need for pensions and the fact that African countries are becoming less needful of expatriates to train their teachers. It was not easy for Hugh to get back into teaching in the U.S. at a time when the teaching field was contracting here, but our only preference was for the East coast where both our sons were in college. Eventually, to our surprise and somewhat to our trepidation, we found ourselves in North Carolina. At the time we left Vermont for Zambia, in 1967, North Carolina was only beginning on the long process of desegregation and the climate was hardly hospitable to interracial marriages. Most of what we knew of the South during the intervening years was what we had read in American and African newspapers, and they tended to report negative rather than positive incidents. However, this is a cosmopolitan and economically well-off city and we have not once, to our knowledge, experienced any kind of discrimination or negativity here, either in housing, work, or recreation.

Hugh became a teacher in a suburban public school with a student ratio of two-thirds White to one-third Black, but a much lower ratio of Black teachers. There is some racial tension among the teachers, the Black teachers usually keeping together and often discussing slights and discrimination, whether real or imagined. Occasionally, Hugh feels pressure from Black teachers to join group activities and to take their side. Reverse prejudice by White teachers, while well-meaning, sometimes causes him discomfort. Both of these situations are infrequent, and would not necessarily be noticed by a casual observer. Both Black and White teachers know that Maris is White but, whatever their feelings, have never commented on the fact.

Maris is lucky enough to be working in a large university which espouses the concept of racial integration, although its percentage of minority students and faculty is too low.

When it came to buying a house we expressed doubts to the real estate agent who took us round, an elderly woman who had lived here all her life, but she reassured us that there would be no problem, and there was not. We are living in a mainly White neighborhood of small houses, and our neighbors on each side were born and raised here. They are all extremely friendly, in fact the neighbors on one side have invited us to some of their family gatherings, and could not have been kinder. It is apparent that the South, or this part of it, has changed dramatically.

Because neither of us feels completely "American" we have always had a sense of standing apart from the places we have lived in since our marriage. This applied even more to the African countries of course. We have looked on them with an objectivity, and perhaps also an uncommittedness and alienness, which may have helped the cohesiveness of our marriage. Although Hugh was raised in Harlem, he does not strongly identify with the culture of Harlem or even particularly with the wider American culture. In fact, he feels happy and at home walking in the streets of London, and after one short visit to Barbados, Maris feels quite at home in Bridgetown and its surrounding countryside. One could say that our marriage has been forged by an amalgam of cultures: American, British and Caribbean, with a touch of African expatriate thrown in.

In practice, however, our friends are mainly White because these are the people with whom we have studied or worked. We have common interests with people who have traveled extensively, who are intellectuals, liberals, and who read widely. As we usually live in White communities, it is difficult to develop contacts with as many Black people as White people who fit this description. We remain close to two of Hugh's cousins who are both lawyers and whose upbringing was the same as his. We are both only children; Hugh's parents are dead, and Maris's father and other relatives are in England. Since her mother's death and her father's remarriage we have less contact with him.

There are great differences between British and Black West Indian family structure. For West Indians, the extended family is important, in contrast to the nuclear family which is the norm in England. While Hugh's mother was alive and we lived in New York and Vermont, we spent time with his aunts, uncles, and cousins. But the fact that we are only children and have lived in so many different places has meant that ours has become a small unit like Maris's in England. Maris's influence has undoubtedly meant that we live a quiet, self-contained life, but neither of us feels that it has been dull or uneventful, and we assume it will not be in the future.

Black West Indians are descended from West African slaves who in some cases came from matriarchal societies, but in any case were forced into a kind of matriarchy by the slavery system. The mother was the stable part of the family and often dominant. There was much illegitimacy, and the father was more peripheral and carried less responsibility. This situation changed among the immigrants who came to the U.S., but it was still true that Hugh's mother was the dominant parent. Family structure in England is (or was) generally patriarchal, with the father playing the dominant role of decision-making and carrying out practical matters. It happened, however, that Maris's mother was the dominant parent in her family and took responsibility for day-to-day running of affairs. It is perhaps not surprising, then, that Maris tended to be the practical one and took on roles which thirty years ago were more usually those of the American male. Hugh, on the other hand, has always earned the main salary.

In personality we could not be more different. Hugh is gregarious, talkative, artistic, interested in philosophy, mysticism, people. He is creative, undisciplined, other-directed, and daydreams about the past. Maris is reserved, quiet, logical, inner-directed, interested in history, anthropology, places, and daydreams about the future. Perhaps these extreme ends of the spectrum have enabled us to adjust to each other more easily than if we had been more similar.

We were each raised to respect the Protestant Ethic of hard work and a conscience about helping others, and with the idea that marriage was permanent. Neither Hugh's parents nor Maris's got on particularly well with each other, but they expected to remain together for life, and they did. This attitude must have influenced both of us: we also married with an expectation of permanency and have never been faced with any overriding reasons why that should change. We have had to make many adjustments to each other, and perhaps Hugh has had to make more than Maris because he is less rigid, more malleable, but so far the adjustments have worked and we each gain an enormous amount from the partnership. One ongoing dispute, which could well be culturally determined, is the question of music on the radio. Hugh likes it to be loud and continuous, Maris prefers it soft and only rarely. Another concerns tidiness and organization with the home. Hugh collects and keeps all forms of papers, while Maris throws everything out immediately. We consider the past thirty-four years to have been a draw and expect the battle to continue indefinitely. Two mechanisms which may have helped in the adjustment process are that we tacitly agreed that we would not go to sleep while there was something between us that had been unresolved; the other was again an unspoken understanding that it is necessary to compromise on inessentials while clearly signalling to the other when something is essential. These understandings have not been abused and as a result are used rarely.

Before our children were born we liked to quote an English limerick: There was a young lady called Sarkie/ Who had an affair with a darkie/ The result of her sins/ Was quads and not quins/ One Black and one White and two Khaki. Well, we had only two children, and owing to the fact that Hugh had considerable White ancestry, we had one Khaki and one White. Perhaps we would have liked a larger family, but economic constraints and the difficulties inherent in intercontinental travel with more than two children dissuaded us.

Our sons are now in their twenties and independent, but not married. We have asked them their thoughts about having interracial, intercultural parents and neither expressed any strong feelings on the subject. Possibly they did not want to articulate certain things to us, but it seems more likely that it genuinely has not been a problem for them. They both feel that they have been fortunate to experience living in several countries and because of this they are able to empathize with the viewpoint of different racial and cultural groups.

Michael, the elder and the one with "khaki" skin, seems to be completely color-blind. He has had girl friends who are light-skinned West Indian, White American, and Black American. Marcus, on the other hand, who passes for White, has had only White girl friends and only a few friendships with Blacks, although in college he roomed with Mexican-Americans.

Our sons went to school on three continents. Michael had a year of public school in Vermont, then they were tutored in Zambia for two years by an American. While Hugh was studying at Columbia University, they attended the laboratory school for three years; when we returned to Africa we did the traditional thing and sent them to boarding school in England, but a progressive Quaker-affiliated school which they more or less enjoyed. When Michael was seventeen and Marcus was fifteen we happened to move to a Nigerian town which had an excellent high school run by American missionaries primarily for their own children, but also for Nigerians and others. Both boys chose to go to that school and live with us. From there they entered Swarthmore and Princeton respectively--where Michael became an active member of the Afro-American students organization, and Marcus did not. After college Michael went into the Peace Corps in West Africa and is now launched on an international career; Marcus started his career in international economics and is now in graduate school.

During their five years at boarding school outside London, one of Maris's aunts looked after them whenever they did not come home to us. In England they met no discrimination because their great-aunt lives in affluent circumstances in the center of London, where race is not important. She took them to concerts, plays, and expensive restaurants, and her chauffeur took them to museums, sports events, and on sight-seeing trips; all of which over-privileged existence gave them a poise which has stood them in good stead as they grew older.

We used to worry about them when they were of school age that they might get hurt, perhaps be permanently scarred by some racial incident, but it apparently did not happen. Now that they are grown we do not worry any more because we feel they are secure enough to withstand and to understand incidents which may occur. However well they may be able to cope, we are aware that they are burdened with the potential of racial incidents against them in the future.

They have both been extraordinarily lucky in that any place they applied where race was in any sense a factor; it benefited them rather than being a detriment. It must have helped them in their college applications, and it has probably helped in all they have done since. We remember making quite a stir as all four members of the family sat in a row waiting for Michael to have an interview at an Ivy League college, but the well-trained interviewer managed to advance towards us after only the briefest of pauses. Neither of the boys can recall any actual instances of prejudice, though they must often have had to deal with at least surprise on the part of school friends or colleagues upon introducing their parents.

Although Michael feels quite at home in the professional Black-American culture, and both feel perfectly at home in England or Nigeria or Barbados, they probably identify most closely with intellectual White American culture.

It is hard for us to think of any real disadvantages we experienced because our marriage is interracial. People used to stare at the two of us a great deal, and even more so when we were all four together. The staring became almost obsessive when Hugh on his own took the small ash-blond, blue-eyed Marcus on the New York subways, but no one was ever actually moved to comment to him personally. Nowadays the staring seems to have diminished, or perhaps we simply notice it less. One recurring irritant is the fact that when we are waiting to pay in a store, or to check in at a hotel, people will usually assume that we just happen to be standing side by side, and one of us has to announce that we are together. We also have the feeling that because we stand out in a crowd and someone is so often watching us, we should always be on our best behavior in public (not necessarily a bad thing!).

Apart from such minor negativities, we feel our interracial marriage has been of nothing but benefit to us. We have been extremely lucky in belonging to a middle-class social and economic stratum which allowed us to choose where we would live, and to take advantage of the educational and work opportunities being offered. We also realize that at the time of our marriage the old racial attitudes in that stratum were already beginning to change.

We have read enough about the attacks on low-income interracial families to understand what a different world that can be, and from our experiences of living in Harlem, East Harlem, and Watts we know the hopelessness and frustration of ghetto life. There is a vast underclass for whom nothing has changed in the last three decades--or if there has been change it has been for the worse. The summer we spent in Los Angeles leading an American Friends Service Committee project happened to be the summer of the Watts riots, as a result of which we had to be hastily evacuated from Watts and were unable to complete the project. Before leaving Los Angeles we went back and saw the devastation where we had been working. We are conscious of the lack of any movement for the lowest socio-economic group towards integration, which had seemed possible in the sixties.

The middle classes, on the other hand, have largely become desegregated in work, housing, and educational opportunity. Hugh had no difficulty in getting public school jobs in New York City, Vermont, and North Carolina. Our interracial marriage was probably considered an advantage in working for the African American Institute in Zambia and in U.S.-sponsored teaching jobs at universities in Uganda and Nigeria. In addition, Hugh's minority status was presumably an asset when he applied to graduate school.

Neither of us really knows whether our marriage has had an impact on any individual or group, because no one has ever expressed anything to us on the subject. We have generally assumed that people were reacting to us as individuals rather than as an abstract interracial couple, though perhaps there has been a slight bias in our favor by people who want to associate with us in part in order to show that they are not racially prejudiced. We have been surprised when someone meets the other of us for the first time, but have not been aware of any particular value judgment. If it is not awkward and out of place to do so, we try to inform people ahead of time so that they do not have to be surprised, but we have not yet encountered anyone who could not handle their surprise with equanimity. Other people when meeting us do have an advantage in being able to assume that we will not be prejudiced on the matter of race and they usually assume that we will be unprejudiced on other social and cultural matters as well. Perhaps this latter assumption is unwarranted, but interracial couples in our experience do tend to be on the liberal end of the scale on most social and political questions. On a very basic level, we feel that the mere presence of an interracial marriage in a community can encourage others' belief in the ultimate possibility of racial harmony, particularly where the marriage is long-lasting.

There has historically been the feeling that an interracial marriage has one strike against it, that it has less chance of succeeding than one in which husband and wife come from similar backgrounds and their two families have a common heritage and can be supportive. Perhaps we saw that as a challenge, and it helped our determination to make our marriage succeed. In any case, nowadays there is no compelling reason not to marry outside of the group. A number of things have changed: there is a wide generation gap and parents and grandparents are no longer so closely involved in supporting their children's marriages; many people have moved far away from their birthplace and their primary group affiliation; and radio and television have provided a common global culture which is shared and understood everywhere.

We also think that the challenge of living in developing countries has been helpful to our marriage. We constantly had to adjust to difficult living conditions, to being without water or electricity, to exposure to coups and violence and political uncertainty, to learning new ways of doing just about everything. There were also the pleasures of feeling useful and appreciated, of rewarding friendships, and of travel to undreamed of places. All this gave us a focus outside the expected routines of marriage, and a great number of unusual experiences which we lived through together. For other couples the focus may be on religion or a consuming hobby or a large family; for us it has been foreign travel and living in Africa and an interest in the world as a whole.

CHAPTER 18

LINKING TRINIDAD, EAST INDIA AND EUROAMERICA

Pearl Ramcharan-Crowley and Daniel J. Crowley

Daniel

After 35 years of a successful mixed marriage, we have come to realize that there are indeed both kinds and degrees of mixture, and that our marriage is in reality not near as "deviant" as it looks. My wife, born Pearl Rita Ritwanti Ramcharan, is a Trinidadian whose ancestors came from North India as indentures in the sugar plantations beginning in the 1850's. One of her maternal great-grandmothers was born in Trinidad, but both her father's parents were themselves indentures from West Bengal. Her family converted to Christianity and was relatively successful economically and politically, her maternal great-uncle Saran Teelucksingh having been the second East Indian member of the Legislative Council. Pearl herself was educated in United Church of Canada Mission Schools, became a teacher and kindergarten specialist, then attended Toronto Normal and the National College of Education in Illinois, became Principal of Naparima (CM) Primary School, and received her M. Ed. from the Indian Institute of Education, Delhi University, in 1957, before ruining her career by marrying me and setting up our own home kindergarten.

Two of my grandparents came from County Cork, Ireland, and two as German-speaking French citizens from Alsace. My father was a successful plumbing contractor, realtor, and Building and Loan executive. I was educated in Catholic schools in Peoria, Illinois, but rejected Notre Dame in favor of Northwestern University near the bright lights of Chicago. While a Lt. (jg.) in the Navy, I contracted poliomyelitis just at the end of World War II, and was left a so-called partial quadruplegic with only limited use of my arms and legs. I wear a left leg brace and a heavy orthopedic corset, and use a wheelchair for long distances, but I can walk, and more important, climb a few steps with a little help. Thus while I appear helpless, I am actually quite healthy and able to take care of myself, providing I am in the right environment and/or have a little help. As proof, I am in the Guinness Book of World Records as "most traveled disabled person," claiming 219 countries (or other political or geographic entities) out of a possible 308 recognized by the Travelers' Century Club.

When I came back from military service as a quadruplegic, I found myself with a substantial Veterans Administration pension and reasonably good health in spite of needing a wheelchair. So what to do with my life? I decided I might as well concentrate on the big problem of my generation: race. I started back to school, studying Art History, particularly African and Oceanic, and soon realized that I could teach as well as any able bodied person. After an M.A. in Art History and two years teaching, I discovered that Anthropology offered me more suitable disciplinary approaches than Art History to the non-Western arts, so I left home for graduate study with Herskovits and Bascom in Northwestern's African Studies

Program. I realized immediately that I had found my life's work, and it has been a most rewarding one. The next winter I began fieldwork in the Bahamas, and Trinidad the following year, so my falling for Pearl was almost inevitable, the logical next step. With Veterans Administration support, I earned a Ph.D. in Anthropology, and have spent my life as a professor commuting between my classes in California and my field research in the Caribbean, Brazil, Africa, India, and elsewhere.

We are indeed an odd-looking couple, a dark Indian woman wearing kaftans or muumuus made of African tie-dye or Indonesian batik pushing the wheelchair of a bald, bearded, disabled man followed by three obviously mixed but otherwise racially-unidentifiable children. We are different in ancestry, skin color, nationality, and religion, and she is able-bodied while I am disabled. But we are similar in family background, class, education, and most attitudes and values, not too surprising when we realize that we have spent nearly half our lives together. She was and is the personification of Trinidad, my Bali-Hai, an authentically exotic and beautiful person who also turned out to be a practical homemaker and loving mother of our children. Most important, although she must help me physically many times a day, and do almost all the household chores, she never makes me feel ashamed of my physical deficiencies.

<u>Why and how did we enter marriage?</u>

We first met in 1955, when Pearl was the Principal of Naparima Preparatory School in San Fernando, Trinidad, and I was Tutor in Anthropology at the fledgling University College of the West Indies in Port-of-Spain. According to her story, as she headed down Naparima Hill on her way to see Gregory Peck in "Spellbound," she ran into some alumnae of Naparima who assumed she was joining them at an Alumnae meeting to hear "some Yonkee mon give a talk about music." Not being able to think of an excuse, she went to my lecture, and at the reception afterwards "over the tepid tea and stale cake," was introduced to the lecturer because "she went to school in your town," she had attended National College of Education and I Northwestern University, both in Evanston, IL, although at different times. Figuratively if not literally, I am fast on my feet, and immediately invented a research project requiring the help of East Indian teachers, a survey of family patterns. I have to admit though that the demure Miss Ramcharan wasn't the only woman there who took my eye; rather, I realized that these charming, shy, East Indian ladies were far more attractive to me than the flamboyant Creoles of Port-of-Spain. So I followed up, arranged the research project for which Pearl provided the meeting room, and let propinquity do its work. We saw each other weekly, occasionally socialized with the group, but with no mention of a date. When my colleague Andrew Pearse decided to leave the UWI for a new assignment in Brazil, the farewell party seemed the right occasion to ask for a date, which I planned carefully.

After we had served as judges in an art show in the refinery compound in South Trinidad, I persuaded Marguerite Wyke to drive me out to Rio Claro, where Pearl was spending the weekend with her family, so I could ask for the date. Later a Senator and hostess for Prime Minister Eric Williams, American-born Marguerite is a fine painter and genuine <u>grande dame</u> of Trinidad society married to Dr. David Wyke, distinguished physician, and she knew Pearl's family through her two cousins in medical school. But when her chauffeur helped me up the steps into Pearl's livingroom, her parents thought I was drunk as I, perspiring freely, commented on "the nice family life" with the brothers and sisters gathered around the dining table playing cards. Marguerite's presence soon explained things, and Pearl agreed to go on the date. By this time, she had her own car (one of the first Indian women to drive) and as we dated more frequently, trying out all the good restaurants in north Trinidad, she would spend the night with her friends, the Jagbandansinghs, in Curepe a few miles from Barataria, where I lived. We played mask at the Beaux Arts Ball, I as a sedan-chair Bacchus in a yellow toga and crown of grapes, Pearl as my hand maiden in a white toga-like sari carrying a jeroboam of champagne, and later we served as judges for the Carnival parade itself. First I ran after her, with few results, and then after a glass of Cointreau at a country restaurant, I got my first kiss. Once I realized that she might actually be interested in me, I froze, wondering what I was getting myself in for. What indeed! I was expecting a self-effacing and dutiful haremgirl, but what I got was a combination of a Canadian Presbyterian old maid and a vociferously independent West Indian marketwoman who just happened to look like an odalisque.

The "how" of our marriage was thus fairly normal in spite of its exotic setting, a classic "boy meets girl." After all, anthropologists really have very limited matrimonial choices, either to marry another anthropologist who is willing to go off to spend years in some muddy malarial village, or to marry one of the natives who is already there. I chose the second alternative. The "why" is much more complicated. To begin with, my parents had what amounted to a mixed marriage. Although both were first-generation Euroamerican Catholics born in the same Illinois city, both families bitterly objected to the marriage on ethnic grounds. "The Irish are all drunks, and keep pigs in their parlors." "Everybody knows French women are immoral painted hussies who spend all their husbands' money on fripperies." Needless to say, my parents didn't fit these ridiculous stereotypes, and once the inlaws realized it, they accepted the marriage. As my Alsation grandfather said, "The young Irish, they ain't like the old Irish." But ever after, family arguments came down ultimately to ethnic differences, with both parents ambivalent about their own and each other's affiliation. My parents had a very good marriage which lasted 53 years, and were also more successful financially and socially than most of their peers and siblings, facts not lost on me as I grew up "a white-collar kid in a blue-collar town." I was idealistic, romantic, studious, and soon hooked on music and the arts, not an easy life for a plumbing contractor's son in Peoria, Illinois. I sometimes think I am simply living out the fantasies I had at age 12 reading the National Geographic Magazine. Certainly I consciously planned to get as far from Peoria as possible, and to have a more meaningful, adventuresome life than I saw around me. I recognize that I felt the need to justify myself to the old home town that saw me as a longhair, to show them that I did indeed live up to my grandiose goals.

I have long thought about how we have managed to get along so well, so long, considering all the strikes against our marriage, not only our differences in race, nationality, religion, and lifestyle, (sometimes I think the gender differences are the biggest cause of friction between men and women), but also my physical disability. Certainly we didn't know each other very well when we married, and we both had a lot of adapting to do, especially during our first year of marriage, as we traveled through the Caribbean, then across South and Central America mostly by bus, heading toward my new job in the Sociology Department at Notre Dame.

At Notre Dame (privately we called it "Notre Dome") I taught sociology courses, including one called "Marriage and the Family." In my first lecture, I told the then-all-male students that I was hired to teach them that their best chances for successful marriage was to marry the girl down the block, of the same religious class, and ethnic background, but that I hadn't followed the rules but still had high hopes for our marriage. Actually, Pearl was quite popular at Notre Dame in spite of the racial tension in South Bend, and some of the students from there are still our close friends, two of them being godfathers of our children. Of course, I had a poor example of a "down the block" marriage; my sister having married an Irish Catholic Peoria lawyer with disastrous results. After five children and a long bout with alcohol, he disappeared with her best friend, never to be seen again, no child support, no nothing. Years later she married another lawyer, a first generation Italian/English one this time, and has been very happy with him.

As far as my expectations of marriage, I doubt if I had formulated them very clearly beforehand. Our courting and honeymoon were largely spent traveling, so the shock of discovering that we had each married a stranger didn't happen until we settled into a rented furnished house in South Bend, Indiana, in September, 1958. Raised in a shopkeeping home where servants did the cooking, Pearl learned to cook in a surprisingly short time, finding in me the perfect audience, and food and entertaining have been a bond ever since. But for love or money, no one in Indiana or California is willing to be a house servant of the sort Pearl was used to, and as an educated professional woman, she still feels demeaned by housework. We decorated our house with our honeymoon souvenirs and wedding gifts, and entertained hordes of relatives, colleagues, students, and junketing Peorians over for the football games. Although my mother treated her home like a museum, nothing out of place, I had to get used to a slower and more casual style of housekeeping, though not without some tension. And Pearl still enjoys cooking and entertaining, but hates the cleanup, and now sometimes gets students or professional help for housecleaning and garden work.

Because my parents didn't get beyond high school, I realized that by marrying an established professional woman, I had to expect a different lifestyle, especially since we lived far from either of our families. One expectation that came true was that Pearl would fit in well with my colleagues and their wives. The first few times I saw her chatting away with the Dean's wife or the Vice Chancellor, I died a little, but she always made a hit, and we've always had more socializing than we really want. One curious fact is that virtually everyone in my world calls Pearl by her first name, not only our class and age peers, but workmen, students, and casual acquaintances, much more so than if she were a white American woman. I don't think it's a lack of respect, but rather a desire to be friendly to a hard-to-place, but easily approachable foreigner.

Even on our honeymoon we did research in Dominica and St. Lucia, and read papers on it at an Americanist Congress in Costa Rica on the way up to Notre Dame. Pearl continued to publish in her field, and has read papers at professional meetings as far away as Mexico, India, and Argentina. Not only does she always edit my papers, but we have collaborated on several articles and a published translation of Fran Olbrechts' Plastiek van Kongo. She and the children have shared the fieldwork as well: two years in Ghana, 1969-71, a year each in Trinidad,

1973-74, and Brazil, 1978-79 as well as every summer traveling, collecting, and writing.

The major factors in our marital success is our similar class background with attendant interests, attitudes, values, and tastes. We both love to travel (Pearl had been around the world before we married); we think that education is never too expensive; and that houses should be clean but not necessarily compulsively neat; of course we have each also changed, sometimes too drastically, to suit the other. Pearl has learned to enjoy wines and beer with food, although she still rarely drinks before dinner; I have increased my taste for herbs, spices, and pepper, and have learned to eat breakfast; but in the last analysis, West Indians in general and Pearl in particular are more adaptable than Americans, maybe because of the famous "wide range of acceptable behavior" in their culture with its roots.

With this paean of praise, it is only fair to list some of my wife's perceived weaknesses as well, especially those that are cultural more than individual. As her brothers warned, she is not just hot tempered and stubborn, but she is also contrary, especially when she thinks I have slighted her or not listened closely enough to her opinions. Although this characteristic has a certain durability in a traditional extended family, I would much prefer a little straight talk beforehand. However, direct communication is rare from Pearl, and indirection is the rule. Even after three decades, I still don't get all the signals, and often say or do exactly the wrong thing. Another version of indirection is her use of a mumbling monologue just loud enough to be noticed, but not to be understood. I would have thought she was losing her mind if I hadn't had a Trinidadian servant who did the same thing during my first year on the island. Another cultural characteristic is that she is always and invariably late for any event or appointment, and not just late but very late, like a half hour late at the dentist's. Another Trinidadian, the architect Glean Chase, once put it well: "It's impolite of you to expect me to be on time." Pearl also registers her degree of disapproval of official events connected with my job by how late she is--very late indeed for departmental parties. Maddeningly enough however, she refuses to watch a film, play, or television show if she misses even the first few seconds, which sometimes happens because it takes me so long to get about. Of course I use my disability to explain always being on "West Indian time," since she usually catches on if I put the time forward. She has a short temper and is an inveterate complainer, presenting me with a fresh list every morning and evening at least. She requires me to do all the contacting of tradesmen and repairmen, although women usually do these things in this country. Finally, she is jealous and possessive, and much threatened by any other women in my world such as colleagues and students, which I find touching and deeply complimentary considering my age and physical condition. Actually as I reread the above, I remember a laughing comment of my sister that Pearl is an Indian duplicate of my mother.

Mixed Marriage and Society

All in all, I don't think our mixed marriage caused as many waves as we expected. In the little California college town where we've spent the last 31 years, Pearl is not a threat to anybody, and has always felt welcome. Occasionally we notice some reaction, such as the time in Sears when Pearl was carrying light-skinned baby Peter and I was wheeling along a few yards behind, and I heard one redneck say to another, "I wonder who scored with that one." Also years later on a train in France, a couple of American women journalists asked me apologetically, "Pardon me, but is Peter adopted?" Before we married, I had the good sense to call in two important women in my family, my father's sister, who is a school teacher, and my mother's niece who was my godmother, and asked them if they would support our marriage. Both readily agreed, and apparently spread the word that Pearl would be an ornament on the family tree, and God help anyone who said otherwise. Nobody did, although I'm sure there was muttering among some of my more rube cousins. Remembering their own experiences, my parents were supportive, glad to have their wandering son settle down at last. Pearl's family had other problems, particularly my physical condition and ability to father children. "Can he get her pregnant, or if so, will he just get her pregnant and then die on her?" After a very curious conversation with her medical cousin, I apparently passed, but then her brothers took me aside and tried to warn me about her independent nature, stubbornness, and devotion to her career. Actually, once we were married, both sets of parents bent over backwards to be supportive, and we got along well. Indian women leave their own families, and belong to their husband's family, so Pearl welcomed my parents spending winters with us in California. In the same way, I played up to my in-laws like all good American men, and they were overwhelmed, since it was not expected. Of course, they were also my informants, real live Trinidadians who could hardly do wrong in the view of this cultural relativist. Actually, we were good friends, and they visited my parents in Peoria and traveled and stayed with us in California. The word went out in Trinidad that I was a right guy, so that even to this day, nearly 26 years after my mother-in-law's death, the curry stocks and chicken population decline precipitously whenever I hit the island as Pearl's female relatives feast us. When we travel to England, Zambia, Switzerland, or virtually any city in Canada or the U.S., there are always pleasant and hospitable Trinidadian relatives and friends on which to sponge. Troubles I've had in my life, but not from my wife's relations.

Before we married, we wondered about the problems our children would face, and indeed, how they might look. Pearl has seen a few Indian/European children in Trinidad, and once I met the son of Judge Saund, an Indian politician from the Imperial Valley who had a Euroamerican wife. Since we were 36 when we got married, we welcomed children, and when I got a substantial and long-hoped-for Ford Foundation Fellowship to do research in Africa a few months after arriving at Notre Dame, we discovered that Pearl was pregnant. We decided to do the museum work in Europe, then settle in England to have the baby, since it was at least as homelike as the U.S. for Pearl. The first Cockney in our family, Peter arrived three weeks early and breech birth, but grew like a weed, and was ready to travel to Europe and Africa six weeks later. Somehow daughter Eve got conceived in the Imperatriz Hotel in Madrid en route, and was born in Dar-es-Salaam, Tanzania, after we had been run out of the then-Belgian Congo. What with two children in 11 months, known in some circles as "Irish twins," the Ford Foundation has never been quite the same toward us, leaving for Africa with two people and returning with four.

Our third child, daughter Magdalene (after seven generations of Alsatian ancestresses) arrived 17 months later in Woodland, California. Like all children of biologically different parents, they have the features of both sides of the family, but don't particularly resemble each other. Peter has the lightest skin and looks rather like me, but is taller. Like me, he is growing bald in his mid-20's. As an Arabist doing field work in the Yemen Arab Republic for his Princeton Ph.D., he is often taken for an American of Arab descent, and in Brazil always passes as a Brazilian. Eve has a golden cast to her skin, but otherwise resembles my sister Pat, who once took her to a Delta Kappa Gamma Teachers' Sorority meeting in Peoria. The good ladies, friends of mine and my parents, complimented her on her good looks, stressing her "beautiful suntan," until she pointed out that she was that color all year round. As a Yale Ph.D. candidate in Anthropology, she is working in Guinea-Bissau, West Africa, where her appearance and fluency in Portuguese Crioulo classify her with the local Cape Verdean mulatto elite. Maggie, a film major at Santa Barbara, looks rather like her mother though a bit lighter, but she is her father's daughter in her commitment to the arts, romanticism, and swashbuckling lifestyle. She has just returned from a backpacking safari in darkest East Africa, meeting us in Bissau to help Eve videotape the Carnival.

Obviously, our children have not suffered by being mixed. The first two went to Andover, and the third to San Domenico, were accepted in the Universities, and two have gotten scholarships to graduate school and grants for field research. Who knows? They may even find gainful employment one day. Interestingly enough, their friends down through the years have often themselves been mixed or non-white, or like our children, have spent years abroad, a fairly frequent circumstance in University towns. They seem to date people with ancestries as unusual as their own, the only common thread being that most of them are also faculty brats! All three of them play with their ethnicity, Peter being notorious for wearing misleading T-shirts from the far corners of the earth, Eve and Mag wearing braids and Mexican huipiles or Chinese cheong-sams or Indian shalwar-kameez. None of them will declare their "race" on forms, describing themselves only as "other," certainly never Asian-Americans. Pearl also will describe herself only as "Trinidadian," never as "Indian" or "Asian," much less "Caucasian," because she feels anyone who asks is innately prejudiced. In our country, the worst prejudice is directed against Blacks, and the growing prejudice against successful Asians has apparently not yet hit our children, who in any case are Americans with no particular sensitivity or chip on their shoulders. As "the last white man in my family," I have had it with the whole idea of race. I make my living studying its ramifications, but for me there is only one race, the human one.

What if I had married someone from my own background? I suspect that my life would have been very similar to what it has been, since my vocation is rather circumscribed, as are the limitations of my physical condition. Only a very unusual woman, of whatever ancestry, would have married me in the first place, or bore my children all over the world, or shared my field research and collecting with such indomitable strength and panache. Although Pearl turned out not to be the shy Arabian Nights enchantress I probably had in mind, I lucked out with a fine trustworthy woman, and am still as fascinated with her as when we first met. Not that we don't have deep and abiding differences, and problems like any other married couple, but they are not directly related to our racial or cultural distinctiveness.

<u>Pearl</u>

Our earliest known ancestor was named Ramdialsingh of the Kshatriya (warrior/landowner caste) who with his wife arrived in the early 1850's as indentures, had among other children a daughter named Jumni, and got land at Sumsum Hill near Claxton Bay in west-central Trinidad, on which was found oil. Jumni was married at an early age to Teelucksingh, a Kshatriya indenture from near Arrah, a city on the Bihar-Uttar Pradesh border 60 miles north of the sacred Hindu city of Banaras. Even before his indenture was over, Teelucksingh was "selling cloth out the back window of the barracks," and in a few years was a successful merchant, importer, and landowner. Although he had seven living children, his wife was active in the business, but when he died at about age 53 in 1897, she found that she had no control of the estate; it having passed to her sons, then teenagers already distinguished for their drinking and wenching. Establishing the pattern of independence and self-reliance among women in our family, she began secreting gold pieces from the case drawer, sewing them into the flounces of her Indian underskirts, and a few years later at age 34, she eloped with a 19 year old bookkeeper from a nearby sugar factory, a "Frenchman" named Sellier who was actually a Martiniquais coloured. He proved to be a gentleman, marrying her after the fourth of their six children. She turned Catholic, changed her name to Christine, and was notorious for driving her carriage by herself from Port-of-Spain to St. Joseph, where she once more established a very successful mercantile business. Although her Indian sons forbade any contact with her, Christine "kidnapped" her two youngest Indian daughters, one of who married an Indian of the same caste, and the other migrated to the States in the '20's and married a Black American.

Having married a nine year old orphan girl named Ramcooarie Harrachsingh, Jumni's eldest son Ramadeen, my grandfather, decided that the whole family should turn Anglican, thus granting the deathbed wish of his favorite brother. He became a leading Indian entrepreneur and landowner, but when he died from typhoid at age 36, his brother took over the estate and forced his widow to work in the fields like a laborer. My mother, the eldest daughter, was forced to give up school and music lessons, and to return to their country estate in Balmain, near Couva, where at age 18 she was married off, along with her 16 year old cousin, to two prosperous but Baniya caste brothers, the Ramcharans. Their father, a literate Bengali from Dumka, had changed his name from Hari Govind Lal to hide his caste (thought unsuitable for laboring), and had married another indenture, a widow of unknown ancestry. This couple, my paternal grandparents, became very successful as importers of Indian goods and spices, but after having four children, separated, living next door to each other. My grandfather converted to Presbyterianism, but later returned to Hinduism. After stripping the business of its assets and leaving it in my father's name, he returned to India where he lost the money and soon returned. The business never recovered, and he was mysteriously murdered in his shop. The wrangling over his estate ultimately caused my parents to cut themselves off from the business at considerable financial loss, and my father proved to be an improvident businessman, going bankrupt when I was a child.

I grew up in the country with my parents, five brothers, and two sisters in a close family relationship. We belonged to and participated in most of our community life. There was little privacy and everybody shared in local events. We were also close with uncles, aunts, cousins, and grandparents in an extended relationship in other parts of the island, even with the poor transportation and little telephone service. There was no identity problem for me, as there has been for Dan. I was always proud and confident of my place in my family, my community, my job, and my island. I might have been often angry, frustrated, and fed up, but rarely ashamed or defeated, and always ready for a challenge or an argument, eager and willing to espouse principles or any cause I believed in, fighting for them and sacrificing for them.

We were surrounded by poverty, poor and struggling ourselves, but money was never the most important goal in the lives of either of my parents or any of my brothers and sisters. I cannot emphasize this fact too much, since most of my siblings are now living outside of Trinidad, and have had to start over with little money. Education was a major goal. Respect and prestige in our community was another. Concern for and service to our people were my parents' gift to their children. They both gave up family inheritances (both were first-born) when a choice had to be made between money and freedom to live independently. They both very much rejected the "money-grubbing" that is supposed to be the characteristic of my father's Hindu caste, the Baniyas or shopkeepers, and certainly was the personality of my mother's Kshatriya male ancestors, who made their considerable fortunes largely through trade and money-lending.

Although I was the first to marry out in my generation, I am certainly not the only one in my family, nor am I the only one to emigrate. Two generations ago, my maternal grandfather Ramadeen had an "outside child" by a Creole woman, my uncle Bob Teelucksingh, who became Licensing Officer of Trinidad. One of my brothers married a Chinese Guyanese, and they are raising their four children in Brandon, Manitoba, where one girl has just returned from an exchange program in the Netherlands speaking Dutch, while another has a scholarship in speech therapy. Another brother has just arrived in Toronto with his Trinidad Hindu wife and three children, and three bachelor brothers spent their lives in Toronto, Montreal, and Nassau, Bahamas, respectively. One sister married a Trinidad Christian Indian who was already an American citizen, and raised their two sons in Long Island, while another married a Trinidad Chinese-Creole physicist in the Ministry of Education, and she is now Deputy Permanent Representative of Trinidad and Tobago to the United Nations in Geneva, after having been Deputy High Commissioner to Canada, where their two sons now attend McGill. One cousin married a Trinidad Muslim in England, and another married an Englishman who took her to the Zambian Copperbelt. Two female cousins, both physicians, married "real" Indians, both Hindu doctors, and spent years in India, where one is now a devotee of Sai Baba, the charismatic. Her American-born son, however, is a very successful software designer in New York. Her now-widowed sister has impressive grants for medical research in Calgary, and her son does computer research in Berkeley. The doctor's brother is an Episcopal priest in South Carolina married to a Trinidadian dogla (Indian/Black) woman, and one of their sons is a U.S. Army major. A few cousins actually married other Trinidad Indians and stayed in the island, but the majority of us have migrated and married out to one degree or another. But in spite of what my husband says, we are never "marginal" because we participate fully in whatever culture we find ourselves.

I have had problems with Dan, but not with his parents. I visited them on the way back home from India in 1957, which influenced my decision about marriage. I had no difficulty relating with them, they being basically so like my parents in many ways--attitudes toward family, food, business, and community. My parents were both readers, and my mother loved to play the piano although my father couldn't carry a tune. At night he would sit in a rocking chair (his feet tucked under him, Indian fashion) holding a baby--there were eight in twenty years-- tunelessly humming a bhajan or local tune, so that my mother could sleep. Dan's parents, for the most part, approved of my methods of child upbringing. After all, this was my specialty, from experience with babies at home in Trinidad and my studies in Early Childhood Education abroad. Dan's mother may have looked askance at my housekeeping, but so did my own mother. His father showed me how to deal with bank statements, and did our income tax returns every year. Unlike my father who couldn't fix a thing around the house, he mended and fixed everything. I still have Dan's mother's and cousin Sybil's handwritten recipes, invaluable and often used. Our parents got along quite well with each other. They had seen the same '20's movies, read similar magazines, played bridge, and often had similar views about people and events.

Even though I am the West Indian and Dan the American, he espouses many aspects of the Creole culture more than I do, and since he expects the same from me, misunderstands the situation. We might have some similarities in background, but respond and behave very differently in the same situation. I have a more Protestant attitude than he realizes, without the Irish puritanism that is part of his background. In my experience, "actions speak louder than words." To me, and an invitation of hospitality is exactly that, and not mere politeness. Friendships are few and lasting, and a basis for security, and family bonds remain loving and strong even when we are far away, and they are always a basis for security.

I accept Dan's list of my faults and imperfections. It is inevitable, living day and night with someone for 36 years and getting older and less healthy, for criticisms to increase, and some tensions to be expressed. However, being an impulsive Trinidadian, I respond immediately to attitudes and beliefs, expressed or not, unlike Dan who says that if they are not seen, heard, or stated, then their existence is doubtful--a Western trait, where the ideal is to categorize, analyze, and evaluate every thought, feeling, belief, and behavior. Rational straight talk beforehand is only possible when emotions are cool and thoughts organized.

In the first 40 years of my life, unlike the West Indian stereotype, I've always been on time for appointments, etc., both from inclination and as a matter of principle. Some of my brothers and sisters are also like this. I could not have functioned efficiently in my job, or gotten the reputation I had for punctuality in my society otherwise. Dan quotes Cardinal Stritch to the effect that "no soul was ever saved after the third minute" of a sermon. There were occasions when he had to be on time, and others when tardiness was desirable, sometimes confusing to me. It is always an effort for me to be on time after marriage, with the bonus of house, children, transportation, and helping Dan. This required starting off very much earlier, and taking more time on arrival, which were always difficult. Alone I was successful, now I had serious problems and I've still not been able to adjust to this situation satisfactorily. I wound up doing the major physical chores, which I hate, with less time for reading and the simple relaxation of doing nothing. I love walking and hiking, but not with a wheelchair in front of me, so I find myself driving all the time, which I do accept since I also love to drive.

I've had to work by myself at duties usually shared by the men in the family, like yard work, putting out garbage, fixing and mending, carrying loads, packing and unpacking the car and the luggage for trips, driving the car, driving Dan to and from his office, classes, and meetings, shopping, and running various errands around town. As a result, I leave Dan to do other duties like sometimes making arrangements with tradesmen and repairmen, writing letters (even to my family), planning trips, reading maps and travel literature, and arranging for passports, visas, drivers' licenses, air tickets, and the like, even though I could do any of these quite successfully. I cannot be a superwoman. In this culture, a woman feels guilty if she is not an efficient housewife along with doing everything else. Relaxation and vacations are planned for, but don't necessarily coincide. In fact, I am usually dead tired at the end of our "exhausting" vacations. I dislike living on a schedule, and miss a relaxed "take it as it comes" lifestyle, the give and take of family games, teasing, and arguments.

One of the biggest sources of disagreement is Dan's insistence on showing off, probably the result of the lack of appreciation he had among his teenage peers. He is out to show everybody that, in spite of it all, he has "got it made." The house, the art, the research, the travel, even the children are part of the show, carried to such extremes that we send out 300 Christmas letters full of our yearly exploits. Although I used to appreciate his interest in my clothes and jewelry, I now resent it because it makes me feel like I'm just another piece in his collection, an exotic brought back as he says "at great effort and expense" to run his house and have his children with maximum eclat. Please, the show is over!

We entertain less and less, because most of the burden of the cooking and cleaning is on me, and in my 60's it is getting very difficult. Dan won't accommodate to simpler cuisine requiring less preparation or courses, and says "life is not worth living" without a gourmet dinner in prospect. He won't live without a hundred or more bottles of liquor, wines, and liqueurs in the house. So we eat and drink too much, which conflicts with my medication for hypertension. Worst of all, he takes it as a slight if I won't join him in eating and drinking at the meal.

More and more, Dan identifies me with his mother, which I think is an American trait. His mother and I were very unlike in basic personality and philosophy, although we both hated tiresome tasks, and Dan's father did many of these for her. I always choose intellectual pursuits over physical activities, and never spend time on long telephone calls with acquaintances, unlike many Americans. I enjoy TV, but unless I can see the entire episode or film, I would rather read a book. As a result, I turn on the TV only for the news and programs I like, a few at night but rarely any in the daytime. Soap operas are a possible future enjoyment, and so are TV dinners, though Dan's pained and disgusted expression when I mention them is amusing to watch.

With aging comes the necessity of choosing priorities. Unlike many Americans, I am not ashamed of my age, and do not choose to spend time and money trying to look younger, although I do still enjoy a favorable compliment. I have to adapt to the fact that youth is idolized by an aging population here, and many basic truths are avoided. Americans don't always come to terms with the inevitability of declining abilities, sickness, loneliness, and death. In marriage, adaptation difficulties are either compounded or lessened with time. It remains to be seen how we continue to adapt to each other. Our final chapter has yet to be written.

Daniel -The Future

At age 70, we are old enough to retire, but I enjoy teaching and am deeply involved in my ongoing research on Carnivals, heading to Santa Cruz de Tenerife in the Canary Islands next February. What we need most is what we needed when we first got married, help. Davis is a fine place to live, mild climate, good library, flat terrain, lots of friends, and a convenient, spacious house full of our art collection, but no help beyond evanescent students. Unlike the Trinidad Indians who expect their sons and daughters-in-law to take care of them in old age, we have successfully encouraged our children to strike out on their own, and we will never stoop to asking them for help in our old age. Indeed, we will be content if they ultimately marry, and allow us to visit our grandchildren, if any. We spent the summer of '85 in India, and in ex-Portuguese Goa found a beautiful palm-fringed coast where the Christian community curries fine local pork and makes an elegant slivovitz-like liquor called feni. Better yet, honest and trustworthy servants are readily available, and living cost relatively low, but the all-pervading somber and humorless asceticism of India makes me depressed, to say nothing of the poverty, injustice, and political unrest. Although virtually all of Pearl's family is gone, Trinidad is still Bali Hai, with the style and wit only Black people have. It was no accident I chose to study their infinitely complicated culture in the first place, but economic depression with increasing theft and violence, political instability, shortages and sky-high costs fueled by inflation, and the indisputable fact that "you can't go home again," all gives us pause. And with all the out-migration, are there any servants left?

CHAPTER 19

CROSSING RACIAL AND CULTURAL BOUNDARIES IN EUROPE
Aaron Davenport and Noa Davenport-Zanolli

Our Backgrounds: Experiences and Expectations

We met in England in 1978 during a seminar on cross-cultural communication. Aaron is a Black-American, and Noa is a Swiss of Italian origin. As it turned out, the seminar must have been successful indeed! At the time, Aaron was 40 and Noa 37. Aaron was in the Army and living in Germany. He was an Equal Opportunity Officer and Race Relations Instructor. Noa was living in Switzerland and working with the Swiss government managing development programs. Both, however, had made up their minds, independently, that it was time for a change. Aaron had planned to leave the Army after 20 years and Noa had decided to work as a free lance consultant-journalist-teacher.

In Aaron's family background there were two almost contradictory tendencies. Aaron's father could be said to have been a Black racist. He did not trust white people at all. Even though his best friend and co-worker was white, it took him 20 years or more before he let Aaron set foot in his house. He was adamantly opposed to any relations with whites. However, Aaron's mother was extremely religious and always encouraged her children to have open minds toward different people. "Even though my experiences with white people and their treatment of me, as a youth and as I grew up, were quite negative, I had my mother's beliefs inculcated in my makeup," says Aaron. "While I was in the Service I had been in so many different countries and I worked with so many different people of all races and color. My outlook started to broaden quite early. I had only been in the Army for 2 years when I was sent to Korea. I meshed into the culture of Korea immediately. I experienced a culture shock, but I adapted to it. These military experiences broadened me," says Aaron. But for him the most broadening experience came when he was 32. He then became involved in the Army's Equal Opportunity and Race Relations Program and was immersed in a very in-depth and soul-searching training program. "I was responsible for conducting workshops and facilitating seminars in which we attempted to change peoples' perceptions and attitudes towards people of other races and cultures. I did this for over 8 years. All of this brought me from my home environment to my relationship with Noa."

For Noa it was different. She cannot remember that race or a different culture had ever been an issue in her upbringing. She was born into a Swiss family of mixed Italian/German/Jewish background and was brought up in a Swiss environment without special alliances to any of the cultural/religious groups. "In my family the question of whether or not people are different based on cultural/racial grounds, and therefore were judged on these grounds, just never, absolutely never, was an issue. We had, as a family, contact with many different people, even though I must add, that the difference was with respect to language and religion, rather than on racial grounds. So I just never perceived, experienced or consciously knew about racial differences until much, much later, when I was in my twenties." Noa's parents were artists. If she heard anything, she heard only positive comments with regard to Blacks, especially from her father who admired their beauty. "I remember a picture that my mother had painted of a group of dancing Black people in a bar that she had observed on a trip to Morocco. The picture hangs in our house, but the fact that Blacks were the subject matter was never a point of discussion or special observation. I remember one other incidence where we visited in southern Switzerland in 1946/47, a group of Sikhs, Indians, that were interned by the British Army, and I believe I there realized for the first time that people have different colors of their skin, or different facial features, because they really looked exotic to me - but in an awesome sense. I was 5 or 6 years old. Maybe I studied anthropology because I was already pre-disposed to having an open minded attitude. During my student years in the U.S., and during my research in Africa, I was in frequent contact with people from diverse cultural backgrounds and with Blacks. It was awfully awkward for me when I returned to Switzerland after one year and everybody was white."

Aaron goes back to earlier cross-cultural/cross-racial experiences and circumstances that might have influenced his decision to marry someone outside of his own culture or race: "My earlier cross-cultural/cross-racial experiences were very negative, except for high school. There was a white girl that I dated for awhile. We met at a special high school program for students who wanted to become business people. She was a beautiful, red-headed girl. But it was one of those things. Because of the attitude of the people we were always sneaking around to meet each other. Her family was from the South, so that relationship did not last long."

Aaron continues, "All the experiences I had with white people, as I grew up, were negative. "There was one exception. There was a boy that I went to junior and senior high school with. We were always at each other's house. I always helped him with his homework. One day, however, his father told me that it was not wise for Ray to associate with me anymore, that it wasn't good for him. He told me that I could not come by the house anymore and Ray could not come to my house. I was very hurt, Ray was hurt and I could not understand it. The last time I saw Ray he had sneaked over to my house to tell me that he was dropping out of high school to join the Navy. I lost track of him after that. I asked my mother about it and the best she could explain to me was that there was nothing wrong with me, that it was the attitude of Ray's father."

Most of Aaron's experiences with white people in the military, etc. were primarily negative. From the time he graduated from high school, when they wouldn't let him into the National Honor Society (he had graduated in the top 10% of his class) and he couldn't get a scholarship because he was Black; up to being kept from going to the Army Officer Candidate School (in spite of very high scores on the Officer Candidate Aptitude Test). Aaron says, "If I were to sum up my experiences with whites, I could very easily be justified in hating all white people. Most white people cannot rationalize why they dislike Blacks. But I did not have that -- I did not have the capacity in me to continue to hate people. I think that that is my mother's influence.

So much has happened to me, not because of who I was, but because of what I was. As a person, I like all people and I try to treat them fairly. But still, today, I am subjected to actions that are directed at me because of my skin color, not because of job performance, social status, or anything else. If I look back on my experiences, there is absolutely nothing that would indicate that I would fall in love with or accept a Caucasian person in my life. Yet and still, one of my best friends is a white person. We have been in contact for over 30 years, even though there have been spans of over 20 years that we haven't seen each other. There was one other white friend like that. I also do not have many close friends. That's probably because most people I associate with are white, and they choose not to include me in any of their social affairs," says Aaron.

The relations that Noa had with people from different cultural and racial backgrounds have always been very positive for her. These experiences were conducive to marrying someone from a different cultural background. "In fact," Noa says, "I never put any emphasis on color, looks, different cultural background with respect to personal relationships. For me it is the personality traits that are of essence and, as far as race or different cultural background is concerned, it just hasn't been an issue." During her student years in the USA, 1964-1966, she had several good friends from Africa and one special friend from Tanzania whom she dated and kept in contact. However, she hardly ever came in contact with Black Americans, although she participated in the civil rights activities on campus.

As far as Aaron's and Noa's expectations of marriage roles are concerned, it is probably atypical for both of them. The culture that Aaron grew up in was different from that of a white family. Both parents worked. His father as a laborer and his mother as a day worker she took care of white people's children, while she had fourteen children of her own. "There were roles in our family," says Aaron. "My mother ran the house and my father made the money; he was the breadwinner in whatever way that he could. The money that my mother brought in was a contribution to the household, but the main money was my father's responsibility. My mother was very emphatic about "her" house. My father's roles were those of disciplinarian and the head of the family. There was never any disagreement on the way to raise the children."

Even though Aaron feels the responsibility of taking care of his own family, based upon the strong male/father image he had been instilled with, he has no problem accepting that marriage works as a partnership and it does not matter whether the husband or the wife is earning the best income. There is no competition in this regard. Aaron also learned from his mother how to take care of the house, cooking, washing, ironing, washing dishes, and so on. Aaron emphasizes, "I had no fixed ideas as to what a man's work is and what is not man's work. I never felt it was beneath my manliness to do the laundry." Aaron's expectation is that marriage is a team-affair, a partnership, and that neither partner pulls in opposite directions and that responsibilities are shared. Noa concurs entirely with this view. Noa's family background is rather non-traditional too, with respect to a white family. There was no strict division of labor between her father and mother. She says: "My mother and father shared the household duties. My father cooked, cleaned, went shopping, and took care of the baby. There were times that my mother was very ill for weeks at a time. It then was a matter of teamwork between my father, sister, and myself to take care of the household. This is also what I expected from my partner: that he should equally contribute to all the daily tasks, if his situation would allow him to do so. My expectation of marriage is similar to Aaron's. I also see it as a partnership, giving each other mutual support and encouraging each other to fulfill one's best. For me, also, it is the expectation that very intimate feelings are being shared, that are not shared with anybody else, and it is a very deep friendship relationship." Noa did not have many expectations concerning in-laws. She only wanted to be accepted. The same was true for Aaron. Both of these expectations were borne out. We both were accepted for what we are. We never gave much thought to expectations with regard to the larger society. This is probably so because we are mature, middle-aged grown-ups. These societal or in-law issues do not affect us in the same way as it could possibly affect a younger, less mature, less traveled couple. In this context, Aaron says, "If there are problems, it is not the couple as such that causes them. Problems are caused for them by other people. Interracial marriages do not cause problems. Small-minded, bigoted individuals with their attitudes cause the problems."

Overcoming Distance, Working Towards Stability, Respecting Differences

When Aaron and Noa met, both were, of course, aware of their racial differences, but it simply was not an issue in their relationship, and this from the very first moment. Noa says, "I somehow wasn't aware of the fact that Aaron was Black."

I saw something in Noa that I had never seen in anyone else," says Aaron, "A great capacity for love, caring, understanding and intelligence. She also wanted to do something for me and she was always looking at what is the best in me. I had never had that experience before." We met every 4 to 6 weeks, after those first two weeks in England. Then Aaron was transferred to the Pacific. We kept in contact by writing each other every couple of days, by weekly phone calls, and by bi-annual visits. This situation continued up to the time that Aaron decided to come to Switzerland to attend graduate school in 1982. We then were together for 1 1/2 - 2 years. As it turned out, in 1984 Aaron decided to return to the US after his graduation because there were no professional options in Switzerland. Noa was very much involved in her profession. She was not ready to give it up, just yet. "So we tried to make the best of it through all these years," Noa says, "Because, basically, there was this bond and love. Only when those periods of long separation became increasingly unbearable for me, only then was I ready to get married and move to the US." All of these years, we have truly had a long-distance romance. At times we were commuting halfway around the globe. We believe that our regular communications, through all the years of separation, were the essence of our lasting relationship. The stability in our relationship has been enhanced through this on-going attempt to maintain communication. Even when we are together, we maintain communication through periodic discussions, even on issues that sometimes Aaron doesn't feel to be important, but are important for Noa. Practically every day we discuss what happened during the day. Even though some of these things seem to be routine, they are not. We have a desire for communication and are aware of what the other person is doing or is involved in. If we feel that we have lost touch in exchanging feelings, schedules, activities, concerns, frustrations and joys, we sit down, more often than not, on the insistence of Noa and balance things out again. "And more important than anything else," says Noa, "I enjoy Aaron's company. There is nobody around that I prefer spending time with than Aaron. Especially here, in this relatively new environment. We do things together, we discuss issues of world concern, we have different opinions, but we respect each other's differences."

There is another factor that is true for our marriage. We cherish our different backgrounds and do not try to deny it in any way. Noa is European, or Swiss with an Italian background, and that is her cultural pattern. Aaron is a Black American and that is his cultural background. Each one of us accepts the other's differences and preferences. We allow each other to be each other and at the same time we are one with each other. Aaron says, "Noa can be my wife and partner, and I can be Noa's husband and partner, but we can also be part of our respective backgrounds." We do, and have done, things that we would not have done had we been married to someone of the same cultural background. Noa has done things with Aaron, gone to places that she would otherwise never had the opportunity to experience and the other way around. For all the things we get involved in in our lives, intellectual discourse, cultural environments, we believe that our relationship is also more enriched.

Aaron adds: "I really believe that it is the downfall of any relationship, if a white person tries to become black or the other way around. This will then be, almost without exceptions, destructive."

In this context, Noa says, "As long as one maintains the interest in the personality and the changing personality of the other partner and in his/her interests and concerns, the fact whether or not the marriage is mixed or non-mixed is not relevant. It is this much more generalized aspect that is distinctive for me of a successful, stable and meaningful marriage. What is of essence here, I believe, is the disposition to being open and receptive for each other's different experiences and really wanting to learn from each other." In our cultural backgrounds there are necessarily differences. Aaron comes from a very religious family. He went to Sunday School and church every Sunday. On Sunday and weekday evenings, he attended church youth activities. Aaron's mother was very active in church-related activities and was rarely at home on Sundays.

Noa, on the other hand, was brought up without a religious background at all. At times she was exposed to a ridiculing of Christians by her father, who believed that they were bigots in most cases. But she was bothered by this and she developed a contrary attitude of total tolerance. She has never personally felt the need to be associated with any particular religious tradition. She respects, however, Aaron's need to associate with a Black church and will join him and pray in her own way.

Other differences exist with respect to attitudes toward sports or dietary tradition. For example, Noa cannot share Aaron's passion for sports. But this does not affect our relationship in a negative way. Noa does her own things during those weekend afternoons or evenings during which watching a major game on television takes priority. As far as dietary customs are concerned, we combine all our traditions in our menus and come up with a very varied cuisine.

We have both lived in each other's culture, separately and together, in Switzerland and in the USA.

"I don't believe that the culture or society in which we live or lived has affected our marriage," says Noa. "I much rather believe that in the beginning, when I came to the U.S., it was a process of structuring my life anew, getting to know my surroundings and not being able to work in my profession, which made my adaptation not so easy at times. But this could have happened in any culture really, and is not dependent on the American way of life. If anything it has made the process even somewhat easier because I encountered so much general acceptance and friendliness and interest."

"For me it was different," says Aaron. "Socially and culturally I have had no problem living in Switzerland. The problem I had while living there was a professional occupation, and that problem might have been worked out - but it would not have been easy. There were some minor incidences of discrimination here and there, but I never encountered overt discrimination in Europe or Switzerland. There is, however, quite a bit of covert discrimination. In the U.S. the overt discrimination is flagrant."

Our perspectives have not changed during our relationship, with respect to gender or sexual roles, family, relationships, moral or ethical issues. This is largely due to the fact that our personal attitudes are similar, irrespective of our differing cultural backgrounds. With the exception of religious commitment and beliefs, we pretty much have the same feelings or attitudes so that these realms have not been a source of conflict. If they were, it would be the pattern of communication that we have established that would help resolve such problems.

All of this is not to say that there are not areas of conflict or friction that have their roots in cross-cultural differences. One of these is Noa's difficulty to adjust to the American passion for watching television. Noa watches certain programs, but it is a constant source of irritation for her walking into a house, wanting to converse with people, and the television is running. For her this is almost a rudeness, as if it took away precious time to talk about "serious" matters. Aaron is not bothered by that at all, in fact quite the contrary. He often watches, for several hours, programs that Noa considers a waste of time. Noa resolves the problem by doing her own thing during that time, but her feelings of frustration persist somewhat. Another area is that Americans, and also Aaron, are accustomed to noise around them. To have music playing in the offices where people work, is for Noa totally alien and very disturbing. Aaron, in fact, works better with background noises. The point is not what Aaron listens to or watches, it is that the noise is needed. Noa usually goes to her room and closes the door.

Another area of conflict is the American car-culture, the dependency on a personal vehicle rather than using public transportation. It is not so much that a car is a luxury item, as it still is to some extent in Europe, but rather a necessity. Whole towns, suburbs and shopping centers are laid out with the idea that access will be via personal auto. But this is a matter of the general culture and Noa, by necessity, is adjusting to it.

"If a mixed marriage lasts, it is probably a much stronger union than any other marriage, because it puts you through a variety of tests that a non-mixed marriage does not," says Aaron. Noa agrees with this, however she views it somewhat differently. For her the question of a mixed or non-mixed marriage and of differences in cultural backgrounds becomes increasingly irrelevant. The only matter in a relationship, married or not, mixed or not, that counts, for her, is the bond between the two individuals, the trust, the love, the respect for each other, and the constant attempt of maintaining an open mind and being tuned into each other. For her, it is of the essence to maintain an intimate relationship that is being sustained by an open and honest pattern of communication. Cultural patterning may hinder this, but it does not mean that it cannot be learned. Aaron and Noa agree that one of the advantages of a cross-cultural marriage is that the broadening of each other's mind is enhanced by this very fact.

Another major advantage which, with much regret does not apply to us, is the beauty and intelligence of the children that result from such a union.

"In general," Aaron adds, "the only weakness that I can think of in a mixed marriage, is when the couple got married for the wrong reasons, like out of the "forbidden fruit" reason, as a form of protest. Also, it is very important for the partner to understand that Black people are very tuned in to any kind of overt or hidden discrimination, and that they are sensitive to that. The partner must understand that these slights are very offensive."

Our Marriage and the Wider Society

As our two cultures, American and Swiss, in very broad and generalized terms, two Western, industrialized cultures, are after all not that fundamentally different, there are really no major areas in the legal or political realm that have affected the conduct of our marriage. If anything it was much easier for Noa to marry an American, receive a Visa, and become a permanent resident with relatively little paperwork and hassle. It would have been more difficult if we had decided to live in Switzerland; the laws of the country would have made things more difficult for Aaron. "But," says Noa, "I don't believe that this would have affected the conduct of our marriage in any way."

Living in the U.S. as a black-white couple is not such an event. Society as a whole has been getting used to this phenomenon and has been more receptive to it, generally. In Switzerland, generally speaking, we have been looked at with more curiosity and heads turning very often, as we walked by people hand-in-hand. "But for me, however, the wider society looks at our relationship," Noa emphasizes, "I feel it is none of the society's business, and I am just not concerned about it." Aaron views this question very similarly: "My experiences have taught me that the problems of mixed marriages were always, without exception, the problems of the wider society, and not the problem of that particular couple. If people have a problem, when they see us together, I just have the attitude that this is their problem, not mine. I do not lose any sleep over it. We have our own world, and we are not concerned about that part of the wider society that might not like our relationship."

"I don't think that our relationship has changed the attitudes of friends, family or any of our professional colleagues. At least, I have not perceived changes," says Noa. If persons would have disapproved of our union, we would not be concerned about that because we do not associate with those circles in the first place. Aaron confirms this perception from his own experiences. There was only one incident where Aaron was of the opinion that it would be more advantageous for him, if he would not openly declare that at that time his fiancee was Caucasian. That was when he was running for a position on the school board in his home town of Pontiac, Michigan and had to attend functions and campaign within the Black community.

In general, we have not encountered adversity because of our mixed marriage, in fact quite the contrary. Living now in the Midwest, we have established relations within these rather conservative communities, we have encountered openness, friendliness and acceptance. We have not noticed or encountered any ill-feelings.

This is possibly linked to the general evolution of how society presently looks at mixed marriages. This is true for Switzerland as well as the U.S. "Generally, I would say," adds Noa, "in Switzerland the occurrences of mixed marriages are somewhat more frequent nowadays, even though they are still rather exceptional." Aaron adds, "For the U.S. the climate has changed from what it was 35 years ago. A lot has to do with mass communication, with the broadening of people's ideas and also through the military. How many servicemen have brought wives from other racial/cultural backgrounds from foreign countries back to the U.S.? So, all of this has really changed."

Aaron was married before to someone from the same home town, neighborhood, background, and race. There were problems in that relationship and, in spite of it being a non-mixed marriage, it did not work out. Aaron explains: "It didn't work out because emotionally and intellectually we could not relate to each other. So, what was important for me was to find someone that was on the same plane as I was. This has nothing to do with racial or cultural differences. It has to do with a loving heart and an open mentality."

CHAPTER 20

THE BRITISH-PAKISTANI CONNECTION IN NIGERIA

Shahina Ghazanfar and Yusuf Martin

Shahina

My marriage to Martin is the first in our family to a man from outside our own country. It is perhaps more common for a Pakistan man to marry a foreigner than for a woman to do so (my youngest brother is married to a Spanish girl). My childhood and education was perhaps slightly unusual for a Pakistani girl. I was educated in English medium schools by English and Irish Christian missionaries. I learned about Christianity at school, and Islam at home. Both my grandfather and my father had a part of their university education in England. (My mother was born in Cambridge while her father was studying there, and one of my brothers was born in Oxford while my father was at that university.) This smattering of contact with England gave a slight western flavor to the lives of myself and my brothers and sister. Later, part of my own university education was also in England.

When my friendship with Martin first began to develop there was no hesitation on my part. I already knew the West and Westerners, both from my family background and from my education. One factor that influenced the development of my friendship with Martin, and kept my mind open to the idea of marriage with a foreigner, was that I have been married before, but to a Pakistani. My first marriage dissolved after fifteen years. Many of those years were unhappy ones. The breaking up of this first marriage led, at least indirectly, to my marriage with Martin. I was not keen to marry another Pakistani. I was already aware of the expectations that a Pakistani man would have of me, and I was no longer prepared to fulfill these expectations. I have worked during all of my adult life, even while bearing children, and I had no wish to be subservient in a second marriage. My parents treated their sons and daughters alike. All of the five children (two girls and three boys) were given an equal opportunity for education. Like myself, my sister has always worked. I came to adulthood expecting to be an equal partner in a marriage. After completing my education in England, I expected to be able to carry out my research and academic interests without social constraints, and found it very difficult when my first marriage prevented this.

When I met Martin in Nigeria (we both came to work in the same university department within a few months of each other), I recognized the importance of the respect which he gave towards my professional life. This filled a large gap that had been lacking in my first marriage.

Since I was already familiar with the English and their culture, it was not difficult for me to establish a friendship with Martin. Moreover, being born in the post-colonial era, I did not have the same respect for the British as did my mother's generation. I did not view the British as a superior race, and it never seemed to me that marriage to an Englishman would be a social advantage.

All of my expectations in a marriage regarding Martin were pleasantly fulfilled. Helping with the housework and looking after the baby came as pleasant surprises. My expectations failed, however, in the attitude of my in-laws. Their refusal to recognize me as their daughter-in-law, their refusal to see their grandson, and finally their expulsion of Martin from his family came as a great shock to me. It took me a long time to adjust to this situation. It is fairly common in my culture for parents to reject their sons if they marry below their status, or to a girl that is not of the parents' choice, but it did not occur to me that such conservative attitudes still existed in Britain. For the first time in my life I was discriminated against because of cultural, color, and religious differences. My second shock was Martin's attitude to his parents' prejudices. He was very disturbed by his parents' reaction, but he was able to say: "It is very stupid of them to feel this way, but if this is how they want it, then let it be." I was surprised by this attitude. In my culture, offspring are required to respect the decisions of their parents, and sons in particular are to a large extent emotionally dependent on their parents. The normal outcome of parental objection to an 'unfavorable' marriage by a son in Pakistan is that the son bows to his parents' wishes. Less frequently the parents may eventually be persuaded to accept the unfavored daughter-in-law, but rarely would a son take it upon himself to risk complete rejection from his family.

In the early stages of our friendship, when it became apparent that Martin's parents were going to give us great problems, I did consider ending our relationship since I had no wish to expose myself to prejudices and unhappiness. However, Martin's evident independence of mind, which is so much more apparent in the young people of Britain than in those of Pakistan, fortunately prevented this.

There was no opposition from my family to my relationship with Martin. My brothers and sisters were at the time widely dispersed around the world, and only my mother and youngest brother met Martin. It would not have been the same had I been living in Pakistan. Marriages there are between families and not between individuals, and it would have been difficult for my extended family to accept Martin without his parents' blessing.

I had to overcome several problems very early on in my friendship with Martin. I was not used to any form of public affection (such as holding hands) and I felt very embarrassed if Martin tried to hold my hand while walking down the street. I have only partly overcome this, and am occasionally prepared to hold hands in public, but preferably under cover of darkness. Swimming in mixed pools was initially an anathema to me, but I am now largely used to this, and do not feel embarrassed unless there are a lot of people about. One of the greatest cross-cultural conflicts early on in our relationship was the fact that Martin had previously lived with a girl for two years without being married to her. It was almost impossible for me to accept that, firstly, this had occurred, and secondly, that it was all over. I found it difficult to understand the idea of 'living together.' It was the passage of time that finally allow me to accept that Martin was no longer emotionally attached to this girl.

Yusuf

It was not difficult to fall in love with Shahina, and I realized very soon after our friendship developed that I wanted to stay with her. I wasn't particularly concerned about being married, but in deference to Shahina's wishes (and also because any children that we might have would, due to the idiosyncratic laws of England and Pakistan, be stateless) I asked her to marry me. It never occurred to me that I could not, or should not, marry her. My parents assured me that if I did marry her all my friends would turn their backs on me. In the event, my friends remained true and my parents rejected us.

I had no reservations about marrying a Pakistani and few, if any, preconceptions about Asians. I was born after the colonial days, and had not been influenced by the mores and morals of that time. I received a moderately liberal Roman Catholic education, during which I was to some extent encouraged to be a free thinker. Perhaps some unfortunate people have fallen in love with someone of a shockingly different background but failed to marry because they had been taught to place family and/or society first. I had no such reservations. If anything at all, besides love and an open mind, what led to my entry into a mixed marriage was a certain longing for adventure, particularly of the cultural sort.

The reaction of my parents when I first told them about Shahina (during my first summer vacation from my work in Nigeria) was straightforward: horror. They did not want this alien as their daughter in-law. Shahina failed as a prospective companion for their son on four counts: she was a Muslim, a Pakistani, she had been married before, and she was too old (Shahina is my elder by seven years). I naturally countered that this was all irrelevant, and pointed out that she was an attractive human being. When I ventured to suggest to them that I loved her, I was told that evidently I did not understand the meaning of love. I tried my best to show them that she was not an illiterate savage. They even met her briefly ("she's terribly thin," my Father said), but all to no avail. Many arguments and much disputation ensued between myself and my parents in the two weeks following their introduction to Shahina. I then retired to the safe distance of Nigeria, and we continued to dispute the matter by letter. I remember suggesting to my brother that perhaps I should send our parents a copy of Shahina's curriculum vitae in order to show them (as though it was important!) that she was as well, if not better, educated than myself.

Naturally we eventually married without the 'blessing' of my parents. My education had not taught me to place family or society before reason and love. I believe that many families have become reconciled to the wayward nature of their offspring's marriage after the birth of the first grandchild. This was not the case in my family. The final break, when my parents decided that they never wanted to see me again, came shortly before the birth of our son, Sikander. Ironically, due to the random nature of inheritance, Sikander is as fair as myself and, if he bears a resemblance to any relative, it is to my Father. However, my parents will never know this, since they have never seen him, and I doubt that they will ever decide to do so.

I may have lost my parents, but I have gained a Mother. Shahina's Mother welcomed me as her own son, and did not seem too perturbed that I was more or less ignorant of her country and culture. I received a similar welcome from her brothers and sister, and the family's friends, both Pakistani and English.

My parents, like myself, were born in Birmingham, a city which has seen a lot of Asian immigration in recent years. The natives have not always welcomed these immigrants, and this may have influenced my parents reaction to a potential Pakistani daughter-in-law. I have always presumed that a great part of my parents' adverse reaction to Shahina was fear of the unknown. This was probably most marked in their antagonism to her religion. In general, Islam receives a bad press in the English media. My mother once said to me after she had learned of the entry of

Shahina into my life: "I hope that you are not going to do anything stupid like becoming a Muslim." I was already seriously considering conversion at the time, but in the hope that I might first be able to persuade them to accept Shahina as a person, and then later educate them about Islam, I replied that no, I was not considering conversion (anything for some peace, I remember thinking at the time). As far as I can tell from casual observation most parents have a prejudice against their sons marrying an older woman. There appears to be no particular rational reason for this as long as the potential wife is still of child-bearing age. Objections appear to be less frequently raised against a younger woman. Shahina's age was of course a side issue, but it compounded her offense: a Muslim, a Pakistani, previously married and <u>older</u>!

It is ironic that my Mother's grandparents were all Italian immigrants into Birmingham. Despite being second generation Italian immigrants, and despite the role of Italy in World War II, my mother and her brothers and sisters managed to marry natives of their settled land, and the family is well assimilated into English life. Unfortunately, this piece of history was conveniently forgotten by my parents, and it did not occur to me at the time to raise this point in my disputations with them. I have since come to the conclusion that this was a strong factor in my parents' opposition to my intending marriage. It is worth noting in this context that the strongest opposition to my intending marriage came from my Mother.

It is perhaps apparent that it is difficult for me to write of my 'expulsion' from my family without bitterness. However, being happily married, and being a pragmatist, I am resigned to the fact that I will never see my parents again. I think that my acceptance of the situation has been made easier by the complete unreasonableness of my family.

All of this has not left Shahina untouched. She feels much bitterness against my family. It is difficult to see prejudice against oneself in an objective light, since it is too personal. I doubt that she could now, in the unlikely event of a reconciliation, ever have a normal relationship with my family.

Shahina

It was not very important to Martin which religion I belonged to. It was however important for me that my husband should have the same religion as myself. I also felt that any children we might have should be raised as Muslims. Martin did not have any objections to this, and when I asked him if he would convert to Islam he said that he would do so, as he said "as long as I don't have to be circumcised." Conversion to Islam is very simple and straightforward, and, fortunately for Martin, circumcision is not absolutely obligatory for an adult convert. The two obligations which affected Martin were the bans on the eating of pork and the drinking of alcohol. We have compromised on the latter and, since I am not a fundamentalist, Martin has not faced any severe constraints or problems following his conversion. Martin has in fact found a much wider acceptance in Muslim communities since his conversion, and I have received much praise for my ability to persuade him to convert!

Yusuf

Islam required that Muslim women only marry fellow Muslims. It was therefore easier for Shahina to live in Muslim society if I converted to Islam before marriage (we were living in the mainly Muslim north of Nigeria at the time of my conversion), and it would also make us both more generally acceptable in a Muslim community. I readily assented to conversion, though I was very hesitant and nervous when I went to the mosque one evening at the Maghreb prayer to meet the Imam. As I recited the Kalma after the Imam he clasped my average-sized hand in his large, warm grip. This both reassured and welcomed me.

My conversion to Islam was a further extension of the cultural adventure that was part of my friendship with Shahina. I discovered that I was happy to be a Muslim. In some inexplicable, perhaps irrational, way I felt 'better' as a Muslim (though not morally so). Perhaps the reason is that when I converted to Islam I didn't only discover a different religion, I joined a whole culture, a whole way of life.

Shahina and Yusuf

We have not found it difficult to live together. Fortunately, neither of us insisted on strict adherence to particular cultural habits. A few things, such as listening to the BBC World Service and the ban on eating pork were not open to negotiation, but generally we have both been flexible. Few of the many compromises were planned beforehand. Cross-cultural problems were faced as they arose. Most conflicts were naturally of the trivial domestic sort, in which it is difficult to distinguish cultural from personal differences. The stability of our friendship and marriage has depended greatly on the compromises which we have both had to make.

Our life together has more of an eastern than a western flavor. The relaxed social habits of the East came to predominate over more reserved western habits. Again, this was not pre-planned, it simply came to pass. It may have been influenced by the fact that Nigeria, where we met and until recently lived, has a more open, relaxed social structure than the West.

It is perhaps significant that many of the good friends that we have made since being together are mixed couples. There appears to be an elusive force that causes mixed couples to gravitate towards each other. This force does not appear to be caused by rejection from the rest of the world, but perhaps results simply from a certain indefinable empathy of spirit between mixed couples. All of the mixed couples of our acquaintance have passed through some traumas, particularly conflicts with family. Thus we all have some common ground of struggle.

Since we have been together we have lived in neither England nor Pakistan, apart from brief vacations. Probably we could not be entirely happy in either country, though we could perhaps live more easily in Pakistan than in England. The racial prejudices in England are to some extent institutionalized and are too great to make life there comfortable for either us or our son. Although, in our brief visits to England, we have not personally met with any prejudice or discrimination, apart from that of Martin's family, we feel that we would inevitably encounter difficulties in a racially divided society. Shahina's mother lives in Handsworth, Birmingham. While we were staying with her in 1984 we witnessed the hatred inspired by the infamous riots that broke out that summer in Handsworth and other parts of Birmingham. We decided then that we had no wish to be a part of such a society and would prefer to continue working outside England.

Pakistan is more or less free of the severe racial problems that permeate British society. It would, therefore, be easier for us to live there as a mixed couple. Additionally, although Pakistan became independent from Britain in 1948, the British are still to some extent looked up to in Pakistan. Since we are both Muslims, we would be more readily accepted into Pakistani society than we would be into British society. However, it would be very difficult for Martin to find employment in Pakistan.

Both of us are subject to visa requirements when visiting each other's country, and our son, being British, is subject to visa requirements when entering Pakistan. It is more difficult to travel around the world on a Pakistani than on a British passport (many countries are apparently afraid that Pakistanis will 'disappear' within their borders) and this greatly restricts our movements as a family. Because of our work, and because Shahina's mother lives in England (she is British, but this has no affect on Shahina's nationality), we go there more frequently than we do to Pakistan. Although our son is British, Shahina has no automatic right to accompany him to England. For Shahina to obtain the right of residence in England, we would have to both live together in England for three years. Because of the present nature of British society, alluded to above, and also because of the difficulty of finding jobs there as academics, we are not at present prepared to do this. These legal constraints are a nuisance, they restrict our travel and they make us feel insecure.

We knew that it would be preferable that any children we might have should be British. However, if we hadn't wished to 'marry', in the traditional sense, any children of our union would have been born stateless. The nationality of children born outside 'legal wedlock' in England passes through the mother, and the putative father has no legal relationship with his children. Additionally, any children of such a union would not be entitled to Pakistani nationality. We feel that this is an intolerable constraint on the lives of people in a civilized community. It means that a British male and a non-British female have to marry if they wish their children to be British.

Living in Nigeria, and now in Oman, has suited us well so far. We are of course treated as foreigners, but we have never met any racial discrimination. The people of Nigeria and Oman have, as far as we can tell, treated us both equally. To some extent a mixed marriage is a source of fascination to other people, and this has helped us to mix with the people of these two countries. However, we have never been able to mix very well with the expatriate Pakistani and British communities. The British and Pakistanis do not naturally seem to mix when they find themselves working as expatriates in the same country, and as a mixed couple we are not accepted fully into either community. In Pakistani society, husbands and wives tend to have separate friends, and any joint friends come more commonly from the husband's circle. Since Shahina works, she has little time to mix with the Pakistani wives, and on the whole Martin has not become close to the Pakistani men. So, the British do not warmly welcome us because of Shahina and the Pakistanis will not accept us very easily because of Martin. We have lost out socially on both sides, and have depended a lot on each other's companionship, perhaps more than would be normal in a non-mixed marriage. Our relationship has had to be strong to enable us to survive this sort of isolation. Our close expatriate friends have on the whole been from a third country: Americans, Poles, and French in particular.

We are both biologists and, although our specialist areas are different, we have much in common professionally. This common ground has helped our relationship. We are both primarily field biologists, and we have been able to fruitfully combine much of our field work. This has on occasions blossomed into joint work. We have therefore found companionship both in our home life and in work. Although many couples might balk at both living and working together, it has helped our friendship.

We feel that, despite the problems we have faced, the advantages of our mixed marriage have far outweighed the disadvantages. Both of us, but particularly Martin, have had to learn to understand a foreign culture. We have not always liked the things that we have learned about each other's country (the racialism in England and the new wave of Islamic fundamentalism in Pakistan, for example) but this has not detracted from the continuing cultural adventure of our marriage. The main psychological obstacle to our marriage was the objection of Martin's parents. Once we had determined that their objection was written in stone, so to speak, we were able to marry with clear, happy minds. Our joys culminated in the birth of Sikander, a Pakistani-Italian-English chimaera. He demonstrates by the very mixture of his genes and the smiles on his face, that mixed marriages can be happy. The only problems that we can presently foresee for us in the future are: further increases in the repressive nature of British immigration law, and the dilemma over where we will eventually settle, if at all.

CHAPTER 21

LEARNING TO LIVE AND LOVE IN DIFFERENT WORLDS

Mary Salawuh Warren and Dennis Michael Warren

Entering the Mixed Marriage

Although we grew up in very different worlds, each of us had several influencing factors which may have helped to program us towards a mixed marriage. Mary, a Nigerian Yoruba, grew up in Ghana where her father worked as a cocoa purchaser and her mother was a petty trader. Growing up as an ethnic minority in coastal Ghana, Mary became very aware of one's distinguishing features at an early age and had to learn to cope with challenges in order to survive. Moving from Cape Coast to Accra, then onto Anloga, and finally to Techiman, Mary acquired bilingual capabilities in Fante, Ga, Ewe, and Ashanti in addition to her native Yoruba. As a seamstress and a trader working and living in a multiethnic environment, Mary became adept at cross-cultural communications.

Mike was born on the Yakima Indian Reservation in the eastern part of Washington State in the United States at a time when there was virtually no opportunity for Anglo and Native American children to meet and get to know one another. This environment, however, did kindle a deep interest in people from other cultures. Mike gained at least superficial cross-cultural friendships by working summers in the orchards and ranches of Washington, Oregon and Idaho, at close quarters with migrant Hispanic and Anglo Americans. As an undergraduate at Stanford, he was active in Civil Rights Movement activities in the early 1960s and became friendly with a number of African Americans and Africans. Partly due to this exposure to other cultures and partly due to Kennedy-era idealism, Mike joined the Peace Corps and went to Ghana in 1964 as a secondary school science teacher. It was in Techiman, in Central Ghana, that Mike had his first intense exposure to another culture. The Bono, an Akan ethnic group, have a culture which is noted for its hospitality towards outsiders. It was here that Mike and Mary met in 1965. Both of them had very close relationships with a large number of Bono, but both of them were outsiders. It was, in fact, a mutual Bono friend, who encouraged their relationship.

After going together for nearly a year, we both declared our love for one another and interest in pursuing a marriage bond. This was to be a difficult task. Mary's parents had long since moved back to Nigeria, and Mary lived with her aunt in Techiman. Mike's mother and stepfather both lived in the United States. Letters were sent to both sets of parents declaring the intention to pursue a marriage. Mike travelled to Nigeria during one of the school holidays and after some difficulty located Mary's mother's family house in the old section of Ibadan, Nigeria. He travelled with two other volunteer teachers from Techiman, one American and one British. Unfortunately, no one at the house had ever heard of Mike as the letter Mary had posted from Ghana had never arrived. After a brief audience when the purpose for his visit became clear, he and his colleagues were asked to return the next day. That was when the interrogation by Mary's family began, a most thorough and exhausting event. It was obvious that they had serious concerns about such a mixed marriage. Mary was born into a family which had been Muslims for several generations and for her to marry a non-Muslim would put her into a state of sin. Her family is a well-known one in Ibadan, and the idea of marrying into an unknown blood line was also troubling. Since Yoruba marriages are agreed to only after considerable discussion between the extended families of both potential spouses, the Yoruba family insisted that Mike's parents enter into communication with them. It took several trips to Nigeria to work out the agreement. Mike's mother entered into a very friendly and fruitful correspondence with Mary's family which helped immensely. A dowry was finally agreed upon, an amount which seemed immense to a Peace Corps volunteer teacher. This money was distributed to the various family members in Nigeria to indicate that the marriage union had been agreed upon.

Because of timing and expense, a surrogate Yoruba ceremony was conducted in Techiman by members of Mary's extended family who were living there. Mike then proceeded to Indiana University where he had been accepted into graduate school in 1966. The plan was for Mary to follow as soon as Mike saved the cash for the airplane ticket and had gotten settled in Bloomington. This turned out to be another difficulty. The United States Embassy in Accra would not accept the traditional African marriage, even though it was recognized as legal in both Nigeria and Ghana. A visa would not be granted to Mary unless Mike returned to Ghana and remarried Mary in either a church or a court. Expenses precluded this. Fortunately, J. Gus Liebenow, the Director of the African Studies Program at Indiana University at the time, travelled to West Africa and managed to work out an arrangement whereby Mary was granted a visa with the assurance that she and Mike would get remarried under American law upon her arrival.

Mary's only formal schooling was a half dozen years in an Islamic school in Cape Coast learning Muslim prayers and basic Arabic. She had picked up basic English prior to leaving for America, but had only rudimentary skills in reading English. She had never been on an airplane and had very little conception of the great distance she would soon be travelling. Because she was never sure when she was expected to get off the plane, she never slept during the entire trip so she wouldn't miss her stop! In June 1967 when she departed for America, interracial marriages were still against the law in Indiana, so it was decided to have her change planes in New York and continue directly onto Portland, Oregon where Mike's aunt was to meet her. A Peace Corps friend had sent a priority cable from Accra with the information on the flights - a cable which still hasn't arrived! Arriving in New York's JFK can be a bewildering experience for the most hardened travellers. An African American assisted Mary to her new departure lounge in New York. In Portland, no one was at the airport to meet her since no word had been received. A thoroughly exhausted Mary was finally assisted by a friendly Oregonian who managed to reach Mike's aunt by telephone and she rushed to the airport and brought her home, then contacted Mike who drove to Portland from The Dalles. After a lovely reunion, Mary and Mike drove to Yakima, Washington, where they got remarried in the court with Mike's mother and stepfather as witnesses.

After the marriage ceremony, a large wedding party which brought together Mike's extended family took place, an event not far removed from its African equivalent. A honeymoon in San Francisco, and then work at a Peace Corps training center in Escondido, California, followed where Mary began her long journey towards understanding the complexities of American society and culture.

Although at the time, the lengthy negotiations for the marriage seemed very irritating, the hindsight view is a positive one. Both of us followed through the discussion over a year's period of time with both sides of the family. Although many traditional steps were bypassed because Mike and Mary were both residing in the third country of Ghana, enough elements were fulfilled to legitimize the bond in the eyes of members of both sides. Both sides, as well as the United States Embassy, were satisfied that this was not a union being entered on a whim. It forced both of us into a path which has been far more complex and challenging than if each of us had married someone from the home culture. Mike seriously began the study of Islam and formally converted in Alexandria, Egypt, in 1971. This has been a positive move for several reasons. Islam recognizes Christianity and hence Mike's family, who are Protestants, are not alienated by the move. And being Muslim, Mike can freely join his in-laws at the mosque and Mary is, according to Islamic tradition, no longer living in a state of sin.

The Mixed Marriage

Mary and Mike have now been married since 1966 (in Africa) and since 1967 (in America). They have lived nearly nine of the past twenty-six years in Ghana, Nigeria, and Zambia, have travelled extensively in Europe, Africa, the Middle East and Asia, and have learned to cope with a mixed marriage in a multitude of environments. The marriage assumed new complexities with the birth of their daughter Medina in 1971 in Indiana. Both Mike and Mary have had to travel the difficult path of learning to understand different cultural perspectives on gender and sex roles and on marriage patterns. This path has been made more confusing at times because the cultural patterns of the Bono of Central Ghana have gotten mixed up with those for the Yoruba and those for the United States. The Bono are a matrilineal Akan group and both Mike and Mary are very familiar with the patterns of this group. Descent and inheritance is determined strictly through the female blood line. Marriage tends to be quite fragile in matrilineal societies as compared with patrilineal types of societies. Many males and females, whether formally married or not, tend to have a number of other partners with a wide range of commitments from those that emerge into polygynist unions to the casual affairs. The Yoruba are patrilineal and marriage and divorce tend to be more rigorously controlled with far more expensive dowries being paid. And then the United States over the past two decades with the so-called sexual revolution, feminism, and the increased range of acceptable marriage unions which now includes homosexual unions increases the difficulty of identifying which set of these changing norms is the one which should be adopted by Mike and Mary. In Ghana, where males follow a fairly free approach to sexual liaisons, it was easy for Mike to get carried away with his many Ghanaian male colleagues. This tended to cause more than its share of conflicts in the household to the point where any female would be viewed with suspicion.

Mary came to describe American marriages as "chicken marriages," a term which refers to the behavior of the cock and hen in the typical barnyard. The apparent ease with which Americans, particularly younger ones, moved in and out of marriage was viewed as pathological at best by Mary. She viewed the occasional philandering by Mike in these terms with the other women taken as potential threats to the stability of the marriage. Mike, on the other hand, tended to view these liaisons from the Ghanaian perspective, as a natural diversion which had no potential negative impact on the marriage itself. Because the gender and sex roles were being viewed from different perspectives and sometimes from confused mixtures of perspectives, communications was sometimes difficult.

One liaison which was established by Mike in Zambia got out of hand and nearly crushed the marriage. It was at that point that Mary and Mike were forced to go through an African style approach to marriage reconciliation. In both Ghana and Nigeria, extended family members (including those in a fictive kin relationship), especially those who have shared in the dowry, are obliged to work to reconcile the differences which inevitably arise between two spouses. This is not nearly so common in America where surrogates may play a similar role - persons playing the role of marriage counsellor. In the case of Mary and Mike, they relied on long-term close friends in Iowa who worked with them to sit down and communicate and sort out their perspectives and options. Although this process was tedious and painful, it was also extremely insightful and therapeutic. Their daughter Medina also took part. The result was a clarity in the understanding of gender and sex roles, attitudes towards marriage and the family which is now commonly agreed upon by the entire nuclear family. Mike also wrote to his inlaws in Nigeria to explain the circumstances and asked that the proper prayers be given at the mosque and before the ancestral shrines to provide guidance and strength. The ancestral shrine which Mike and Mary maintain at their home in the United States was used to call upon the spirits of Mike's deceased father and mother and that of his father-in-law to assure that the union would be maintained. These are behavioral patterns which are adaptive within the African and the American contexts to assure stability and to reduce stress in a formalized approach to conflict resolution. Mary and Mike had used these approaches with friends of theirs whose own marriages were going through rough periods both in America and in Africa. In several instances the techniques were very beneficial and helped the marriages to survive in a strengthened way. Having gone through the same approach they used with other friends, they now have come to the point where they have reached the highest level of understanding in more than twenty-seven years of marriage. Not only has it been therapeutic at the individual and marital level, it has added a strength and understanding to the marriage bond which has never before existed at this level.

It is apparent to Mike and Mary as they communicated their differences, that marriage norms and sex and gender roles are changing in Africa quite as much as they have been in America. The tendency for younger Africans to move into formal polygynist unions is far less these days, partly because the economic basis for such unions in an agrarian setting is less now than a few decades ago. Post-partum sex taboos which prohibited sex between marriage partners for up to three years have now been greatly relaxed, making the physical need for a male partner to go outside the marriage union to satisfy sexual needs less. On the other hand, as economic conditions worsen in many African countries, the need for multiple relationships established through a sexual union which can facilitate a degree of economic stability, especially for many younger women who are most vulnerable to economic difficulties, may encourage multiple liaisons outside of the marriage. In the United States the free-wheeling sexual revolution seems to have been tamed by a new moralism coupled with a fear of the contraction of AIDS. In any case, the agreed standard in the Warren household is the traditional marriage bond linking one man with one woman without any external intrusions. This standard has been sealed before the ancestral shrine.

Another factor which has entered into the scene in terms of views of gender and sex roles is the new feminism which as had an impact on both Mary and Mike. Yoruba women tend to be viewed as quite strong individuals. Mary is no exception and is not inclined to be pushed around by anyone. One major difference one finds between many African cultures and that of the United States is the African view that one must voice out problems rather than harbor them inside so they eat away at one's soul. In both the short and long term, Mike has learned that this approach is far more therapeutic than the American tendency to hide one's feelings. For many years, this tendency in Mary to express her feelings openly to others was unnerving for Mike as much as for the others who were getting blasted verbally. Among the Bono, there is an annual eleven day festival during which everyone in the community is expected to voice out all misgivings which have been accumulated during the previous year. The idea is that each human has a spirit and that the spirit of the community is comprised of the collective spirits of the individuals living there. Over the period of a year the hidden difficulties make the community less pleasant to live in and this has a detrimental impact on individual and community health. In Techiman, where Mike and Mary used to take part in these festivals, at the end of the eleven days there is a symbolic sweeping of all ill feelings to the edge of town indicating that the individual and collective spirits of the community are fresh again. Mike has found this to be a very useful approach to clearing up conflicts and it is the expected behavior in the marriage.

The Mixed Marriage and Society

Mixed marriages by definition find themselves in a minority situation in any society. Responsiveness to a mixed marriage can vary greatly from one society to another, and from one point in time to another. West Africa has seen interracial and cross-cultural mixing at both the formal and informal levels for five hundred years when the first Europeans arrived. This phenomenon is nothing new and many of the well-known families of the Fante, Ga and Yoruba have lineages which have established European and Brazilian strains. In Techiman there are persons from more than sixty ethnic groups from eight West African nations residing in this district capital, with numerous cross-cultural marriages. When the Peace Corps arrived in Ghana, the advent of American cross-cultural and interracial marriages was added. Mike was in the fifth Peace Corps group sent to Ghana in 1964 which was comprised of twenty-five men and twenty-five women. Three of the men in this group married African women and one of the women married a Ghanaian. That's a high percentage of individuals moving into a mixed marriage situation. Five American and British men have taken wives home from the town of Techiman in the past twenty years. And there were others who tried and failed - one women from Gravel Switch, Kentucky, had her parents contact their Congressional representatives to stop her from marrying a Ghanaian. The pressure worked but there were some deep scars left on the woman.

When Mike and Mary arrived together in Bloomington, Indiana in August 1967 it was still several months before the Supreme Court overruled all of the laws in Indiana and other states which prohibited interracial marriages. Despite the overt activity of the Ku Klux Klan, there were numerous cross-cultural and interracial marriages represented among the graduate student population. Within shouting distance of our married housing unit were several such couples, Black and White Americans, a Ghanaian and a Briton, a Finn and a Vietnamese, a White American and a Greek, a Nigerian male and a White American female. We all had had similar types of problems to face and almost automatically found each other - an inherent support group of individuals who knew the scene and could interact freely with one another.

The African Studies Program at Indiana University was a fruitful venue for former Peace Corps volunteers, Africans and African Americans to meet and become friendly. Each weekend there was an excellent African style party which was invariably interracial and multinational. Several mixed marriages emerged from individuals who used to come to our parties. In a sense, the fact that so many of us had ventured into such unions seemed to provide a role model and the strength for others to follow along.

In 1972 Mike, Mary and Medina moved to Ames, Iowa, where Mike took up a faculty appointment at Iowa State University. At that time there were probably less than a half dozen mixed marriages in the entire community, and very few African Americans. The community was definitely small town USA and we met constant difficulties, as did others like us. For a period there was overt racism by one of the city police; there was also overt action by a number of us resulting in his being taken off the streets and placed at a desk. Mike and Mary used to expect that everytime they went to the supermarket there would be questions asked Mary about the tribal marks on her cheeks. After dozens of such sessions, one gets both tired of it and more thick-skinned. One time we were in Safeway and heard someone in the next aisle say, "Hey, come and look at the colored kid!" Being in a minority situation does provide grist for the sensitivity mill. In terms of ethnicity, race, and the mixed marriage, both Mike and Mary had been exposed to the minority role in both Africa and America. This is probably the only true way in which an individual can begin to empathize with the constant crap that ethnic and racial minorities face on a daily basis.

Much has been written by social psychologists about the offspring from mixed marriages. The "marginal man" is a term coined by one of these professors to express the ambiguity faced by such individuals. The person faces the dilemma of not fitting into the culture of either parent in a nice neat way. This marginality became evident as Medina made it into school. On several occasions she came home crying because she had been taunted and ridiculed by being called "nigger." This was a situation faced by a number of other children from pure Black heritage as well. Several years later Medina faced the other side of the coin when a African American female called her a "fucking half-breed bitch." Mary and Mike recall one summer when the family went to Ibadan to visit Mary's relatives. Medina, about five years old then, made the observation that in America she is called "Black" and in Ibadan, Nigeria, the Yoruba kids all called here "oyinbo," a term usually used to refer to Whites. She said, "What am I?"

In independent Black Africa, the mixed marriage is received in a very positive way. The family has never faced any overt negative problems in their travels from one end of Africa to the other. During 1982-85, they lived in Zambia where there were numerous mixed marriages. Zimbabwe, the next country to the south of Zambia, was only newly independent and interracial marriages had been outlawed in former Rhodesia. All of the interracial couples and families who visited Zimbabwe for holidays invariably faced considerable scrutiny by both Blacks and Whites. On several occasions the family travelled through Johannesburg, South Africa, to visit Lesotho, Swaziland and Botswana, and faced no overt difficulties other than the frequent stares and occasional disbelief.

The most uncomfortable environment which Mike and Mary found themselves in was Pakistan and India in 1971, much to the chagrin of the long-term Pakistani and Indian friends with whom they stayed. The South Asians are not terribly inclined towards interracial marriages and there is considerable stress on skin tone. We were frequently stopped on the street and queried about our status and why Mike would marry someone like Mary. Much of this was simple curiosity but it became very old, very quickly.

But things change, and Mike, Mary and Medina have themselves been forces in social change. Ames, Iowa is a much more cosmopolitan and enlightened community in 1993 than it was in 1972. The number of interracial and cross-cultural marriages on the faculty and in the community has grown by a hundred times. The number of minority students has increased many times over, and the international student population now exceeds 2,500 individuals representing 106 countries. There are now many more opportunities to meet a wider variety of people and to get to know them as human beings. And Mike and Mary have changed. Prejudice is not nearly so irritating as it once was. They view it as a lack of opportunity for those individuals to be exposed to other types of human beings and to grow as humans themselves. They are relieved that they needn't carry the burden of hate, prejudice and dislike that so many others feel so important to maintain. Mike sees his role in teaching as providing insights for students about the nature of human prejudice and how we can learn to better understand this human universal.

In Ghana and Nigeria now, Mike has moved from being viewed as a "small boy" to a "big man". He speaks the Akan language very well and the Yoruba language reasonably well. He is commited to Africa, and he and Mary have built houses in Ibadan as well as in Ara, the town where Mary's father's family live. They intend to retire to Nigeria where things have changed, but not so much that old people are put out to pasture in nursing homes. These Euro-American institutions haven't yet reached Africa, where the elderly are still greatly respected. Mike now assumes the status of elder in many family discussions and his opinions are highly regarded. He was installed as a chief in Ara, Nigeria, and in both Krobo and Tanoboase in Ghana in 1990, while Mary was installed as a queenmother in Tanoboase, Ghana in 1992.

Regarding the "marginal person," Mike and Mary see Medina evolving far beyond the realm of marginality. She has double the options of most of her friends. She knows the rules for appropriate behavior for Africa as well as America. She is both African and American and can take advantage of both worlds. Her breadth of understanding of human interactions and problems exceeds that of most adults. This does not mean that she isn't caught in the middle sometimes. Mary does not like the way many American children, especially teenagers, treat their parents. She doesn't like the way American teenagers are given so much freedom that many end up with difficulties such as unwanted pregnancies, drug problems, and alcoholism. Medina is controlled considerably more tightly and this sometimes is irritating to her, but hopefully in the long run she will find that an African approach can have an excellent result.

Conclusion

Thinking through the mixed marriage was not an easy task for Mary and Mike. None of the issues they discussed was terribly clear-cut. There were many fuzzy edges and as many emotional as rational decisions made over the years. It did provide them an opportunity to talk through many sensitive issues which they may never have done otherwise. One primary conclusion out of their discussions is that the mixed marriage is almost by definition more complicated than the non-mixed one. The spouses must deal with a wider array of issues, but that provides opportunities for increased human growth and understanding and that may make it all worthwhile.